CONCISE
CHINESE-ENGLISH
USAGE DICTIONARY

A STUDY REFERENCE TO THE 500 MOST
ESSENTIAL CHINESE CHARACTERS

CONCISE
CHINESE-ENGLISH
USAGE DICTIONARY

A STUDY REFERENCE TO THE 500 MOST
ESSENTIAL CHINESE CHARACTERS

YONG HO

HIPPOCRENE BOOKS, INC.
New York

For further information, address:
HIPPOCRENE BOOKS, INC.
171 Madison Avenue
New York, NY 10016
www.hippocrenebooks.com

Previous edition ISBN: 978-0-7818-0842-2

Library of Congress Cataloging-in-Publication Data

Ho, Yong.
[Chinese-English frequency dictionary.]
Concise Chinese-English usage dictionary : a study reference to the 500
most essential Chinese characters / Yong Ho. -- Rev. ed.
    p. cm.
  ISBN-13: 978-0-7818-1293-1
  ISBN-10: 0-7818-1293-3
  "This is a greatly revised version of Chinese-English Frequency
Dictionary: A Study Guide to Mandarin Chinese's 500 Most Frequently
Used Words, first published in 2003."
    Includes index.
1. Chinese language--Dictionaries--English. I. Title. II. Title: Study
reference to the 500 most essential Chinese characters.
PL1455.H67 2012
495.1'321--dc23
                                                2012025270

Printed in the United States of America.

INTRODUCTION

This is a greatly revised version of my book entitled *Chinese-English Frequency Dictionary: A Study Guide to Mandarin Chinese's 500 Most Frequently Used Words*, first published in 2003. Like the earlier version, the current book is written primarily for students of Chinese, from beginning to advanced levels, and for teachers of Chinese. As it is a reference guide, it deals with both relatively simple points and more complicated problems of the language.

The Foreign Service Institute of the U.S. State Department categorizes Chinese as a "Group III" language. Under the State Department criteria, Group III languages are considered to be exceptionally difficult for native speakers of English to master, with other languages in this group including Arabic, Japanese, and Korean. It is generally thought that what makes Chinese difficult is its writing system, which is not phonetic but rather logographic. This is true to a large extent, but grammar and usage often present equally great challenges for students. Since Chinese is not inflectional in nature, much of the burden of the grammatical meaning is carried by lexical items. For this reason, a reference book focused on the words in a dictionary format may be a more effective guide for students than an overview of grammatical structures in a grammar book.

This book selects the 500 most frequently used Chinese characters, arranged alphabetically according to *pinyin* Romanization, and provides detailed phonologic and syntactic explanations. These 500 characters were chosen primarily on the basis of the frequency wordlist developed by the National Office of Teaching Chinese as a Foreign Language in China, and secondarily, the prevailing textbooks for foreign students of Chinese, including those written by this author. Although 500 characters only account for a fraction of the lexical universe in Chinese, the mastery of them and their associated compounds would enable the student to gain 70 percent reading fluency in Chinese.

To say, as some might be tempted to, that the 500 entries listed in the book are 500 *words* is not entirely correct. They are, instead, 500 *characters*. Though Chinese was once a monosyllabic language where each character represented just a single word, the language has evolved over the millennia into a predominantly disyllabic language, where the majority of words consist of two characters. In spite of this development, we can't say that the component characters of disyllabic or polysyllabic words are not words themselves. The overwhelming majority of them are free-form words on their own with similar or different meanings in set expressions left over from the classical Chinese. Additionally, most of the most frequently used words in modern Chinese remain monosyllabic.

For this reason, this book adopts the prevailing practice of Chinese dictionaries to use single characters as entries. While a comprehensive treatment is given to the entry character, frequently used disyllabic and polysyllabic words and expressions with the entry character as the first element are also listed and explained. The actual number of words listed and explained in the book thus far exceeds 500. The listing of such compounds with definitions and explanations is expected to be of great help to students, as present-day idiomatic Chinese abounds in compounds—so much so that many linguists regard modern Chinese as "a language of compound words."

Two additional features have been added to the current edition. First, the book includes under each entry commonly used words where the entry character appears as the second character. This is useful for students, as they would otherwise have no way to look up such words except in a reverse dictionary or concordance, which are not commonly available. Second, the book lists after certain nouns the classifiers that are associated with them. This is especially useful to students of Chinese, as the choice of the correct classifier for some nouns often presents a challenge.

The Chinese system of writing is not phonetic, but takes the form of contiguous strings of discrete characters. Until about 100 years ago, punctuation marks were not even used, leaving the boundary of words, phrases, and sentences for the reader to decipher. Since this book is primarily intended for English-speaking students of Chinese, *pinyin* (a system devised in China in the 1950s for transcribing Chinese) is provided side by side with characters. In transcribing Chinese words in *pinyin*, tones are included to indicate the correct pronunciation. Note that the apostrophe is used in a polysyllabic word to separate the preceding syllable from the following syllable that begins with a, o, or e such as *nǚ'er* (*daughter*).

While this book is written with the foreign students of Chinese in mind, it is not a replacement for a study course or a textbook. Meanings of Chinese words are heavily dependent upon context, and the grammaticality of a linguistic item is heavily dependent upon syllabic structure. For example, a monosyllabic word may be given the same glossary as a disyllabic word, but the correct use of them depends on their syllabic collocation with other words. For this reason, the best approach is to use this book as a supplement to a textbook. To facilitate easy reference and study, two indices are provided at the end of the book, one listing the 500 characters according to the frequency with which they appear in general texts and the other listing the 500 characters according to the number of strokes in the entry character.

GRAMMATICAL TERMS EXPLAINED

Adverbial
A word, phrase, or clause that functions to modify a verb, an adjective, or another adverb, providing such information as time, place, manner, reason, condition, and so on.

Aspect
Manner in which an action takes place. English distinguishes four aspects: indefinite, continuous, perfect, and perfect continuous, whereas Chinese distinguishes indefinite, continuous, and perfect. The indefinite aspect indicates the habitual or repeated action. The continuous aspect indicates the continuation or progression of the action. The perfect aspect indicates the completion of an action.

Classifier
A word used between a numeral and a noun to show a sub-class to which the noun belongs.

Complement
That part of the sentence that follows and completes the verb. As such, they are also called verb complements. The most common complements in Chinese are those of direction, result, and degree. Directional complements indicate the direction of the action in relation to the speaker and are not separated from the verb by any particle. Result and degree complements indicate the result and the degree of the action expressed by the verb and they are separated from the verb by the particle 得 de.

Existential sentence

This refers to a type of sentence that is similar to the "there is/are" structure in English. The pattern for existential sentences in Chinese is (在 zài) Adverbial of Place + 有 (yǒu, *there is/are*) + Subject. The adverbial of place precedes instead of follows the verb 有 (yǒu). *There is a Bank of China in Chinatown* is thus expressed in Chinese as 中国城有中国银行 (Zhōngguóchéng yǒu Zhōngguó yínháng). In an existential sentence, the initial 在 zài is always dropped.

Object

A noun, pronoun, phrase, or clause that is used after, and affected in some way by, a transitive verb. If it is affected in a direct way, it is called the direct object. If it is affected in an indirect way, it is called the indirect object. In the sentence *"he gave me a book,"* *a book* is the direct object and *me* is the indirect object.

Particle

A word that has only grammatical meaning, but no lexical meaning, such as *ma*, *ne*, and *ba* in Chinese.

Predicate

That part of a sentence that states or asserts something about the subject. This role is only assumed by the verb in English, but can also be assumed by the adjective in Chinese.

Predicative adjective

An adjective used after the verb *to be* in English, as in *"the book is interesting,"* which is opposed to an attributive adjective used before a noun, as in *"this is an interesting book."* The predicative adjective in Chinese is used without the verb *to be*, and functions as the predicate of the sentence.

Subject

Something about which a statement or assertion is made in the rest of the sentence.

Transitive and intransitive verbs

A transitive verb is one that needs to take an object such as the underlined verbs in the following sentences:

我们 学习 中文。
Wǒmen xuéxí Zhōngwén.
We study Chinese.

你 能 教 我 开车 吗?
Nǐ néng jiāo wǒ kāichē ma?
Can you teach me how to drive?

An intransitive verb is one that does not take an object such as the underlined verbs in the following sentences:

你 什么 时候 走?
Nǐ shénme shíhou zǒu
When are you leaving?

犯人 跑 了。
Fànrén pǎo le.
The prisoner escaped.

Note that a transitive verb in English may be intransitive in Chinese, and vice versa.

VO verbs

A large number of verbs in Chinese are formed by a verb and an object such as 见面 jiànmiàn (meet), 结婚 jiéhūn (marry), and 帮忙 bāngmáng (help). Many of these verbs would be transitive in English, but they are not to be followed by an object in Chinese, as there is already an "embedded object." The idea that would be expressed by an object in English are usually expressed in China by an adverbial before the verb or an attribute before the embedded object: 跟他见面 gēn tā jiànmiàn (meet with him), 跟同事结了婚 gēn tóngshì jié le hūn (married a colleague), 帮了我的忙 bāng le wǒde máng (helped me; did me a favor).

ABBREVIATIONS

adjective	adj.
adverb	adv.
classifier	cl.
compare	cf.
grammar	gram.
medicine	med.
military	mil.
noun	n.
somebody	sb.
something	sth.
usually	usu.
verb	v.

啊 à; a

1. sentence-final particle used to indicate exclamation: 长城多壮观啊 Chángchéng duō zhuàngguān à (*how splendid the Great Wall is!*); 你要好好学习啊 nǐ yào hǎohao xuéxi à (*you must study well!*)

2. used to mark the topic: 电影啊, 我根本没有时间看 diànyǐng a, wǒ gēnběn méi you shíjiān kàn (*speaking of the movies, I simply don't have time to see them*). When used in this sentence, the word is pronounced in the neutral tone.

3. used in enumerating things: 动物园有很多动物, 老虎啊, 狮子啊, 熊啊, … dòngwùyuán yǒu hěn duō dòngwù, lǎohǔ a, shīzi a, xióng a, … (*there are many animals in the zoo such as tigers, lions, bears, ...*). When used in this sentence, the word is pronounced in the neutral tone.

爱 ài

1. *love, like*

2. *fall in love with*, often used with 上 shàng (*up*): 他爱上了中国菜 tā ài shàng le Zhōngguó cài (*he fell in love with Chinese food*)

3. *apt to, be in the habit of*: 那个孩子爱生气 nà ge háizi ài shēngqì (*that child is apt to get angry*)

Also appears in the following words: 敬爱 jìng'ài (*respectable; dear*); 可爱 kě'ài (*cute; lovely*); 亲爱 qīn'ài (*dear*); 热爱 rè'ài (*ardently love*); 做爱 zuò'ài (*make love*)

爱护	àihù	*take good care*, usu. followed by an object noun: 爱护公物 àihù gōngwù (*take good care of public property*)
爱慕	àimù	*adore, admire*
爱情	àiqíng	(*romantic*) *love* (n.)
爱人	àirén	*spouse*

安 ān

1. *peaceful, at ease*: 麻烦你这么多, 我觉得很不安 máfan nǐ zhème duō, wǒ juéde hěn bù ān (*I feel very uneasy about having given you so much trouble*)

2. *install*: 安电话 ān diànhuà (*install a telephone*)

Also appears in the following words: 保安 bǎo'ān (*ensure public security; security personnel*); 公安 gōng'ān (*public security*); 平安 píng'ān (*safe and sound*); 晚安 wǎn'ān (*good night*); 治安 zhì'ān (*public security*)

安家	ānjiā	*settle down; set up a residence*
安静	ānjìng	*quiet; peaceful*

安排 ānpái	arrange; arrangement
安全 ānquán	safe; safety
安心 ānxīn	content with; at ease
安慰 ānwèi	console
安装 ānzhuāng	install

吧 ba; bā

When pronounced in the neutral tone:

Sentence-final particle used to indicate:

1. suggestion, request or command: 我们去吧 wǒmen qù ba (*let's go*)

2. concurrence, often used in conjunction with 就 jiù: 我就明天来吧 wǒ jiù míngtiān lái ba (*okay, I'll come tomorrow then*)

3. confirmation or supposition: 你是中国人吧 nǐ shì Zhōngguórén ba (*you are Chinese, aren't you?*)

When pronounced in the first tone:

bar; *bar-like stores*: 酒吧 jiǔbā (*bar*); 网吧 wǎngbā (*internet café*); 书吧 shūbā (*book bar*; *bookstore with a café*)

八 bā

eight

Pronounced in the second tone before a fourth-tone word: 八块钱 bá kuài qián (*$8*).

| 八方 bāfāng | all directions; all over; everywhere, often used with 四面 sìmiàn (all sides): 我们学校的学生来自四面八方 wǒmen xuéxiào de xuésheng lái zì sìmiàn bāfāng (students at our school come from all over the country) |
| 八角 bājiǎo | aniseed; octagonal |

把 bǎ

1. *classifier* used for things that one can hold by making a fist such as a chair, umbrella, flag, spade, scissors, screwdriver, bouquet of flowers, knife and pistol

2. grammatical device used to shift the object before the verb: 把书放在桌上 bǎ shū fàng zài zhuō shang (*put the book on the table*); 把饭吃完 bǎ fàn chī wán (*finish eating the food*). For an object to be shifted to the front, it has to meet the following conditions: **a)** the object must be a definite or specified one; **b)** the verb must be a complex one, i.e. it must be followed by a complement such as 在桌子上 zài zhuōzi shang or 完 wán；**c)** the verb must be one that can produce a tangible result in the object, such as causing it to change hands, location, form, state, or to disappear and so on. When there is a choice, the sentence that uses the 把 *ba*-construction differs in meaning from the one that doesn't. Although both 他吃了饭 tā chī le fàn and 他把饭吃了 tā bǎ fàn chī le can be translated as *he ate the food*, the foci of the sentences are different. 他吃了饭 tā chī le fàn answers the question *what did he do*, whereas 他把饭吃了 tā bǎ fàn chī le answers the question *what did he do to the food*.

3. grammatical particle used before a pronoun object to mean *cause sb. to do sth.*: 这件事把我气死了 zhè jiàn shì bǎ wǒ qì sǐ le (*this matter greatly angered me*)

把关 **bǎguān**	*provide inspection or guarantee* (about the quality or the legality of a product or a matter)
把握 **bǎwò**	*being sure; assurance; confidence*, usu. used with the verb 有 yǒu: 你有没有把握赢这次比赛 nǐ yǒu méi you bǎwò yíng zhè cì bǐsài (*are you confident that you can win this match?*)

爸 bà

father, usu. taking the disyllabic form of 爸爸 bàba

白 bái

1. *white*

2. *plain; blank*: 白纸 báizhǐ (*blank paper*); 白话 báihuà (*vernacular*); 白饭 báifàn (*plain rice*)

3. *in vain; for no purpose*: 白做 báizuò (*do a fruitless or thankless job*); 白费时间 báifèi shíjiān (*spend one's time for no purpose*)

4. *at no cost*: 白吃 báichī (*eat at someone else's expense*)

Also appears in the following words: 表白 biǎobái (*profess*); 蛋白 dànbái (*egg white*); 空白 kòngbái (*blank space; gap*); 明白 míngbai (*understand; clear*); 清白 qīngbái (*innocent*); 自白 zìbái (*confess; confession*); 坦白 tǎnbái (*confess*); 雪白 xuěbái (*snow white; pure white*); 开场白 kāichǎngbái (*opening gambit*)

白菜 **báicài**	*Chinese cabbage*
白痴 **báichī**	*idiot*

白酒 báijiǔ	liquor
白天 báitiān	daytime
白血病 báixuěbìng	leukemia

百 bǎi

hundred: 一百 yìbǎi (one hundred); 五百 wǔbǎi (five hundred)

百分比 bǎifēnbǐ	percentage
百分之 bǎifēnzhī	percent: 百分之一 bǎifēnzhī yī (one percent)
百货公司 bǎihuògōngsī	department store
百科全书 bǎikēquánshū	encyclopedia
百万 bǎiwàn	million: 一百万 yì bǎiwàn (one million)
百姓 bǎixìng	common people, also expressed as 老百姓 lǎobǎixìng

搬 bān

move (heavy object): 搬桌子 bān zhuōzi (move the table); 搬家具 bān jiājù (move the furniture). If what is moved is a light object, verbs such as 拿 ná should be used.

搬家 bānjiā	1. move house
	2. (of stores, etc.) move to different location: 那个银行搬 家了 nà ge yínháng bānjiā le (that bank moved to a different location)
搬用 bānyòng	apply discriminately; copy mechanically
搬运 bānyùn	transport; carry; move: 搬运工 bānyùngōng (mover); 搬运公司 bānyùn gōngsī (moving company)

班 bān

1. class: 中文班 Zhōngwénbān (Chinese class); 培训班 péixùnbān (training class)

2. shift: 白班 báibān (day shift); 夜班 yèbān (night shift); 上班 shàngbān (go to work, literally go to one's shift); 下班 xiàbān (get off work, literally leave one's shift)

3. squad (mil.): 班长 bānzhǎng (squad leader)

4. means of transportation at regular intervals: 班车 bānchē (shuttle bus); 班机 bānjī (scheduled flight)

班车	**bānchē**	*shuttle bus*
班机	**bānjī**	*scheduled flight*
班级	**bānjí**	*classes and grades in a school*
班长	**bānzhǎng**	(mil.) *squad leader*; (school) *class monitor*
班子	**bānzi**	(management) *group*; *team*: 领导班子 lǐngdǎo bānzi (*management team*)

半 bàn

1. *half*: 三点半 sān diǎn bàn (*3:30*); 半天 bàn tiān (*half a day*); 半个月 bàn ge yuè (*half a month*). When used after a number, it follows the classifier: 五个半小时 wǔ ge bàn xiǎoshí (*five and a half hours*)

2. *in the middle of*: 半夜 bànyè (*midnight*); 半山腰 bànshānyāo (*halfway up the mountain*)

3. *partially*: 半新的汽车 bàn xīnde qìchē (*a partially new car*); 门半敞着 mén bàn chǎng zhe (*the door is partially open*)

4. *semi-*: 半官方 bànguānfāng (*semi-official*); 半决赛 bànjuésài (*semi-final*)

Also appears in the following words: 大半 dàbàn (*a greater part*); 对半 duìbàn (*half and half*); 多半 duōbàn (*probably*; *mostly*); 过半 guòbàn (*more than half*); 小半 xiǎobàn (*a small part*); 夜半 yèbàn (*midnight*)

半径	**bànjìng**	*radius*
半路	**bànlù**	*halfway*; *on the way*
半球	**bànqiú**	*hemisphere*
半职	**bànzhí**	*part-time* (work)

办 bàn

1. *handle*: 他很会办事 tā hěn huì bàn shì (*he handles things well*)

2. *start*; *run* (a business or organization): 我的朋友办了一个学校 wǒde péngyou bàn le yí ge xuéxiào (*my friend started a school*)

3. *go through formalities*: 办签证 bàn qiānzhèng (*apply for a visa*); 办结婚证 bàn jiéhūnzhèng (*apply for a marriage certificate*)

Also appears in the following words: 承办 chéngbàn (*take charge of*; *undertake*; *accept an assignment*); 筹办 chóubàn (*make preparations for*); 创办 chuàngbàn (*establish*; *break ground*); 举办 jǔbàn (*conduct*; *hold*); 民办 mínbàn (*privately run*); 主办 zhǔbàn (*sponsor*; *hold*)

| 办法 | **bànfǎ** | *solution*; *means*; *method* |

| 办公 **bàngōng** | handle official business: 办公室 bàngōngshì (office) |
| 办理 **bànlǐ** | process (an application, etc.) |

帮 **bāng**

help; assist: 我的同事来帮我搬家 wǒde tóngshì lái bāng wǒ bānjiā (my colleagues came to help me move house)

帮忙 **bāngmáng**	help: 我们去帮忙 wǒmen qù bāngmáng (let's go to help); 帮忙 bāngmáng cannot take an object as it is a Verb + Object structure, but a possessive pronoun or a possessive noun can be placed between 帮 bāng and 忙 máng: 你帮了我的大忙 nǐ bāng le wǒde dà máng (you have done me a big favor); 我不能帮他的忙 wǒ bù néng bāng tāde máng (I can't help him)
帮手 **bāngshǒu**	helper; assistant
帮凶 **bāngxiōng**	accomplice
帮助 **bāngzhù**	help (n. and v.): 这本书对我的帮助很大 zhè běn shū duì wǒde bāngzhù hěn dà (this book has helped me a lot); 谢谢你的帮助 xièxie nǐde bāngzhù (thank you for your help)

包 **bāo**

1. wrap: 包礼物 bāo lǐwù (wrap a present)

2. bag; package: 书包 shūbāo (schoolbag); 钱包 qiánbāo (wallet; purse)

3. classifier for bagged objects: 一包香烟 yì bāo xiāngyān (a pack of cigarettes)

4. charter (a bus, plane, etc.): 包一条船 bāo yì tiáo chuán (charter a boat)

5. include; cover: 房租包水电吗 fángzū bāo shuǐdiàn ma (does the rent include utilities?); 包吃包住 bāo chī bāo zhù (room and board provided)

Also appears in the following words: 背包 bèibāo (knapsack); 打包 dǎbāo (pack up); 承包 chéngbāo (contract with)

包庇 **bāobì**	cover up; shield
包袱 **bāofu**	burden; weight: 搬家成了我们的包袱 bānjiā chéng le wǒmende bāofu (moving house has become a burden for us)
包裹 **bāoguǒ**	parcel
包括 **bāokuò**	include; consist of
包扎 **bāozhā**	dress a wound

| 包装 **bāozhuāng** | *package*: 包装商品 bāozhuāng shāngpǐn (*package a product*) |
| 包子 **bāozi** | *stuffed bun*. Cl: 个 gè |

报 bào

1. *report*; *declare*; *announce*

2. *newspaper*; *journal*; *bulletin*: 日报 rìbào (*daily paper*); 晚报 wǎnbào (*evening paper*). Cl: 份 fèn; 张 zhāng

Also appears in the following words: 公报 gōngbào (*communique*; *gazette*); 海报 hǎibào (*poster*; *flyer*); 画报 huàbào (*pictorial magazine*); 回报 huíbào (*repay a favor*); 警报 jǐngbào (*alarm*; *alert*); 墙报 qiángbào (*wall newspaper*; *bulletin*); 情报 qíngbào (*intelligence*); 通报 tōngbào (*circular*; *bulletin*); 预报 yùbào (*forecast*)

报酬 **bàochóu**	*compensation*; *remuneration*; *reward*. Cl: 份 fèn
报仇 **bàochóu**	*revenge*; *avenge*
报答 **bàodá**	*repay*
报到 **bàodào**	*check in*; *register*
报导 **bàodǎo**	*(news) report*
报复 **bàofù**	*retaliate*
报告 **bàogào**	*report (v. and n.)*. Cl: 份 fèn; 篇 piān; 个 gè
报关 **bàoguān**	*declare at customs*
报警 **bàojǐng**	*report a case to the police*
报刊 **bàokān**	*newspaper and magazines*. Cl: 份 fèn
报名 **bàomíng**	*sign up*; *register*
报社 **bàoshè**	*newspaper headquarters*; *newspaper office*. Cl: 家 jiā
报税 **bàoshuì**	*file a tax return*
报纸 **bàozhǐ**	*newspaper*. Cl: 份 fèn; 张 zhāng

杯 bēi

cup; *glass*; *mug*: 茶杯 chábēi (*tea cup*); 酒杯 jiǔbēi (*wine glass*). Also used as classifier: 一杯咖啡 yì bēi kāfēi (*a cup of coffee*); 两杯酒 liǎng bēi jiǔ (*two glasses of wine*)

| 杯子 **bēizi** | *cup*; *glass*; *mug*. Cl: 只 zhī; 个 gè |

背 bēi; bèi

When pronounced bēi:

carry on the back: 背行李 bēi xíngli (*carry the luggage on the back*)

背包 bēibāo	*knapsack*
背包袱 bēi bāofu	*take on a mental burden*; *have a weight on one's mind*
背债 bēi zhài	*be in debt*

When pronounced bèi:

1. *back*: 背痛 bèitòng (*backache*); 椅背 yǐbèi (*back of a chair*)

2. *with one's back towards*: 换胶卷时要背光 huàn jiāojuǎn shí yào bèiguāng (*when changing the film, you need to do it with your back towards the light*)

3. *hide sth. from*; *do sth. behind sb.'s back*, often used with 着 zhe: 秘书背着老板接受了很多礼物 mìshū bèi zhe lǎobǎn jiēshòu le hěn duō lǐwù (*the secretary accepted many gifts behind her boss's back*)

4. *recite from memory*: 老师要我们明天背诗 lǎoshī yào wǒmen míngtiān bèi shī (*the teacher asked us to recite the poem tomorrow*)

5. *remote*; *out of the way*: 那个地方很背，消息不灵通 nà ge dìfāng hěn bèi, xiāoxi bù língtōng (*that place is out of the way, with poor access to information*)

背后 bèihòu	**1**. *at the back*; *behind*: 房子背后有一个花园 fángzi bèihòu yǒu yí ge huāyuán (*there is a garden behind the house*) **2**. *behind sb.'s back*: 在人背后议论他们的私事不好 zài rén bèihòu yìlùn tāmende sīshì bù hǎo (*it is not nice to discuss people's private affairs behind their back*)
背景 bèijǐng	*background*; *backdrop*: 小说的历史背景 xiǎoshuō de lìshǐ bèijǐng (*the historical backdrop of the novel*)
背离 bèilí	*deviate from*; *depart from*: 他们的行为背离了组织的章程 tāmende xíngwéi bèilí le zǔzhí de zhāngchéng (*their behavior deviated from the charter of the organization*)
背面 bèimiàn	*the reverse side*: 写在纸的背面 xiě zài zhǐ de bèimiàn (*write on the reverse side of the paper*)
背叛 bèipàn	*betray*
背书 bèishū	*recite a text from memory*
背诵 bèisòng	*recite from memory*
背心 bèixīn	*a sleeveless piece of clothing* (waistcoat, vest, tank top). Cl: 件 jiàn; 个 gè
背约 bèiyuē	*break an agreement*; *go back on one's word*

北 běi

north; *northern*: 北部 běibù (*northern part*); 北边 běibian (*north side*). In expressing northeast and northwest, Chinese places east and west first: 东北 dōngběi (*northeast*); 西北 xīběi (*northwest*).

北边 běibian	(*to the*) *north of:* 美国在墨西哥的北边 Měiguó zài Mòxīgē de běibian (*the United States lies to the north of Mexico*); 中国的北边有两个国家 Zhōngguó de běibian yǒu liǎng ge guójiā (*there are two countries to the north of China*)
北方 běifāng	*northern part of a country:* 北方人 běifāngrén (*northerner*)
北极 běijí	*the North Pole*

被 bèi

by, used in the passive sentence to introduce the agent: 他被老师批评了 tā bèi lǎoshī pīpíng le (*he was criticized by the teacher*). The agent can often be omitted from the sentence, but 被 bèi must be retained: 他被批评了 tā bèi pīpíng le (*he was criticized*); 汽车被偷了 qìchē bèi tōu le (*the car was stolen*). Sentences using 被 bèi tend to suggest undesirable situations, as shown in the examples cited above.

被单 bèidān	*bed sheet*
被动 bèidòng	*passive*
被告 bèigào	*accused*; *defendant*
被害人 bèihàirén	*victim* (in a crime)
被迫 bèipò	*be forced to*
被子 bèizi	*quilt*. Cl: 条 tiáo; 床 chuáng; 个 gè

本 běn

1. (of money or funds) *capital*; *principal*

2. *original*; *originally*: 这不是我的本意 zhè bú shì wǒde běnyì (*this is not my original intention*); 她本不是美国人 tā běn bú shì Měiguórén (*she was originally not American*)

3. *this*; *our*; *present*: 本公司 běn gōngsī (*our company*); 本月 běn yuè (*this month*)

4. *book*: 照相本 zhàoxiàngběn (*photo album*); 笔记本 bǐjìběn (*notebook*). Cl: 个 gè

5. classifier for bound printed materials such as books, magazines, dictionaries

and photo albums: 五本书 wǔ běn shū (*five books*); 十本杂志 shí běn zázhì (*ten magazines*)

本地 **běndì**	*local*: 本地人 běndìrén (*local person*)
本科 **běnkē**	*undergraduate study*: 本科生 (*undergraduate student*)
本来 **běnlái**	*original; originally*: 本来的计划 běnláide jìhuà (*original plan*); 本来这儿没有桥 běnlái zhèr méi you qiáo (*originally there was no bridge here*)
本领 **běnlǐng**	*skill; ability*
本能 **běnnéng**	*instinct*
本钱 **běnqián**	*(of funds) capital; principal*
本人 **běnrén**	*oneself; in person*
本性 **běnxìng**	*natural instinct; true nature*
本意 **běnyì**	*original intention*
本着 **běnzhe**	*in conformity with; on the basis of*: 本着合作的精神 běnzhe hézuò de jīngshen (*in the spirit of cooperation*)
本质 **běnzhì**	*essence; nature; intrinsic quality*
本子 **běnzi**	*notebook*. Cl: 个 gè; 本 běn.
本族语 **běnzúyǔ**	*native language*

比 bǐ

1. *than*: 飞机比火车快 fēijī bǐ huǒchē kuài (*the plane is faster than the train*); 我姐姐比我大三岁 wǒ jiějie bǐ wǒ dà sān suì (*my older sister is three years older than I*). In a negative sentence, 不 bù appears before 比 bǐ: 香港的东西不比日本的东西贵 Xiānggǎng de dōngxi bù bǐ Rìběn de dōngxi guì (*things in Hong Kong are not more expensive than those in Japan*).

2. *compare*: 比力气大 bǐ lìqi dà (*compare physical strength*); 比谁学习努力 bǐ shuí xuéxí nǔlì (*compare who studies harder*)

3. *compare sth. to*, used with 把 bǎ: 把图书馆比作知识的海洋 bǎ túshūguǎn bǐ zuò zhīshi de hǎiyáng (*compare the library to an ocean of knowledge*)

4. *to* (in a score or rate): 美元对人民币是一比八 Měiyuán duì Rénmínbì shì yī bǐ bā (*the exchange ratio between U.S. dollars and Renminbi is 1 to 8*)

Also appears in the following words: 对比 duìbǐ (*contrast*); 相比 xiāngbǐ (*compared to*); 评比 píngbǐ (*evaluate; appraise through comparison*); 无比 wúbǐ (*matchless; be without equal*)

比方说 **bǐfāngshuō**	*for example*
比分 **bǐfēn**	*(sports) score*
比较 **bǐjiào**	**1.** *compare; contrast*: 比较一下新房子和旧房子 bǐjiào

yíxià xīn fángzi hé jiù fángzi (*compare the new house with the old house*)

2. *comparatively*; *relatively*; *rather*: 这家旅馆的条件比较好 zhè jiā lǚguǎn de tiáojiàn bǐjiào hǎo (*conditions at this hotel are rather good*)

3. *comparative*: 比较文学 bǐjiào wénxué (*comparative literature*)

4. *comparison*: 没有比较, 就不知道区别 méi you bǐjiào, jiù bù zhīdao qūbié (*without comparison, we won't know the differences*)

比例	bǐlì	*proportion*
比率	bǐlǜ	*ratio*; *rate*
比起	bǐqǐ	*compare with*: 比起城市, 农村还很穷 bǐqǐ chéngshì, nóngcūn hái hěn qióng (*compared with the cities, the countryside is still rather poor*)
比如	bǐrú	*for example*
比赛	bǐsài	*competition*; *contest*; *match*. Cl: 场 chǎng; 次 cì
比喻	bǐyù	*metaphor*; *figure of speech*

笔 bǐ

writing instrument: 钢笔 gāngbǐ (*fountain pen*); 铅笔 qiānbǐ (*pencil*); 毛笔 máobǐ (*writing brush*); 粉笔 fěnbǐ (*chalk*). Cl: 枝 zhī

Also appears in the following words: 败笔 bàibǐ (*a faulty stroke in calligraphy or painting*); 亲笔 qīnbǐ (*in one's own handwriting*); 手笔 shǒubǐ (*one's own hand-writing*); 执笔 zhíbǐ (*write*; *pencraft*); 主笔 zhǔbǐ (*editor*; *act as the main author*)

笔法	bǐfǎ	*technique of writing*; *style of calligraphy*
笔画	bǐhuà	*strokes of a Chinese character*
笔记	bǐjì	*notes*. Cl: 本 běn
笔迹	bǐjī	*a person's handwriting*
笔录	bǐlù	*notes*; *written statement*; *record*
笔名	bǐmíng	*pen name*; *pseudonym*. Cl: 个 gè
笔试	bǐshì	*written exam*
笔顺	bǐshùn	*stroke order of a Chinese character*
笔筒	bǐtǒng	*pen container*. Cl: 只 zhī; 个 gè
笔译	bǐyì	*written translation*
笔直	bǐzhí	*perfectly straight*

必 bì

1. *certainly*; *necessarily*: 我们的队必胜 wǒmende duì bì shèng (*our team will certainly win*)

2. *must*: 故宫是必去的地方 Gùgōng shì bì qù de dìfāng (*the Palace Museum is a place that one must visit*)

必定 bìdìng	*be sure to*: 教育必定要改革 jiàoyù bìdìng yào gǎigé (*education will surely be reformed*)
必然 bìrán	**1.** *inevitable*: 必然的后果 bìránde hòuguǒ (*inevitable consequence*) **2.** *surely*; *certainly*: 你如果经常锻练，身体必然会好 nǐ rúguǒ jīngcháng duànliàn, shēntǐ bìrán huì hǎo (*if you exercise regularly, your health will surely be good*)
必修课 bìxiūkè	(for students) *required course*. Cl: 门 mén
必须 bìxū	*must*; *have to*: 作业必须按时完成 zuòyè bìxū ànshí wánchéng (*assignment must be finished on time*). The negative form is 不必 búbì: 不必担心 búbì dānxīn (*don't have to worry*).
必需 bìxū	*indispensable*: 电脑是学生必需的工具 diànnǎo shì xuésheng bìxūde gōngjù (*the computer is an indispensable tool for the students*); 必需品 bìxūpǐn (*necessities*)
必要 bìyào	*necessary*; *indispensable*; *need*: 必要的条件 bìyàode tiáojiàn (*necessary conditions*); 没有必要送礼 méi you bìyào sòng lǐ (*there is no need to give presents*)

边 biān

1. *side*, often pronounced in the neutral tone: 东边 dōngbian (*east side*); 左边 zuǒbian (*left side*); 双边会谈 shuāngbiān huìtán (*bilateral talk*)

2. *edge*; *margin*: 水边 shuǐbian (*water margin*); 桌边 zhuōbian (*edge of the table*)

3. *limit*; *bound*: 无边的田野 wú biān de tiányě (*boundless fields*)

Also appears in the following words: 靠边 kàobiān (*move to the side*); 里边 lǐbian (*inside*); 旁边 pángbiān (*beside*; *on the side*); 身边 shēnbiān (*at one's side*); 手边 shǒubiān (*at hand*); 外边 wàibian (*outside*)

边 … 边 … biān … biān …	Used in pairs to indicate two actions are taking place simultaneously; interchangeable with 一边 … 一边 yìbiān … yìbiān. However if the subjects are different, only 一边 … 一边… can be used. See under 一 yī.

边际 biānjì	bound; boundary
边疆 biānjiāng	frontier; border area
边界 biānjiè	boundary; border
边境 biānjìng	border area
边缘 biānyuán	edge; brink
边远 biānyuǎn	remote (area)

变 biàn

1. *change*: 这个城市完全变了 zhè ge chéngshì wánquán biàn le (*this city has completely changed*); 教学方法应该多变 jiàoxué fāngfǎ yīnggāi duō biàn (*teaching methods should be varied*)

2. *change into*, often followed by the verb complement 成 chéng or 为 wéi: 坏事变好事 huàishì biàn hǎoshì (*a bad thing becomes a good thing*); 水变成了气 shuǐ biàn chéng le qì (*water changed into gas*)

3. *an unexpected turn of events* (political): 事变 shìbiàn (*political incident*); 政变 zhèngbiàn (*coup*)

Also appears in the following words: 改变 gǎibiàn (*alter; change*); 剧变 jùbiàn (*shake-up*); 叛变 pànbiàn (*mutiny*); 演变 yǎnbiàn (*evolve; evolution*); 转变 zhuǎnbiàn (*change; transformation*).

变动 biàndòng	change (n.); *alteration*: 人事变动 rénshì biàndòng (*personnel change*)
变卦 biànguà	go back on one's word
变化 biànhuà	change (n. and v.): 气候变化很大 qìhòu biànhuà hěn dà (*climate changes greatly*); 我的工作有了变化 wǒde gōngzuò yǒu le biànhuà (*there has been a change in my job*)
变相 biànxiàng	in a disguised form: 变相征税 biànxiàng zhēng shuì (*exact tax in a disguised form*)
变心 biànxīn	change heart; cease to be faithful

遍 biàn

1. *once; one time*: 请再说一遍 qǐng zài shuō yí biàn (*please say it one more time*); 这本书我看过两遍 zhè běn shū wǒ kàn guo liǎng biàn (*I've read this book twice*). 遍 biàn differs from 次 cì (*time; occurrence*) in that it suggests the action proceeds in its entirety from beginning to end, whereas 次 cì does not have the implication. Cf. 这部电影我看过三遍 zhè bù diànyǐng wǒ kàn guo sān biàn (*I've seen the movie three times* – from beginning to end); 这部

电影我看过三次 zhè bù diànyǐng wǒ kàn guo sān cì (*I've seen the movie three times – maybe didn't finish seeing it each time*).

2. *all over; throughout*, as a verb complement: 走遍中国 zǒu biàn Zhōngguó (*travel throughout China*); 看遍纽约的博物馆 kàn biàn Niǔyuē de bówùguǎn (*visit every museum in New York*)

遍布 **biànbù**	*spread all over; be found everywhere*: 电视台遍布全国 diànshìtái biànbù quánguó (*TV stations can be found all over the country*)	
遍地 **biàndì**	*everywhere; all over*: 遍地是垃圾 biàndì shì lājī (*there is trash all over the place*)	
遍及 **biànjí**	*extend all over*: 他的研究遍及世界 tāde yánjiū biànjí shìjiè (*his research extended to the entire world*)	

表 biǎo

1. *wrist watch*. Cl: 只 zhī; 块 kuài; 个 gè

2. *table; form*: 时间表 shíjiānbiǎo (*timetable*); 申请表 shēnqǐngbiǎo (*application form*). Cl: 个 gè; 张 zhāng; 份 fèn

3. *meter*: 电表 diànbiǎo (*electricity meter*); 水表 shuǐbiǎo (*water meter*). Cl: 只 zhī; 个 gè

4. *surface; external*, usu. used as part of the word 表面 biǎomiàn

5. *express; show*: 表心意 biǎo xīnyì (*show a token of thanks*)

Also appears in the following words: 代表 dàibiǎo (*represent; representative; representation*); 发表 fābiǎo (*publish*); 课表 kèbiǎo (*class schedule*); 图表 túbiǎo (*chart; diagram*); 外表 wàibiǎo (*surface; appearance; exterior*)

表层 **biǎocéng**	*surface layer*	
表达 **biǎodá**	*express*	
表格 **biǎogé**	*table; form*. Cl: 份 fèn; 张 zhāng	
表决 **biǎojué**	*decide by vote*	
表面 **biǎomiàn**	*surface*: 表面现象 biǎomiàn xiànxiàng (*surface phenomenon*)	
表明 **biǎomíng**	*make clear; clearly state*	
表情 **biǎoqíng**	*facial expression*	
表示 **biǎoshì**	*indicate; show*	
表态 **biǎotài**	*declare one's position*	
表现 **biǎoxiàn**	**1.** *(work) performance*	
	2. *manifest; manifestation*. Cl: 种 zhǒng	
表演 **biǎoyǎn**	*perform; performance*	
表扬 **biǎoyáng**	*praise* (n. & v.)	

别 bié

1. *other*, often taking the form of 别的 biéde: 别的国家 biéde guójiā (*other countries*); 别的公司 biéde gōngsī (*other companies*)

2. *don't*, often used in conjunction with 了 le: 别去了 bié qù le (*don't go*); 别说了 bié shuō le (*don't talk*)

3. *difference*: 性别 xìngbié (*gender*); 区别 qūbié (*distinction*)

4. *leave; part*: 别了父母 bié le fùmǔ (*said good-bye to parents*)

Also appears in the following words: 差别 chābié (*difference*); 分别 fēnbié (*leave each other*); 告别 gàobié (*say goodbye*); 个别 gèbié (*individual*); 离别 líbié (*leave; bid farewell*); 识别 shíbié (*identify; distinguish*); 特别 tèbié (*special*)

别名 **biémíng**	*another name; alias*
别人 **biérén**	*someone else; other people*
别针 **biézhēn**	*safety pin.* Cl: 个 gè
别字 **biézì**	*a Chinese character written or pronounced incorrectly.* Cl: 个 gè

病 bìng

1. *sick; ill*: 病人 bìngrén (*sick person; patient*)

2. *become sick; fall sick*: 我太太病了一个星期 wǒ tàitai bìng le yí ge xīngqī (*my wife has been sick for a week*)

3. *sickness; disease*: 我的病已经好了 wǒde bìng yǐjīng hǎo le (*I have recovered from my sickness*); 心脏病 xīnzàngbìng (*heart disease*); 传染病 chuánrǎnbìng (*contagious disease*)

Also appears in the following words: 疾病 jíbìng (*disease*); 发病 fābìng (*fall sick*); 毛病 máobìng (*fault; defect*); 职业病 zhíyèbìng (*occupational disease*)

病床 **bìngchuáng**	*hospital bed; sickbed.* Cl: 张 zhāng
病毒 **bìngdú**	*virus*
病房 **bìngfáng**	*hospital ward.* Cl: 间 jiān
病故 **bìnggù**	*die of a disease*
病假 **bìngjià**	*sick leave*
病历 **bìnglì**	*medical record; medical history.* Cl: 份 fèn; 本 běn
病情 **bìngqíng**	*patient's condition*
病人 **bìngrén**	*patient.* Cl: 个 gè; 位 wèi; 名 míng
病因 **bìngyīn**	*cause of disease*
病愈 **bìngyù**	*recover from an illness*

并 bìng

1. *combine*; *merge*, often taking the form of 合并 hébìng: 把两个班并成一个班 bǎ liǎng ge bān bìng chéng yí ge bān (*combine the two classes into one class*); 三家电话公司合并了 sān jiā diànhuà gōngsī hébìng le (*the three telephone companies have merged*)

2. used before a negative word to indicate a strong denial or emphasis: 他并不是律师 tā bìng bú shì lùshī (*he is by no means a lawyer*)

3. *and also*: 我们吃了饭并看了电影 wǒmen chī le fàn bìng kàn le diànyǐng (*we ate a meal and we also saw a movie*)

并排 **bìngpái**	*side by side*: 并排坐 bìng pái zuò (*sit side by side*)
并且 **bìngqiě**	*besides*; *moreover*: 他赢了第一名，并且也打破了全国纪录 tā yíng le dìyīmíng, bìngqiě yě dà pò le quánguó jìlù (*he won first place; besides, he also broke the national record*)

不 bù

In isolation, it is pronounced in the fourth tone, but when followed by a fourth-tone word, it is pronounced in the second tone: 不来 bù lái (*not come*); 不去 bú qù (*not go*). 不 bù is pronounced in the neutral tone when used in the "verb/adjective – 不 bu – verb/adjective" yes/no question form: 你今天忙不忙 nǐ jīntiān máng bu máng (*are you busy today?*); 你太太工作不工作 nǐ tàitai gōngzuò bu gōngzuò (*does your wife work?*).

no; *not*, used before all the adjectives, adverbs, and verbs except 有 yǒu (*have*):

    A: 你知道路吗? nǐ zhīdào lù ma? (*Do you know the way?*)
    B: 不，我不知道 bù, wǒ bù zhīdào (*No, I don't.*)

To negate a verb followed by a complement, 不 bù is placed between the verb and the complement: 字写得不好看 zì xiě de bú hǎokàn (*the characters were not written nicely*); 我说不清楚 wǒ shuō bù qīngchǔ (*I can't explain it clearly*); 他看不见黑板上的字 tā kàn bú jiàn hēibǎn shang de zì (*he can't see the words on the blackboard*).

不必 **búbì**	*not necessary*; *don't have to*; *no need*: 你不必给我钱 nǐ búbì gěi wǒ qián (*you don't have to give me money*). 不必 búbì can be used interchangeably with 不用 búyòng.
不错 **búcuò**	*not bad*; *pretty good*
不但 … 而且 **búdàn … érqiě**	*not only … but also*, adverbs such as 也 yě (*also*), 还 hái (*still*) or 又 yòu (*further*) are often used in the second clause: 他不但会说上海话，而且也会说广东话 tā

búdàn huì shuō Shànghǎihuà, érqiě yě huì shuō Guǎngdōnghuà (*he can speak not only Shanghai dialect, but also Guangdong dialect*). 而且 érqiě can be substituted by 还 hái. If the two clauses introduced by 不但 búdàn and 而且 érqiě share the same subject, the subject appears before 不但 búdàn. However if the two clauses do not share the same subject, the two subjects appear after the conjunctions respectively: 不但我不知道这个字，而且我的老师也不知道这个字 búdàn wǒ bù zhīdào zhè ge zì, érqiě wǒde lǎoshī yě bù zhīdào zhè ge zì (*not only do I not know this character, but my teacher doesn't know this character either*).

不敢当 **bùgǎndāng**	Response to a compliment, literally meaning *I don't deserve it*. Another commonly used expression with the similar meaning is 哪里 nǎlǐ.
不管 **bùguǎn**	*no matter* (*what, who, when, how, etc.*). The presence of 都 dōu, 也 yě or 还是 háishi is required in the main clause to suggest that there is no exception: 不管明天下不下雨，我也要去公园 bùguǎn míngtiān xià bu xià yǔ, wǒ yě yào qù gōngyuán (*I'm going to the park tomorrow whether it rains or not*); 不管我怎么说，他都不听 bùguǎn wǒ zěnme shuō, tā dōu bù tīng (*no matter what I say, he refuses to listen*).
不过 **búguò**	*nevertheless*
不好意思 **bùhǎoyìsī**	*embarrassed; I'm sorry*
不仅 … 而且 **bùjǐn … érqiě**	*not only … but also*, used mostly in written language
不久 **bùjiǔ**	*soon; before long*
不客气 **búkèqī**	*you are welcome* (as a response to *thank you*)
不论 **búlùn**	*no matter* (*what, who, when, how, etc.*), used interchangeably with 不管 bùguǎn. 不论 búlùn is more formal than 不管 bùguǎn.
不如 **bùrú**	*not as good as*; *not as … as*: 我的中文不如你的中文 wǒde Zhōngwén bùrú nǐde Zhōngwén (*my Chinese is not as good as your Chinese*)
不是 … 吗? **bú shì … ma?**	used in a rhetorical question to expect an affirmative answer: 这个字不是很难写吗 zhè ge zì bú shì hěn nán xiě ma (*isn't this character difficult to write?*)
不同 **bùtóng**	*not the same; different*
不要 **búyào**	*don't*, used in an imperative sense
不一定 **bùyídìng**	*not necessarily; not particularly*
不用 **búyòng**	*not necessary; don't have to*, used interchangeably with 不必 búbì

部 bù

1. *part*; *section*: 北部　běibù (*northern part*); 校部　xiàobù (*campus section, as opposed to living quarters of a school*)

2. (of government) *ministry*: 外交部　wàijiāobù (*foreign ministry*)

3. *head office*; *headquarters*: 编辑部　biānjíbù (*editorial board*)

4. classifier for movies, novels, machines, etc.: 一部电影　yí bù diànyǐng (*a movie*); 两部小说　liǎng bù xiǎoshuō (*two novels*)

Also appears in the following words: **局部** júbù (*part*; *local*); **内部** nèibù (*internal*; *inside*); **全部** quánbù (*whole*; *entire*); **外部** wàibù (*external*; *outside*); **俱乐部** jùlèbù (*club*)

部队　bùduì	*army*; *troops*. Cl: 支 zhī
部分　bùfēn	**1.** *part* (n. and adj.); *some*: 这篇课文分三个部分　zhè piān kèwén fēn sān ge bùfēn (*this text consists of three parts*); 部分地区　bùfēn dìqū (*some areas*)
	2. *partly*; *partially*: 部分正确　bùfēn zhèngquè (*partially correct*)
部件　bùjiàn	(of machines) *parts*; *components*. Cl: 个 gè
部落　bùluò	*tribe*. Cl: 个 gè
部门　bùmén	*department* (in a company or an organization)
部署　bùshǔ	*deploy*
部位　bùwèi	*body part*; *position of body parts*. Cl: 个 gè

步 bù

1. *step*; *stride*: 大步走　dà bù zǒu (*walk in big strides*); 下一步　xiàyī bù (*next step*)

2. *walk* (v.): 步入会场　bù rù huìchǎng (*walk into the auditorium*)

Also appears in the following words: **初步** chūbù (*initial*; *preliminary*); **地步** dìbù (*extent*); **脚步** jiǎobù (*footsteps*); **进步** jìnbù (*progress*); **跑步** pǎobù (*run*; *jog*); **让步** ràngbù (*concede to*; *yield*); **散步** sànbù (*take a walk*; *stroll*); **退步** tuìbù (*retrograde*; *backslide*)

步兵　bùbīng	*infantry*; *foot soldier*
步伐　bùfá	*step*: 加快步伐　jiākuài bùfá (*quicken steps*)
步枪　bùqiāng	*rifle*. Cl: 枝 zhī
步行　bùxíng	*go on foot*
步骤　bùzhòu	*step*; *measure*
步子　bùzi	*step*; *pace*: 建设的步子　jiànshè de bùzi (*the pace of construction*)

才 cái

1. *talent*: 人才 réncái (*talented person*)

2. adverb with the meaning of *later than expected* or *worse than expected*. 才 cái in this sense is often opposed to 就 jiù, which suggests *earlier than expected* or *better than expected*. Cf. 九点上课, 他十点才来 jiǔ diǎn shàng kè, tā shí diǎn cái lái (*class started at 9, but he didn't come until 10*); 九点上课, 他八点就来了 jiǔ diǎn shàng kè, tā bā diǎn jiù lái le (*class started at 9, but he came as early as 8*)

3. *only*, with the implied meaning of *too few, too little*: 我才看过一部中国电影 (*I've only seen one Chinese movie*)

4. used to indicate that one situation is conditional upon another: 你做完作业才能看电视 nǐ zuò wán zuòyè cái néng kàn diànshì (*you can only watch TV after you finish your homework*); 我只有星期天才有时间 wǒ zhǐyǒu xīngqītiān cái yǒu shíjiān (*I only have time on Sunday*)

Also appears in the following words: 刚才 gāngcái (*just now*); 口才 kǒucái (*eloquence; speechcraft*); 天才 tiāncái (*genius*)

才华	**cáihuá**	*literary or artistic talent*
才能	**cáinéng**	*ability and talent*
才学	**cáixué**	*talent and knowledge*

菜 cài

1. *dish*: 所有的菜都好吃 suǒyǒude cài dōu hǎochī (*all the dishes are delicious*). Cl: 个 gè; 道 dào; 盘 pán

2. *vegetable*: 菜汤 càitāng (*vegetable soup*). Cl: 棵 kē

菜场	**càichǎng**	*food market; vegetable market*
菜单	**càidān**	*menu*. Cl: 份 fèn; 张 zhāng; 个 gè
菜刀	**càidāo**	*kitchen knife*. Cl: 把 bǎ
菜地	**càidì**	*vegetable plot*. Cl: 块 kuài
菜农	**càinóng**	*vegetable farmer*. Cl: 个 gè; 位 wèi

参 cān

join: 参政 cānzhèng (*participate in government or political process*); 参战 cānzhàn (*enter a war*); 参赛 cānsài (*enter a competition*). When followed by a disyllabic or polysyllabic object, it takes the disyllabic form of 参加 cānjiā: 参加会议 cānjiā hūnlǐ (*attend a wedding*); 参加运动会 cānjiā yùndònghuì (*take part in a sports meet*)

参观	cānguān	*visit* (a place)
参加	cānjiā	*join*; *attend*; *take part in*
参见	cānjiàn	*refer to* (a document)
参军	cānjūn	*join the military*
参考	cānkǎo	*read sth. for reference*; *consult*: 参考书 cānkǎoshū (*reference books*)
参议员	cānyìyuán	*senator*. Cl: 个 gè; 位 wèi; 名 míng
参议院	cānyìyuàn	*The Senate*
参与	cānyù	*participate in*; *be involved in*; *have a hand in*
参赞	cānzàn	(diplomatic) *counselor*; *councilor*. Cl: 个 gè; 位 wèi; 名 míng
参选	cānxuǎn	*enter an election*; *be a candidate*

餐 cān

meal; *food*: 早餐 zǎocān (*breakfast*); 午餐 wǔcān (*lunch*); 晚餐 wǎncān (*dinner*); 中餐 zhōngcān (*Chinese food*); 西餐 xīcān (*Western food*); 快餐 kuàicān (*fast food*)

餐车	cānchē	*dining car* (on a train)
餐馆	cānguǎn	*restaurant*. Cl: 家 jiā; 个 gè
餐巾	cānjīn	*napkin*. Cl: 条 tiáo; 块 kuài
餐具	cānjù	*tableware*; *silverware*; *dining set*. Cl: 件 jiàn; 套 tào
餐厅	cāntīng	*cafeteria*; *dining room*; *restaurant*. Cl: 个 gè; 间 jiān; 家 jiā

草 cǎo

1. *grass*; *weed*; *straw*; *hay*

2. *careless*; *slipshod*; *slovenly*, used as part of another word

草案	cǎo'àn	*a draft plan*
草包	cǎobāo	*duffer*; *good-for-nothing*. Cl: 个 gè
草草	cǎocǎo	*carelessly*; *quickly*; *hastily*; *perfunctorily*: 草草地检查了一下儿 cǎocǎode jiǎnchá le yíxiàr (*gave a hasty inspection*)
草地	cǎodì	*grassland*; *pasture*. Cl: 片 piàn; 块 kuài
草房	cǎofáng	*thatched house*. Cl: 间 jiān
草稿	cǎogǎo	*draft* (of an article or a book). Cl: 个 gè; 篇 piān; 张 zhāng
草帽	cǎomào	*straw hat*. Cl: 个 gè; 顶 dǐng
草书	cǎoshū	*cursive handwriting in Chinese calligraphy*
草率	cǎoshuài	*careless*; *perfunctory*; *rash*: 这个案子处理得很草率 zhège ànzi chǔli de hěn cǎoshuài (*this case was handled in a very careless manner*)
草药	cǎoyào	*herbal medicine*. Cl: 服 fú; 剂 jì

草原 cǎoyuán   *prairie.* Cl: 片 piàn
草纸 cǎozhǐ   *toilet paper.* Cl: 张 zhāng

层 céng

1. *layer; tier; stratum:* 表层 biǎocéng (*surface layer*); 下层阶级 xiàcéng jiējí (*lower class*)

2. *floor; story:* 第三层 dìsān céng (*the third floor*); 十层楼 shí céng lóu (*a ten-story building*)

差 chā; chà; chāi

When pronounced as chā:

1. *difference:* 时差 shíchā (*time difference*); 温差 wēnchā (*difference in temperature*); 反差 fǎnchā (*contrast*)

2. *error,* usu. taking such disyllabic forms as 偏差 piānchā (*error*) and 差错 chācuò (*mistake*)

差别 chābié   *difference; disparity*
差错 chācuò   *mistake; error; mishap; accident*
差距 chājù   *disparity; gap*
差异 chāyì   *difference; divergence; discrepancy*

When pronounced as chà:

1. *fall short of; differ from:* 我的中文水平差远了 wǒde Zhōngwén shuǐpíng chà yuǎn le (*my Chinese level is far from being adequate*)

2. *wanting; missing; short of:* 差5分3点 chà wǔ fēn sān diǎn (*5 minutes before 3; 2:55*); 我们团还差一个人 wǒmen tuán hái chà yí ge rén (*our group is missing one person*)

3. *poor; inferior; wanting:* 产品的质量很差 chǎnpǐn de zhìliàng hěn chà (*the quality of the product is very poor*)

差不多 chàbuduō   *more or less; approximately; roughly*
差点儿 chàdiǎnr   *almost; nearly:* 他差点儿没来 tā chàdiǎnr méi lái (*he almost didn't make it*)
差得多 chàdeduō   *far from (being enough); very different*

When pronounced as chāi:

errand; *job*: 出差 chūchāi (*go on a business trip*); 邮差 yóuchāi (*mailman*)

差事 chāishi   *errand*; *assignment*. Cl: 个 gè; 件 jiàn; 项 xiàng

---

茶 chá

tea: 茶杯 chábēi (*tea cup*); 茶馆 cháguǎn (*teahouse*); 绿茶 lǜchá (*green tea*);
红茶 hóngchá (*black tea*)

茶点 chádiǎn	*tea and refreshments*
茶壶 cháhú	*teapot*. Cl: 把 bǎ; 个 gè
茶具 chájù	*tea set*. Cl: 套 tào
茶叶 cháyè	*tea leaves*

产 chǎn

1. *produce*: 中国产油 Zhōngguó chǎn yóu (*China produces oil*)

2. *maternity*: 产妇 chǎnfù (*woman in labor*); 产房 chǎnfáng (*maternity ward*)

3. *property*; *estate*; *wealth*: 房产 fánghǎn (*housing property*; *estate*);
家产 jiāchǎn (*family property*)

Also appears in the following words: 财产 cáichǎn (*property*; *possessions*); 出产 chūchǎn (*produce*); 破产 pòchǎn (*bankruptcy*; *go bankrupt*); 生产 shēngchǎn (*produce*; *production*); 特产 tèchǎn (*special local product*); 土产 tǔchǎn (*local product*); 物产 wùchǎn (*product*); 遗产 yíchǎn (*heritage*; *inheritance*); 早产 zǎochǎn (*premature delivery*); 资产 zīchǎn (*assets*)

产地 chǎndì	*place of production*
产假 chǎnjià	*maternity leave*
产科 chǎnkē	*maternity department* (*in a hospital*)
产量 chǎnliàng	*production output*
产生 chǎnshēng	*produce* (*a result*); *engender*: 产生了好的结果 chǎngshēng le hǎo de jiéguǒ (*produced good results*)
产物 chǎnwù	*outcome*; *final product*

长 cháng

long

Also appears in the following words: 擅长 shàncháng (*be adept at; be clever at*); 特长 tècháng (*one's strong suit; specialty*); 延长 yáncháng (*prolong; extent*); 专长 zhuāncháng (*specialty*)

长城 chángchéng	*Great Wall*	
长处 chángchù	*strong point; merit*	
长度 chángdù	*length*	
长方形 chángfāngxíng	*rectangle*	
长江 chángjiāng	*Yangtze River*	
长跑 chángpǎo	*long-distance running*	
长期 chángqī	*long term; protracted*	
长途 chángtú	*long distance*: 长途汽车 chángtú qìchē (*long-distance bus*); 长途电话 chángtú diànhuà (*long-distance telephone call*)	
长远 chángyuǎn	*long range*: 长远目标 chángyuǎn mùbiāo (*long-range goal*)	

常 cháng

1. *often; frequently*: 我们常吃日本菜 wǒmen cháng chī Rìběn cài (*we often eat Japanese food*)

2. *ordinary; common; average*: 在中国这是常事 zài Zhōngguó zhè shì cháng shì (*in China, this is a common occurrence*)

Also appears in the following words: 反常 fǎncháng (*abnormal*); 非常 fēicháng (*very*); 经常 jīngcháng (*often; frequently*); 平常 píngcháng (*usually; common*); 日常 rìcháng (*day-to-day; everyday*); 通常 tōngcháng (*as a rule; customarily*); 照常 zhàocháng (*as usual*); 正常 zhèngcháng (*normal; normally*)

常常 chángcháng	*often; frequently*
常规 chángguī	*convention; routine practice*
常见 chángjiàn	*common occurrence*: 这里三月下雪是常见的 zhèlǐ sānyuè xiàxuě shì chángjiàn de (*snowing in March is a common occurrence here*)
常年 chángnián	*throughout the year; perennial*
常识 chángshí	*general knowledge*
常用 chángyòng	*in common use*: 常用术语 chángyòng shùyǔ (*terms in common use*)

场 chǎng

1. *place; open space; field*: 运动场 yùndòngchǎng (*sports ground*);
飞机场 fēijīchǎng (*airport*); 剧场 jùchǎng (*theater*)

2. classifier used for a showing of a movie, sports events, etc.: 一场电影
yì chǎng diànyǐng (*a movie*); 两场表演 liǎng chǎng biǎoyǎn (*two
performances*)

Also appears in the following words: 操场 cāochǎng (*playground*); 当场 dāngchǎng
(*on the spot*); 官场 guānchǎng (*officialdom*); 广场 guǎngchǎng (*square; plaza*);
立场 lìchǎng (*position; stand*); 商场 shāngchǎng (*shopping center; bazaar*); 市场
shìchǎng (*market*); 现场 xiànchǎng (*locale; scene*); 战场 zhànchǎng (*battlefield*)

场地	**chǎngdì**	*site; space*
场合	**chǎnghé**	*occasion*
场面	**chǎngmiàn**	*scene* (of an event)
场所	**chǎngsuǒ**	*site; place*

唱 chàng

sing

Also appears in the following words: 独唱 dúchàng (*vocal solo*); 歌唱 gēchàng
(*sing*); 合唱 héchàng (*chorus*); 演唱 yǎnchàng (*sing in a performance*)

唱反调 **chàng fǎndiào**	*deliberately speak or act contrary to*
唱歌 **chànggē**	*sing (a song)*
唱机 **chàngjī**	*gramophone.* Cl: 台 tái; 个 gè
唱片 **chàngpiàn**	*gramophone record.* Cl: 张 zhāng; 套 tào
唱戏 **chàngxì**	*sing and act in an opera*

车 chē

1. *vehicle*: 火车 huǒchē (*train*); 汽车 qìchē (*motor vehicle*); 卡车 kǎchē
(*truck*); 摩托车 mótuōchē (*motorcycle*). Cl: 辆 liàng; 部 bù

2. *wheeled machinery or device*: 马车 mǎchē (*horse-drawn carriage*);
水车 shuǐchē (*waterwheel*). Cl: 部 bù; 台 tái

Also appears in the following words: 倒车 dàochē (*back out a car*); 候车 hòuchē
(*wait for a bus*); 赛车 sàichē (*racing car*); 自行车 zìxíngchē (*bicycle*); 超车
chāochē (*overtake a vehicle*)

车祸	chēhuò	*traffic accident*
车库	chēkù	*garage.* Cl: 个 gè; 间 jiān
车轮	chēlún	*(vehicle) wheel.* Cl: 只 zhī; 个 gè
车票	chēpiào	*bus or train ticket.* Cl: 张 zhāng
车站	chēzhàn	*(train or bus) station.* Cl: 个 gè; 座 zuò

成 chéng

1. *become*: 三年前, 她成了我的太太 sān nián qián, tā chéng le wǒde tàitai (*she became my wife three years ago*)

2. *succeed*: 事情没有成 shìqing méiyou chéng (*the matter was not accomplished*)

3. verb complement of result indicating the successful accomplishment of an action: 桥建成了 qiáo jiàn chéng le (*the bridge has been built*)

4. *into*, used after a verb: 美元换成了日元 Měiyuán huàn chéng le Rìyuán (*U.S. dollars were changed into Japanese yen*)

5. *grown*: 成人 chéngrén (*grown-up*; *adult*)

Also appears in the following words: **构成** gòuchéng (*constitute*; *make up*); **速成** sùchéng (*crash course*); **完成** wánchéng (*complete*); **现成** xiànchéng (*ready-made*); **形成** xíngchéng (*form*); **赞成** zànchéng (*agree*; *approve*)

成本	chéngběn	*production cost*
成份	chéngfèn	*composition; ingredient*
成功	chénggōng	*succeed; success*
成果	chéngguǒ	*achievement; gain.* Cl: 个 gè; 项 xiàng
成绩	chéngji	*result; achievement.* Cl: 项 xiàng
成家	chéngjiā	*get married*
成见	chéngjiàn	*bias; prejudice; preconceived idea*
成就	chéngjiù	*attainment; accomplishment*
成立	chénglì	*establish; found; establishment; founding*
成名	chéngmíng	*become famous*
成年	chéngnián	*come of age*: 成年人 chéngniánrén (*adult*)
成品	chéngpǐn	*finished product.* Cl: 个 gè; 件 jiàn
成人	chéngrén	*adult*
成熟	chéngshú	*mature*
成为	chéngwéi	*become; turn into*
成效	chéngxiào	*effect*
成语	chéngyǔ	*idiom*
成长	chéngzhǎng	*grow up*

城 chéng

1. *city*; *town*: 进城 jìn chéng (*go to town*); 中国城 Zhōngguóchéng (*China-town*); 古城 gǔchéng (*ancient city*). Cl: 座 zuò

2. *city wall*: 长城 Chángchéng (*the Great Wall*)

城里	chénglǐ	*inside the city*; *in town*: 城里人 chénglǐrén (*city people*)
城门	chéngmén	*city gate*
城墙	chéngqiáng	*city wall*
城区	chéngqū	*the city proper*; *urban area*
城市	chéngshì	*city*. Cl: 座 zuò; 个 gè

吃 chī

1. *eat*

2. *take*: 吃药 chī yào (*take medicine*)

3. *capture*; *wipe out* (in battles or board games): 吃了敌人的一个连 chī le dírén de yí ge lián (*wiped out the enemy's entire company*); 吃了对方的马 chī le duìfāng de mǎ (*captured the opponent's knight*)

Also appears in the following words: 口吃 kǒuchī (*stammer; stutter*); 小吃 xiǎochī (*snack*)

吃不下 chī bú xià	*be unable to eat any more*: 我吃了很多, 吃不下了 wǒ chī le hěn duō, chī bú xià le (*I ate a lot and can't eat any more*). The opposite is 吃得下 chī de xià.
吃不消 chī bù xiāo	*be unable to stand or put up with*: 你现在如果不睡觉, 一定会吃不消 nǐ xiànzài rúguǒ bú shuìjiào, yídìng huì chī bù xiāo (*if you don't go to sleep now, you surely won't be able to stand it*). The opposite is 吃得消 chī de xiāo.
吃醋 chīcù	*be jealous*, usu. of a rival in a love affair
吃饭 chīfàn	**1.** *eat*; *eat a meal*
	2. *make a living*: 靠打鱼吃饭 kào dǎyú chīfàn (*make a living by fishing*)
吃惊 chījīng	*be surprised*; *be shocked*
吃苦 chīkǔ	*bear hardship*
吃亏 chīkuī	*suffer losses*; *be in a disadvantageous position*: 不老实会吃亏 bù lǎoshi huì chīkuī (*those who are dishonest will suffer at the end*)
吃素 chīsù	*be a vegetarian*: 我吃素 wǒ chī sù (*I'm a vegetarian*)

出 chū

1. *go out; exit*: 出门要带伞 chū mén yào dài sǎn (*when you leave the house, you need to take an umbrella with you*)

2. *exceed*: 不出五年 bù chū wǔ nián (*in less than five years*)

3. *issue; offer*: 出证明 chū zhèngmíng (*issue a certificate*); 出主意 chū zhǔyì (*offer an idea*)

4. *produce*: 中国出石油 Zhōngguó chū shíyóu (*China produces petroleum*)

5. (*unpleasant things or situations*) *happen; arise*: 出问题 chū wèntí (*problem arises*); 出了事故 chū le shìgù (*accident happened*). 出 chū is often used with 来 lái or 去 qù to form a complex directional complement to a verb to show the direction of the movement indicated by the verb in relation to where the speaker is. If the verb takes an object that indicates a place, the object should be placed between 出 chū and 来 lái or 去 qù: 他走出学校来了 tā zǒu chū xuéxiào lái le (*he walked out of the school—in the direction of the speaker*). If the object is other than a place, it can be placed either between 出 chū and 来 lái/去 qù or after 来 lái/去 qù: 他从口袋里拿出来十块钱 tā cóng kǒudài lǐ ná chū lái shí kuài qián (*he took out ten dollars from his pocket*) or 他从口袋里拿出十块钱来 tā cóng kǒudài lǐ ná chū shí kuài qián lái.

6. *out*, used after a verb: 取出 qǔ chū (*take out*); 寄出 jì chū (*mail out*); 写出 xiě chū (*write out*); 找出 zhǎo chū (*find out*); 想出主意 xiǎng chū zhǔyì (*come up with an idea*)

Also appears in the following words: 杰出 jiéchū (*outstanding*); 日出 rìchū (*sunrise*); 输出 shūchū (*output*); 突出 tūchū (*outstanding*); 退出 tuìchū (*quit; retreat from*); 演出 yǎnchū (*perform*); 指出 zhǐchū (*point out*)

出版 **chūbǎn**	*publish*: 出版社 chūbǎnshè (*publishing house*)	
出差 **chūchāi**	*go on a business trip*: 去外地出差 qù wàidì chūchā (*go out of town for business*)	
出产 **chūchǎn**	*produce*	
出处 **chūchù**	*source of information*	
出发 **chūfā**	*set out; start off; depart*	
出国 **chūguó**	*go abroad*	
出口 **chūkǒu**	*exit* (n.); *export* (n. and v.)	
出路 **chūlù**	*way out*	
出门 **chūmén**	*leave home*	
出气 **chūqì**	*vent anger*	
出身 **chūshēn**	*class origin; family background*	
出生 **chūshēng**	*be born; birth*: 我是在中国出生的 wǒ shì zài Zhōngguó chūshēng de (*I was born in China*); 出生日期 chūshēng rìqī (*date of birth*)	

出席	chūxí	*attend* (a meeting or an event); *be present*
出现	chūxiàn	*appear*; *emerge*
出院	chūyuàn	*be discharged from hospital*
出租	chūzū	*rent* (v.): 出租车 chūzūchē (*taxi*); 你有没有房子出租 nǐ you méi you fángzi chūzū (*do you have a room to rent?*)

处 chǔ; chù

When pronounced chǔ:

1. *get along with*: 我们处得很好 wǒmen chǔ de hěn hǎo (*we get along very well*); 她很好处 tā hěn hǎo chǔ (*she is easy to get along with*)

2. *sentence; punish*: 处三年刑 chǔ sān nián xíng (*sentence to three years' imprisonment*)

处罚	chǔfá	*punish; penalize*
处方	chǔfāng	(med.) *prescription*
处分	chǔfèn	*punishment; penalty; disciplinary action*
处境	chǔjìng	*situation; plight*
处决	chǔjué	*execute; put to death*
处理	chǔlǐ	1. *handle* (business); *deal with; treat*
		2. *dispose of*: 处理污水 chǔlǐ wūshuǐ (*dispose of sewage*); 处理垃圾 chǔlǐ lājī (*dispose of garbage*)
处女	chǔnǚ	*maiden; virgin*
处于	chǔyú	*be in* (a situation): 处于有利的形势 chǔyú yǒulìde xíngshì (*be in a favorable situation*)

When pronounced chù:

1. *place; location*: 付款处 fùkuǎnchù (*cashier*, literally *place where payment is made*); 问讯处 wènxúnchù (*information desk*, literally *place where inquiries can be made*)

2. *department; office*: 办事处 bànshìchù (*branch office*); 管理处 guǎnlǐchù (*management office*)

Also appears in the following words: **长处** chángchù (*strength; long suit*); **短处** duǎnchù (*shortcoming; weakness*); **出处** chūchù (*source of information*); **到处** dàochù (*everywhere*); **害处** hàichu (*harm; detriment*); **好处** hǎochù (*benefit*); **坏处** huàichu (*harm; disadvantage*); **难处** nánchu (*difficulty; trouble*); **去处** qùchù (*place to turn to*); **用处** yòngchu (*use; usefulness*); **原处** yuánchù (*original place*)

| 处处 | chùchù | *everywhere; at every turn* |
| 处所 | chùsuǒ | *place; location* |

穿 chuān

1. *wear* (clothing; but not to be used for items such as hats, scarves, and gloves)

2. *pierce through*: 穿耳洞 chuān ěrdòng (*pierce a hole in the ear*); 在墙上穿洞 zài qiáng shang chuān dòng (*drill a hole in the wall*)

3. *cross*; *pass through*, often used with 过 guò: 穿马路 chuān mǎlù (*cross the street*); 穿过公园 chuān guò gōngyuán (*cut across the park*)

4. *through*: used as a verb complement: 看穿 kàn chuān (*see through*)

Also appears in the following words: 贯穿 guànchuān (*run through*; *penetrate*); 戳穿 chuōchuān (*expose*; *puncture*); 说穿 shuōchuān (*reveal*; *disclose*)

穿插 **chuānchā**	*insert*; *weave in*: 儿童的节目里穿插着大人的节目 értóng de jiémù lǐ chuānchā zhe dàrén de jiémù (*the adults' performance was weaved into the children's performance*)
穿梭 **chuānsuō**	*shuttle back and forth*: 穿梭外交 chuānsuō wàijiāo (*shuttle diplomacy*)
穿针 **chuānzhēn**	*thread a needle*

船 chuán

boat; *ship*: 渡船 dùchuán (*ferryboat*); 帆船 fānchuán (*sailboat*); 轮船 lúnchuán (*steamboat*; *streamship*); 游船 yóuchuán (*yacht*); 渔船 yúchuán (*fishing boat*). Cl: 只 zhī; 条 tiáo

船厂 **chuánchǎng**	*shipyard*
船队 **chuánduì**	*fleet of ships*
船票 **chuánpiào**	*boat ticket*. Cl: 张 zhāng
船员 **chuányuán**	*crew*; *sailor*. Cl: 个 gè; 位 wèi; 名 míng
船长 **chuánzhǎng**	*captain*; *skipper*. Cl: 个 gè; 位 wèi; 名 míng

传 chuán

1. *pass*: 传球 chuán qiú (*pass the ball*); 把书传给我 bǎ shū chuán gěi wǒ (*pass the book to me*)

2. *spread*: 这个消息传遍了校园 zhè ge xiāoxi chuán biàn le xiàoyuán (*the news spread throughout the campus*)

3. *summon*: 传证人 chuán zhèngrén (*summon the witness*)

Also appears in the following words: 家传 jiāchuán (*run in the blood; hand down in the family*); 口传 kǒuchuán (*from mouth to mouth; hearsay*); 流传 liúchuán (*spread; go around*); 宣传 xuānchuán (*publicize; disseminate*); 遗传 yíchuán (*heredity; inheritance*); 祖传 zǔchuán (*handed down from one's ancestors*)

传播 **chuánbō**	*disseminate; spread*
传达 **chuándá**	*relay* (information, instruction, etc.)
传单 **chuándān**	*leaflet.* Cl: 张 zhāng; 份 fèn
传道 **chuándào**	*preach; deliver a sermon*
传家宝 **chuánjiābǎo**	*family heirloom*
传票 **chuánpiào**	*subpoena; summons.* Cl: 张 zhāng
传染 **chuánrǎn**	*infect; contagious*: 传染病 chuánrǎnbìng (*contagious disease*)
传授 **chuánshòu**	*pass on* (knowledge; skill, etc.); *teach*
传说 **chuánshuō**	*legend; the legend has it that*
传送 **chuánsòng**	*convey*: 传送带 chuánsòngdài (*conveyor belt*)
传统 **chuántǒng**	*tradition; traditional*: 传统社会 chuántǒng shèhuì (*traditional society*)
传闻 **chuánwén**	*it is said; rumor; hearsay*
传真 **chuánzhēn**	*fax*: 发传真 fā chuánzhēn (*send a fax*). Cl: 份 fèn

词 cí

word: 同义词 tóngyìcí (*synonym*); 反义词 fǎnyìcí (*antonym*); 欢迎词 huānyíngcí (*welcome remarks*); 开幕词 kāimùcí (*opening speech*); 生词 shēngcí (*new words*)

Also appears in the following words: 措词 cuòcí (*wording*); 歌词 gēcí (*lyrics*); 台词 táicí (*actor's lines*)

词典 **cídiǎn**	*dictionary.* Cl: 部 bù; 本 běn
词汇 **cíhuì**	*vocabulary*
词类 **cílèi**	*parts of speech*
词素 **císù**	*morpheme*
词条 **cítiáo**	*entry* (in a dictionary)
词序 **cíxù**	*word order*
词义 **cíyì**	*meaning of a word*
词语 **cíyǔ**	*words and expressions*
词源 **cíyuán**	*etymology; word origin*
词组 **cízǔ**	*phrase*

次 cì

1. *time; occurrence:* 三次 sān cì (*three times*); 第一次 dìyī cì (*the first time*)

2. *substandard; second-rate:* 次品 cìpǐn (*defective products*)

3. *second; secondary:* 次日 cìrì (*second day*)

4. *classifier for things that recur:* 三次会议 sān cì huìyì (*three meetings*); 二次大战 Èr Cì Dà Zhàn (*World War II*)

5. *poorer than; inferior to*, followed by preposition 于 yú and used in negative comparative sentences only: 美国汽车不次于日本汽车 Měiguó qìchē bú cì yú Rìběn qìchē (*American cars are not inferior to Japanese cars*)

次数 cìshù	*number of times; frequency:* 出现的次数 chūxiàn de cìshù (*frequency of occurrences*)
次序 cìxù	*sequence; order*
次要 cìyào	*of secondary importance*

从 cóng

1. *from:* 他从中国来 tā cóng Zhōngguó lái (*he is from China*); 从今年起 cóng jīnnián qǐ (*starting from this year*); 从上到下 cóng shàng dào xià (*from top to bottom*)

2. *by way of; through:* 从我家去 cóng wǒ jiā qù (*leave from my house*); 从海上运 cóng hǎishàng yùn (*ship from the sea*)

3. *ever,* usu. used in negative sentences: 这儿冬天从不下雪 zhèr dōngtiān cóng bú xiàxuě (*it has never snowed here in winter*)

Also appears in the following words: 服从 fúcóng (*obey; submit; comply with*); 随从 suícóng (*attendant*); 听从 tīngcóng (*defer to; comply with*); 自从 zìcóng (*since; ever since*)

从此 cóngcǐ	*from this/that time on*
从来 cónglái	*always; ever*, used in negative sentences: 我从来没有吃过日本菜 wó cónglái méiyou chī guo Rìběn cài (*I have never had Japanese food before*)
从前 cóngqián	*before; a long time ago*
从事 cóngshì	*be engaged in:* 从事商业 cóngshì shāngyè (*be engaged in commerce*)
从头 cóngtóu	*from the beginning*
从小 cóngxiǎo	*since childhood*

错 cuò

1. *wrong*; *mistaken*; *incorrect*; *erroneous*, often used as a verb complement: 坐错了汽车 zuò cuò le qìchē (*took the wrong bus*); 说错了话 shuō cuò le huà (*said the wrong thing*); 写错了字 xiě cuò le zì (*wrote the character wrong*)

2. *bad*; *poor*, used with the negative word 不: 不错 bú cuò (*not bad*; *very good*)

3. *alternate*; *stagger*; *avoid*, used with the verb complement 开 kāi: 错开上下班的时间 cuò kāi shàngxī kāibān de shíjiān (*avoid the rush hours*; *stagger the hours to go to and leave work*)

Also appears in the following words: 差错 chācuò (*error*; *mishap*); 过错 guòcuò (*fault*; *offence*); 认错 rèncuò (*acknowledge mistakes*)

错怪 **cuòguài**	*blame sb. wrongly*
错过 **cuòguò**	*miss*; *let slip* (an opportunity)
错觉 **cuòjué**	*illusion*; *wrong impression*; *misconception*
错开 **cuò kāi**	*stagger*; *avoid*
错误 **cuòwù**	*mistake*; *error*; *wrong*; *mistaken*; *incorrect*; *erroneous*

答 dá

answer; *reply*, usu. taking the disyllabic form of 回答 huídá

Also appears in the following words: 报答 bàodá (*repay*); 对答 duìdá (*answer*; *reply*); 解答 jiědá (*answer*; *explain*); 问答 wèndá (*questions and answers*)

答案 **dá'àn**	*answer* (n.): 找到了答案 zhǎo dào le dá'àn (*found the answer*)
答辩 **dábiàn**	*answer*; *reply*; *defend* (a thesis, dissertation, etc.)
答复 **dáfù**	(a formal) *answer*; *reply* (n. and v.)
答谢 **dáxiè**	*return thanks*; *reciprocate kindness*

打 dǎ

1. *hit*; *beat*; *strike*; *break*; *fight*: 打人 dǎi rén (*hit someone*); 打钟 dǎ zhōng (*strike the clock*); 打了盘子 dǎ le pánzi (*broke the plate*)

2. *pack*: 打行李 dǎ xínglǐ (*pack luggage*)

3. *knit*; *weave*: 打毛衣 dǎ máoyī (*knit a sweater*)

4. *play* (a game): 打球 dǎ qiú (*play a ball game*); 打牌 dǎ pái (*play cards*); 打麻将 dǎ májiàng (*play mahjong*)

5. *hold up*: 打伞 dǎ sǎn (*hold an umbrella*)

6. *send*; *dispatch*: 打电话 dǎ diànhuà (*make a phone call*)

7. *fetch*; *go and buy*: 打水 dǎ shuǐ (*fetch water*); 打饭 dǎ fàn (*go and buy the meal*)

8. *buy*: 打车票 dǎ chēpiào (*buy a bus ticket*)

9. *do*; *work*: 打工 dǎ gōng (*work as a laborer*)

10. used with many nouns to form set expressions (see below)

打扮 **dǎbàn**	*dress up*; *make up*
打倒 **dǎdǎo**	*overthrow*; *down with*
打动 **dǎdòng**	*touch*; *move*
打赌 **dǎdǔ**	*bet*; *wager*
打断 **dǎduàn**	*interrupt*
打官司 **dǎguānsī**	*engage in a lawsuit*
打击 **dǎjī**	*crack down*; *strike*; *attack*
打架 **dǎjià**	*fight*; *scuffle*
打交道 **dǎjiāodào**	*come into contact with*; *deal with*
打搅 **dǎjiǎo**	*disturb*
打开 **dǎkāi**	*open* (v.): 打开箱子 dǎkāi xiāngzi (*open the suitcase*); 打开窗子 dǎkāi chuāngzi (*open the window*)
打猎 **dǎliè**	*hunt*
打乱 **dǎluàn**	*disrupt*; *upset* (a plan, etc.)
打破 **dǎpò**	*break* (an object, a record, etc.)
打气 **dǎqì**	1. *inflate* (a tire)
	2. *bolster up* (the morale, etc.)
打扫 **dǎsǎo**	*sweep*; *clean*
打算 **dǎsuàn**	*plan* (n. and v.): 你毕业后有什么打算 nǐ bìyè hòu yǒu shénme dǎsuàn (*what's your plan after graduation?*); 我打算继续学习 wǒ dǎsuàn jìxù xuéxí (*I plan to continue my studies*)
打碎 **dǎsuì**	*break into pieces*
打胎 **dǎtāi**	*have an abortion*
打听 **dǎtīng**	*inquire about*; *ask around*
打退 **dǎtuì**	*beat back*: 打退敌人的进攻 dǎtuì dírén de jìngōng (*beat back the enemy's attack*)
打消 **dǎxiāo**	*give up* (an idea, etc.): 打消旅行的念头 dǎxiāo lǚxíng de niàntou (*give up the idea of traveling*)
打印 **dǎyìn**	*print*: 打印机 dǎyìnjī (*printer*)
打杂 **dǎzá**	*do odd jobs*
打仗 **dǎzhàng**	*fight a war or a battle*

打招呼 dǎzhāohū	1. *greet*; *say hello*
	2. *inform*; *notify*
打折扣 dǎzhékòu	1. *give a discount*
	2. *fall short of expectation*: 安全问题不能打折扣 ānquán wèntí bù néng dǎ zhékòu (*we can't cut corners regarding safety issues*)
打字 dǎzì	*typewrite*: 打字机 dǎzìjī (*typewriter*); 打字员 dǎzìjīyuán (*typist*)

大 dà

1. *big*; *large*; *great*; *heavy*

2. *very*; *greatly*: 他妈妈的身体已大好 tā māma de shēntǐ yǐ dà hǎo (*his mother's health has greatly improved*); 我不大清楚 wǒ bú dà qīngchǔ (*I'm not very sure*); 这家旅馆不大干净 zhè jiā lǚguǎn bú dà gānjìng (*this hotel is not very clean*)

3. *old*, used in questions and comparative sentences: 你今年多大 nǐ jīnnián duō dà (*how old are you this year?*); 我哥哥比我大三岁 wǒ gēge bǐ wǒ dà sān suì (*my brother is three years older than I*)

4. *often*, used with 不 bù: 这儿冬天不大下雪 zhèr dōngtiān bú dà xiàxuě (*it doesn't often snow here*)

Also appears in the following words: 放大 fàngdà (*enlarge*; *magnify*); 高大 gāodà (*lofty*; *tall*); 广大 guǎngdà (*vast*; *immense*); 巨大 jùdà (*huge*); 夸大 kuādà (*exaggerate*); 扩大 kuòdà (*broaden*; *expand*); 强大 qiángdà (*powerful*; *mighty*); 伟大 wěidà (*great*; *grand*)

大白菜 dàbáicài	*Chinese cabbage*. Cl: 棵 kē
大半 dàbàn	*greater part*; *more than half*; *most*, interchangeable with 大部分 dàbùfēn and 大多数 dàduōshù: 大半的老师会说英语 dàbàn de lǎoshī huì shuō Yīngyǔ (*most teachers can speak English*)
大便 dàbiàn	*human excrement*; *defecate*
大伯 dàbó	*father's older brother*
大部分 dàbùfēn	*greater part*; *more than half*; *most*, interchangeable with 大半 dàbàn and 大多数 dādàduōshù
大胆 dàdǎn	*bold*; *daring*
大豆 dàdòu	*soybean*
大多数 dàduōshù	*great majority*, interchangeable with 大半 dàbàn and 大部分 dàbùfēn
大方 dàfang	*generous*; *unaffected*; *tasteful*
大概 dàgài	*general*; *rough*; *generally*; *roughly*; *probably*

大号 **dàhào**	(of clothing) *large size*	
大会 **dàhuì**	*plenary meeting; convention*	
大家 **dàjiā**	*everyone*	
大街 **dàjiē**	*street.* Cl: 条 tiáo	
大局 **dàjú**	*overall situation*	
大考 **dàkǎo**	*final exam*	
大量 **dàliàng**	*a large number; a large quantity*	
大陆 **dàlù**	*continent; mainland*	
大米 **dàmǐ**	(raw) *rice*	
大批 **dàpī**	*a large number; a large quantity*	
大人 **dàren**	*adult*	
大人物 **dàrénwù**	*big shot; VIP*	
大声 **dàshēng**	*loudly; in a loud voice*	
大使 **dàshǐ**	*ambassador*	
大事 **dàshì**	*major event*	
大蒜 **dàsuàn**	*garlic.* Cl: 头 tóu	
大厅 **dàtīng**	*lobby; hall*	
大头针 **dàtóuzhēn**	*pin*	
大西洋 **dàxīyáng**	*the Atlantic Ocean*	
大写 **dàxiě**	*capital letters; capital Chinese numerals*	
大型 **dàxíng**	*large-scale; giant; full-length*	
大熊猫 **dàxióngmāo**	*giant panda.* Cl: 只 zhī	
大学 **dàxué**	*university.* Cl: 所 suǒ; 个 gè	
大衣 **dàyī**	*overcoat.* Cl: 件 jiàn	
大意 **dàyi**	*careless*	
大意 **dàyì**	*main idea; gist*	
大约 **dàyuē**	*approximately*	
大运河 **dàyùnhé**	*the Grand Canal*	

带 dài

1. *take; bring; carry*: 今天会下雨, 你要带伞 jīntiān huì xiàyǔ, nǐ yào dài sǎn (*it is going to rain today, so you need to take an umbrella*); 我带了中饭 wǒ dài le zhōngfàn (*I brought lunch*)

2. *come with*: 这本中文书带光盘 zhè běn zhōngwén shū dài guāngpán (*this Chinese book comes with CDs*)

3. *take; lead*: 老师带全班同学去参观博物馆 lǎoshī dài quán bān tóngxué qù cānguān bówùguǎn (*the teacher took the whole class to visit the museum*)

4. *look after; bring up* (a child): 谁给你带孩子 shuí gěi nǐ dài háizi (*who takes care of your child?*)

5. *belt; lace*: 皮带 pídài (*leather belt*); 鞋带 xiédài (*shoelace*); 传送带 chuánsòngdài (*conveyor belt*). Cl: 条 tiáo; 根 gēn

6. *tape*; *ribbon*: 录音带 lùyīndài (*audio tape*); 录象带 lùxiàngdài (*video tape*). Cl: 盘 pán

7. *area*; *zone*: 这一带很安全 zhè yí dài hěn ānquán (*this area is very safe*); 热带 rèdài (*torrid zone*)

Also appears in the following words: **绷带** bēngdài (*bandage*); **磁带** cídài (*magnetic tape*); **海带** hǎidài (*seaweed*); **寒带** hándài (*frigid zone*); **领带** lǐngdài (*tie*); **声带** shēngdài (*vocal cords*); **温带** wēndài (*temperate zone*)

带领 **dàilǐng**	*lead*; *guide*
带路 **dàilù**	*show the way*; *lead the way*
带头 **dàitóu**	*set an example*; *take the lead*
带子 **dàizi**	*belt*; *tape, band, ribbon*. Cl: 条 tiáo; 根 gēn

代 dài

1. *be in place of*; *on behalf of*: 老板有病，我代他去开会 lǎobǎn yǒu bìng, wǒ dài tā qù kāi huì (*my boss is sick, so I'm going to the meeting in his place*); 请代我向你父母问好 qǐng dài wǒ xiàng nǐ fùmǔ wènhǎo (*please give my regards to your parents*)

2. *era*; *dynasty*; *generation*: 古代 gǔdài (*ancient times*); 现代 xiàndài (*modern times*)

Also appears in the following words: **朝代** cháodài (*dynasty*); **当代** dāngdài (*the contemporary era*); **年代** niándài (*decade*); **时代** shídài (*age*; *epoch*; *era*)

代表 **dàibiǎo**	**1.** *represent*
	2. *representative*. Cl: 个 gè; 位 wèi; 名 míng
	3. *representation*
代号 **dàihào**	*code name*
代价 **dàijià**	*price* (for doing something)
代理 **dàilǐ**	**1.** *agent*; *act as an agent*
	2. *act on behalf*
代替 **dàitì**	*replace*; *substitute*

戴 dài

put on; *wear*. Note that the word is used for things such as gloves, scarves, glasses, earrings, hats, watches, and masks. For things such as clothing, 穿 chuān should be used instead.

单 dān

1. *list*; *form*: 名单 míngdān (*name list*); 菜单 càidān (*menu*); 传单 chuándān (*leaflet*); 订单 dìngdān (*order form*); 清单 qīngdān (*detailed list; inventory*); 账单 zhàngdān (*bill; check*); 成绩单 chéngjìdān (*school report card*)

2. *one*; *single*: 单人间 dānrénjiān (*single room*); 单人床 dānrénchuáng (*single bed*)

3. *odd* (number): 单号 dānhào (*odd number*); 单日 dānrì (*odd number day of the month*)

Also appears in the following words: **被单** bèidān (*bed sheet*); **床单** chuángdān (*bed sheet*); **孤单** gūdān (*lonely*); **简单** jiǎndān (*simple*)

单程 dānchéng	*one way*: 单程票 dānchéngpiào (*one-way ticket*)
单纯 dānchún	1. *simple; pure*
	2. *merely; purely*
单词 dāncí	*individual word*
单调 dāndiào	*monotonous; tedious*
单独 dāndú	*alone; by oneself*
单方面 dānfāngmiàn	*one-side; unilateral*
单人床 dānrénchuáng	*single bed.* Cl: 张 zhāng
单人间 dānrénjiān	*single room*
单身 dānshēn	*single; unmarried*: 单身汉 dānshēnhàn (*bachelor*)
单数 dānshù	(*gram*) *singular*
单位 dānwèi	*unit; workplace*
单向道 dānxiàngdào	*one-way street*
单一 dānyī	*unitary; single*
单元 dānyuán	*unit*
单子 dānzi	*list; bill; form.* Cl: 个 gè

蛋 dàn

egg: 鸡蛋 jīdàn (*chicken egg*); 鸭蛋 yādàn (*duck egg*); 下蛋 xià dàn (*lay eggs*). Cl: 个 gè; 只 zhī

Also appears in the following words: **笨蛋** bèndàn (*fool; idiot*); **捣蛋** dǎodàn (*make trouble*); **滚蛋** gǔndàn (*get lost!*); **坏蛋** huàidàn (*bad guy*); **完蛋** wándàn (*fall from grace; be finished*)

蛋白 dànbái	*egg white*
蛋白质 dànbáizhì	*protein*
蛋糕 dàngāo	*cake.* Cl: 块 kuài; 个 gè
蛋黄 dànhuáng	*yolk*

| 蛋卷 dànjuǎn | egg roll |
| 蛋壳 dànké | eggshell |

但 dàn

but; *yet*, often taking the disyllabic form of 但是 dànshì

Also appears in the following expression: 不但 búdàn … 而且 érqiě (*not only, but also*)

| 但愿 | *hope*; *if only it were true* |

当 dāng

1. *just as*; *just when*, used in conjunction with 时候 shíhou: 当我们在准备考试的时候，他在玩 dāng wǒmen zài zhǔnbèi kǎoshì de shíhou, tā zài wán (*when we were preparing for the exam, he was playing*)

2. *work as*; *act as*; *become*: 我儿子长大后想当老师 wǒ érzi zhǎng dà hòu xiǎng dāng lǎoshī (*my son wants to become a teacher when he grows up*)

3. *at the time or place*: 当时 dāngshí (*at that time*); 当地 dāngdì (*at that spot*)

Also appears in the following words: 充当 chōngdāng (*serve as*); 相当 xiāngdāng (*quite; fairly*); 应当 yīngdāng (*should*); 正当 zhèngdàng (*legitimate*); 不敢当 bùgǎndāng (*far from being the case – as a response to a compliment*)

当场 dāngchǎng	*on the spot*
当初 dāngchū	*at the beginning*
当家 dāngjiā	(of household or business affairs) *manage*; *be in charge of*: 你们公司谁当家 nǐmen gōngsī shuí dāngjiā (*who is in charge in your company?*)
当局 dāngjú	(of government) *authorities*
当面 dāngmiàn	*in one's presence*; *face to face*; *in person*: 我想和你当面谈一谈 wǒ xiǎng hé nǐ dāngmiàn tán yi tán (*I'd like to have a face-to-face talk with you*).
当然 dāngrán	1. *without doubt*; *of course*; *certainly*: 他是中国人，当然会说中文 tā shì Zhōngguórén, dāngrán huì shuō Zhōngwén (*he is Chinese and can certainly speak Chinese*) 2. *only natural*: 孩子们学得很好，家长们当然很高兴 háizimen xué de hěn hǎo, jiāzhǎngmen dāngrán hěn gāoxìng (*the children did a good job with their studies and it is only too natural that their parents feel happy*)

当中 **dāngzhōng**	1. *during:* 假期当中 jiàqī dāngzhōng (*during the vacation*)
	2. *between; in the middle,* usu. used in conjunction with 在 zài: 邮局在银行和书店的当中 yóujú zài yínháng hé shūdiàn de dāngzhōng (*the post office is between the bank and the bookstore*)
当作 **dāngzuò**	*regard as,* usu. used in the 把 *bǎ-* or 被 *bèi-* construction: 把老师当作朋友 bǎ lǎoshī dāngzuò péngyou (*regard the teacher as a friend*); 电脑现在被当作不可少的工具 diànnǎo xiànzài bèi dāngzuò bùkěshǎode gōngjù (*the computer is now regarded as an indispensable tool*)

刀 dāo

knife: 菜刀 càidāo (*kitchen knife*); 水果刀 shuǐguǒdāo (*fruit knife*); 手术刀 shǒushùdāo (*scalpel*); 剃须刀 tìxūdāo (*shaver*). Cl: 把 bǎ

Also appears in the following words: 剪刀 jiǎndāo (*scissors*); 军刀 jūndāo (*saber*); 剃刀 tìdāo (*razor; shaver*); 屠刀 túdāo (*butcher's knife*)

刀叉 **dāochā**	*knife and fork*
刀口 **dāokǒu**	*the edge of knife; blade*
刀片 **dāopiàn**	*razor blade*
刀子 **dāozi**	*knife; pocketknife.* Cl: 把 bǎ

倒 dǎo; dào

When pronounced dǎo:

fall down; collapse, often used as a verb complement: 房子倒了 fángzi dǎo le (*the house collapsed*); 他不小心摔倒了 tā bù xiǎoxīn shuāi dǎo le (*he fell down by accident*)

Also appears in the following words: **打倒** dǎdǎo (*down with; overthrow*); **颠倒** diāndǎo (*upside down*); **推倒** tuīdǎo (*overturn; topple*)

倒闭 **dǎobì**	(business) *close down; go bankrupt*
倒车 **dǎochē**	*change trains or buses:* 去电影院要不要倒车 qù diànyǐngyuàn yào bu yào dǎo chē (*do I need to change buses to go to the movie theater?*)
倒台 **dǎotái**	*be overthrown*

When pronounced dào:

1. *reverse; invert*: 倒车 dào chē (*reverse the car*); 这两个字倒了 zhè liǎng ge zì dào le (*these two words were inverted*)

2. *pour; empty; dump*: 倒茶 dào chá (*pour tea*); 倒垃圾 dào lājī (*dump garbage*)

3. *on the contrary; rather*: 他不仅不认错，倒说是别人的责任 tā bùjǐng bú rèn cuò, dào shuō shì biérén de zérèn (*he not only refuses to admit his mistake, but also blames others*)

倒立 **dàolì**	*stand on one's head*
倒数 **dàoshǔ**	*count backwards*
倒退 **dàotuì**	*go backwards; retrogress*: 这样做等于倒退 zhèyàng zuò děngyu dàotuì (*to do this is tantamount to regression*)
倒置 **dàozhì**	*misplace; reverse*: 轻重倒置 qīngzhòng dàozhì (*wrongly assign the order of importance*)

道 dào

road; way; path. Cl: 条 tiáo

Also appears in the following words: 报道 bàodào (*report; cover*); 赤道 chìdào (*equator*); 传道 chuándào (*preach; evangelize*); 地道 dìdào (*underground passage*); 街道 jiēdào (*street; neighborhood*); 频道 píndào (*TV channel*); 渠道 qúdào (*channel; ditch*); 人道 réndào (*humane*); 隧道 suìdào (*tunnel*); 铁道 tiědào (*railroad*); 味道 wèidào (*taste*); 知道 zhīdao (*know*); 人行道 rénxíngdào (*sidewalk*)

道德 **dàodé**	*moral; ethical; morality; ethics*
道教 **dàojiào**	*Taoism*
道理 **dàoli**	*reason; rationality; truth*: 他的话有道理 tāde huà yǒu dàoli (*there is truth in what he says*)
道路 **dàolù**	*road; way.* Cl: 条 tiáo

到 dào

1. *arrive; reach; go*: 火车到了站 huǒchē dào le zhàn (*the train has arrived at the station*); 到南京大学怎么走 (*how to get to Nanjing University?*)

2. *to; up until; up to*: 从早到晚 cóng zǎo dào wǎn (*from morning till night*); 从亚洲到欧洲 cóng Yàzhōu dào Ōuzhōu (*from Asia to Europe*)

3. used after a verb to indicate a place or a time that the action extends to: 寄到中国 jì dào Zhōngguó (*mail to China*); 玩到十点 wán dào shí diǎn (*play till ten o'clock*)

4. used after a verb as a complement to suggest the successful accomplishment of an action that involves a certain amount of difficulty and effort. Cf. 买了电影票 mǎi le diànyǐngpiào (*bought the movie ticket*—no difficulty suggested), 买到了电影票 mǎi dào le diànyǐngpiào (*succeeded in buying the movie ticket*—difficulty suggested); 吃了北京烤鸭 chī le Běijīng kǎoyā (*ate Peking Duck*—no difficulty suggested; it was easily available), 吃到了北京烤鸭 chī dào le Běijīng kǎoyā (*managed to eat Peking Duck*—difficulty suggested; there may have been many people waiting in line)

5. used after certain verbs to mean *touch upon*: 他说到了你 shuō dào le nǐ (*he mentioned you*); 文章写到了这件事 wénzhāng xiě dào le zhè jiàn shì (*the article touched upon this matter*); 老师问到了这个问题 lǎoshī wèn dào le zhè ge wèntí (*the teacher brought up this question*)

Also appears in the following words: 报到 bàodào (*check in*; *register*); 迟到 chídào (*be late for*); 得到 dédào (*receive*; *get*); 感到 gǎndào (*feel*); 遇到 yùdào (*run into*; *encounter*); 周到 zhōudao (*thoughtful*; *considerate*)

到处 **dàochù**	*everywhere*	
到达 **dàodá**	*arrive*	
到底 **dàodǐ**	**1**. *at the end*; *at last*; *finally*: 他到底告诉了我事情的真相 tā dàodǐ gàosù le wǒ shìqing de zhēnxiàng (*he finally told me the truth of the matter*)	
	2. *exactly*, used in questions: 这本书到底是谁的 zhè běn shū dàodǐ shì shuíde (*who exactly does this book belong to?*)	
到来 **dàolái**	*advent*; *arrival*; *arrive*	
到期 **dàoqī**	*expire*; *become due*	
到手 **dàoshǒu**	*come into one's possession*	

的 de

1. possessive marker used **a**) after a personal pronoun to form a possessive adjective or a possessive pronoun: 我的 wǒde (*my, mine*); 你的 nǐde (*your, yours*, singular); 他的 tāde (*his*); 她的 tāde (*her, hers*); 它的 tāde (*its*); 我们的 wǒmende (*our, ours*); 你们的 nǐmende (*your, yours*, plural); 他们的 tāmende (*their, theirs*); and **b**) after a noun to show a possessive relationship: 老师的 lǎoshī de shū (*the teacher's book*); 美国的公司 Měiguó de gōngsī (*America's companies*). When a modifying noun describes the property of another noun instead of showing a possessive relationship, 的 de is not used: 英语报纸 Yīngyǔ bàozhǐ (*English language newspaper*); 法国菜 Fǎguó cài (*French food*—法国 Fǎguó is a noun in Chinese). When the name of a country is used as a modifier, the presence and absence of 的 de makes a difference in meaning: 中国的餐馆 Zhōngguó de cānguǎn (*China's restaurants*, i.e. *restaurants in China*); 中国餐馆 Zhōngguó cānguǎn (*Chinese* *restaurants, which can be anywhere in the world).* 的 de is often left out from the possessive pronoun when: **a)** it is monosyllabic (我 wǒ, 你 nǐ, 他 tā, and 她 tā) and followed by a noun indicating a close relationship, particularly a family relationship: 我爸爸 wǒ bàba (*my father*); 你哥哥 nǐ gēge (*your older brother*); 她朋友 tā péngyou (*her friend*); and **b)** it is followed by a noun indicating a place that the person represented by the pronoun is affiliated with: 我们学校 wǒmen xuéxiào (*our school*); 他们工厂 tāmen gōngchǎng (*their factory*). 的 de is obligatory when what follows is an object: 我的电脑 (*my computer*); 你的汽车 (*your car*).

2. modifier marker used **a)** after an adjective to indicate its attributive relationship with the following noun. 的 de is obligatory after disyllabic or polysyllabic adjectives: 高兴的事 gāoxìngde shì (*happy event*); 有意思的电影 yǒuyìsīde diànyǐng (*interesting movie*). A monosyllabic attributive adjective modified by an adverb also requires the use of 的 de before a noun: 很好的人 hěn hǎode rén (*very good person*); 非常热的夏天 fēicháng rède xiàtiān (*extremely hot summer*). 的 de is optional, but usu. left out after a monosyllabic attributive adjective: 新房子 (*new house*); 旧书 (*old book*), unless an emphasis or a contrast is intended: 这是新的书，不是旧的书 (*this is a new book, not an old book*); and **b)** after an attributive prepositional phrase or sentence to define a noun that follows it: 关于中国的电影 guānyú Zhōngguó de diànyǐng (*movie about China*); 你昨天买的书 nǐ zuótiān mǎi de shū (*the book that you bought yesterday*). Prepositional phrases and relative clauses follow the nouns they modify in English, but they precede the nouns in Chinese. Given enough contexts, the noun defined by an adjective + 的 de, a verb + 的 de, or a sentence + 的 de can often be left out, resulting in a nominal construction: 好的 (人) 多 hǎode (rén) duō, 坏的 (人) 少 huàide (rén) shǎo (*there are more good people than bad people*); 我说的 (话)，你懂不懂 wǒ shuō de (huà), nǐ dǒng bù dǒng (*do you understand what I say?*)

3. used at the end of a statement to indicate certainty: 我会告诉她的 wǒ huì gàosù tā de (*I'll certainly tell her*); 你知道这件事的 nǐ zhīdao zhè jiàn shì de (*you are definitely aware of this matter*)

是 … 的 shì … de	See under 是 shì (#4).
… 的话 … dehuà	Used at the end of a conditional or hypothetical clause in connection with conjunctions such as 如果 rúguǒ, 假如 jiǎrú, and 要是 yàoshì: 如果天下雨的话 rúguǒ tiān xià yǔ dehuà (*if it rains*); 假如你有钱的话 jiǎrú nǐ yǒu qián dehuà (*if you have money*); 要是我是你的话 yàoshì wǒ shì nǐ dehuà (*if I were you*). In the previous examples, either the conjunction or 的话 dehuà can be left out.
… 的时候 … de shíhou	*time when*, used at the end of a phrase or a clause: 吃饭的时候 (*when eating*); 你学习的时候 (*when you study*). If the subordinate clause shares the same subject as the main

clause, only one subject is present: 我在美国的时候去过华盛顿 wǒ zài Měiguó de shíhou qù guò Huáshèngdùn (*when I was in America, I had been to Washington*); 上班的时候不要看报纸 shàngbān de shíhou búyào kàn bàozhǐ (*don't read newspapers when you are at work*)

得 de; děi; dé

When pronounced de:

Used after a verb to mark a complement of degree or result: 他写得好 tā xiě de hǎo (*he writes well*); 火车今天到得早 huǒchē jīntiān dào de zǎo (*the train arrived early today*). When the sentence takes the negative form, 不 bù is placed after 得 de: 他写得不好 tā xiě de bù hǎo (*he doesn't write well*); 火车今天到得不早 huǒchē jīntiān dào de bù zǎo (*the train did not arrive early today*). If the verb takes an object, the object needs to be placed immediately after the verb, thus creating a conflict with the complement marker 得 de, which should also be placed immediately after the verb. To satisfy both conditions, the object will be placed after the verb, but the verb will be repeated after the object so that it can immediately precede 得 de: 他说中文说得很流利 tā shuō Zhōngwén shuō de hěn liúlì (*he speaks Chinese fluently*). There are two ways commonly used in Chinese to avoid the repetitiveness: **a**) leave out the initial verb: 他中文说得很流利 tā Zhōngwén shuō de hěn liúlì, and **b**) shift the object to the front: 中文他说得很流利 Zhōngwén tā shuō de hěn liúlì.

When pronounced as děi:

1. *have to*; *must*: 我得走了 wǒ děi zǒu le (*I must be going*)

2. *require*: 从北京坐火车去上海得15个小时 cóng Běijīng zuò huǒchē qù Shànghǎi děi 15 ge xiǎoshí (*it takes 15 hours to go to Shanghai from Beijing by train*)

When pronounced as dé:

1. *get*; *obtain*: 这次考试他得了满分 zhè cì kǎoshì tā dé le mǎnfēn (*he received a full score in this exam*)

2. *can*; *may*, usu. used in the negative: 考试的时候不得查词典 kǎoshì de shíhou bùdé chá cídiǎn (*dictionaries are not to be used during the exam*)

Also appears in the following words: **获得** huòdé (*gain; obtain*); **难得** nándé (*rare; hard to come by*); **取得** qǔdé (*achieve; acquire*); **只得** zhǐdé (*have no alternative but*)

得到 dédào   *get; receive; acquire; obtain*

地 de

Suffix used after a disyllabic adjective to turn it into an adverb, similarly to
–*ly* in English: 高兴地说 gāoxìngde shuō (*talk happily*); 努力地工作 nǔlǐde
gōngzuò (*work hard*). The adverb thus formed always precedes the verb it
modifies. 地 de is not used for monosyllabic adjectives, which can directly
modify a verb in Chinese. Cf. 快走 kuài zǒu (*walk fast*) and 快快地走
kuàikuaide zǒu (*walk fast*). Some disyllabic adjectives can modify verbs
directly if they are habitually used together: 认真学习 rènzhēn xuéxí
(*earnestly study*) or 认真地学习 rènzhēnde xuéxí (*earnestly study*); 详细调查
xiángxì diàochá (*investigate meticulously*) or 详细地调查 xiángxìde diàochá
(*investigate meticulously*).

等 děng

1. *wait*: 别担心, 我们等你 bié dānxīn, wǒmen děng nǐ (*don't worry, we'll wait for
you*)

2. *so on*, often taking the form of 等等 děngděng: 北京有很多著名的大学:
北京大学, 清华大 学, 等等 Běijīng yǒu hěn duō zhùmíngde dàxué:
Běijīng Dàxué, Qīnghuá Dàxue, děngděng (*there are many famous universities
in Beijing: Beijing University, Qinghua University and so on*)

3. *class*; *grade*; *rate*: 头等舱 tóuděngcāng (*first class cabin*)

Also appears in the following words: 不等 bùděng (*vary*); 初等 chūděng (*elementary*; *primary*); 高等 gāoděng (*higher*; *high level*); 对等 duìděng (*equity*; *reciproc-
ity*); 平等 píngděng (*equal*; *equality*); 上等 shàngděng (*highest quality*; *superior
grade*); 中等 zhōngděng (*medium grade*); 下等 xiàděng (*inferior quality*; *inferior
grade*); 同等 tóngděng (*equivalent*; *equivalence*); 相等 xiāngděng (*equality*;
equation*)

等待 děngdài	*wait*	
等级 děngjí	*class*; *grade*; *rank*	
等同 děngtóng	*be equal*; *equate*	
等于 děngyú	**1.** *equal*: 二加二等于四 èr jiā èr děngyú sì (*two plus two equals four*)	
	2. *tantamount to*: 这样做等于自杀 zhèyàng zuò děngyú zìshā (*doing this is tantamount to committing suicide*)	

低 dī

1. *low*: 低声 dīshēng (*in a low voice*); 低工资 dī gōngzī (*low salary*); 低地 dīdì (*lowland*); 低年级 dīniánjí (*junior classes in school*)

2. *lower*; *let droop*: 低头 dītóu (*lower one's head*)

Also appears in the following words: **贬低** biǎndī (*belittle*); **减低** jiǎndī (*lower; decrease*); **降低** jiàngdī (*reduce*)

低潮	**dīcháo**	*low tide*; *low ebb*
低调	**dīdiào**	*low-key*
低估	**dīgū**	*underestimate*; *underrate*
低级	**dījí**	1. *elementary*; *rudimentary*; *lower*
		2. *vulgar*; *low*: 低级趣味 dījí qùwèi (*vulgar and bad taste*)
低能	**dīnéng**	*mental deficiency*; *feeble-mindedness*: 低能儿 dīnéng'ér (*imbecile*; *retarded child*)
低声	**dīshēng**	*in a low voice*; *under one's breath*
低头	**dītóu**	1. *lower one's head*; *bow one's head*
		2. *yield*; *submit*: 绝不低头 jué bù dītóu (*will never yield*)
低温	**dīwēn**	*low temperature*
低音	**dīyīn**	(music) *bass*

底 dǐ

1. *bottom*: 井底 jǐngdǐ (*bottom of a well*); 海底 hǎidǐ (*bottom of the sea*)

2. (of the year or the month) *end*: 月底 yuèdǐ (*end of the month*); 年底 niándǐ (*end of the year*)

3. *background*: 白底黑字 bái dǐ hēi zì (*black characters on white background*)

4. (of a document) *copy*: 我没有留底 wǒ méiyou liú dǐ (*I didn't keep a copy*)

Also appears in the following words: **彻底** chèdǐ (*downright*; *completely*); **到底** dàodǐ (*to the end*; *through*); **谜底** mídǐ (*answer to a riddle*)

底层	**dǐcéng**	1. *first floor*
		2. *bottom* (of society)
底稿	**dǐgǎo**	(of a document) *original*; *manuscript*; *draft*
底片	**dǐpiàn**	*negative* (film). Cl: 张 zhāng; 卷 juàn
底细	**dǐxì**	1. *inside story*; *ins and outs*.
		2. *background* (of a person): 不知道他的底细 bù zhīdao tāde dǐxì (*don't know his background*)
底下	**dǐxià**	1. *bottom*: 箱子底下有一条领带 xiāngzi dǐxià yǒu yì tiáo

língdài (*there is a tie at the bottom of the suitcase*)
2. *under; below*: 照片底下有说明 zhàopiàn dǐxià yǒu shuōmíng (*there is a caption under the photo*); 钥匙在席子底下 yàoshi zài xízi dǐxià (*the key is under the mat*) **3.** *later; remaining*: 看电影时我睡着了，不知道底下发生了什么事 kàn diànyǐng shí wǒ shuì zháo le, bù zhīdao dǐxià fāshēng le shénme shì (*I fell asleep at the movies and I don't know what happened afterwards*). 底下 dǐxià is considered as a noun in Chinese.

底子 **dǐzi** **1.** *foundation* (for a skill): 他的表演底子很好 tāde biǎoyǎn dǐzi hěn hǎo (*she has a good foundation in performing*)
2. (of a document) *original; draft*

第 dì

Prefix used before a cardinal number to make it an ordinal number: 第一 dìyī (*the first*); 第二 dì'èr (*the second*); 第十 dìshí (*the tenth*)

地 dì

1. *land; soil*: 草地 cǎodì (*grassland*); 高地 gāodì (*highland*). Cl: 块 kuài; 片 piàn

2. *earth*: 地层 dìcéng (*earth stratum*); 地震 dìzhèn (*earthquake*)

3. *place*: 世界各地 shìjiè gèdì (*all over the world*); 外地 wàidì (*out of town; other places in the country*). When unmodified, it usually takes the disyllabic form of 地方 dìfang.

Also appears in the following words: **本地** běndì (*this locality*); **产地** chǎndì (*place of product origin*); **场地** chǎngdì (*site; venue*); **当地** dāngdì (*local*); **工地** gōngdì (*construction site*); **内地** nèidì (*hinterland*)

地板 **dìbǎn**	*floor; floor board*. Cl: 块 kuài.
地道 **dìdao**	**1.** *authentic*: 地道的中国菜 dìdao de Zhōngguó cài (*authentic Chinese food*) **2.** *pure; idiomatic*: 地道的英语 dìdào de Yīngyǔ (*idiomatic English*)
地道 **dìdào**	*tunnel*. Cl: 条 tiáo
地点 **dìdiǎn**	*place; site; spot*
地方 **dìfang**	**1.** *place; region*: 你是什么地方人 nǐ shì shénme dìfangrén (*what part of the country are you from?*)

2. *local*: 地方政府 dìfang zhèngfǔ (*local government*)

3. *part*; *aspect*: 电影中最感人的地方 diànyǐng zhōng zuì gǎnrén de dìfang (*the most touching part of the movie*)

地雷	dìléi	*land mine.* Cl: 颗 kē; 个 gè
地理	dìlǐ	*geography*
地球	dìqiú	*the earth*; *the globe*
地毯	dìtǎn	*carpet*; *rug.* Cl: 块 kuài; 张 zhāng
地图	dìtú	*map.* Cl: 张 zhāng; 本 běn; 册 cè
地位	dìwèi	*position*; *standing*; *status*
地下	dìxià	*underground*
地震	dìzhèn	*earthquake*
地址	dìzhǐ	*address*: 回信地址 huíxìn dìzhǐ (*return address*)

点 diǎn

1. *point*; *dot*; *speck*: 一点五 yì diǎn wǔ (*1.5*); 沸点 fèidiǎn (*boiling point*); 雨点 yǔdiǎn (*raindrop*); 起点 qǐdiǎn (*point of departure*)

2. *o'clock*: 两点 liǎng diǎn (*two o'clock*)

3. *stain*; *spot*: 污点 wūdiǎn (*stain*)

4. *count*: 点钱 diǎn qián (*count money*); 点数 diǎn shù (*count numbers*)

5. *light*; *kindle*: 点火 diǎn huǒ (*light a fire*)

6. *appointed time*: 准点 zhǔndiǎn (*on time*, for trains, buses, etc.); 晚点 wǎndiǎn (*behind schedule*, for trains, buses, etc.)

7. *a little*; *somewhat*, taking the form of 一点儿 yìdiǎnr or 有点儿 yǒu diǎnr: 会说一点儿中文 huì shuō yìdiǎnr Zhōngwén (*can speak a little Chinese*); 吃了一点儿东西 chī le yìdiǎnr dōngxi (*ate a little*); 我有点儿累 wǒ yǒudiǎnr lèi (*I'm a little tired*); 她有点儿气 tā yǒudiǎnr qì (*she is a little angry*). 有点儿 yǒudiǎnr differs from 一点儿 yìdiǎnr in two ways: it is used before a verb or adjective instead of after it as 一点儿 yìdiǎnr is; it is used with a verb or adjective that indicates an undesirable condition or action. 一 yī in colloquial speech is often left out.

Also appears in the following words: 标点 biāodiǎn (*punctuation mark*); 茶点 chádiǎn (*tea and refreshments*); 地点 dìdiǎn (*location*; *spot*); 顶点 dǐngdiǎn (*peak*; *zenith*); 观点 guāndiǎn (*viewpoint*); 焦点 jiāodiǎn (*focus*); 论点 lùndiǎn (*argument*); 缺点 quēdiǎn (*shortcoming*; *blemish*); 特点 tèdiǎn (*characteristic*; *trait*); 要点 yàodiǎn (*main point*); 出发点 chūfādiǎn (*point of departure*); 早点 zǎodiǎn (*breakfast*); 终点 zhōngdiǎn (*end point*; *destination*); 重点 zhòngdiǎn (*key point*)

点菜	diǎncài	*order food* (in a restaurant)
点名	diǎnmíng	*roll call*; *take attendance*

点燃	**diǎnrán**	*light; kindle*
点头	**diǎntóu**	*nod; agree*
点心	**diǎnxīn**	*refreshments*
点子	**diǎnzi**	*idea*

店 diàn

1. *store*; *shop*: 书店 shūdiàn (*bookstore*); 花店 huādiàn (*florist*); 药店 yàodiàn (*drugstore*; *pharmacy*); 珠宝店 zhūbǎodiàn (*jewelry store*); 文具店 wénjùdiàn (*stationery store*); 理发店 lǐfàdiàn (*barber's*); 面包店 miànbāodiàn (*bakery*); 杂货店 záhuòdiàn (*grocery store*).When used without modification, it often takes the disyllabic form of 商店 shāngdiàn: 街上有很多商店 jiē shàng yǒu hěn duō shāngdiàn (*there are many stores in the street*). Cl: 家 jiā; 个 gè

2. *inn*; *restaurant*: 旅店 lǚdiàn (*inn*); 饭店 fàndiàn (*restaurant*). Cl: 家 jiā; 个 gè

电 diàn

electric; *electricity*

Also appears in the following words: 充电 chōngdiàn (*charge with electricity*); 触电 chùdiàn (*get an electric shock*); 发电 fādiàn (*generate electricity*); 雷电 léidiàn (*thunderbolt*); 闪电 shǎndiàn (*lightning*); 手电 shǒudiàn (*flashlight*); 无线电 wúxiàndiàn (*wireless radio*)

电报	**diànbào**	*telegram; cable*
电表	**diànbiǎo**	*electric meter*
电冰箱	**diànbīngxiāng**	*refrigerator*. Cl: 个 gè; 台 tái
电车	**diànchē**	*tram; trolley bus*. Cl: 辆 liàng
电池	**diànchí**	*battery*
电灯	**diàndēng**	*electric light*
电工	**diàngōng**	*electrician*. Cl: 个 gè; 位 wèi; 名 míng
电话	**diànhuà**	*telephone*: 打电话 dǎ diànhuà (*make a phone call*). Cl: 个 gè; 部 bù
电力	**diànlì**	*electric power*
电炉	**diànlú**	*electric stove; hot plate*
电脑	**diànnǎo**	*computer*. Cl: 台 tái
电钮	**diànniǔ**	*push button* (n.)
电器	**diànqì**	*electric appliances*
电视	**diànshì**	*television*. Cl: 台 tái
电台	**diàntái**	*radio station*

电梯 diàntī	elevator
电线 diànxiàn	electric wire
电影 diànyǐng	movie: 电影院 diànyǐngyuàn (*movie theater*). Cl: 个 gè; 部 bù; 场 chǎng
电邮 diànyóu	*e-mail*
电源 diànyuán	*power supply*
电子 diànzǐ	*electronic; electronics*: 电子信 diànzǐxìn (*e-mail*)

掉 diào

1. *drop; fall*: 掉下山去 diào xià shān qù (*fall off the mountain*); 价格掉了 jiàgé diào le (*the price has fallen*)

2. *lose*: 掉了钱包 diào le qiánbāo (*lost a wallet*)

3. *leave out; drop; miss out*: 参观博物馆时，我们班掉了三个人 cānguān bówùguǎn shí, wǒmen bān diào le sān ge rén (*when we were visiting the museum, three people were missing from our class*)

4. *turn*: 掉头看 diào tóu kàn (*turn one's head*)

5. *away; off*, used as a verb complement: 跑掉 pǎo diào (*run away*); 飞掉 fēi diào (*fly away*)

掉队 diàoduì	*fall behind*
掉换 diàohuàn	*change; exchange*: 掉换商品 diàohuàn shāngpǐn (*exchange merchandise*); 掉换座位 diàohuàn zuòwèi (*change seats*)
掉色 diàosè	*fade; lose color*: 这种衣服不掉色 zhè zhǒng yīfu bú diàosè (*this kind of clothing does not fade*)
掉头 diàotóu	*turn; turn back*: 掉头走 diàotóu zǒu (*walk back*); 汽车在这里不能掉头 qìchē zài zhèlǐ bù néng diàotóu (*the vehicle can't make a U-turn here*)

顶 dǐng

1. *top; peak; summit*: 山顶 shāndǐng (*mountaintop*); 房顶 fǎngdǐng (*roof*); 头顶 tóudǐng (*top of the head*)

2. *carry on one's head*: 顶篮子 dǐng lánzi (*carry a basket on the head*)

3. *prop up*: 用棍子顶门 yòng gùnzi dǐng mén (*use a stick to prop up the door*)

4. *against; under*: 顶着很大压力 dǐng zhe hěn dà yālì (*under a lot of pressure*); 顶风行船 dǐng fēng xíng chuán (*sail against the wind*)

5. classifier for hats and caps: 一顶帽子 yì dǐng màozi (*a hat*)

6. *the most*: 顶想当老师 dǐng xiǎng dāng lǎoshī (*wish most to become a teacher*); 顶好吃的菜 dǐng hǎochīde cài (*the most delicious dish*)

顶点 **dǐngdiǎn**	*apex; zenith; pinnacle*
顶多 **dǐngduō**	*at most*
顶峰 **dǐngfēng**	*peak; summit; pinnacle; zenith*
顶少 **dǐngshǎo**	*at least*
顶替 **dǐngtì**	*substitute; take the place*: 很多新老师顶替了退休的老师 hěn duō xīn lǎoshī dǐngtì le tuìxiūde lǎoshī (*many new teachers have replaced the retired teachers*)
顶头上司 **dǐngtóu shàngsī**	*one's immediate superior or supervisor*
顶针 **dǐngzhēn**	*thimble*
顶撞 **dǐngzhuàng**	*contradict* (a parent, elder, or superior) *defiantly*
顶嘴 **dǐngzuǐ**	*talk back*

订 dìng

1. *subscribe to* (a newspaper, magazine, etc.): 订报纸 dìng bàozhǐ (*subscribe to a newspaper*)

2. *book* (v.); *reserve*: 订机票 dìng jīpiào (*book a plane ticket*); 订房间 dìng fángjiān (*reserve a hotel room*)

3. *corrections*, usu. in words such as 修订 xiūdìng (*revise*) and 订正 dìngzhèng (*correct*)

4. *draw up; conclude*: 订条约 dìng tiáoyuē (*draw up a treaty*)

订单 **dìngdān**	(goods) *order*: 下订单 xià dìngdān (*place an order*)
订购 **dìnggòu**	*place an order*
订户 **dìnghù**	*subscriber*
订婚 **dìnghūn**	*be engaged to; be betrothed to*
订书机 **dìngshūjī**	*stapler*
订正 **dìngzhèng**	*corrections; amend*

定 dìng

1. *fix*: 学生们的眼睛都定在黑板上 xuéshengmen de yǎnjing dōu dìng zài hēibǎn shang (*the students all fixed their eyes on the blackboard*)

2. *stable; restful; calm*: 形势不定 xíngshì bú dìng (*the situation is not stable*)

3. *decide; set*: 计划已定 jìhuà yǐ dìng (*the plan has already been made*)

4. *certainly; definitely*, often taking the disyllabic form of 一定 yídìng 定有

原因 dìng yǒu yuányīn (*there is certainly a reason*); 明天我一定来 míngtiān wǒ yídìng lái (*I'll definitely come tomorrow*)

5. *still*, used as a verb complement: 站定 zhàn dìng (*stand still*); 坐定 zuò dìng (*sit still*)

Also appears in the following words: 安定 āndìng (*stability*); 必定 bìdìng (*be bound to*; *without fail*); 法定 fǎdìng (*legal*; *legally permitted*); 否定 fǒudìng (*negative*); 固定 gùdìng (*fix*; *fixed*); 规定 guīdìng (*regulate*; *regulation*); 假定 jiǎdìng (*presume*); 鉴定 jiàndìng (*authenticate*); 决定 juédìng (*decide*; *decision*); 肯定 kěndìng (*affirmative*; *affirmation*); 确定 quèdìng (*make certain*); 稳定 wěndìng (*stable*; *stability*); 限定 xiàndìng (*limit*; *restrict*); 预定 yùdìng (*prearrange*; *schedule*); 镇定 zhèndìng (*calm*); 制定 zhìdìng (*formulate*; *draft*)

定婚	dìnghūn	*be engaged; be betrothed*
定居	dìngjū	*settle down; take up residence*
定局	dìngjú	*foregone conclusion*
定论	dìnglùn	*final conclusion*
定期	dìngqī	*regularly; periodically*
定义	dìngyì	*definition*
定做	dìngzuò	*have sth. custom-made; made to order*

东 dōng

1. *east*; *eastern*: 东部 dōngbù (*eastern part*); 东边 dōngbian (*east side*)

2. *owner*; *master*; *host*, used as part of another word: 房东 fángdōng (*landlord*); 做东 zuò dōng (*play the host*)

东边	dōngbian	*east; east side*
东道国	dōngdàoguó	*host country*
东方	dōngfāng	*the East*
东西	dōngxi	*things; stuff*

懂 dǒng

understand; *know*: 懂中文 dǒng Zhōngwén (*know Chinese*), often used as a verb complement after verbs 看 kàn (*read*) and tīng 听 (*listen*): 看懂了这个故事 kàn dǒng le zhè ge gùshì (*understood the story through reading*); 听不懂这段对话 tīng bù dǒng zhè duàn duìhuà (*do not understand this dialog*)

懂得	dǒngde	*understand; know; grasp*
懂事	dǒngshì	*intelligent; sensible*

动 dòng

1. *to move*: 别动 bié dòng (*don't move; freeze*)

2. *used as a verb complement to indicate possession of strength to move sth.*:
这张桌子太重，你一个人搬不动 zhè zhāng zhuōzi tài zhòng, nǐ yí ge rén bān bú dòng (*this table is too heavy for you to move by yourself*)

3. *touch; arouse*: 谁动了我的书 shuí dòng le wǒde shū (*who touched my book?*); 这部电影动了很多人的感情 zhè bù diànyǐng dòng le hěn duō rén de gǎnqíng (*this movie moved many people*)

4. *change*: 他写的文章一个字都不需要动 tā xiě de wénzhāng yì ge zì dōu bù xūyào dòng (*not a word needs to be changed in the articles he writes*)

5. *use; resort to*: 动武 dòngwǔ (*use force*); 动火 dònghuǒ (*use fire*)

Also appears in the following words: **暴动** bàodòng (*rebellion; insurrection*); **被动** bèidòng (*passive*); **变动** biàndòng (*change*); **冲动** chōngdòng (*impulse; impulsion*); **打动** dǎdòng (*touch; move*); **发动** fādòng (*launch*); **感动** gǎndòng (*move; touch*); **活动** huódòng (*activity*); **激动** jīdòng (*excited*); **劳动** láodòng (*labor; work*); **推动** tuīdòng (*impel; drive*); **行动** xíngdòng (*action*); **运动** yùndòng (*movement; exercise; sports; campaign*); **主动** zhǔdòng (*act on one's own initiative*); **自动** zìdòng (*automatic*)

动词 dòngcí	*verb*	
动荡 dòngdàng	*upheaval; turmoil*	
动画片 dònghuàpiàn	*cartoon.* Cl: 部 bù	
动机 dòngjī	*motive*	
动力 dònglì	*motivation*	
动乱 dòngluàn	*upheaval; turmoil*	
动脉 dòngmài	*artery*	
动人 dòngrén	*moving; touching*	
动身 dòngshēn	*set out; start on a journey*	
动手 dòngshǒu	*begin work; use force*	
动手术 dòngshǒushù	*perform an operation*	
动听 dòngtīng	*pleasant to listen to*	
动物 dòngwù	*animal:* 动物园 dòngwùyuán (*zoo*)	
动向 dòngxiàng	*trend; tendency*	
动心 dòngxīn	*become interested in; become desirous of:* 对买房子动了心 duì mǎi fángzi dòng le xīn (*become interested in buying a house*)	
动摇 dòngyáo	*waver; vacillate*	
动用 dòngyòng	*employ; use; appropriate*	
动员 dòngyuán	*mobilize*	
动作 dòngzuò	*action; movement.* Cl: 个 gè	

都 dōu

1. *both; all*: 我们都喜欢中国菜 wǒmen dōu xǐhuan Zhōngguócài (*we all like Chinese food*). 都 dōu in Chinese is an adverb. As such it can only appear before a verb. When 都 dōu refers to the object, the object must be placed at the beginning of the sentence: 米饭和面条我都喜欢 mǐfàn hé miàntiáo wǒ dōu xǐhuan (*I like both rice and noodles*). In response to a question such as 你喜欢米饭还是面条 nǐ xǐhuan mǐfàn háishi miàntiáo (*do you like rice or noodles?*), the object is always left out: 我都喜欢 wǒ dōu xǐhuan (*I like both*) or 我都不喜欢 wǒ dōu bù xǐhuan (*I like neither*). It is ungrammatical to say 我都喜欢米饭和面条 wǒ dōu xǐhuan mǐfàn hé miàntiáo (*I like both rice and noodles*). The only way to include the object in the sentence is to relocate it to the beginning of the sentence: 米饭和面条我都喜欢 mǐfàn hé miàntiáo wǒ dōu xǐhuan. However, when 都 dōu refers to the subject, the relocation of the object is not needed: 我和我太太都喜欢面条 wǒ hé wǒ tàitai dōu xǐhuan miàntiáo (*both my wife and I like noodles*).

2. *even*, often used in special structures in conjunction with 连 lián and interrogative words: 他的中国朋友连中国城都没有去过 tāde Zhōngguó péngyou lián Zhōngguóchéng dou méiyou qù guo (*his Chinese friend has not even been to Chinatown*); 我什么都不想吃 wǒ shénme dou bù xiǎng chī (*I don't want to eat anything*). Used in this sense, 都 dōu is pronounced in the neutral tone.

3. *already*, with 了 le used at the end of the sentence: 你都六岁了，还不会系鞋带 nǐ dōu liù suì le, hái bú huì jì xiédài (*you are already six, but still can't tie your shoelaces*). This use differs from 已经 yǐjīng (*already*) in that 都 suggests an unfulfilled condition or expectation as shown in the previous example, whereas 已经 yǐjīng doesn't carry the implication.

读 dú

1. *read*: 我读过这本书 wǒ dú guo zhè běn shū (*I've read this book*)

2. *read aloud*: 读课文 dú kèwén (*read the text aloud*)

3. *attend school; study*: 读中学 dú zhōngxué (*attend a middle school*); 读博士 dú bóshì (*study in a doctoral program*)

读本 dúběn	*textbook; reader*: 英语读本 Yīngyǔ dúběn (*English reader*)
读书 dúshū	**1.** *read; study*: 喜欢读书 xǐhuan dúshū (*enjoy reading*) **2.** *attend school*: 在大学读书 zài dàxué dúshū (*study at a college*); 读书人 dúshūrén (*scholar*)
读物 dúwù	*reading material; books*

读者 dúzhě   *reader*: 读者和作者 dúzhě hé zuòzhě (*readers and authors*)

度 dù

1. *degree* (of intensity, temperature, angle, etc.): 长度 chángdù (*intensity*); 热度 rèdù (*degree of heat*); 温度 wēndù (*temperature*); 180 度 dù (*180 degrees*)

2. *limit*: 过度饮酒 guòdù yǐnjiǔ (*drink excessively*)

3. *spend* (time); *celebrate*, often used in conjunction with 过 guò: 我在巴黎度过了美好的时光 wǒ zài Bālí dù guò le měihǎo de shíguāng (*I have had a wonderful time in Paris*)

Also appears in the following words: 程度 chéngdù (*degree; extent*); 尺度 chǐdù (*measure; yardstick*); 调度 diàodù (*dispatch*); 风度 fēngdù (*grace; style*); 幅度 fúdù (*scope; extent*); 高度 gāodù (*height; altitude*); 过度 guòdù (*excessive; excessively*); 季度 jìdù (*quarter of a year*); 角度 jiǎodù (*angle; perspective*); 进度 jìndù (*rate of progress*); 难度 nándù (*level of difficulty*); 深度 shēndù (*depth*); 速度 sùdù (*speed*); 态度 tàidù (*attitude*); 制度 zhìdù (*system*)

度假 dùjià   *go on vacation*

短 duǎn

1. *short; brief*: 短文 duǎnwén (*short passage*); 短距离 duǎn jùlí (*short distance*). Note the word cannot be used to describe the height of person, for which 矮 ǎi should be used.

2. *shortcoming; weak point; fault*

Also appears in the following words: 长短 chángduǎn (*length*); 简短 jiǎnduǎn (*brief; brevity*); 缩短 suōduǎn (*shorten*)

短波 duǎnbō	*shortwave*	
短处 duǎnchù	*weakness; shortcoming; disadvantage*	
短见 duǎnjiàn	1. *shortsighted view*	
	2. *suicide*	
短裤 duǎnkù	*shorts*	
短路 duǎnlù	*short circus*	
短跑 duǎnpǎo	*sprint; dash*	
短期 duǎnqī	*short-term*	
短缺 duǎnquē	*shortage; deficit*	
短途 duǎntú	*short distance*	

短袜 duǎnwà	socks
短文 duǎnwén	short essay; passage
短语 duǎnyǔ	phrase
短暂 duǎnzàn	of short duration; transient

对 duì

1. *correct; right*

2. *to; for; in; regarding*: 他对我说 tā duì wó shuō (*he said to me*); 英语对我的帮助很大 Yīngyǔ duì wǒ de bāngzhù hěn dà (*English is a great help to me*); 她对音乐没有兴趣 tā duì yīnyuè méi you xìngqù (*she is not interested in music*)

3. *opposite*: 对面 duìmiàn (*opposite side*); 对岸 duì'àn (*opposite bank*); 对方 duìfāng (*the opposing side; the other side*)

4. *against; as opposed to*: 美国队对中国队 Měiguó duì duì Zhōngguó duì (*the American team against the Chinese team*); 美元对人民币 Měiyuan duì Rénmínbì (*US dollars versus Renminbi*).

5. *couple; pair*: 一对情人 yí duì qíngrén (*two lovers*); 两对鸭子 liǎng duì yāzi (*two pairs of ducks*)

Also appears in the following words: **查对** cháduì (*check; verify*); **敌对** díduì (*hostile; hostility*); **反对** fǎnduì (*oppose*); **校对** jiàoduì (*proofread*); **绝对** juéduì (*absolute; absolutely*); **相对** xiāngduì (*relatively*); **针对** zhēnduì (*aim at*); **作对** zuòduì (*set oneself against*)

对比 duìbǐ	contrast
对不起 duìbuqǐ	sorry
对策 duìcè	countermeasure; countermove
对待 duìdài	treat; handle
对付 duìfu	deal with; cope with
对话 duìhuà	dialogue. Cl: 句 jù; 段 duàn; 组 zǔ
对 … 来说 duì … láishuō	as far as ... is concerned: 对我来说，这是一件小事 duì wǒ láishuō, zhè shì yí jiàn xiǎo shì (*as far as I am concerned, this is a trivial matter*)
对抗 duìkàng	oppose; opposition; confront; confrontation
对了 duì le	1. *correct; right*, used when the interlocutor made several attempts before getting the right answer 2. used to signal the change of the topic or a thought that suddenly comes to mind in the middle of a conversation
对联 duìlián	couplet. Cl: 副 fù
对面 duìmiàn	the opposite side; the other side

对手 **duìshǒu**	*opponent*. Cl: 个 gè; 位 wèi
对象 **duìxiàng**	*target; object*
对于 **duìyú**	*concerning; regarding; in terms of*

队 duì

1. *team; brigade*: 篮球队 lánqiúduì (*basketball team*); 消防队 xiāofángduì (*fire brigade*)

2. *line; queue*: 买东西的人很多，队很长 mǎi dōngxi de rén hěn duō, duì hěn cháng (*there are many shoppers and the line is very long*); 排队 pái duì (*line up*)

Also appears in the following words: 部队 bùduì (*troop*); 舰队 jiànduì (*fleet*); 军队 jūnduì (*armed forces; army*); 乐队 yuèduì (*band; orchestra*)

| 队员 **duìyuán** | *team member*. Cl: 个 gè; 名 míng; 位 wèi |
| 队长 **duìzhǎng** | *captain of the team*. Cl: 个 gè; 名 míng; 位 wèi |

多 duō

1. *many; much*, often used predicatively: 那个城市的人很多 nà ge chéngshì de rén hěn duō (*there are a lot of people in that city*). When used attributively before a noun, it needs to be preceded by 很 hěn: 她有很多中国朋友 tā yǒu hěn duō Zhōngguó péngyou (*she has many Chinese friends*).

2. *more*: 你要多说中文 nǐ yào duō shuō Zhōngwén (*you need to speak more Chinese*)

3. *more than*: 五个多星期 wǔ ge duō xīngqī (*more than five weeks*); 八十多岁 bāshí duō suì (*over eighty years old*). 多 duō is used after the classifier when the number is smaller than ten, but before the classifier when the number is larger than ten. Cf. 六个多月 liù ge duō yuè (*more than six months*); 十多本书 shí duō běn shū (*more than ten books*)

4. *how*, used to ask a question about degree or intensity: 多大 duō dà (*how big?*); 多长 duō cháng (*how long?*); 多远 duō yuǎn (*how far?*); 多贵 duō guì (*how expensive?*)

5. *how*, used with 啊 a to indicate exclamation: 今年的冬天多冷啊 jīnnián de dōngtiān duō lěng a (*how cold this winter is!*)

Also appears in the following words: 大多 dàduō (*mostly; for the most part*); 好多 hǎoduō (*a good many*); 许多 xǔduō (*many*); 众多 zhòngduō (*in great numbers*); 差不多 chàbùduō (*almost; more or less*)

多半 **duōbàn**	*the majority*; *most*: 商店里的东西多半是日本货 shāngdiàn lǐ de dōngxi duōbàn shì Rìběn huò (*most of the merchandise at the store is made in Japan*)
多亏 **duōkuī**	*luckily*; *thanks to*: 多亏你的帮助，我找到了工作 duōkuī nǐde bāngzhù, wǒ zhǎo dào le gōngzuò (*thanks to your help, I've found a job*)
多么 **duōme**	(exclamatory) *how*; *what*: 今天的天气多么好 jīntiān de tiānqì duōme hǎo (*what a fine day today!*)
多少 **duōshao**	*how many*; *how much*: 上海有多少大学 Shànghǎi yǒu duōshao dàxué (*how many universities are there in Shanghai?*); 你身上有多少钱 ní shēn shang yǒu duōshao qián (*how much money do you have on you?*)
多数 **duōshù**	*the majority*; *most*: 他们中的多数是大学生 tāmen zhōng de duōshù shì dàxuésheng (*most of them are college students*)
多心 **duōxīn**	*oversensitive*; *suspicious*
多样化 **duōyànghuà**	*diversity*
多余 **duōyú**	*superfluous*

儿 ér

1. *child*

2. *son*: 儿女 érnǚ (*son and daughter*)

3. suffix in the form of 儿 -r attached to a noun or occasionally a verb, a feature of pronunciation typical of the Beijing dialect. It does not affect meaning: 歌儿 gēr (*song*); 花儿 huār (*flower*).

Also appears in the following words: 孤儿 gū'ér (*orphan*); 孩儿 hái'ér (*child*); 女儿 nǚ'ér (*daughter*); 混血儿 hùnxuě'ér (*half-breed*; *children of interracial marriage*)

儿歌 **érgē**	*nursery rhymes*. Cl: 支 zhī; 首 shǒu
儿科 **érkē**	*pediatrics*; *pediatric department*: 儿科医生 érkē yīshēng (*pediatrician*)
儿童 **értóng**	*children*
儿媳 **érxí**	*daughter-in-law*. Cl: 个 gè
儿子 **érzi**	*son*. Cl: 个 gè

二 èr

two. For differences from 两 liǎng, see under 两 liǎng.

二心	èrxīn	*half-hearted; half-heartedness*
二月	èryuè	*February*

发 fā

1. *send; dispatch* (fax, telegraph, email, etc., but not letters, parcels, etc.)

2. *distribute* (handout, leaflets, news dispatches, goods, etc.)

3. *develop; come into; become:* 发财 fācái (*come into fortune*); 发病 fābìng (*develop a disease*); 发炎 fāyán (*become infected*)

4. *utter:* 发音 fāyīn (*pronounce; utter sounds*)

Also appears in the following words: 爆发 bàofā (*break out; erupt*); 出发 chūfā (*set out; depart*); 分发 fēnfā (*distribute*); 揭发 jiēfā (*expose*); 开发 kāifā (*open up; develop*); 散发 sànfā (*emit; emanate*); 蒸发 zhēngfā (*evaporate*)

发表	fābiǎo	*publish; issue*
发布	fābù	*issue* (a report, release, etc.); *promulgate*
发达	fādá	*developed:* 发达国家 fādá guójiā (*developed country*)
发电	fādiàn	*generate electricity:* 发电厂 fādiànchǎng (*power plant*)
发动	fādòng	*start; launch* (a campaign, war, etc.)
发疯	fāfēng	*go crazy; become mad*
发挥	fāhuī	*give play to* (one's talent, etc.)
发觉	fājué	*detect; find*
发明	fāmíng	*invent; invention.* Cl: 个 gè; 项 xiàng; 种 zhǒng
发胖	fāpàng	*gain weight*
发脾气	fāpíqì	*lose temper*
发票	fāpiào	*receipt; invoice.* Cl: 张 zhāng
发烧	fāshāo	*have a fever*
发生	fāshēng	*happen; occur*
发现	fāxiàn	*discover; discovery.* Cl: 个 gè; 项 xiàng
发言	fāyán	*make a speech.* Cl: 个 gè; 份 fèn
发音	fāyīn	*pronounce; pronunciation*
发展	fāzhǎn	*develop; development*

法 fǎ

1. *law*: 刑事法 xíngshìfǎ (*criminal law*); 民事法 mínshìfǎ (*civil law*)

2. *method*; *way*, short for 方法 fāngfǎ: 教法 jiāofǎ (*teaching methods*); 说法 shuōfǎ (*way of saying things*). Cl: 个 gè; 种 zhǒng

Also appears in the following words: **办法** bànfǎ (*means*; *way*); **不法** bùfǎ (*illegal*); **犯法** fànfǎ (*violate the law*); **非法** fēifǎ (*illegal*); **国法** guófǎ (*state law*); **合法** héfǎ (*be within the law*); **军法** jūnfǎ (*military law*); **立法** lìfǎ (*legislation*; *legislate*); **设法** shèfǎ (*manage*; *try*); **手法** shǒufǎ (*ploy*; *technique*); **司法** sīfǎ (*judicature*); **违法** wéifǎ (*break the law*); **宪法** xiànfǎ (*constitution*); **想法** xiǎngfǎ (*idea*; *thinking*); **语法** yǔfǎ (*grammar*); **执法** zhífǎ (*enforce the law*); **作法** zuòfǎ (*practice*; *way of doing things*)

法典	**fǎdiǎn**	*law book*; *statute book*. Cl: 部 bù; 套 tào
法官	**fǎguān**	*judge* (n.). Cl: 名 míng; 位 wèi; 个 gè
法国	**fǎguó**	*France*: 法国人 Fǎguórén (*the French*)
法令	**fǎlìng**	*decree* (n.). Cl: 项 xiàng; 条 tiáo; 个 gè
法律	**fǎlǜ**	*law*. Cl: 条 tiáo; 项 xiàng
法庭	**fǎtíng**	*court*
法语	**Fǎyǔ**	*French language*
法院	**fǎyuàn**	*courthouse*

反 fǎn

1. *reverse*; *opposite*; *inside out*: 反面 fǎnmiàn (*the reverse side*); 反向 fǎnxiàng (*the opposite direction*); 毛衣穿反了 máoyī chuān fǎn le (*the sweater was put on inside out*)

2. *turn over*: 把纸反过来 bǎ zhǐ fǎn guò lái (*turn over the paper*)

3. *counter*: 反问 fǎnwèn (*retort*; *counter with a question*); 反击 fǎnjī (*counterattack*)

4. *oppose*; *combat*: 反贪污 fǎn tānwū (*oppose embezzlement*); 反间谍 fǎn jiāndié (*combat espionage*)

反驳	**fǎnbó**	*retort*; *refute*
反常	**fǎncháng**	*abnormal*; *unusual*
反动	**fǎndòng**	*reactionary*
反对	**fǎnduì**	*fight against*; *oppose*
反而	**fǎn'ér**	*on the contrary*; *instead*, used to indicate a situation contrary to expectation or to what is previously stated: 这个学生住得最远，可他反而最先到 zhè ge xuésheng zhù de zuì yuǎn, kě tā fǎn'ér zuì xiān dào (*this student lived the farthest, but he was the first one to arrive*)

反复 fǎnfù	1. *repeatedly*
	2. *reverse; relapse; reversal*
反感 fǎngǎn	*be disgusted with*
反话 fǎnhuà	*irony; facetious remark.* Cl: 句 jù
反悔 fǎnhuǐ	*go back on one's word*
反抗 fǎnkàng	*revolt; resist*
反面 fǎnmiàn	1. *reverse side*
	2. *negative side*: 反面意见 fǎnmiàn yìjiàn (*negative opinion*)
反叛 fǎnpàn	*revolt*
反义词 fǎnyìcí	*antonym*
反应 fǎnyìng	*reaction*
反映 fǎnyìng	*reflect; reflection*
反正 fǎnzhèng	*anyway; in any case*: 我帮你查这本书；我反正要去图书馆 wǒ bāng nǐ chá zhè běn shū; wǒ fǎnzhèng yào qù túshūguǎn (*let me check this book for you; I'm going to the library anyway*)

饭 fàn

1. *meal; food*: 早饭 zǎofàn (*breakfast*); 中饭 zhōngfàn (*lunch*); 晚饭 wǎnfàn (*dinner*); 中国饭 Zhōngguófàn (*Chinese food*). Cl: 顿 dùn; 份 fèn

2. *cooked rice; noodles* (or other starch-based staple food)

饭店 fàndiàn	*hotel; restaurant.* Cl: 家 jiā; 个 gè
饭馆 fànguǎn	*restaurant.* Cl: 家 jiā; 个 gè
饭盒 fànhé	*lunch box; mess tin.* Cl: 个 gè
饭厅 fàntīng	*dining hall; cafeteria.* Cl: 个 gè
饭碗 fànwǎn	*rice bowl; means of livelihood.* Cl: 个 gè
饭桌 fànzhuō	*dining table.* Cl: 张 zhāng

方 fāng

1. *square*: 方桌 fāngzhuō (*square table*)

2. *direction; place*: 前方 qiánfāng (*front*); 后方 hòufāng (*rear*); 西方 xīfāng (*west*)

3. *side*: 我方 wǒfāng (*our side*); 双方 shuāngfāng (*both sides*); 对方 (*the other party*)

Also appears in the following words: 处方 chǔfāng (*prescription*); 地方 dìfang (*place*); 对方 duìfāng (*the other side; counterpart*); 前方 qiánfāng (*the front;*

ahead); 东方 dōngfāng (*the East*); 西方 xīfāng (*the West*); 远方 yuǎnfāng (*distant place*)

方案	fāng'àn	*plan*. Cl: 个 gè; 种 zhǒng; 套 tào
方便	fāngbiàn	*convenient*
方法	fāngfǎ	*method*; *way*.Cl: 个 gè; 种 zhǒng
方面	fāngmiàn	*aspect*; *side*.Cl: 个 gè
方式	fāngshì	*way*; *manner*. Cl: 个 gè; 种 zhǒng
方向	fāngxiàng	*direction*
方言	fāngyán	*dialect*. Cl: 种 zhǒng
方针	fāngzhēn	*policy*; *principle*

房 fáng

1. *house*: 民房 mínfáng (*residential housing*); 楼房 lóufáng (*multi-level building*). Cl: 栋 dòng; 座 zuò; 所 suǒ; 幢 zhuàng

2. *room*: 卧房 wòfáng (*bedroom*); 客房 kèfáng (*guestroom*); 厨房 chúfáng (*kitchen*). Cl: 间 jiān; 个 gè

Also appears in the following words: 病房 bìngfáng (*sickroom*; *ward*); 牢房 láofáng (*jail*); 楼房 lóufáng (*storied building*); 票房 piàofáng (*box office*; *ticket office*); 药房 yàofáng (*drugstore*; *pharmacy*); 营房 yíngfáng (*barracks*)

房地产	fángdìchǎn	*real estate*
房顶	fángdǐng	*roof*
房东	fángdōng	*landlord*; *landlady*. Cl: 家 jiā; 位 wèi; 个 gè
房间	fángjiān	*room*. Cl: 个 gè
房客	fángkè	*tenant*. Cl: 个 gè; 位 wèi; 名 míng
房主	fángzhǔ	*owner of a house*. Cl: 个 gè; 位 wèi
房子	fángzi	*house*: 买房子 mǎi fángzi (*buy a house*). Cl: 间 jiān; 所 suǒ; 栋 dòng; 幢 zhuàng
房租	fángzū	*rent* (for an apartment, a house, etc.)

放 fàng

1. *put*; *place*, 把钱放在银行里 bǎ qián fàng zài yínháng lǐ (*put the money in the bank*); 窗前放着桌子 chuāng qián fàng zhe zhuōzi (*in front of the window is a table*)

2. *set free*; *release*: 鸽子被放了 gēzi bèi fàng le (*the pigeons were released*)

3. *let off*; *let out*: 放风筝 fàng fēngzhēng (*fly a kite*); 放学 fàngxué (*school is dismissed*); 放假 fàngjià (*have a holiday*)

4. *readjust; make relaxed:* 放松思想 fàngsōng sīxiǎng (*relax thoughts*); 放慢速度 fàngmàn sùdù (*slow down the speed*)

5. *put animals out to pasture:* 放养 fàngyǎng (*put the sheep out to pasture*)

6. *show; play back:* 放电影 fàng diànyǐng (*show a movie*); 放录音 fàng lùyīn (*play back a recording*); 放音乐 (*play music*)

7. *lay aside; sit around:* 牛奶不能放得太久 niúnǎi bù néng fàng de tài jiǔ (*the milk can't be laid aside for too long*)

Also appears in the following words: **存放** cúnfàng (*deposit; trust with*); **发放** fāfàng (*distribute; issue*); **解放** jiěfàng (*liberate*); **开放** kāifàng (*be open to*); **释放** shìfàng (*set free; release*)

放大 fàngdà	*enlarge* (a picture, etc.)	
放过 fàngguò	*let off; let sb. get away with; let sth. slip by:* 不能放过这个错误 bù néng fàngguò zhè ge cuòwù (*can't let this mistake slip by*)	
放火 fànghuǒ	*set on fire; commit arson*	
放假 fàngjià	*have a holiday; have a day off*	
放宽 fàngkuān	*loosen restrictions; relax; extend* (a deadline, etc.)	
放弃 fàngqì	*give up; abandon*	
放手 fàngshǒu	*have a free hand:* 这件事你可以放手做 zhè jiàn shì nǐ kěyǐ fàngshǒu zuò (*you have a free hand to do it*)	
放松 fàngsōng	*relax; loosen*	
放心 fàngxīn	*rest assured; set one's mind at ease*	

飞 fēi

1. *fly*

2. *rapidly; swiftly:* 飞跑 fēi pǎo (*dash; run swiftly*); 汽车在公路上飞驰 qìchē zài gōnglù shang fēi chí (*the car is speeding along on the highway*)

飞弹 fēidàn	**1.** *missile* **2.** *stray bullet* Cl: 颗 kē
飞机 fēijī	*airplane:* 飞机场 fēijīchǎng (*airport*); 直升飞机 zhíshēng fēijī (*helicopter*). Cl: 架 jià
飞快 fēikuài	*rapidly; at lightening speed:* 形势在飞快地变化 xíngshì zài fēikuàide biànhuà (*the situation is changing rapidly*)
飞行 fēixíng	*flight; aviation:* 飞行员 fēixíngyuán (*pilot; aviator*)
飞涨 fēizhàng	*(of price) soar; skyrocket:* 价格飞涨 jiàgé fēizhàng (*the price skyrocketed*)

非 fēi

1. *no; not; non*, remnant of literary Chinese used mostly in written language or set expressions: 非赢利 fēiyínglì (*nonprofit*); 非凡 fēifán (*extraordinary*)

2. *wrong*: 不分是非 bù fēn shìfēi (*do not distinguish between right and wrong*)

3. *must; have to*, used with negative expressions such as 不可 bùkě, 不行 bùxíng, or 不成 bùchéng: 他非明天来不可 tā fēi míngtiān lái bùkě (*he must come tomorrow*); 学外语的时候，你非练不行 xué wàiyǔ de shíhou, nǐ fēi liàn bùxíng (*when learning a foreign language, it won't do if you don't practice it*)

Also appears in the following words: 除非 chúfēi (*unless; only if*); 是非 shìfēi (*right and wrong*); 无非 wúfēi (*nothing but; simply*)

非常 fēicháng	**1.** *very; extremely*: 非常高兴 fēicháng gāoxìng (*extremely happy*)
	2. *extraordinary; unusual*: 非常事件 fēicháng shìjiàn (*unusual incident*)
非得 fēidé	*have to; must*: 我非得赢这盘棋 wǒ fēidé yíng zhè pán qí (*I must win this chess game*)
非法 fēifǎ	*illegal; unlawful*
非洲 Fēizhōu	*Africa*

费 fèi

1. *fee, dues, expenses, charge*: 经费 jīngfèi (*funds; outlay; budget*); 旅费 lǚfèi (*traveling expenses; fare*); 免费 miǎnfèi (*be exempted of fees; free of charge*); 小费 xiǎofèi (*gratuity; tip*); 学费 xuéfèi (*tuition*); 运费 yùnfèi (*shipping charge*); 自费 zìfèi (*self fund; at one's own expense*)

2. *cost; consume*: 费力 fèilì (*require great efforts*); 费时 fèishí (*take time; be time-consuming*)

Also appears in the following words: 白费 báifèi (*go to waste; waste*); 稿费 gǎofèi (*author's remuneration; royalty*); 耗费 hàofèi (*expend*); 花费 huāfèi (*expend; spend*); 经费 jīngfèi (*funds; budget*); 浪费 làngfèi (*waste*); 破费 pòfèi (*spend money*); 消费 xiāofèi (*consume*)

费解 fèijiě	*hard to understand, obscure*
费钱 fèiqián	*cost money; be costly*
费时 fèishí	*take time; be time-consuming*
费用 fèiyòng	*cost; expense.* Cl: 笔 bǐ

分 fēn

1. *divide*: 把学生分成三组 bǎ xuésheng fēn chéng sān zǔ (*divide the students into three groups*)

2. *distribute; allocate; assign*: 我们分到了新的住房 wǒmen fēn dào le xīnde zhùfáng (*we have been assigned new housing*)

3. *branch of* (a company, school, etc.); *subsidiary*: 分公司 fēngōngsī (*branch company*); 分行 fēnháng (*branch bank*); 分校 fēnxiào (*branch school*). Cl: 家 jiā; 个 gè

4. *cent* (monetary unit in China)

5. *minute*

6. *fraction*, used in such constructions as 百分之九十 bǎifēn zhī jiǔshí (*90 percent*); 五分之四 wǔfēn zhī sì (*four-fifths*), where 分 fēn literally means "parts" and 之 zhī is the the remnant of the classical Chinese, which is equivalent to the modern 的 de.

Also appears in the following words: **划分** huàfēn (*carve up*); **区分** qūfēn (*differentiate; distinguish*); **十分** shífēn (*very*); **万分** wànfēn (*very much; extremely*)

分辨 **fēnbiàn**	*decipher; distinguish*	
分别 **fēnbié**	1. *say good-bye; part*	
	2. *differently*: 分别对待 fēnbié duìdài (*treat differently*)	
分布 **fēnbù**	*be distributed over; be dispersed*	
分担 **fēndān**	*share responsibility; share the burden*	
分隔 **fēngé**	*separate; divide*	
分工 **fēngōng**	*division of labor; divide work*	
分机 **fēnjī**	(telephone) *extension.* Cl: 部 bù; 个 gè	
分解 **fēnjiě**	*dissolve; dissect*	
分居 **fēnjū**	(of husband and wife, or members of a family) *live apart; separate*	
分开 **fēnkāi**	*separate; divide*	
分类 **fēnlèi**	*classify*	
分裂 **fēnliè**	*split; break up*	
分配 **fēnpèi**	*assign; allot*	
分批 **fēnpī**	*in batches; taking turns*: 分批参观 fēnpī cānguān (*take turns to visit*)	
分歧 **fēnqí**	*different opinions; divergence*	
分清 **fēnqīng**	*distinguish*: 分清是非 fēnqīng shìfēi (*distinguish between right and wrong*)	
分散 **fēnsàn**	*disperse; scatter*: 组织的成员分散在全国各地 zǔzhī de chéngyuán fēnsàn zài quánguó gèdì (*members of the organization are scattered around the country*)	

分手 fēnshǒu	*part company*
分析 fēnxī	*analysis; analyze:* 分析师 fēnxīshī (*analyst*)
分享 fēnxiǎng	*share* (joy, happiness, etc.) *with*
分钟 fēnzhōng	*minute*

风 fēng

wind

Also appears in the following words: 伤风 shāngfēng (*catch a cold*); 台风 táifēng (*typhoon*); 通风 tōngfēng (*ventilation*); 中风 zhòngfēng (med. *stroke*); 作风 zuòfēng (*style of work*)

风暴 fēngbào	*storm.* Cl: 阵 zhèn; 场 chǎng; 次 cì
风波 fēngbō	*disturbance; incident.* Cl: 场 chǎng; 个 gè
风车 fēngchē	*windmill.* Cl: 架 jià; 个 gè
风格 fēnggé	(writing, etc.) *style*
风光 fēngguāng	*view; scene*
风景 fēngjǐng	*scenery*
风气 fēngqì	*trend;* (social) *mode*
风琴 fēngqín	*organ:* 弹风琴 tán fēngqín (*play the organ*). Cl: 架 jià; 个 gè
风趣 fēngqù	*humorous; witty*
风声 fēngshēng	*wind* (of something); *news*
风水 fēngshuǐ	*geomancy*
风俗 fēngsú	*custom*
风味 fēngwèi	*flavor:* 当地风味 dāngdì fēngwèi (*local flavor*)
风筝 fēngzhēn	*kite.* Cl: 个 gè; 只 zhī

服 fú

1. *clothes:* 军服 jūnfú (*military uniform*); 便服 biànfú (*plain clothes*); 工作服 gōngzuòfú (*overalls; work clothes*). Cl: 件 jiàn; 套 tào

2. *be accustomed to:* 不服水土 bù fú shuǐtǔ (*not accustomed to the local climate*)

3. *accept* (a fact): 很多人不服他当经理 hěn duō rén bù fú tā dāng jīnglǐ (*many people don't accept the fact that he was appointed manager*)

Also appears in the following words: 口服 kǒufú (med. *take orally*); 佩服 pèifú (*admire*); 屈服 qūfú (*knuckle under; yield*); 舒服 shūfú (*comfortable*); 说服 shuìfú (*persuade; convince*); 驯服 xùnfú (*tame; domesticate*); 征服 zhēngfú (*conquer*)

服从 fúcóng	obey; submit to: 少数服从多数 shǎoshù fúcóng duōshù (the minority should go along with the majority)
服气 fúqì	be convinced; accept (a fact)
服输 fúshū	acknowledge defeat; concede a loss
服务 fúwù	serve; service: 为人民服务 wèi rénmín fúwù (serve the people); 服务员 fúwùyuán (waiter; waitress; hotel attendant; flight attendant). Note that 服务 fúwù is an intransive verb in Chinese. As such, it cannot be followed by an object.
服装 fúzhuāng	clothing: 服装厂 fúzhuāngchǎng (garment factory); 服装店 fúzhuāngdiàn (clothing store)

父 fù

father, usu. taking the disyllabic form of 父亲 fùqin, which is primarily used as a term of reference as opposed to 爸爸 bàba, which is used as a term of address as well as a term of reference.

Also appears in the following words: 继父 jìfù (*stepfather*); 祖父 zǔfù (*paternal grandfather*); 岳父 yuèfù (*father-in-law*)

父辈 fùbèi	father's generation; the previous generation
父母 fùmǔ	parents
父女 fùnǚ	father and daughter
父亲 fùqin	father
父子 fùzǐ	father and son

该 gāi

1. *should; ought to*: 我该走了 wǒ gāi zǒu le (*I should be leaving*); 你不该在上课的时候说话 nǐ bù gāi zài shàngkè de shíhou shuōhuà (*you shouldn't talk in class*)

2. *deserve*: 他开车超速，该罚 tā kāichē chāosù, gāi fá (*he was speeding and deserved to be fined*)

3. *be one's turn*: 上次是你请的客；这次该我了 shàng cì shì nǐ qǐng de kè; zhè cì gāi wǒ le (*you treated me last time; it is my turn this time*)

4. *the said; the aforementioned*, used in formal language as a demonstrative pronoun to refer to an antecedent: 该公司 gāi gōngsī (*this company*); 该书 gāi shū (*that book*)

Also appears in the following words: 活该 huógāi (*serve sb. right*); 应该 yīnggāi (*should; ought to*)

该死 gāisǐ Used in colloquial speech to indicate annoyance, resentment, anger, etc.: 该死，又下雨了 gāisǐ, yòu xiàyǔ le (*damn it, it is raining again*); 该死的汽车老是出问题 gāisǐ de qìchē lǎoshì chū wèntí (*the damned car keeps breaking down*)

改 gǎi

1. *revise; correct; alter*: 衣服太长，需要改一改 yīfu tài cháng, xūyào gǎi yi gǎi (*the clothes are too long and need alteration*); 老师在改学生的作业 lǎoshī zài gǎi xuésheng de zuòyè (*the teacher is correcting the students' work*); 这篇文章不用改 zhè piān wénzhāng bú yòng gǎi (*this article does not need revision*)

2. *switch over to; do instead*: 改用电脑写 gǎi yòng diànnǎo xiě (*use the computer to write instead*); 改坐火车 gǎi zuò huǒchē (*switch over to the train*)

Also appears in the following words: 更改 gēnggǎi (*alter*); 修改 xiūgǎi (*revise; amend*)

改编 gǎibiān *adapt*: 把小说改编成电影 bǎ xiǎoshuō gǎibiān chéng diànyǐng (*adapt the novel into a movie*)

改变 gǎibiàn *change* (n. and v.): 中国有了很大的改变 Zhōngguó yǒu le hěn dàde gǎibiàn (*there have been great changes in China*); 人们改变了对他的看法 rénmen gǎibiàn le duì tāde kànfa (*people have changed their opinion of him*)

改掉 gǎidiào *give up; drop* (an undesirable habit; behavior): 改掉迟到的习惯 gǎidiào chídào de xíguàn (*drop the habit of being constantly late*)

改革 gǎigé *reform* (n. and v.). Cl: 项 xiàng

改行 gǎiháng *change one's profession*

改换 gǎihuàn *change over to; replace*: 改换教材 gǎihuàn jiàocái (*change the textbook*); 改换政府 gǎihuàn zhèngfǔ (*replace the government*)

改进 gǎijìn *improve*: 改进工作 gǎijìn gōngzuò (improve work).

改期 gǎiqī *change the date*: 演出已经改期 yǎnchū yǐjīng gǎiqī (*the date for the performance has been changed*)

改日 gǎirì *another day; some other day*, also expressed as 改天 gǎitiān: 你今天没有时间，我们改日再谈吧 nǐ jīntiān méi you shíjiān, wǒmen gǎirì zài tán ba (*since you don't have time today, let's talk about it some other day*)

改善 gǎishàn *improve; improvement*: 我们的生活有了很大的改善 wǒmende shēnghuó yǒu le hěn dàde gǎishàn (*there has been a lot of improvement in our life*)

| 改造 **gǎizào** | *transform*; *remake*: 改造旧城市 gǎizào jiù chéngshì (*transform the old city*) |
| 改正 **gǎizhèng** | *to correct*: 改正错误 gǎizhèng cuòwu (*correct mistakes*) |

干 **gān**; **gàn**

When pronounced gān:

1. *dry*: 干衣服 gān yīfu (*dry clothes*)

2. *dry* (v.): 油漆未干 yóuqī wèi gān (*wet paint*; *the paint has not dried yet*); 口干 kǒu gān (*thirsty*)

3. *connection*: 这个决定和我们无干 zhè ge juédìng hé wǒmen wú gān (*this decision has nothing to do with us*)

干杯 **gānbēi**	(proposing a toast) *bottoms up*; *cheers*
干脆 **gāncuì**	**1.** *not mince words*; *straightforward*; *frank*: 办事干脆 bànshì gāncuì (*be straightforward in doing things*) **2.** *had better*: 你不知道就干脆说不知道 nǐ bù zhīdao jiù gāncuì shuō bù zhīdao (*if you don't know, you had better say so*)
干饭 **gānfàn**	*cooked rice*
干旱 **gānhàn**	*dry weather*; *drought*
干净 **gānjìng**	*clean*
干扰 **gānrǎo**	*disturb*; *jam*; *interfere with*
干涉 **gānshè**	*interfere with*; *meddle in*
干洗 **gānxǐ**	*dry cleaning*
干燥 **gānzào**	(of weather) *dry*

When pronounced gàn:

1. *do*: 你今天晚上干什么 nǐ jīntiān wǎnshang gàn shénme (*what are you going to do tonight?*)

2. *trunk* (of a tree): 树干 shùgàn (*tree trunk*)

干部 **gànbù**	*cadre.* Cl: 个 gè; 名 míng; 位 wèi
干活 **gànhuó**	*work* (v.)
干劲 **gànjìng**	*vigor*; *drive*; *enthusiasm*

赶 **gǎn**

1. *catch up with*, often used with 上 shàng or 上来 shàng lái: 对方赶上来了 duìfāng gǎn shàng lái le (*the opponent has caught up*); 我缺了很多课，赶不

上班里的同学了 wǒ quē le hěn duō kè, gǎn bú shàng bān lǐ de tóngxué le (*I missed a lot of classes and can't catch up with the rest of the class*)

2. *make a dash for; try to catch*: 我没有时间和你说话，我要赶汽车 wǒ méi you shíjiān hé nǐ shuōhuà, wǒ yào gǎn qìchē (*I don't have time to talk to you because I need to hurry up to catch the bus*)

3. *rush to do sth.*: 记者每天晚上要赶稿子 jìzhě měitiān wǎnshang yào gǎn gǎozi (*reporters have to rush to write articles every night*)

4. *drive away*, usu. used with the verb complement 走 zǒu or 跑 pǎo: 用蚊香赶走蚊子 yòng wénxiāng gán zǒu wénzi (*use the mosquito-repellent incense to drive away the mosquitoes*)

5. *find oneself in a situation; catch someone doing sth.*, usu. used with 上 shàng: 我去他家时，正赶上他吃晚饭 wǒ qù tā jiā shí, zhèng gǎn shàng tā chī wǎnfàn (*when I went to his house, he was eating his dinner*)

赶集	gǎnjí	*go to market* (used in rural China)
赶紧	gǎnjǐn	*hasten to do*: 你丢了护照，要赶紧去报失 nǐ diū le hùzhào, yào gǎnjǐn qù bàoshī (*you lost your passport and you need to report the loss right away*)
赶快	gǎnkuài	*at once; quickly*: 电影要开始了，请大家赶快坐下 diànyǐng yào kāishǐ le, qǐng dàjiā gǎnkuài zuò xià (*the movie is about to start, please sit down quickly, everyone!*)

感 gǎn

1. *feel*, often used with 到 dào: 感到很舒服 gǎndào hěn shūfu (*feel very comfortable*)

2. *move; touch*: 这部电影非常感人 zhè bù diànyǐng fēicháng gǎn rén (*this movie is very touching*)

3. *sense; feelings*: 责任感 zérèngǎn (*sense of responsibility*)

Also appears in the following words: 反感 fǎngǎn (*repulsion; repugnance*); 好感 hǎogǎn (*favorable impression*); 快感 kuàigǎn (*pleasant sensation*); 灵感 línggǎn (*inspiration*); 流感 liúgǎn (*flu*); 敏感 mǐngǎn (*sensitive*); 情感 qínggǎn (*emotion*); 同感 tónggǎn (*sympathy*); 性感 xìnggǎn (*sexy*); 预感 yùgǎn (*hunch*).

感动	gǎndòng	*move; touch*
感激	gǎnjī	*feel grateful*
感觉	gǎnjué	**1.** *feeling; sense; sensation*: 这是我们共同的感觉 zhè shì wǒmen gòngtóngde gǎnjué (*this is our common feeling*)
		2. *feel*: 你感觉怎么样 nǐ gǎnjué zěnmeyàng (*how are you feeling?*)

感冒 gǎnmào	catch cold
感情 gǎnqíng	emotion; affection; feeling
感想 gǎnxiǎng	impression; reflection; thoughts
感谢 gǎnxiè	express thanks: 感谢信 gǎnxièxìn (letter of thanks; thank-you letter)

刚 gāng

1. *just*; *a moment ago*: 雨刚停 yǔ gāng tíng (*the rain has just stopped*); 医生刚给我检查了身体 yīshēng gāng gěi wǒ jiǎnchá le shēntǐ (*the doctor gave me a physical just now*)

2. *first*: 他刚来美国的时候，一点儿英语也不会 tā gāng lái Měiguó de shíhou, yìdiǎnr Yīngyǔ yě bú huì (*when he first came to America, he could barely speak English*)

3. *just*; *exactly*: 水不冷也不热；刚好 shuǐ bù lěng yě bú rè; gāng hǎo (*the water is neither cold nor hot; it is just right*)

刚才 gāngcái	just now; a moment ago: 我的中国朋友刚才在这儿 wǒde Zhōngguó péngyou gāngcái zài zhèr (*my Chinese friends were here just now*); 风比刚才小了 fēng bǐ gāngcái xiǎo le (*the wind is less intense than it was just now*). 刚才 gāngcái is a noun in Chinese.
刚刚 gānggāng	1. *a moment ago*; *just now*: 孩子刚刚入睡 háizi gānggāng rùshuì (*the child has just fallen asleep*) 2. *only*; *exactly, just*: 我们进大学到现在刚刚一年 wǒmen jìn dàxué dào xiànzài gānggāng yì nián (*it is exactly one year since we entered college*)
刚好 gānghǎo	1. *it so happened that*: 我们想去吃中国饭，刚好学校旁边就有一个中国餐馆 wǒmen xiǎng qù chī Zhōngguófàn, gānghǎo xuéxiào pángbiān jiù yǒu yí ge Zhōngguó cānguǎn (*just when we wanted to eat Chinese food, we saw a Chinese restaurant near the school*) 2. *just*; *exactly*: 这件上衣100块钱，我刚好带了100块钱 zhè jiàn shàngyī 100 kuài qián, wǒ gānghǎo dài le 100 kuài qián (*this jacket cost 100 kuai and it just so happened that I brought exactly 100 kuai*)
刚…就… gāng…jiù…	as soon as: 他刚从大学毕业就找到了工作 tā gāng cóng dàxué bìyè jiù zhǎo dào le gōngzuò (*he found a job as soon as he graduated from college*)
刚强 gāngqiáng	(of a person's character) firm; staunch
刚直 gāngzhí	(of a person) upright; outspoken

高 gāo

high; tall: 高山 gāo shān (*high mountain*); 高楼 gāo lóu (*tall building*)

Also appears in the following words: 崇高 chónggāo (*sublime; lofty*); 提高 tígāo (*raise; enhance*); 增高 zēnggāo (*raise; heighten*)

高潮	**gāocháo**	*high tide; climax*
高等	**gāoděng**	*of a higher level:* 高等学校 gāoděng xuéxiào (*schools of higher learning; colleges and universities*)
高度	**gāodù**	1. (of objects) *height*
		2. (of degree) *high; highly:* 高度的热情 gāodùde rèqíng (*high enthusiasm*); 高度赞扬 gāodù zànyáng (*praise highly*)
高峰	**gāofēng**	*summit; peak:* 高峰会议 (*summit meeting*). Cl: 座 zuò
高贵	**gāoguì**	*noble; lofty*
高级	**gāojí**	*high-ranking; superior; luxury:* 高级宾馆 gāojí bīnguǎn (*luxury hotel*); 高级官员 gāojí guānyuán (*high-ranking official*)
高明	**gāomíng**	*wise; brilliant*
高速	**gāosù**	*high speed:* 高速公路 gāosù gōnglù (*expressway*)
高温	**gāowēn**	*high temperature*
高兴	**gāoxìng**	*happy; glad*
高血压	**gāoxuèyā**	*high blood pressure*
高原	**gāoyuán**	*highland; plateau*
高中	**gāozhōng**	*high school:* 高中生 gāozhōngshēng (*high school student*)

告 gào

1. *tell; inform; report,* used in set expressions, otherwise taking the disyllabic form of 告诉 gàosù: 无可奉告 wú kě fènggào (*nothing to inform; no comment*)

2. *bring a lawsuit against:* 告政府 gào zhèngfǔ (*bring a lawsuit against the government*)

Also appears in the following words: 报告 bàogào (*report*); 被告 bèigào (*defendant; the accused*); 布告 bùgào (*notice; bulletin*); 祷告 dǎogào (*pray*); 广告 guǎnggào (*advertisement; commercial*); 警告 jǐnggào (*warn; warning*); 控告 kònggào (*accuse; charge*); 通告 tōnggào (*announcement*); 预告 yùgào (*foretell; report in advance*); 原告 yuángào (*plaintiff*); 忠告 zhōnggào (*advice*)

告别	**gàobié**	*say good-bye to; bid farewell*
告发	**gàofā**	*report an offense*

告急 gàojí	report an emergency; request help with an emergency situation
告密 gàomì	inform against someone
告示 gàoshì	official notice; bulletin. Cl: 张 zhāng; 个 gè
告诉 gàosù	tell; inform
告状 gàozhuàng	bring a lawsuit: 去法院告状 qù fǎyuàn gàozhuàng (go to the court to file a suit)

歌 gē

song: 唱歌 chàng gē (sing a song). Cl: 支 zhī; 个 gè; 首 shǒu

Also appears in the following words: 儿歌 érgē (children's song; nursery rhyme); 国歌 guógē (national anthem); 民歌 míngē (folk song); 诗歌 shīgē (poetry); 赞歌 zàngē (hymn; song of praise)

歌唱 gēchàng	sing: 歌唱家 gēchàngjiā (singer).
歌词 gēcí	lyrics of a song. Cl: 句 jù; 段 duàn
歌剧 gējù	opera. Cl: 出 chū
歌谱 gēpǔ	music of a song
歌曲 gēqǔ	song. Cl: 首 shǒu; 支 zhī
歌手 gēshǒu	singer. Cl: 个 gè; 位 wèi; 名 míng
歌颂 gēsòng	sing the praise of
歌舞 gēwǔ	song and dance
歌谣 gēyáo	ballad. Cl: 句 jù; 首 shǒu; 个 gè

个 gè

Classifier, pronounced in the neutral tone. It is the most frequently used classifier in Chinese for people, places and most objects.

个别 gèbié	isolated; specific: 个别现象 gèbié xiànxiàng (isolated phenomena)
个人 gèrén	individual: 这件事在于个人 zhè jiàn shì zài yú gèrén (this matter is up to the individuals)
个性 gèxìng	individual character; personality
个子 gèzi	height of a person

各 gè

each; every. 各 gè differs from 每 měi in that it can be used directly with a noun without a classifier, whereas 每 měi, with a few exceptions, requires a classfier when used with a noun. Cf. 各人 gè rén; 各公司 gè gōngsī; 每个人 měi ge rén; 每个公司 měi ge gōngsī

各界 gèjiè	*all walks of life*
各自 gèzì	*each; respective; one's own*: 我们要做好各自的工作 wǒmen yào zuò hǎo gèzì de gōngzuò (*we must do a good job with our own work*)

给 gěi

1. *give*: 学校给了他奖学金 xuéxiào gěi le tā jiǎngxuéjīn (*the school has given him a scholarship*)

2. *for*: 给电话公司工作 gěi diànhuà gōngsī gōngzuò (*work for a telephone company*); 给学校买书 gěi xuéxiào mǎi shū (*buy books for the school*)

3. *to*: 给我妈妈打电话 gěi wǒ māma dǎ diànhuà (*call my mother*); 给我朋友写信 gěi wǒ péngyou xiě xìn (*write a letter to my friend*)

4. *by*: 汽车给撞坏了 qìchē gěi zhuàng huài le (*the car was damaged in the crash*)

跟 gēn

1. *with; and*: 你跟谁去旅行 nǐ gēn shuí qù lǚxíng (*who are you going to travel with?*); 这件事跟我没有关系 zhè jiàn shì gēn wǒ méi you guānxi (*this matter has nothing to do with me*)

2. *from*: 我跟他借钱 wǒ gēn tā jiè qián (*I borrowed money from him*)

3. *to*: 老师跟我们说明天要考试 lǎoshī gēn wǒmen shuō míngtiān yào kǎoshì (*the teacher told us that there would be an exam tomorrow*). 跟 gēn in this usage is interchangeable with 对 duì.

4. *as*: 纽约跟上海一样挤 Niǔyuē gēn Shànghǎi yíyàng jǐ (*New York is as congested as Shanghai*). 跟 gēn in this usage is interchangeable with 和 hé.

5. *heel*: 脚跟 jiǎogēn (*heel*); 高跟鞋 gāogēnxié (*high-heeled shoes*)

6. *follow*: 狗跟着我 gǒu gēn zhe wǒ (*the dog follows me*)

跟前 gēnqián	*at hand; in one's presence*: 你跟前有没有照相机 nǐ gēnqián yǒu méi you zhàoxiàngjī (*do you have a camera*

at hand?*); 请来我跟前 qǐng lái wǒ gēnqián (*please come before me*)

跟随 gēnsuí   *follow someone* (as an aide or attendant): 他的秘书跟随了他二十年 tāde mìshū gēnsuí le tā èrshí nián (*his secretary has followed him for twenty years*)

跟头 gēntou   1. *fall* (n.) *to the ground,* usu. used with verbs such as 摔 shuāi or 跌 dié: 摔了跟头 shuāi le gēntou (*had a fall*)
2. *somersault,* always used with the verb 翻 fān: 翻跟头 fān gēntou (*do a somersault*).
Cl: 个 gè

更 gèng

even more: 洛杉矶大, 纽约更大 Luòshānjī dà, Niǔyuē gèng dà (*Los Angeles is large, but New York is even larger*); 会说中文后, 外国学生更喜欢中国了 huì shuō Zhōngwén hòu, wàiguó xuésheng gèng xǐhuan Zhōngguó le (*having learned to speak Chinese, the foreign students like China even more*)

更加 gèngjiā   *even more,* usu. used before disyllabic adjectives or verbs: 装饰过以后, 房子更加漂亮了 zhuāngshì guo yǐhòu, fángzi gèngjiā piàoliang le (*after decorating, the house is even prettier*)

工 gōng

1. *worker,* usu. taking the disyllabic form of 工人 gōngrén

2. *work; project*: 分工 fēngōng (*divide work; division of work*)

3. *industry*: 化工 huàgōng (*chemical industry*); 重工 zhònggōng (*heavy industry*)

Also appears in the following words: 罢工 bàgōng (*strike; walkout*); 技工 jìgōng (*mechanic*); 加工 jiāgōng (*process*); 开工 kāigōng (*start a construction job*); 人工 réngōng (*manpower; manual work*); 童工 tónggōng (*child labor*); 员工 yuángōng (*employee; personnel*); 职工 zhígōng (*employee; staff*)

工厂 gōngchǎng   *factory*

工程 gōngchéng   *engineering; engineering project; construction.* Cl: 个 gè; 项 xiàng

工地 gōngdì   *construction site*

工夫 gōngfu   1. *time*: 一星期的工夫 yì xīngqī de gōngfu (*a week's time*)
2. *effort; work*: 花了很多工夫 huà le hěn duō gōngfu (*devoted a lot of efforts*)

工会 gōnghuì	trade union
工匠 gōngjiàng	craftsman; artisan. Cl: 名 míng; 个 gè
工具 gōngjù	tool; instrument. Cl: 件 jiàn; 样 yàng
工科 gōngkē	engineering major
工龄 gōnglíng	years of employment; seniority
工人 gōngrén	worker. Cl: 名 míng; 个 gè
工业 gōngyè	industry
工艺 gōngyì	technique; craft
工资 gōngzī	salary; pay. Cl: 份 fèn
工作 gōngzuò	work; job. Cl: 件 jiàn; 个 gè; 份 fèn; 项 xiàng

公 gōng

1. *public; state-owned; official*: 公立学校 gōnglì xuéxiào (*public school*)

2. *official business*: 办公 bàn gōng (*handle official business*)

3. *metric*: 公里 gōnglǐ (*kilometer*); 公斤 gōngjīn (*kilogram*)

4. *(of animals) male*: 公鸡 gōngjī (*rooster*); 公牛 gōngniú (*bull*)

公安 gōngān	*public security*: 公安局 gōngānjú (*public security bureau; police department*), 公安员 gōngānyuán (*police*)
公布 gōngbù	*make public; promulgate; announce*
公差 gōngchāi	*public errand; travel on official business*
公告 gōnggào	*announcement; bulletin.* Cl: 张 zhāng
公共 gōnggòng	*public; communal*: 公共汽车 gōnggòng qìchē (*bus*); 公共厕所 gōnggòng cèsuǒ (*public bathroom*)
公公 gōnggong	*husband's father; maternal grandfather*
公开 gōngkāi	*public; open*: 公开信 gōngkāixìn (*open letter*); 公开场合 gōngkāi chǎnghé (*public occasion*)
公款 gōngkuǎn	*public fund.* Cl: 笔 bǐ
公路 gōnglù	*highway.* Cl: 条 tiáo
公民 gōngmín	*citizen.* Cl: 个 gè; 位 wèi
公平 gōngping	*fair; just; impartial*
公认 gōngrèn	*generally acknowledged*
公式 gōngshì	*formula*
公事 gōngshì	*public affairs.* Cl: 件 jiàn
公文 gōngwén	*official document.* Cl: 件 jiàn; 份 fèn
公务 gōngwù	*official business*
公用 gōngyòng	*for public use*: 公用电话 gōngyòng diànhuà (*pay phone*)
公寓 gōngyù	*apartment.* Cl: 所 suǒ; 座 zuò; 栋 dòng
公元 gōngyuán	*the Christian era*
公园 gōngyuán	*park.* Cl: 个 gè; 所 suǒ
公章 gōngzhāng	*official seal*

公证 gōngzhèng	notarize; notarization: 公证员 gōngzhèngyuán (notary public)
公众 gōngzhòng	the public; people
公主 gōngzhǔ	princess

共 gòng

1. *share*: 共用厨房 gòng yòng chúfáng (*share the kitchen*)

2. *altogether; in total*: 共花了一百块钱 gòng huā le yì bǎi kuài qián (*altogether spent $100*)

Also appears in the following words: 公共 gōnggòng (*public*); 一共 yígòng (*altogether*); 总共 zǒnggòng (*in total*)

共产党 gòngchǎndǎng	Communist Party
共产主义 gòngchǎnzhǔyì	Communism
共存 gòngcún	coexist
共计 gòngjì	in total; altogether
共同 gòngtóng	1. *common*: 共同的目标 gòngtóngde mùbiāo (*common goal*); 共同的语言 gòngtóngde yǔyán (*common language*) 2. *jointly; collectively*: 共同主办 gòngtóng zhǔbàn (*jointly sponsor*)

够 gòu

1. *enough; sufficient*: 这台电视要一千块，你的钱够不够 zhè tái diànshì yào yì qiān kuài, nǐde qián gòu bu gòu (*this television costs 1,000 kuài; do you have enough money?*). 够 gòu in this sense is often used as a verb complement: 睡够 shuì gòu (*have enough sleep*); 玩够 wán gòu (*have enough fun*); 看够 kàn gòu (*see enough*)

2. *reach* (a point or degree), often used with the complement 着 zháo: 天花板太高，我够不着 tiānhuābǎn tài gāo, wǒ gòu bù zháo (*the ceiling is too high, I can't reach it*)

3. *really*: 这条河真够宽 zhè tiáo hé zhēn gòu kuān (*this river is really wide*)

Also appears in the following words: 能够 nénggòu (*be able to; can*); 足够 zúgòu (*enough*).

| 够格 gòugé | qualified: 没有学过教育的人不够格当老师 méiyou xué guo jiàoyù de rén bú gòugé dāng lǎoshī (*those who have not studied education are not qualified to be teachers*) |

| 够呛 gòuqiàng | *excessively; unbearably*: 今年冬天冷得够呛 jīnnián dōngtiān lěng de gòuqiàng (*this winter is unbearably cold*) |

古 gǔ

ancient: 古人 gǔrén (*ancient people*); 古时候 gǔshíhou (*ancient times*)

古巴 **Gǔbā**	*Cuba*
古板 **gǔbǎn**	*old-fashioned and inflexible*
古代 **gǔdài**	*ancient times*: 古代史 gǔdàishǐ (*ancient history*)
古典 **gǔdiǎn**	*classical*: 古典文学 gǔdiǎn wénxué (*classical literature*); 古典音乐 gǔdiǎn yīnyuè (*classical music*)
古董 **gǔdǒng**	*antique*. Cl: 件 jiàn
古怪 **gǔguài**	*eccentric; odd*: 古怪的性格 gǔguàinde xìnggé (*eccentric personality*)
古话 **gǔhuà**	*old saying*
古迹 **gǔjì**	*historic site*. Cl: 处 chù
古籍 **gǔji**	*ancient books; classics*
古老 **gǔlǎo**	*age-old; ancient*: 古老的城市 gǔlǎode chéngshì (*ancient city*)
古物 **gǔwù**	*ancient objects; antiques*

挂 guà

1. *hang; put up*: 把地图挂在墙上 bǎ dìtú guà zài qiáng shàng (*hang the map on the wall*)

2. (phone) *hang up; ring off*: 不要挂电话 búyào guà diànhuà (*don't hang up; hold the line*)

3. *register at a hospital*: 挂内科 guà nèikē (*register for the internal medicine department*)

挂号 **guàhào**	*register at a hospital; send letter registered*: 挂号信 guàhàoxìn (*registered letter*). Cl: 封 fēng
挂面 **guàmiàn**	*fine dried noodle; vermicelli*. Cl: 把 bǎ
挂名 **guàmíng**	*titular; nominal; only in name*
挂失 **guàshī**	*report the loss of sth.*
挂图 **guàtú**	*wall map; hanging chart*. Cl: 张 zhāng; 幅 fú
挂钟 **guàzhōng**	*wall clock*

关 guān

1. *close; shut:* 关窗子 guān chuāngzi (*close the window*); 商店关门了 shāngdiàn guān mén le (*the store is closed now*)

2. *turn off; switch off:* 关电视 guān diànshì (*turn off the television*); 关灯 guān dēng (*turn off the light*)

3. *lock up:* 老虎被关在笼子里 lǎohǔ bèi guān zài lóngzi lǐ (*the tiger is locked up in the cage*)

4. *pass:* 海关 hǎiguān (*customs*); 要关 yàoguān (*strategic pass*)

5. *connection:* 这事和我无关 zhè shì hé wǒ wú guān (*this matter has nothing to do with me*); 植物的生长和天气有关 zhíwù de shēngzhǎng hé tiānqì yǒu guān (*the growth of plants has to do with the weather*)

Also appears in the following words: **把关** bǎguān (*make checks*); **报关** bàoguān (*declare at customs*); **海关** hǎiguān (*customs*); **机关** jīguān (*government offices*); **开关** kāiguān (*switch*); **双关** shuāngguān (*have a double meaning*); **相关** xiāngguān (*correlated*); **有关** yǒuguān (*related*)

关键	**guānjiàn**	*key; crux*
关联	**guānlián**	*be connected; be related*
关门	**guānmén**	(*of a store or business*) *close; be closed*
关系	**guānxi**	**1.** *relation; relationship; connection:* 雇主和雇员的关系很好 gùzhǔ hé gùyuán de guānxi hěn hǎo (*the employer maintains a good relationship with the employees*); 这两个国家有外交关系 zhè liǎng ge guójiā yǒu wàijiāo guānxi (*these two countries have diplomatic relations with each other*)
		2. *impact; significance:* 你来晚一点儿没有关系 nǐ lái wǎn yìdiǎnr méi you guānxi (*it doesn't matter if you come a little late*)
		3. *due to; because of,* used with 因为 yīnwei or 由于 yóuyú: 由于身体的关系，他决定辞职 yóuyú shēntǐ de guānxi, tā juédìng cízhí (*due to health issues, he has decided to resign*)
		4. *affect:* 教师的质量关系到学校的名声 jiàoshī de zhìliàng guānxi dào xuéxiào de míngshēng (*the teachers' quality affects the reputation of the schools*)
关心	**guānxīn**	*show concern or interest for:* 我妈妈对我很关心 wǒ māma duì wǒ hěn guānxīn (*my mother shows great concern for me*); 他对国际事务很关心 tā duì guójì shìwù hěn guānxīn (*he is very interested in international affairs*)
关于	**guānyú**	*regarding; about,* always used before the subject: 关于这

个问题，大家有很多看法 guányú zhè ge wèntí, dàjiā yǒu hěn duō kànfa (*people have many opinions about the issue*); 关于中国的电影 guānyú Zhōngguó de diànyǐng (*movie about China*)

馆 guǎn

1. *accommodations for guests*: 旅馆 lǚguǎn (*hotel*); 宾馆 bīnguǎn (*guesthouse*). Cl: 家 jiā; 个 gè; 座 zuò; 所 suǒ

2. *a diplomatic office*: 大使馆 dàshǐguǎn (*embassy*); 领事馆 lǐngshìguǎn (*consulate*). Cl: 座 zuò; 处 chù

3. *a service venue*: 饭馆 fànguǎn (*restaurant*); 茶馆 cháguǎn (*teahouse*); 咖啡馆 kāfēiguǎn (*coffee shop*). Cl: 家 jiā; 个 gè

4. *public facilities; a place of cultural activities*: 图书馆 túshūguǎn (*library*); 博物馆 bówùguǎn (*museum*); 美术馆 měishùguǎn (*gallery*); 展览馆 zhǎnlǎnguǎn (*exhibition hall*). Cl: 座 zuò; 个 gè

管 guǎn

1. *manage; supervise; be in charge*: 管账 guǎn zhàng (*keep accounts*); 谁管这件事 shuí guǎn zhè jiàn shì (*who is in charge of the matter?*)

2. *control; bother about; boss around*: 我哥哥总是管我 wǒ gēge zǒngshì guǎn wǒ (*my older brother always bosses me around*); 别管她 bié guǎn tā (*leave her alone; don't bother her*)

3. *tube; pipe*: 水管 shuǐguǎn (*pipe*); 试管 shìguǎn (*test tube*)

Also appears in the following words: 保管 bǎoguǎn (*safekeeping*); 尽管 jǐnguǎn (*in spite of*); 看管 kānguǎn (*take charge; attend to*); 只管 zhǐguǎn (*by all means; merely*); 主管 zhǔguǎn (*person in charge*)

管道 **guǎndào**	*pipeline*. Cl: 条 tiáo	
管家 **guǎnjiā**	*butler; manager; housekeeper*	
管教 **guǎnjiào**	*subject sb. (usu. a child) to discipline*	
管理 **guǎnlǐ**	*manage; supervise; run; administer*: 管理人员 guǎnlǐ rényuán (*management personnel; administrative staff*)	
管辖 **guǎnxiá**	*have jurisdiction over*	
管弦乐 **guǎnxiányuè**	*orchestral music*	
管制 **guǎnzhì**	*control (by force)*: 交通管制 jiāotōng guǎnzhì (*traffic control*); 货币管制 huòbì guǎnzhì (*currency control*)	
管子 **guǎnzi**	*tube; pipe*. Cl: 根 gēn; 节 jié; 段 duàn	

光 guāng

1. *light*: 灯光 dēngguāng (*lamplight*); 月光 yuèguāng (*moonlight*)

2. *honor*; *glory*: 为国家争光 wèi guójiā zhēng guāng (*win honor for one's country*)

3. *glossy*; *smooth*: 桌面很光 zhuōmiàn hěn guāng (*the tabletop is very glossy*)

4. *use up*, used as a verb complement: 吃光 chī guāng (*eat up*); 花光了钱 huā guāng le qián (*spent all the money*)

5. *bare*; *naked*: 光头 guāng tóu (*bare head*)

6. *only*: 光有钱还不够 guǎng yǒu qián hái bú gòu (*it is not enough just to have money*)

Also appears in the following words: 风光 fēngguāng (*scenery*; *landscape*); 观光 guānguāng (*sightseeing*); 日光 rìguāng (*daylight*); 阳光 yángguāng (*sunlight*)

光顾	**guānggù**	*patronize*
光滑	**guānghuá**	(of objects) *smooth*; *glossy*
光洁	**guāngjié**	*bright and clean*
光临	**guānglín**	*presence* (of a visitor, guest, etc.)
光年	**guāngnián**	*light-year*
光谱	**guāngpǔ**	*spectrum*
光荣	**guāngróng**	*glory*; *glorious*
光线	**guāngxiàn**	*light*; *ray*. Cl: 条 tiáo; 道 dào

贵 guì

1. *expensive*; *costly*

2. *distinguished*; *honorable*: 贵宾 guìbīn (*distinguished guest*; *VIP*). Cl: 位 wèi

3. *your*, used as an honorific before the name of a person, a country or an organization to show respect: 您贵姓 nín guì xìng (*what is your last name?*); 贵国 guì guó (*your country*); 贵公司 guì gōngsī (*your company*)

Also appears in the following words: 宝贵 bǎoguì (*valuable*; *previous*); 高贵 gāoguì (*noble*); 可贵 kěguì (*esteemable*); 名贵 míngguì (*rare and famous*); 珍贵 zhēnguì (*precious*)

贵宾	**guìbīn**	*distinguished guest*; *VIP*. Cl: 位 wèi
贵重	**guìzhòng**	*valuable*; *precious*
贵族	**guìzú**	*aristocrat*; *noble*

国 guó

1. *country; state; nation*

2. used to translate names of foreign countries: 英国 Yīngguó (*Britain*); 法国 Fǎguó (*France*); 德国 Déguó (*Germany*). When used unmodified, 国家 guójiā, instead of 国 guó, should be used: 三个国家 sān ge guójiā (*three countries*); 国家的利益 guójiā de lìyì (*national interest*).

Also appears in the following words: 出国 chūguó (*go abroad*); 帝国 dìguó (*empire*); 外国 wàiguó (*foreign country*); 祖国 zǔguó (*motherland*); 共和国 gònghéguó (*republic*)

国产 guóchǎn	*made in one's own country; domestically made*
国防 guófáng	*national defense*
国歌 guógē	*national anthem*
国画 guóhuà	*traditional Chinese painting.* Cl: 张 zhāng; 幅 fú
国会 guóhuì	*Congress; Parliament*
国籍 guójí	*nationality; citizenship*
国际 guójì	*international*
国内 guónèi	*(of a country) domestic*
国旗 guóqí	*national flag.* Cl: 面 miàn
国庆节 guóqìngjié	*national day*
国外 guówài	*overseas; abroad*
国王 guówáng	*king*
国语 guóyǔ	*Mandarin Chinese*

果 guǒ

1. *fruit*

2. *result*

Also appears in the following words: 成果 chéngguǒ (*outcome; achievement*); 后果 hòuguǒ (*consequence; aftermath*); 结果 jiéguǒ (*result*); 如果 rúguǒ (*if*); 糖果 tángguǒ (*candy*); 效果 xiàoguǒ (*effect*)

果断 guǒduàn	*resolute; decisive*
果酱 guǒjiàng	*jam* (fruit)
果然 guǒrán	*as expected; sure enough*: 天气报告说有台风，台风果然来了 tiānqì bàogào shuō yǒu táifēng, táifēng guǒrán lái le (*the weather forecast said that there would be a typhoon; sure enough a typhoon arrived*)
果实 guǒshí	1. *fruit* 2. *result*: 改革的果实 gǎigé de guǒshí (*result of the reform*)

果树 **guǒshù**	*fruit tree.* Cl: 棵 kē
果园 **guǒyuán**	*orchard*
果汁 **guǒzhī**	*fruit juice*

过 guò

1. *cross; pass*: 过马路 guò mǎlù (*cross the street*); 过了很多天 guò le hěn duō tiān (*many days passed*)

2. *spend* (time); *observe* (an occasion): 过年 guò nián (*celebrate the New Year*); 过生日 guò shēngrì (*celebrate one's birthday*)

3. *exceed; go beyond*: 牛奶已经过期了 (*the milk has expired*); 我爸爸已经过60岁了 (*my father is over 60*)

4. *across; past; through*, used after a verb: 穿过隧道 chuān guò suídào (*go through a tunnel*); 游过河 yóu guò hé (*swim across the river*)

5. *excessively; too*: 速度过快 sùdù guò kuài (*the speed is excessive*); 裤子过长 kùzi guò cháng (*the pants are too long*)

6. *go over; review*: 过课文 guò kèwén (*go over the text*); 过生词 guò shēngcí (*review the new words*)

7. *as good as; better than* (in a competition), used after a verb: 你能跑过他吗 nǐ néng pǎo guò tā ma (*can you run as fast as he does?*). Additionally, it is often preceded by 得 de in affirmative sentences and 不 bù in negative sentences: 我们的队打得过他们的队 wǒmende duì dǎ de guò tāmende duì (*our team can beat their team*); 我们的队打不过他们的队 wǒmende duì dǎ bú guò tāmende duì (*our team is no match for their team*).

8. aspect particle used after a verb to indicate **a)** a past event or experience: 你去过香港吗 nǐ qù guo Xiāng Gǎng ma (*have you been to Hong Kong before?*); **b)** the completion of an action: 衣服洗过了 yīfu xǐ guo le (*the clothes have been washed*); 她看过医生了 tā kàn guo yīshēng le (*she has seen the doctor*)

9. aspect particle used after an adjective to suggest a situation contrary to the present: 我们的村子穷过 wǒmende cūnzi qióng guo (*our village was once poor*)

When used as an aspect particle, 过 is pronounced in the neutral tone: guo. The negative form of the aspect 过 guo is 没有 méiyou: 我没有去过欧洲 wǒ méiyou qù guo Ōuzhōu (*I have not been to Europe*).

Also appears in the following words: 超过 chāoguò (*exceed*); 错过 cuòguò (*miss out*); 放过 fàngguò (*let off*); 经过 jīngguò (*pass*); 路过 lùguò (*pass by*); 难过 nánguò (*sad*); 通过 tōngguò (*pass; pass through*)

过来 guò lái　*come over*, often used after another verb: 请过来一下儿 qǐng guò lái yíxiàr (*please come over for a minute*); 走过来 zǒu guò lái (*walk over*)

过去 guò qù　1. (*of time or a state*) *pass*; *be gone*: 三年过去了 sān nián guò qù le (*three years have passed*); 雨季过去了 yǔjì guò qù le (*the monsoon season is gone*)

2. *across*; *over* (a distance), often used after another verb: 游过河去 yóu guò hé qù (*swim across the river*); 拿过去 ná guò qù (*take sth. over*)

还 hái

1. *also*; *else*; *additionally*: 你还要买什么 nǐ hái yào mǎi shénme (*what else would you like to buy?*); 除了杭州，我们还去了苏州 chúle Hángzhōu, wǒmen hái qù le Sūzhōu (*besides Hangzhou, we also went to Suzhou*)

2. *still*; *yet*: 春天还没有来 chūntiān hái méiyou lái (*spring has not come yet*); 九点上课，现在还早呢 jiǔ diǎn shàng kè, xiànzài hái zǎo ne (*class starts at nine; it is still early now*)

还好 háihǎo　*all right*; *not bad*

还是 háishi　1. *or*, used in questions only: 你在家吃中饭还是在公司吃中饭 nǐ zài jiā chī zhōngfàn háishi zài gōngsī chī zhōngfàn (*do you eat lunch at home or at work?*)

2. *it is better that*: 现在下雨，你还是别走吧 xiànzài xiàyǔ, nǐ háishi bié zǒu ba (*it's raining, it is better that you don't leave now*). This expression is used when a decision or suggestion made out of alternatives: 这个问题你还是问他吧 zhè ge wèntí nǐ háishi wèn tā ba (*it's better for you to ask him the question—implying that I'm not the right person to answer your question*).

3. *nevertheless*; *just the same*; *after all*: 大家都以为他不会来了，可是他还是来了 dàjiā dōu yǐwéi tā bú huì lái le, kěshì tā háishi lái le (*everybody thought that he was not coming, but he came after all*)

4. *still*: 我们中饭吃面条，晚饭还是吃面条 wǒmen zhōngfàn chī miàntiáo, wǎnfàn háishì chī miàntiáo (*we had noodles for lunch and we had noodles for dinner again*)

孩 hái

child; children, taking the disyllabic form of 孩子 háizi when unmodified:
男孩 nánhái (*boy*); 女孩 nǚhái (*girl*); 小孩 xiǎohái (*child*)

孩子 háizi	*child; children.* Cl: 个 gè; 群 qún
孩子气 háizìqi	*childish; childishness*

海 hǎi

sea

海岸 hǎi'àn	*seashore*
海产 hǎichǎn	*sea products*
海底 hǎidǐ	*seabed; bottom of the sea*
海港 hǎigǎng	*port; harbor.* Cl: 座 zuò
海关 hǎiguān	*customs*
海军 hǎijūn	*navy.* Cl: 支 zhī
海绵 hǎimián	*sponge.* Cl: 块 kuài
海外 hǎiwài	*overseas*
海峡 hǎixiá	*strait; channel*
海鲜 hǎixiān	*seafood*
海洋 hǎiyáng	*ocean.* Cl: 片 piàn
海员 hǎiyuán	*seaman; sailor.* Cl: 个 gè; 名 míng; 位 wèi

好 hǎo

1. *good; nice; kind*

2. *get better; get recovered*: 她的病还没有好 tāde bìng hái méiyou hǎo (*she has not recovered from her illness*)

3. *so; very*, often used in exclamations: 好累啊 hǎo lèi a (*so tired*)

4. *quite a few; a good number of*, often used before words such as 几 jǐ, 些 xiē, and 多 duō: 好几本日语书 hǎo jǐ běn Rìyǔ shū (*several Japanese books*); 好些年 hǎo xiē nián (*many years*); 好多人 hǎo duō rén (*many people*)

5. *easy*: 今天出租车不好找 jīntiān chūzūchē bù hǎo zhǎo (*it is not easy to find a taxi today*); 这本字典很好用 zhè běn zìdiǎn hěn hǎo yòng (*this dictionary is easy to use*)

6. used as a verb complement to indicate that a desired state has been reached: 饭做好了 fàn zuò hǎo le (*the meal is ready*); 你的汽车修好了 nǐde qìchē xiū hǎo le (*your car has been fixed*)

Also appears in the following words: 刚好 gānghǎo (*just*; *exactly*); 讨好 tǎohǎo (*kiss up to*); 要好 yàohǎo (*be on good terms with*); 友好 yǒuhǎo (*friendly*)

好吃	hǎochī	*delicious*; *tasty*
好处	hǎochù	*benefit*; *advantage*; *gain*
好多	hǎoduō	*many*; *a good number of*
好感	hǎogǎn	*favorable impression*
好看	hǎokàn	*good-looking* (for people and objects); *interesting* (for books, movies, etc.)
好事	hǎoshì	*good deeds*. Cl: 件 jiàn
好听	hǎotīng	*pleasant to listen to*
好玩	hǎowán	*fun*; *interesting* (for toys, places, etc.): 北京很好玩 Běijīng hěn hǎowán (*Beijing is a fun place*)
好象	hǎoxiàng	*seem*; *look like*: 天好象要下雨 tiān hǎoxiàng yào xiàyǔ (*it looks like rain*)
好笑	hǎoxiào	*laughable*; *ridiculous*; *absurd*
好意	hǎoyì	*good intention*
好在	hǎozài	1. *fortunately*; *luckily*: 好在我们有药 hǎozài wǒmen yǒu yào (*fortunately we have medicine*) 2. *good because of*: 这部电影好在情节 zhè bù diànyǐng hǎozài qíngjié (*this movie is good for its plot*)
好转	hǎozhuǎn	*change for the better*; *improve*

和 hé

1. *and*, used to link two individual words, but not sentences. When more than two items are enumerated, 和 hé appears before the last item: 我爸爸，我妈妈，我哥哥和我 wǒ bàba, wǒ māma, wǒ gēge hé wǒ (*my father, my mother, my older brother and myself*)

2. *with*: 谁和你去看电影 shuí hé nǐ qù kàn diànyǐng (*who is going to see the movie with you?*)

和好	héhǎo	*become reconciled*
和睦	hémù	*harmony*
和平	hépíng	*peace*
和气	héqì	*gentle*; *cordial*; *amicable*
和谐	héxié	*harmonious*

河 hé

river

Also appears in the following words: 拔河 báhé (*tug-of-war*); 银河 yínhé (*Milky Way*)

河岸 hé'àn	*riverbank*
河床 héchuáng	*riverbed*
河马 hémǎ	*hippopotamus.* Cl: 只 zhī; 头 tóu

合 hé

1. *join*; *combine*: 合资 hézī (*pool funds*; *joint venture*)

2. *share*: 合住 hézhù (*share a room*); 合用 héyòng (*share the use of*)

3. *suit*; *agree*: 不合我的意 bú hé wǒde yì (*does not suit my needs*); 合法 héfǎ (*legal*; *in accordance with the law*)

Also appears in the following words: 场合 chǎnghé (*occasion*; *scene*); 凑合 còuhé (*make do*); 汇合 huìhé (*join*; *converge*); 联合 liánhé (*unite*); 巧合 qiǎohé (*coincidence*); 适合 shìhé (*suit*; *suitable*)

合并 hébìng	*combine*; *merge*: 这两个公司合并了 zhè liǎng ge gōngsī hébìng le (*these two companies are merged*)
合唱 héchàng	*chorus*
合法 héfǎ	*legal*; *lawful*
合格 hégé	*qualified*; *up to standard*: 合格人选 hégé rénxuǎn (*qualified candidate*); 合格产品 hégé chǎnpǐn (*products that have passed inspection*)
合伙 héhuǒ	*form a partnership*
合理 hélǐ	*reasonable*; *rational*
合身 héshēn	(*of clothes*) *fit*
合适 héshì	*suitable*; *proper*; *appropriate*
合同 hétóng	*contract.* Cl: 份 fèn; 项 xiàng; 种 zhǒng
合作 hézuò	*cooperate*; *collaborate*; *cooperation*; *collaboration*

汉 hàn

Chinese

汉人 hànrén	*ethnic Chinese*; *the Chinese people*
汉学 hànxué	*Chinese studies*; *Sinology*
汉语 hànyǔ	*Chinese language*

汉字 hànzì	Chinese characters
汉族 hànzú	ethic Chinese; the Han nationality

号 hào

1. *date*: 今天几号 jīntiān jǐ hào (*what is the date today?*)

2. *number*: 你住几号房间 nǐ zhù jǐ hào fángjiān (*what's your room number?*)

3. *size*: 大号 dàhào (*large size*); 中号 zhōnghào (*medium size*); 小号 xiǎohào (*small size*)

4. (punctuation) *mark*: 句号 jùhào (*full stop*); 问号 wènhào (*question mark*)

Also appears in the following words: 暗号 ànhào (*code; password*); 符号 fúhào (*symbol; sign*); 记号 jìhào (*mark; notation*); 外号 wàihào (*nickname*); 信号 xìnhào (*signal*)

号码 hàomǎ	*number*: 电话号码 diànhuà hàomǎ (*telephone number*); 房间号码 fángjiān hàomǎ (*room number*). Cl: 个 gè
号召 hàozhào	*call; appeal*: 国家的号召 guójiā de hàozhào (*nation's call*)

黑 hēi

1. *black; dark*

2. *illegal*: 黑货 hēihuò (*contraband*); 黑车 hēichē (*unlicensed vehicle*)

黑暗 hēi'àn	*dark*, usu. used metaphorically: 黑暗的社会 hēi'ànde shèhuì (*dark society*)
黑白 hēibái	*black and white; right and wrong*: 黑白电视 hēibái diànshì (*black and white TV*); 不分黑白 bù fēn hēibái (*do not distinguish between right and wrong*)
黑板 hēibǎn	*blackboard*. Cl: 块 kuài
黑名单 hēimíngdān	*blacklist*. Cl: 张 zhāng
黑人 hēirén	*black people*. Cl: 个 gè; 位 wèi
黑色 hēisè	*black color*: 黑色的衣服 hēisè de yīfu (*black clothes*)
黑市 hēishì	*black market*
黑眼镜 hēiyǎnjìng	*sunglasses*

很 hěn

very; *very much*: 很高兴 hěn gāoxìng (*very happy*); 很喜欢 hěn xǐhuan (*like very much*). 很 hěn is usu. obligatory when an adjective functions as a stative verb without qualification: 今天很冷 jīntiān hěn lěng (*it is cold today*). In this case, 很 hěn serves a grammatical function and may not carry the meaning of *very*. With the exception of 多 duō, adjectives modified by 很 hěn require the use of 的 de when preceding nouns: 很好的人 hěn hǎo de rén (*a very good person*); 很热的天 hěn rè de tiān (*a very hot day*).

后 hòu

1. *back*; *rear*: 后门 hòumén (*back door*); 后座 hòuzuò (*back seat*)

2. *rear*; *back*; *behind*; *in the rear*; *at the back*, used after a noun, as the word is considered as a noun in Chinese, and in conjunction with 在 zài: 生词表在书后 shēngcíbiǎo zài shū hòu (*the glossary is at the back of the book*); 公园后有一条河 gōngyuán hòu yǒu yì tiáo hé (*there is a river behind the park*). 在 zài is often left out when appearing at the beginning of an existential sentence. See under 在 zài. In this sense, 后 hòu is often but not always interchangeable with 后边 hòubian, 后面 hòumian, and 后头 hòutou. When used as an attribute modifying a noun or when used by itself as an adverbial of place, only the disyllabic form is possible: 后边的车 hòubiān de chē (*the car behind*); 后边有个车库 hòubian yǒu ge chēkù (*there is a garage in the back*).

3. *last*: 后两个问题 hòu liǎng ge wèntí (*the last two questions*)

4. *after*, used at the end of a phrase or a clause: 来美国后，我在纽约学习 lái Měiguó hòu, wǒ zài Niǔyuē xuéxí (*after coming to America, I studied in New York*); 酒后开车 jiǔ hòu kāi chē (*drive after drinking*); 课后 kè hòu (*after class*)

Also appears in the following words: **落后** luòhòu (*lag behind*); **幕后** mùhòu (*behind the scene*); **随后** suíhòu (*subsequently*)

后辈	hòubèi	*the younger generation; descendant*
后边	hòubian	*rear; back; behind; in the rear; at the back*
后方	hòufāng	(*of a region*) *rear*
后果	hòuguǒ	*consequence*
后患	hòuhuàn	*potential or future trouble*
后悔	hòuhuǐ	*regret*
后来	hòulái	*afterwards; later on*
后路	hòulù	*room for retreat.* Cl: 条 tiáo
后妈	hòumā	*stepmother*
后门	hòumén	*back door; connection; influence*

后面 **hòumian**	*rear; back; behind; in the rear; at the back*
后天 **hòutiān**	*the day after tomorrow*
后头 **hòutou**	*rear; back; behind; in the rear; at the back*

花 **huā**

1. *flower.* Cl: 朵 duǒ; 枝 zhī; 束 shù

2. *flower-like object:* 雪花 xuěhuā (*snowflakes*); 浪花 lànghuā (*spray; spindrift*). Cl: 片 piàn

3. *colorful; colored:* 花衣服 huā yīfu (*patterned clothes*)

4. *blurred; dim:* 年龄大了，眼也花了 niánlíng dà le, yǎn yě huā le (a*s the age advanced, the eyes have also become blurred*)

5. *spend; cost* (time or money): 花时间 huā shíjiān (*spend time*); 花钱 huā qián (*spend money*)

Also appears in the following words: **火花** huǒhuā (*spark*); **棉花** miánhua (*cotton*)

花白 **huābái**	(of hair) *gray*
花茶 **huāchá**	*scented tea*
花房 **huāfáng**	*greenhouse.* Cl: 间 jiān
花费 **huāfèi**	*spend; cost* (time or money)
花盆 **huāpén**	*flowerpot.* Cl: 个 gè
花生 **huāshēng**	*peanut.* Cl: 棵 kē; 颗 kē; 粒 lì
花样 **huāyàng**	*variety:* 这家餐馆的菜有很多花样 zhè jiā cānguǎn de cài yǒu hěn duō huāyàng (*this restaurant has many varieties of dishes*)
花园 **huāyuán**	*garden.* Cl: 处 chù; 座 zuò; 个 gè

话 **huà**

1. *language; speech; dialect:* 中国话 (*Chinese language*); 广东话 (*Cantonese*)

2. *talk; word; message:* 留话 liú huà (*leave a message*); 我能跟你说句话吗 wǒ néng gēn nǐ shuō jù huà ma (*can I have a word with you?*); 我不懂你的话 wǒ bù dǒng nǐde huà (*I don't understand what you said*)

Also appears in the following words: **粗话** cūhuà (*foul language*); **大话** dàhuà (*big talk*); **神话** shénhuà (*myth; mythology*)

| 话剧 **huàjù** | *play* (n.). Cl: 场 chǎng; 台 tái |
| 话题 **huàtí** | *topic; theme; subject.* Cl: 个 gè |

化 huà

1. *melt; dissolve*: 冰化了 bīng huà le (*the ice has melted*)

2. *change into; turn into*: 化悲痛为力量 huà bēitòng wéi lìliang (*turn grief into strength*)

3. suffix used after nouns and adjectives to turn them into verbs or verbal nouns: 现代化 xiàndàihuà (*modernize; modernization*); 美化 měihuà (*beautify; beautification*); 简化 jiǎnhuà (*simplify; simplification*)

Also appears in the following words: 变化 biànhuà (*change*); 恶化 èhuà (*worsen; deteriorate*); 腐化 fǔhuà (*corruption*); 激化 jīhuà (*intensify*); 简化 jiǎnhuà (*simplify*); 进化 jìnhuà (*evolution*); 文化 wénhuà (*culture*); 消化 xiāohuà (*digest*); 工业化 gōngyèhuà (*industrialization*); 现代化 xiàndàihuà (*modernization*)

化肥 huàféi	*chemical fertilizer*. Cl: 种 zhǒng; 袋 dài	
化工 huàgōng	*chemical industry*	
化名 huàmíng	*alias*	
化石 huàshí	*fossil*. Cl: 块 kuài	
化学 huàxué	*chemistry*	
化验 huàyàn	*(lab) test*	
化装 huàzhuāng	1. *make up*	
	2. *disguise oneself*	

画 huà

1. *drawing; painting*: 国画 guóhuà (*Chinese painting*); 油画 yóuhuà (*oil painting*). Cl: 张 zhāng; 幅 fú

2. *draw; paint*: 画画 huà huà (*paint a picture*)

画板 huàbǎn	*drawing board*
画笔 huàbǐ	*paintbrush*. Cl: 支 zhī; 枝 zhī; 管 guǎn
画家 huàjiā	*painter; artist*. Cl: 名 míng; 位 wèi; 个 gè
画廊 huàláng	*gallery*. Cl: 条 tiáo; 座 zuò
画室 huàshì	*studio*
画像 huàxiàng	1. *paint a portrait*
	2. *portrait*. Cl: 张 zhāng; 幅 fú
画展 huàzhǎn	*art exhibition*. Cl: 个 gè; 次 cì

坏 huài

1. *bad*: 坏人 huàirén (*bad person*); 坏习惯 huài xíguàn (*bad habit*); 坏主意 huài zhǔyì (*bad idea*)

2. *go bad*; *spoil*; *break* (down); *ruin*: 牛奶坏了 niúnǎi huài le (*the milk has gone bad*); 汽车坏了 qìchē huài le (*the car broke down*)

3. *badly*; *very*, used as verb complement: 饿坏了 è huài le (*starving*); 累坏了 lèi huài le (*exhausted*)

Also appears in the following words: **毁坏** huǐhuài (*destroy*); **破坏** pòhuài (*sabotage*); **损坏** sǔnhuài (*damage*)

坏处 **huàichù**	*harm; disadvantage*
坏蛋 **huàidàn**	*scoundrel; bastard.* Cl: 个 gè; 群 qún
坏话 **huàihuà**	*vicious talk; malicious remarks.* Cl: 句 jù

还 huán

give back; *return (an object)*; *repay*: 去图书馆还书 qù túshūguǎn huán shū (*go to the library to return books*); 还银行的贷款 huán yínháng de dàikuǎn (*return the bank's loan*)

换 huàn

1. *change*: 换衣服 huàn yīfu (*change clothes*)

2. *exchange*; *trade*: 我在哪儿可以换钱 wǒ zài nǎr kěyǐ huànqián (*where can I exchange money?*)

Also appears in the following words: **撤换** chèhuàn (*dismiss and replace*); **掉换** diàohuàn (*exchange*); **轮换** lúnhuàn (*in rotation*); **退换** tuìhuàn (*exchange a purchase*)

换车 **huànchē**	*change trains or buses*
换机 **huànjī**	*change planes; make a flight connection*
换人 **huànrén**	(sports) *substitute players in the middle of a game*
换算 **huànsuàn**	(math) *convert; conversion*
换牙 **huànyá**	(of a child) *grow permanent teeth*

回 huí

1. *return* (to a place); *go back to*: 回家 huí jiā (*go home*); 回国 huí guó (*go back to one's own country*)

2. directional complement: 收回诺言 shōu huí nuòyán *(take back one's promise)*; 飞回中国 fēi huí Zhōngguó (*fly back to China*)

3. *reply* (to a letter, message, etc.): 回信 huí xìn (*reply to a letter*); 回电话 huí diànhuà (*return a phone call*)

回报 **huíbào**	*repay* (a favor, etc.); *retaliate*	
回避 **huíbì**	*avoid*; *dodge*; *evade*	
回答 **huídá**	*answer*; *reply*: 回答问题 huídá wèntí (answer questions); 正确的回答 zhèngquède huídá (*correct answer*). Cl: 个 gè	
回顾 **huígù**	*look back on* (an event)	
回话 **huíhuà**	*give a reply*	
回教 **huíjiào**	*Islam*	
回声 **huíshēng**	*echo*	
回收 **huíshōu**	*recover* (a used item); *recycle*; *reclaim*	
回头 **huítóu**	1. *turn around*; *mend one's ways* 2. *later*: 回头见 huítóu jiàn (*see you later*)	
回想 **huíxiǎng**	*think back*; *recollect*	
回旋 **huíxuán**	*maneuver*	
回忆 **huíyì**	*recall*; *reminisce*: 回忆录 huíyìlù (*memoirs*). Cl: 段 duàn	

会 huì

1. *know how to*; *can*; *to be able to, to be good at*: 会说中文 huì shuō Zhōngwén (*know how to speak Chinese*); 会做饭 huì zuò fàn (*to be good at cooking*)

2. *to be likely or possible*; *will*: 明天不会下雨 míngtiān bú huì xiàyǔ (*it won't rain tomorrow*); 他会来帮助你 tā huì lái bāngzhù nǐ (*he will come to help you*)

3. *meeting*; *party*: 开会 kāihuì (*hold a meeting*), 运动会 yùndònghuì (*sports meet*); 欢送会 huānsònghuì (*farewell party*)

4. (of an organization) *society*; *association*: 会费 huìfèi (*membership fee*); 会员 huìyuán (*member*). Cl: 名 míng; 位 wèi; 个 gè

会餐 **huìcān**	*get-together meal*
会场 **huìchǎng**	*meeting place*; *site of a meeting*
会费 **huìfèi**	*membership dues*. Cl: 笔 bǐ

会话 huìhuà	conversation: 会话课 huìhuà kè (conversation class)
会见 huìjiàn	meet, used on formal occasions
会谈 huìtán	talk; negotiation
会议 huìyì	meeting; conference. Cl: 个 gè; 次 cì; 届 jiè
会员 huìyuán	member in an association; membership

活 huó

1. *live*: 乌龟可以活很多年 wūguī kěyǐ huó hěn duō nián (*the turtle can live for many years*)

2. *alive*; *live*: 这条鱼是活的 zhè tiáo yú shì huó de (*this fish is alive*)

3. *lively*; *active*: 思想很活 sīxiǎng hěn huó (*active mind*)

4. *work*: 脏活 zāng huó (*dirty work*); 轻活 qīng huó (*light work*)

活动 huódòng	1. *activity*; *event*
	2. *exercise* (v.)
	3. *loose*; *shaky*; *flexible*
活该 huógāi	serve one right
活力 huólì	vigor; vitality
活泼 huópo	(of people) lively
活象 huóxiàng	look exactly like; bear striking resemblance to
活页 huóyè	loose-leaf
活跃 huóyuè	active; dynamic

火 huǒ

1. *fire*

2. *firearms*: 开火 kāihuǒ (*open fire*)

3. *anger*; *be mad*: 发火 fāhuǒ (*become angry*)

火把 huǒbǎ	torch. Cl: 个 gè
火柴 huǒchái	match: 火柴盒 huǒcháihé (matchbox). Cl: 根 gēn; 盒 hé; 包 bāo
火车 huǒchē	train: 火车站 huǒchēzhàn (train station). Cl: 节 jié; 列 liè
火花 huǒhuā	spark
火化 huǒhuà	cremate; cremation
火鸡 huǒjī	turkey. Cl: 只 zhī
火急 huǒjí	urgent: 火急回国 huǒ jí huí guó (urgently rush back to one's country).
火箭 huǒjiàn	rocket. Cl: 支 zhī

火警 **huǒjǐng**	*fire alarm*
火炬 **huǒjù**	*torch*. Cl: 只 zhī
火热 **huǒrè**	**1.** *burning hot*
	2. *intimate*: 他们的关系火热 tāmende guānxi huǒrè (*they have an intimate relationship*)
火头 **huǒtou**	*height of one's anger*
火腿 **huǒtuǐ**	*ham*. Cl: 块 kuài; 只 zhī; 个 gè
火星 **huǒxīng**	*Mars*
火药 **huǒyào**	*gunpowder*

或 huò

or, used in declarative sentences, often taking the disyllabic form of 或者 huòzhě. In questions, *or* is expressed by 还是 háishi

或许 **huòxǔ**	*maybe*; *perhaps*: 今年或许没有雪 jīnnián huòxǔ méi you xuě (*perhaps there is no snow this year*)
或者 **huòzhě**	*or*, used in declarative sentences: 我明天或者后天来 wǒ míngtiān huòzhě hòutiān lái (*I'll come either tomorrow or the day after tomorrow*)

机 jī

1. *machine*; *engine*: 飞机 fēijī (*airplane*). Cl: 架 jià; 电视机 diànshìjī (*television set*). Cl: 台 tái

2. *opportunity*: 良机 liángjī (*good opportunity*); 乘机 chèngjī (*take advantage of the opportunity*)

Also appears in the following words: 班机 bānjī (*flight*); 耳机 ěrjī (*earphone*; *headphone*); 时机 shíjī (*timing*); 司机 sījī (*driver*); 投机 tóujī (*speculate*; *speculation*); 危机 wēijī (*crisis*)

机场 **jīchǎng**	*airport*. Cl: 个 gè; 座 zuò
机动 **jīdòng**	**1.** *motor-driven*: 机动车 jīdòngchē (*motor vehicle*)
	2. *flexible*: 机动的议程 jīdòngde yìchéng (*flexible agenda*)
机工 **jīgōng**	*mechanic*; *machinist*, interchangeable with 机师 jīshī
机构 **jīgòu**	*organization*; *institution*; *department*: 政府机构 zhèngfǔ jīgòu (*government departments*); 金融机构 jīnróng jīgòu (*financial institutions*)
机关 **jīguān**	(government) *office*; *organ*; *institution*: 我太太在机关工作 wǒ tàitai zài jīguān gōngzuò (*my wife works for the government*)

机会 jīhuì	opportunity; chance; occasion
机灵 jīlíng	quick-witted; smart; shrewd
机密 jīmì	secret; confidential: 国家机密 guójiā jīmì (state secret)
	Cl: 个 gè; 件 jiàn
机器 jīqì	machine: 机器人 jīqìrén (robot)
机师 jīshī	mechanic; machinist, interchangeable with 机工 jīgōng
机械 jīxiè	machinery: 机械化 jīxièhuà (mechanize; mechanized)
机油 jīyóu	machine oil; engine oil
机智 jīzhì	quick-witted; resourceful

鸡 jī

chicken. The word shows no gender distinction, as is the case with all the Chinese words for animals. To indicate the distinction, gender words for animals 公 gōng (male) and 母 mǔ (female) should be used: 公鸡 gōngjī (rooster) and 母鸡 mǔjī (hen).

鸡蛋 jīdàn	chicken egg. Cl: 个 gè; 只 zhī
鸡肉 jīròu	chicken meat
鸡尾酒 jīwěijiǔ	cocktail: 鸡尾酒会 jīwěi jiǔhuì (cocktail party)
鸡眼 jīyǎn	(med) corn; clavus

急 jí

1. impatient; anxious; eager, often used with 于 yú or 着 zhe: 别急 bié jí (don't be impatient); 急于得到答案 jí yú dédào dá'àn (anxious to get the answer); 急着去赶汽车 jí zhe qù gǎn qìchē (in a hurry to catch the bus)

2. worry: 飞机票买不到，我很急 fēijīpiào mǎi bú dào, wǒ hěn jí (I'm worried because I can't get the plane ticket)

3. swift; sudden; rapid; violent: 火烧得很急 huǒ shāo de hěn jí (the fire is burning rapidly); 急病 jíbìng (acute and sudden disease)

4. urgent: 急信 jíxìn (urgent letter)

Also appears in the following words: 焦急 jiāojí (anxious; anxiety); 紧急 jǐnjí (emergency); 危急 wēijí (critical); 性急 xìngjí (impatient)

急病 jíbìng	acute disease
急促 jícù	quick; rapid
急电 jídiàn	urgent cable
急件 jíjiàn	urgent dispatch. Cl: 个 gè; 份 fèn
急进 jíjìn	radical

急救 jíjiù	first aid; emergency treatment
急剧 jíjù	drastic; sudden; rapid: 身体急剧恶化 shēntǐ jíjù èhuà (health rapidly worsened)
急忙 jímáng	in a hurry; hastily
急迫 jípò	urgent; pressing
急性 jíxìng	acute (disease): 急性病 jíxìngbìng (acute and sudden disease)
急性子 jíxìngzi	impetuous
急需 jíxū	in an urgent need for
急于 jíyú	be eager to; be impatient to
急噪 jízào	impetuous; impatient
急诊 jízhěn	emergency treatment: 急诊室 jízhěnshì (emergency room)
急转弯 jízhuǎnwān	a sudden turn on the road

极 jí

1. *extremely*, often used with 了 le after an adjective: 极好看的电影 jí hǎokàn de diànyǐng (*an extremely interesting movie*); 忙极了 máng jí le (*extremely busy*); 高兴极了 gāoxìng jí le (*extremely happy; elated*)

2. *extreme; pole*: 南极 nánjí (*the South Pole*); 北极 běijí (*the North Pole*)

Also appears in the following words: 积极 jījí (*positive; active*); 消极 xiāojí (*passive; negative*)

极点 jídiǎn	the limit; the extreme: 逼到极点 bī dào jídiǎn (be forced to the limit)
极度 jídù	extremely, exceedingly: 极度兴奋 jídù xīngfèn (extremely excited)
极端 jíduān	extreme; extremely, often used to describe an undesirable action: 极端敌视 jíduān díshì (extremely hostile); 走向另一个极端 zǒu xiàng lìng yí ge jíduān (go to the other extreme)
极力 jílì	do one's utmost; try by every means: 极力反对 jílì fǎnduì (go all out to oppose); 极力主张 jílì zhǔzhāng (enthusiastically advocate)
极其 jíqí	extremely; exceedingly: 极其重要 jíqí zhòngyào (extremely important)
极限 jíxiàn	the limit; the maximum: 十五人是我们的极限 shíwǔ rén shì wǒmende jíxiàn (15 people is our limit)

几 jǐ

1. interrogative word for asking questions about numbers: 你家有几口人 nǐ jiā yǒu jǐ kǒu rén (*how many people are there in your family?*); 现在几点 xiànzài jǐ diǎn (*what time is it now?*); 今天星期几 jīntiān xīngqī jǐ (*what day is today?*); 今天几号 jīntiān jǐ hào (*what is the date today?*). In asking for a quantity, 几 jǐ is usu. used when the speaker assumes that the answer will be a number less than ten. If the answer is assumed to be a larger or unknown number, 多少 duōshao should be used: 你们的公司有多少人 nǐmende gōngsī yǒu duōshao rén (*how many people are there in your company?*).

2. *several*; *a few*, always followed by a classifier: 她也有几个中国朋友 tā yě yǒu jǐ ge Zhōngguó péngyou (*she also has a few Chinese friends*)

记 jì

1. *note down*; *write down*: 记日记 jì rìjì (*write a diary*); 记名字 jì míngzi (*note down the names*)

2. *remember*; *learn by heart*

Also appears in the following words: **笔记** bǐjì (*notes*); **登记** dēngjì (*check in*; *register*); **日记** rìjì (*diary*); **书记** shūji (*secretary*); **忘记** wàngjì (*forget*); **传记** zhuànjì (*biography*)

记得 jìde	*remember*: 我不记得她的名字 wǒ bú jìde tāde míngzi (*I don't remember her name*)	
记号 jìhào	*mark*; *sign*. Cl: 个 gè; 处 chù	
记性 jìxing	*memory*	
记忆 jìyì	*memory*: 记忆力 jìyìlì (*the faculty of memory*)	
记载 jìzǎi	*record in books* (n. and v.)	
记者 jìzhě	*reporter*; *journalist*. Cl: 位 wèi; 名 míng; 个 gè	
记住 jìzhù	*remember*; *learn by heart*	

寄 jì

1. *send*; *mail*: 寄信 jì xìn (*send a letter*); 寄钱 jì qián (*remit money*)

2. *depend on*; *attach oneself to*: 寄生 jìshēng (*parasitic*)

3. *entrust*; *deposit*: 寄卖 jìmài (*consign for sale for commission*)

寄存 jìcún	*deposit* (an item); *leave with*: 寄存行李 jìcún xíngli (*deposit luggage*)
寄卖 jìmài	*consign for sale for commission*

寄生 jìshēng	*parasitic*: 寄生虫 jìshēngchóng (*parasite*); 寄生病 jìshēngbìng (*parasitic disease*)
寄宿 jìsù	*lodge; put up*: 寄宿学校 jìsù xuéxiào (*boarding school*)
寄托 jìtuō	*leave with; entrust to the charge of sb.*: 把希望寄托在年轻人身上 bǎ xīwàng jìtuō zài niánqīngrén shēn shang (*pin hope on young people*)
寄信人 jìxìnrén	*sender of a letter*

家 jiā

1. *family; house; household; home*

2. classifier used for nouns denoting certain commercial establishments such as companies, stores, restaurants, movie theaters, and banks

3. *specialist*: 科学家 kēxuéjiā (*scientist*); 语言学家 yǔyánxuéjiā (*linguist*); 作家 zuòjiā (*writer*). Cl: 个 gè; 位 wèi; 名 míng

4. *domestic*: 家畜 jiāchù (*domestic animal*); 家禽 jiāqín (*domestic poultry*)

Also appears in the following words: 搬家 bānjiā (*move house*); 成家 chéngjiā (*get married*); 大家 dàjiā (*everyone*); 公家 gōngjia (*the public*); 管家 guǎnjiā (*housekeeper*); 国家 guójiā (*country; nation; state*); 画家 huàjiā (*painter*); 老家 lǎojiā (*hometown*); 专家 zhuānjiā (*expert; specialist*); 作家 zuòjiā (*writer; author*)

家常 jiācháng	*homely; simple; trivial*: 家常饭 jiāchángfàn (*homely food*); 家常话 jiāchánghuà (*small talk*)
家传 jiāchuán	*handed down the generations in the family*
家当 jiādàng	*family possessions*
家伙 jiāhuo	*fellow; guy*
家具 jiājù	*furniture*. Cl: 件 jiàn; 样 yàng; 套 tào; 组 zǔ
家里人 jiālǐrén	*family members*
家谱 jiāpǔ	*genealogy*. Cl: 本 bēn; 部 bù
家属 jiāshǔ	*family members; dependents in the family*
家庭 jiātíng	*family*
家务 jiāwù	*household chores*
家乡 jiāxiāng	*hometown*
家长 jiāzhǎng	*parents; head of a household*. Cl: 个 gè; 位 wèi; 名 míng
家族 jiāzú	*clan*. Cl: 个 gè

加 jiā

1. *plus; add*: 三加四等于七 sān jiā sì děngyú qī (*3 plus 4 is 7*); 咖啡要不要加糖 kāfēi yào bu yào jiā táng (*do you want to add sugar to your coffee?*)

2. *increase:* 加工资 jiā gōngzī (*raise the salary*)

3. used before certain adjectives to turn them into verbs: 加长 jiācháng (*lengthen*); 加宽 jiākuān (*widen*); 加高 jiāgāo (*heighten*); 加热 jiārè (*heat*); 加深 jiāshēn (*deepen*)

Also appears in the following words: 参加 cānjiā (*join; attend; take part in*); 附加 fùjiā (*additional; append*); 更加 gèngjiā (*all the more*); 增加 zēngjiā (*increase*)

加班 jiābān	*work overtime*
加倍 jiābèi	*double; redouble:* 加倍努力 jiābèi nǔlì (*redouble efforts*)
加法 jiāfǎ	(*of mathematics*) *addition*
加工 jiāgōng	**1.** *process; processing:* 加工食品 jiāgōng shípǐn (*process foodstuff*); 食品加工 shípǐn jiāgōng (*food processing*)
	2. *polish; improve:* 这篇文章需要加工 zhè piān wénzhāng xūyào jiāgōng (*this article needs polishing*)
加快 jiākuài	*quicken; accelerate*
加强 jiāqiáng	*strengthen*
加入 jiārù	*join* (a party, organization, etc.)
加油 jiāyóu	**1.** *lubricate; refuel*
	2. *come on*, uttered by spectators of a sports game to urge on players

---

假 jiǎ; jià

When pronounced as jiǎ:

fake; phony; false; pseudo-; sham; artificial

Also appears in the following words: 虚假 xūjiǎ (*false; phony*); 装假 zhuāngjiǎ (*feign*)

假定 jiǎdìng	*presume; suppose; assume*
假发 jiǎfà	*wig*
假话 jiǎhuà	*lie; falsehood*
假名 jiǎmíng	*pseudonym*
假如 jiǎrú	*if; supposing; in case*
假设 jiǎshè	*assume; suppose*
假使 jiǎshǐ	*if; in case; in the event that*
假释 jiǎshì	*release on parole*
假象 jiǎxiàng	*false appearance*
假牙 jiǎyá	*false tooth; denture*. Cl: 颗 kē
假造 jiǎzào	*falsify; counterfeit; fabricate; forge*
假肢 jiǎzhī	*artificial limb*
假装 jiǎzhuāng	*pretend; make believe; feign*

When pronounced as jià:

1. *holiday*; *vacation*; *day off*: 放假 fàngjià (*have a holiday or vacation*; *have a day off*); 度假 dùjià (*spend vacation*; *go on vacation*); 寒假 hánjià (*winter vacation*); 暑假 shǔjià (*summer vacation*)

2. *leave of absence*: 病假 bìngjià (*sick leave*); 产假 chǎnjià (*maternity leave*); 请假 qǐngjià (*ask for leave*)

Also appears in the following words: **度假** dùjià (*go on vacation*); **婚假** hūnjià (*marital leave*); **年假** niánjià (*annual leave*); **请假** qǐngjià (*ask for leave*); **事假** shìjià (*personal leave*); **休假** xiūjià (*on vacation*)

假期 jiàqī	*vacation*; *period of leave*	
假日 jiàrì	*holiday*; *day off*	

间 jiān

1. *between*; *among*, used after a noun, as the word is considered as a noun in Chinese. In this usage, 间 can also be expressed as 之间 zhījiān: 朋友（之）间不必客气 péngyou jiān búbì kèqi (*don't be formal between friends*).

2. *during*; *in*, often taking the form of 期间 qījiān: 暑假期间 shǔjià qījiān (*during the summer vacation*)

3. *room*: 双人间 shuāngrénjiān (*double room*); 单人间 dānrénjiān (*single room*); 洗衣间 xǐyījiān (*laundry room*); 卫生间 wèishēngjiān (*washroom*)

4. classifier, used for rooms: 三间教室 sān jiān jiàoshì (*three classrooms*)

见 jiàn

1. *see*: 明天见 míngtiān jiàn (*see you tomorrow*); 我们很久没见了 wǒmen hěn jiǔ méi jiàn le (*we haven't seen each other for a long time*)

2. *meet*: 我能不能见你们的经理 wǒ néng bu néng jiàn nǐmende jīnglǐ (*can I see your manager?*)

3. *disappear*; *be lost*, used in the negative: 我的自行车不见了 wǒde zìxíngchē bú jiàn le (*my bicycle disappeared*)

Also appears in the following words: **常见** chángjiàn (*common*); **成见** chéngjiàn (*prejudice*); **看见** kànjian (*see*); **碰见** pèngjiàn (*bump into*); **偏见** piānjiàn (*prejudice; bias*); **听见** tīngjiàn (*hear*); **预见** yùjiàn (*foresee; predict*); **再见** zàijiàn (*good-bye*)

见怪 jiànguài	*take offense*
见好 jiànhǎo	(*of health*) *get better*; *improve*
见解 jiànjiě	*view*; *opinion*

见面 jiànmiàn	*meet.* 见面 jiànmiàn is an intransitive verb and can't take an object. It is only grammatical to say 我和他明天见面 wǒ hé tā míngtiān jiànmiàn (*I'll meet him tomorrow*), but not 我明天见面他 wǒ míngtiān jiànmiàn tā.
见识 jiànshi	*experience*; *knowledge*: 长见识 zhǎng jiànshi (*gain knowledge*)
见外 jiànwài	*treat sb. as a stranger*
见闻 jiànwén	*what's heard and seen*
见证 jiànzhèng	*witness*; *testimony*

件 jiàn

1. classifier for items such as clothing, furniture, luggage, matters, etc.: 一件大衣 yí jiàn dàyī (*an overcoat*); 两件家具 liǎng jiàn jiājù (*two pieces of furniture*), 三件行李 sān jiàn xíngli (*three pieces of luggage*)

2. *document*; *letter*: 文件 wénjiàn (*document*). Cl: 个 gè; 份 fèn; 叠 dié; 信件 xìnjiàn (*letter*)

3. *item*; *piece*: 大件 dà jiàn (*big item*); 快件 kuài jiàn (*express mail*)

Also appears in the following words: 案件 ànjiàn (*legal case*); 部件 bùjiàn (*parts*; *component*); 附件 fùjiàn (*attachment*); 稿件 gǎojiàn (*contribution to a publications, etc.*); 零件 língjiàn (*parts*); 软件 ruǎnjiàn (*software*); 事件 shìjiàn (*event*; *incident*); 条件 tiáojiàn (*condition*; *term*); 文件 wénjiàn (*document*); 硬件 yìngjiàn (*hardware*); 邮件 yóujiàn (*mail*); 证件 zhèngjiàn (*identification*; *papers*)

建 jiàn

build; *construct*; *found*

Also appears in the following words: 创建 chuàngjiàn (*establish*; *found*); 封建 fēngjiàn (*feudalism*); 兴建 xīngjiàn (*build*; *establish*); 修建 xiūjiàn (*build*; *construct*)

建国 jiànguó	*establish a state*
建立 jiànlì	*establish*; *found*
建设 jiànshè	*build*; *construct* (a state, system, etc.)
建设性 jiànshèxìng	*constructive* (suggestions, etc.)
建议 jiànyì	*suggest*; *propose*; *suggestion*; *proposal.* Cl: 条 tiáo; 项 xiàng
建筑 jiànzhù	**1.** *build*; *construct* (buildings, bridges, etc.) **2.** *architecture*: 现代建筑 xiàndài jiànzhù (*modern architecture*); 建筑师 jiànzhùshī (*architect*)

将 jiāng

1. *be going to; be about to*, usu. used in written language: 学生们将在五月毕业 xuéshengmen jiāng zài wǔyuè bìyè (*the students are going to graduate in May*)

2. *will*: 我们将永远不忘这一天 wǒmen jiǎng yǒngyuǎn bú wàng zhè yì tiān (*we will never forget this day*)

将近 **jiāngjìn**	*nearly; almost*: 将近三百人 jiāngjìn sǎnbǎi rén (*almost three hundred people*)
将就 **jiāngjiù**	*make do with*: 没有时间做饭，就吃剩饭将就一下儿吧 méi you shíjiān zuòfàn, jiù chì shèngfàn jiāngjiù yíxiàr ba (*there is no time to cook; let's make do with the leftovers*)
将军 **jiāngjūn**	(mil.) *general.* Cl: 名 míng; 位 wèi; 个 gè
将来 **jiānglái**	*future*: 美好的将来 měihǎode jiānglái (*bright future*)
将要 **jiāngyào**	*be going to; be about to*: 高速公路就要通车了 gāosù gōnglù jiāngyào tōngchē le (*the expressway is about to be open to traffic*)

讲 jiǎng

1. *speak; say; tell*: 讲英语 jiǎng Yīngyǔ (*speak English*); 讲故事 jiǎng gùshì (*tell a story*); 讲了很多话 jiǎng le hěn duō huà (*talked a lot*)

2. *explain; describe*: 老师给我们讲课文 lǎoshī gěi wǒmen jiǎng kèwén (*the teacher explained the text to us*); 电影讲的是战争的故事 diànyǐng jiǎng de shì zhànzhēng de gùshì (*the movie is about a war story*)

3. *emphasize; be particular about*: 讲合作 jiǎng hézuò (*stress cooperation*); 讲吃讲穿 jiǎng chī jiǎng chuān (*be particular about food and clothing*)

讲稿 **jiǎnggǎo**	*script for a speech*
讲话 **jiǎnghuà**	*talk; speak; speech*: 做了一个讲话 zuǒ le yí ge jiǎnghuà (*made a speech*); 他不喜欢讲话 tā bù xīhuan jiǎnghuà (*she does not like to talk*)
讲价 **jiǎngjià**	*bargain; haggle over price*: 这个店不讲价 zhè ge diàn bù jiǎng jià (*there is no bargaining in this store*)
讲解 **jiǎngjiě**	*explain*
讲究 **jiǎngjiu**	1. *be particular about; emphasize*: 讲究文明 jiǎngjiu wénmíng (*emphasize civic behavior*) 2. *exquisite; tasteful*: 穿得很讲究 chuān de hěn jiǎngjiu (*exquisitely dressed*)
讲课 **jiǎngkè**	*teach a class*

讲理 jiǎnglǐ	reason with sb.; argue
讲师 jiǎngshī	lecturer. Cl: 位 wèi; 名 míng; 个 gè
讲述 jiǎngshù	relate; describe; narrate: 讲述自己的经历 jiǎngshù zìjǐ de jīnglì (describe one's experience)
讲台 jiǎngtái	dais; lectern. Cl: 个 gè
讲学 jiǎngxué	give lectures
讲演 jiǎngyǎn	give a speech
讲义 jiǎngyì	teaching material. Cl: 份 fèn; 页 yè
讲座 jiǎngzuò	lecture. Cl: 个 gè; 次 cì

交 jiāo

1. *hand in*; *submit*; *pay*: 交作业 jiāo zuòyè (*hand in an assignment*); 交稿 jiāo gǎo (*submit the manuscript*); 交电费 jiāo diànfèi (*pay the electricity bill*)

2. *establish friendship*: 交朋友 jiāo péngyou (*make friends*)

3. *intercourse*: 性交 xìngjiāo (*sexual intercourse*)

4. *business transaction*; *deal*: 没有成交 méiyou chéng jiāo (*the deal was not made*)

Also appears in the following words: **建交** jiànjiāo (*establish diplomatic relationships*); **结交** jiéjiāo (*make friends with*); **社交** shèjiāo (*socialize*); **外交** wàijiāo (*diplomacy; foreign affairs*)

交叉 jiāochā	intersect; cross: 两条公路在这儿交叉 liǎng tiáo gōnglù zài zhèr jiāochā (the two highways intersect here)
交代 jiāodài	1. explain; brief: 市长在度假前向他的助手交代工作 shìzhǎng zài dùjià qián xiàng tāde zhùshǒu jiāodài gōngzuò (the mayor explained to his assistant about work to be done before he went on vacation)
	2. confess: 交代问题 jiāodài wèntí (confess mistakes or crimes committed)
	3. face; account for: 如果不能通过考试, 孩子没法向父母交代 rúguǒ bù néng tōngguò kǎoshì, háizi méifǎ xiàng fùmǔ jiāodài (if the child doesn't pass the exam, he can't face his parents)
交换 jiāohuàn	(physical) exchange: 交换老师 jiāohuà lǎoshī (exchange teachers); 交换货币 jiāohuàn huòbì (exchange currencies)
交际 jiāojì	socialize; socialization
交流 jiāoliú	exchange: 国际交流 guójì jiāoliú (international exchange); 交流经验 jiāoliú jīngyàn (share experiences)
交情 jiāoqing	friendship
交涉 jiāoshè	make representations with; take matters up with

交谈 jiāotán	chat; talk with each other
交通 jiāotōng	1. traffic: 交通事故 jiāotóng shìgù (traffic accident)
	2. transportation: 交通便利 jiāotōng biànlì (the transportation is convenient)
交往 jiāowǎng	associate; contact; association; friendship: 他们交往了三十多年 tāmen jiāowǎng le sānshí duō nián (they have been friends with each other for more than 30 years)
交响乐 jiāoxiǎngyuè	symphony: 交响乐队 jiāoxiǎngyuèduì (philharmonic orchestra)
交易 jiāoyì	business deal; transaction: 交易所 jiāoyìsuǒ (stocks exchange)

教 jiāo; jiào

When pronounced jiāo:

teach; instruct: 教英语 jiāo Yīngyǔ (teach English). 教 jiāo is a transitive verb and needs to be followed by an object. Otherwise, 教书 jiāoshū should be used: 我爸爸在大学教书 wǒ bàba zài dàxué jiāoshū (my father teaches at a university)

When pronounced jiào:

1. teaching; instruction: 教室 jiàoshì (classroom). Cl: 间 jiān; 个 gè; 教案 jiào'àn (lesson plan). Cl: 份 fèn

2. religion: 佛教 fójiào (Buddhism); 道教 dàojiào (Taoism); 信教 xìn jiào (believe in religion; religious)

Also appears in the following words: 传教 chuánjiào (evangelize); 管教 guǎnjiào (subject sb. to discipline); 请教 qǐngjiào (consult)

教材 jiàocái	textbook; text material. Cl: 本 běn; 份 fèn
教程 jiàochéng	course of study
教皇 jiàohuáng	pope. Cl: 位 wèi
教会 jiàohuì	church (as an organization)
教练 jiàoliàn	(of sports) coach. Cl: 位 wèi; 名 míng; 个 gè
教师 jiàoshī	teacher. Cl: 位 wèi; 名 míng; 个 gè
教室 jiàoshì	classroom
教授 jiàoshòu	professor. Cl: 位 wèi; 名 míng
教堂 jiàotáng	church (as a physical site). Cl: 座 zuò
教养 jiàoyǎng	upbringing
教育 jiàoyù	educate; education

叫 jiào

1. *cry; shout*

2. *call; be named*: 你叫什么名字 nǐ jiào shénme míngzi (*what is your name?*)

3. *summon; ask*: 叫警察 jiào jǐngchá (*call the police*); 老师叫我告诉你 lǎoshī jiào wǒ gàosù nǐ (*the teacher asked me to tell you*)

4. *by*, used in a passive structure: 我没带伞，叫雨淋了 wǒ méi dài sǎn, jiào yǔ lín le (*I didn't bring an umbrella and got wet in the rain*)

5. *cause sb. to do sth.*: 这件事叫我感到很难过 zhè jiàn shì jiào wǒ gǎndào hěn nánguò (*this matter made me feel very sad*)

叫喊 jiàohǎn	*shout; yell*
叫苦 jiàokǔ	*complain of hardship or difficulty*
叫醒 jiàoxǐng	*wake up sb.*
叫做 jiàozuò	*be called; be referred to as*: 英国人把 *elevator* 叫做 *lift* Yīngguórén bǎ *elevator* jiàozuò *lift* (*English people call an elevator a lift*)

接 jiē

1. *connect; join*: 接电线 jiē diànxiàn (*connect wires*)

2. *catch*: 接球 jié qiú (*catch the ball*)

3. *pick up; meet*: 接孩子 jié háizi (*pick up a child*); 到机场接人 dào jīchǎng jiē rén (*go to the airport to pick up sb.*)

4. *receive*: 接电话 jiē diànhuà (*answer the phone*); 接信 jiē xìn (*receive a letter*)

5. *replace; take over*: 谁接你的工作 shuí jiē nǐde gōngzuò (*who is going to take over your work?*)

Also appears in the following words: 间接 jiànjiē (*indirect*); 紧接 jǐnjiē (*immediately after*); 连接 liánjiē (*connect*); 迎接 yíngjiē (*greet; meet*); 直接 zhíjiē (*direct*)

接触 jiēchù	*come into contact with*
接待 jiēdài	*receive and entertain* (people)
接见 jiējiàn	*grant an interview* (by a person in a higher position)
接近 jiējìn	*approach; get close to*
接连 jiēlián	*successively; in a row*: 接连上了四节课 jiēlián shàng le sì jié kè (*had four classes back to back*)
接洽 jiēqià	*make business contact*
接生 jiēshēng	*practice midwifery*: 接生员 jiēshēngyuán (*midwife*)

接收 jiēshōu	*receive*
接受 jiēshòu	*accept*: 接受建议 jiēshòu jiànyì (*accept suggestions*)
接替 jiētì	*take over* (a job)
接吻 jiēwěn	*kiss* (v.)

街 jiē

street: 大街 dàjiē (*main street*). Cl: 条 tiáo; 上街 shàng jiē (*go to the street*)

街道 jiēdào	*street.* Cl: 条 tiáo
街头 jiētóu	*street corner; street*
街心 jiēxīn	*center of a street; street crossing center garden*

结 jié

1. *knot*: 打结 dǎ jié (*tie a knot*); 解结 jiě jié (*untie a knot*); 死结 sǐ jié (*fast knot*); 活结 huó jié (*slipknot*)

2. *form a tie*: 结为夫妻 jié wéi fūqī (*be tied in wedlock*); 结为姐妹城市 jié wéi jiěmèi chéngshì (*become sister cities*)

Also appears in the following words: 冻结 dòngjié (*freeze*); 连结 liánjié (*link; connect*); 团结 tuánjié (*unite*); 小结 xiǎojié (*summary*); 总结 zǒngjié (*sum up; summary*)

结冰 jiébīng	*freeze*: 湖结冰了 hú jiébīng le (*the lake is frozen over*)
结构 jiégòu	*structure*
结果 jiéguǒ	1. *result; outcome*: 考试的结果怎么样 kǎoshì de jiéguǒ zěnmeyàng (*how is the result of the test?*)
	2. *as a result; consequently*: 他病了，结果没能来 tā bìng le, jiéguǒ méi néng lái (*he was sick; as a result, he was not able to come*)
	3. *finally*: 结果坏人被抓住了 jiéguǒ huàirén bèi zhuā zhù le (*finally the bad guys were caught*)
结合 jiéhé	1. *integrate; combine*: 结合各种方法 jiéhé gè zhǒng fāngfǎ (*combine various methods*)
	2. *marry; marriage*: 他们的结合是父母包办的 tāmende jiéhé shì fùmǔ bāobàn de (*their marriage was arranged by their parents*)
结核 jiéhé	*tuberculosis*, often expressed as 结核病 jiéhèbìng or 肺结核 fèijiéhé (*tuberculosis*)
结婚 jiéhūn	*get married*: 我妹妹下个星期结婚 wǒ mèimei xià ge xīngqī jiéhūn (*my younger sister is getting married next week*); 我没有结婚 wǒ méiyou jiéhūn (*I'm not married*);

她和谁结婚 tā hé shuí jiéhūn (*whom is she marrying?*).
结婚 jiéhūn cannot take an object as it is a Verb + Object structure. The English sentence "he married his college sweetheart" is expressed in Chinese as 他和他的大学同学结婚了 tā hé tāde dàxué tóngxué jiéhūn le (literally, *he and his college classmate got married*)

结交	jiéjiāo	*become friends with*
结论	jiélùn	*conclusion*
结识	jiéshí	*become acquainted with*
结束	jiéshù	*finish; end; conclusion*: 结束工作 jiéshù gōngzuò (*finish work*); 会议的结束 huìyì de jiéshù (*the end of the meeting*)
结尾	jiéwěi	*ending*: 小说的结尾 xiǎoshuō de jiéwěi (*the ending of the novel*)
结业	jiéyè	*complete a course of study*
结余	jiéyú	*surplus*
结帐	jiézhàng	*balance accounts; pay bills*

节 jié

1. *festival; holiday*: 春节 Chūnjié (*Spring Festival/Chinese New Year*); 圣诞节 Shèngdànjié (*Christmas*); 国庆节 Guóqìngjié (*National Day*)

2. (classifier) *period* (of a class); *section*: 我们每天有四节课 wǒmen měi tiān yǒu sì jié kè (*we have four periods of classes everyday*); 这列火车有十节车厢 zhè liè huǒchē yǒu shí jié chēxiāng (*this train has ten cars*)

3. *economize*, often used in the disyllabic form of 节约 jiéyuē

Also appears in the following words: 关节 guānjié (*joint*); 环节 huánjié (*link*); 季节 jìjié (*season*); 礼节 lǐjié (*etiquette; protocol*); 情节 qíngjié (*plot; story*); 细节 xìjié (*details; particulars*)

节俭	jiéjiǎn	*thrifty; frugal*
节录	jiélù	*extract; excerpt*
节目	jiémù	*program; item* (on a program): 电视节目 diànshì jiémù (*TV program*); 节目单 jiémùdān (*program; playbill*). Cl: 个 gè; 套 tào
节日	jiérì	*festival; holiday*
节省	jiéshěng	*economize; cut down on; save*
节育	jiéyù	*birth control*
节约	jiéyuē	*economize; save; practice thrift*
节制	jiézhì	*control; check; be moderate in*
节奏	jiézòu	*rhythm*

解 jiě

1. *untie*; *undo*: 解鞋带 jiě xiédài (*untie the shoelace*)

2. *separate*; *dissolve*, often used as part of another word: 化解 huàjiě (*dissolve*); 调解 tiáojiě (*mediate*)

3. *allay*; *relieve*: 解热 jiě rè (*allay a fever*); 解痛 jiě tòng (*relieve pain*)

4. *solve*; *explain*: 解题 jiě tí (*solve a mathematics problem*)

Also appears in the following words: 分解 fēnjiě (*break down*); 和解 héjiě (*become reconciled*); 讲解 jiǎngjiě (*explain*); 理解 lǐjiě (*comprehend*; *understand*); 谅解 liàngjiě (*understanding*); 了解 liǎojiě (*knowledgeable about*)

解除 jiěchú		*remove* (someone from his post); *terminate* (a contract, etc.); *lift* (a ban, etc.)
解答 jiědá		*explain*; *answer*
解放 jiěfàng		*liberate*; *emancipate*; *liberation*; *emancipation*
解雇 jiěgù		*dismiss*; *lay off*; *fire sb.*
解救 jiějiù		*save*; *rescue*
解决 jiějué		*solve*; *resolve*
解开 jiěkāi		*undo*; *untie*: 解开上衣 jiě kāi shàngyī (*unbutton the jacket*)
解渴 jiěkě		*quench thirst*
解剖 jiěpōu		*dissect*
解释 jiěshì		*explain*; *explanation*
解脱 jiětuō		*extricate oneself from*
解围 jiěwéi		*help sb. out of a predicament*
解职 jiězhí		*remove from office*

借 jiè

1. *borrow*: 向银行借钱 xiàng yínháng jiè qián (*borrow money from the bank*); 从图书馆借书 cóng túshūguǎn jiè shū (*borrow books from the library*)

2. *lend*: 银行借钱给商家 yínháng jiè qián gěi shāngjiā (*the bank lends money to businesses*); 图书馆借书给学生 túshūguǎn jiè shū gěi xuésheng (*the library lends books to the students*)

3. *make use of*; *take advantage of*: 借此机会 jiè cǐ jīhuì (*take this opportunity*)

借故 jiègù		*find an excuse*
借方 jièfāng		*debtor*; *borrower*
借鉴 jièjiàn		*draw lessons from*; *draw on experience from*: 借鉴外国的经验 jièjiàn wàiguó de jīngyàn (*learn from the experience of the foreign countries*)

借口 jièkǒu	excuse; pretext
借款 jièkuǎn	loan (n. & v.); borrow money
借书证 jièshūzhèng	library card
借债 jièzhai	borrow money
借助 jièzhù	have the aid of; with the help of

今 jīn

1. *today*; *now*, usu. taking the disyllabic form of 今天: 今早 jīnzǎo (*this morning*); 至今 zhìjīn (*up to now*; *to this day*)

2. *this*; *present*: 今年 jīnnián (*this year*)

Also appears in the following words: 迄今 qìjīn (*thus far*; *up to now*); 现今 xiànjīn (*nowadays*)

今后 jīnhòu	from now on
今年 jīnnián	this year
今日 jīnrì	today; now, interchangeable with, but more formal than, 今天 jīntiān
今天 jīntiān	today; now
今昔 jīnxī	the present and the past

紧 jǐn

1. *tight*: 鞋子太紧 xiézi tài jǐn (*the shoes are too tight*); 时间很紧 shíjiān hěn jǐn (*time is very tight*)

2. *fast*; *firm*, used as a verb complement: 抓紧时间 zhuā jǐn shíjiān (*grasp the time*; *make good use of time*); 关紧门 guān jǐn mén (*close the door tightly*)

3. *close to*: 上海紧靠长江 Shànghǎi jǐn kào Chángjiāng (*Shanghai is right on the Yangtze River*)

4. *urgent*: 这篇文章报社要得很紧 zhè piān wénzhāng bàoshè yào de hěn jǐn (*the newspaper wants this article urgently*)

Also appears in the following words: 赶紧 gǎnjǐn (*hasten*; *hurry up*); 要紧 yàojǐn (*important*); 抓紧 zhuājǐn (*grasp*)

紧凑 jǐncòu	(of writings, agendas, etc.) *compact*; *terse*; *tight*
紧跟 jǐngēn	*follow closely*
紧急 jǐnjí	*urgent*; *emergent*; *pressing*: 紧急状况 jǐnjí zhuàngkuàng (*emergency state*); 紧急任务 jǐnjí rènwù (*urgent assignment*)

| 紧要 jǐnyào | critical; crucial: 紧要关头 jǐnyào guāntóu (critical moment) |
| 紧张 jǐnzhāng | nervous; tense |

进 jìn

1. *enter*; *get into*: 请进 qǐng jìn (*please come in*); 进了北京大学 jìn le Běijīng Dàxué (*got into Beijing University*)

2. *advance*; *progress*: 两国的关系进了一步 liǎng guó de guānxi jìn le yí bù (*the relationship between the two countries has advanced a step further*)

3. *accept*; *receive*; *admit*: 百货公司进了一批日本货 bǎihuò gōngsī jìn le yì pī Rìbén huò (*the department store has received a shipment of Japanese goods*)

4. used as a directional complement after certain verbs to indicate an action that moves from outside to inside: 跑进教室 pǎo jìn jiàoshì (*run into the classroom*); 放进书包 fàng jìn shūbāo (*put in the book bag*); 搬进厨房 bān jìn chúfáng (*move into the kitchen*)

5. *eat*; *drink*: used in idioms and formal language; the object is usu. 餐 cān (*food*) or 食 shí (*food*): 病人已经三天没有进食了 bìngrén yǐjīng sān tiān méiyou jìn shí le (*the patient has not eaten anything for three days*)

Also appears in the following words: 促进 cùjìn (*promote*); 改进 gǎijìn (*improve on*); 激进 jījìn (*radical*); 前进 qiánjìn (*advance*; *progress*); 推进 tuījìn (*advance*); 先进 xiānjìn (*advanced*); 增进 zēngjìn (*enhance*)

进步 jìnbù	progress (n. and v.): 进步很快 jìnbù hěn kuài (*the progress is rapid*)
进城 jìn chéng	go into town
进程 jìnchéng	course; process; progress
进度 jìndù	pace; rate of progress
进攻 jìngōng	attack (n. & v.)
进化 jìnhuà	evolution
进口 jìnkǒu	1. entrance. Cl: 个 gè; 处 chù 2. import: 进出口公司 jìnchūkǒu gōngsī (*import and export company*)
进入 jìnrù	enter, go into
进行 jìnxíng	1. carry out; engage in: 进行调查 jìnxíng diàochá (*carry out an investigation*) 2. be under way: 会议正在进行 huìyì zhèng zài jìnxíng (*the meeting is under way*)
进一步 jìnyībù	further; go one step further

进展 jìnzhǎn   *progress* (n. & v.)

近 jìn

1. *near; close:* 我家离学校很近 wó jiā lí xuéxiào hěn jìn (*my home is very close to the school*)

2. *recent:* 近几天 jìn jǐ tiān (*last several days*); 近年 jìn nián (*recent years*)

3. *close to:* 来参观的人近五百 lái cānguān de rén jìn wǔbǎi (*those who came to visit were close to 500*)

Also appears in the following words: 附近 fùjìn (*vicinity*); 将近 jiāngjìn (*nearly; almost*); 接近 jiējìn (*approach*); 临近 línjìn (*draw near; close to*); 亲近 qīnjìn (*intimate*); 最近 zuìjìn (*recently; shortly*)

近代 jìndài	*modern times*
近况 jìnkuàng	*recent situation*
近来 jìnlái	*recently; of late*
近路 jìnlù	*shortcut*
近期 jìnqī	*in the near future*
近亲 jìnqīn	*close relative*
近视 jìnshì	*myopia; nearsightedness*

经 jīng

1. *scripture:* 圣经 shèngjīng (*Bible*); 佛经 fójīng (*Buddhist scripture*). Cl: 本 běn; 册 cè; 部 bù; 卷 juàn

2. *after; through:* 经研究 jīng yánjiù (*after consideration*); 经检查 jīng jiǎnchá (*through inspection*)

Also appears in the following words: 财经 cáijīng (*finance and economics*); 曾经 céngjīng (*once; at one time*); 神经 shénjīng (*nerve*); 已经 yǐjīng (*already*); 月经 yuèjīng (*menstruation*)

经常 jīngcháng	*often; frequently*
经典 jīngdiǎn	*classics*
经费 jīngfèi	*allocated funds; operating funds; budget.* Cl: 笔 bǐ
经过 jīngguò	1. *pass by; pass through; go through.*
	2. *process* (n.); *course:* 事情的经过 shìqing de jīngguò (*the ins and outs of an event*)
经纪人 jīngjìrén	*broker.* Cl: 个 gè; 位 wèi; 名 míng
经济 jīngjì	*economy; economic; economical:* 经济学 jīngjìxué (*economics*)

经理 jīnglǐ	*manager*. Cl: 位 wèi; 名 míng; 个 gè
经历 jīnglì	*experience* (v. and n.); *go through*
经受 jīngshòu	*withstand*: 经受考验 jīngshòu kǎoyàn (*withstand a test*)
经销 jīngxiāo	*distribute* (a product)
经验 jīngyàn	*experience* (n.)
经营 jīngyíng	*manage*; *operate* (a business)

九 jiǔ

nine

| 九月 jiǔyuè | *September* |

酒 jiǔ

liquor; *wine*; *spirits*; *alcoholic drink*: 白酒 báijiǔ (*liquor*); 葡萄酒 pútáojiǔ (*wine*); 啤酒 píjiǔ (*beer*)

Also appears in the following words: 敬酒 jìngjiǔ (*propose a toast*); 醉酒 zuìjiǔ (*drunk*); 祝酒 zhùjiǔ (*toast*)

酒吧 jiǔbā	*bar*. Cl: 间 jiān; 家 jiā
酒杯 jiǔbēi	*wine glass*
酒厂 jiǔchǎng	*brewery*; *winery*; *distillery*
酒店 jiǔdiàn	*wine shop*; *liquor store*; *hotel*. Cl: 家 jiā
酒馆 jiǔguǎn	*pub, tavern*. Cl: 家 jiā
酒会 jiǔhuì	*cocktail party*; *reception*
酒精 jiǔjīng	*ethyl alcohol*
酒窝 jiǔwō	*dimple*
酒席 jiǔxí	*banquet*; *feast*

就 jiù

1. adverb used for emphasis: 银行就在那儿 yínháng jiù zài nàr (*the bank is right there*)

2. adverb with the meaning of *earlier than expected* or *better than expected*. 就 jiù in this sense is often opposed to 才 cái, which means *later than expected* or *worse than expected*. Cf. 九点上课，他八点就来了 jiǔ diǎn shàng kè, tā bā diǎn jiù lái le (*class started at 9, but he came as early as 8*); 九点上课，他十点才来 jiǔ diǎn shàng kè, tā shí diǎn cái lái (*class started at 9, but he didn't come until 10*).

3. *then*: 如果天不好，我就不去野餐 rúguǒ tiān bù hǎo, wǒ jiù bú qù yěcān (*if the weather is not good, then I won't go for the picnic*); 他看到老师，就走了过去 tā kàn dào lǎoshī, jiù zǒu le guò qù (*when he saw the teacher, he walked over*). Note that 就 jiù occurs before the verb and after the subject. This is different from *then* in English, where it is placed before the subject.

4. adverb indicating that one action closely follows another: 他们下了班就去飞机场 tāmen xià le bān jiù qù fēijīchǎng (*they will go to the airport as soon as they get off work*)

5. *just about*, often used with 要 yào and/or 了 le: 天就要下雨了 tiān jiù yào xiàyǔ le (*it is about to rain*); 晚饭十分钟就好了 wǎnfàn shí fēnzhōng jiù hǎo le (*dinner will be ready in ten minutes*)

6. *only*: 我就会说英语 wǒ jiù huì shuō Yīngyǔ (*I can only speak English*); 中国他就去过北京 Zhōngguó tā jiù qù guo Běijīng (*he has only been to Beijing in China*)

就是 jiùshì	1. used to indicate agreement with the listener 2. *even if*: 我就是不告诉你，你也应该知道 wǒ jiùshì bú gàosù nǐ, nǐ yě yīnggāi zhīdao (*even if I didn't tell you, you should still know it*) 3. *still*: 我劝了他半天，他就是不听 wǒ quàn le tā bàntiān, tā jiùshì bù tīng (*I tried a long time to persuade him, but he still refused to listen*) 4. used for emphasis, often as a rebuttal: 我们就是要这样做 wǒmen jiùshì yào zhèyàng zuò (*we insist on doing this way*)
就是说 jiùshìshuō	*that is to say*
就要 jiù yào	*to be about to*, used with 了 le: 冬天就要来了 dōngtiān jiù yào lái le (*winter is about to come*)
就业 jiùyè	*get employed*

旧 jiù

1. *old*; *past*; *outdated*: 旧政权 jiù zhèngquán (old regime); 旧社会 jiù shèhuì (old society).

2. *used*; *secondhand*: 旧书 jiù shū (used books); 旧汽车 jiù qìchē (used car). 旧 jiù differs from 老 lǎo in that 旧 jiù refers to condition, whereas 老 lǎo refers to age. Cf. 旧汽车 jiù qìchē (old car—not in good condition); 老汽车 lǎo qìchē (old-model car—a car with history, but may be worth a lot)

旧货 jiùhuò	*secondhand goods*: 旧货店 jiùhuòdiàn (*secondhand store*)
旧交 jiùjiāo	*old acquaintance*. Cl: 位 wèi

旧居 **jiùjū**	*former residence*
旧历 **jiùlì**	*lunar calendar*
旧式 **jiùshì**	*old-fashioned*
旧约 **jiùyuē**	*the Old Testament*

决 jué

1. *decide*, used in set expressions or in the disyllabic form of 决定 juédìng:
决一死战 jué yī sǐzhàn (*fight a last-ditch battle*)

2. *absolutely*; *definitely*, used in the negative to indicate emphasis: 我决不相信他的话 wǒ jué bù xiāngxìn tāde huà (*I never believe what he says*)

Also appears in the following words: **表决** biǎojué (*vote*); **否决** fǒujué (*vote down; reject*); **坚决** jiānjué (*resolute*); **解决** jiějué (*solve*)

决策 **juécè**	*strategic decision*
决定 **juédìng**	*decide; decision*: 她已决定辞职 tā yǐ juédìng cízhí (*she had decided to resign*); 她已做了决定 tā yǐ zuò le juédìng (*she has already made the decision*)
决赛 **juésài**	(of sports) *finals*
决心 **juéxīn**	*determination; resolution; determined; resolve*: 我们队有决心赢这场比赛 wǒmen duì yǒu juéxīn yíng zhè chǎng bǐsài (*our team has the determination to win the game*); 他决心学好中文 tā juéxīn xué hǎo Zhōngwén (*he is determined to do a good job with his study of Chinese*)
决议 **juéyì**	*resolution*: 会议的决议得到代表们的通过 huìyì de juéyì dédào dàibiǎomen de tōngguò (*the resolution of the conference was approved by the delegates*). Cl: 个 gè; 项 xiàng
决战 **juézhàn**	*decisive battle*

军 jūn

army; military: 陆军 lùjūn (*army*); 海军 hǎijūn (*navy*); 空军 kōngjūn (*air force*)

Also appears in the following words: **裁军** cáijūn (*disarmament*); **参军** cānjūn (*join the army*); **冠军** guànjūn (*champion*); **将军** jiāngjūn (*military general*)

军队 **jūnduì**	*armed forces*. Cl: 支 zhī
军官 **jūnguān**	*military officer*. Cl: 个 gè; 位 wèi; 名 míng
军火 **jūnhuǒ**	*ammunition*. Cl: 个 gè; 位 wèi; 名 míng

军人	jūnrén	soldier; military personnel
军事	jūnshì	military affairs
军装	jūnzhuāng	military uniform. Cl: 件 jiàn; 套 tào

开 kāi

1. *open*: 开门 kāi mén (*open the door*)

2. *turn on*: 开灯 kāi dēng (*turn on the light*); 开电视 kāi diànshì (*turn on TV*)

3. *operate*: 开车 kāi chē (*drive*); 开飞机 kāi fēijī (*fly a plane*)

4. *come loose*: 鞋带开了 xiédài kāi le (*the shoelace came undone*)

5. *bloom*: 花开了 huā kāi le (*the flower bloomed*)

6. *set up*; *start*; *operate* (a business): 开店 kāi diàn (*start a store*)

7. *hold* (meeting, show, party, etc.): 开会 kāi huì (*hold a meeting*)

8. *boil*: 水不开不能喝 shuǐ bù kāi bù néng hē (*the water is not drinkable if it is not boiled*)

9. *clear*; *move away*: used after a verb: 把桌上的东西拿开 bǎ zhuō shang de dōngxi ná kái (*take the stuff off the table*); 走开 zǒu kāi (*go away*)

10. *begin*: 开头 kāitóu (*start*); 开工 kāigōng (*begin production*); 开先例 kāi xiānlì (*set a precedent*)

11. *issue*; *write out*: 开支票 (*issue a check*); 开处方 (*write a prescription*)

Also appears in the following words: **分开** fēnkāi (*separate*); **离开** líkāi (*leave*; *depart*); **展开** zhǎnkāi (*unfold*); **召开** zhàokāi (*convene*).

开除	kāichú	expel (from a school, organization, political party, etc.)
开创	kāichuàng	initiate (a movement); *found* (an organization, etc.)
开刀	kāidāo	perform a surgery
开发	kāifā	develop; reclaim
开放	kāifàng	open to the public
开关	kāiguān	(electric) switch
开始	kāishǐ	begin; start
开心	kāixīn	feel happy
开学	kāixué	school starts
开展	kāizhǎn	launch (a campaign); unfold
开张	kāizhāng	(businesses) open
开支	kāizhī	expenses. Cl: 项 xiàng; 笔 bǐ

看 kàn

1. *see; look; watch*

2. *read*: 看书 kàn shū (*read a book*); 看报 kàn bào (*read a newspaper*)

3. *think*: 我看明天不会下雨 wǒ kàn míngtiān bú huì xiàyǔ (*I don't think it is going to rain tomorrow*); 你看怎么样 (*what do you think?*)

4. *depend on*, often used with 要 yào or 得 děi: 我能不能去旅行要看我有没有钱 wǒ néng bu néng qù lǚxíng yào kàn wǒ yǒu méi you qián (*whether I can travel depends on whether I have money*)

Also appears in the following words: 观看 guānkàn (*look on*; *watch*); 好看 hǎokàn (*good-looking*); 难看 nánkàn (*ugly*); 小看 xiǎokàn (*belittle*)

看病 **kànbìng**	*see a doctor*
看不惯 **kàn bú guàn**	*frown upon*
看不起 **kàn bù qǐ**	*look down upon*
看出 **kànchū**	*detect; tell*
看穿 **kānchuān**	*see through*
看待 **kàndài**	*treat; regard*
看法 **kànfǎ**	*viewpoint; opinion*
看见 **kànjiàn**	*see*
看来 **kànlái**	*it seems*
看破 **kànpò**	*see through*
看起来 **kàn qǐlái**	*it seems*, 起 qǐ can be left out: 看起来你不赞成 kàn qǐlái nǐ bú zànchéng (*it seems that you do not agree*)
看上 **kànshàng**	*take a liking to*
看望 **kànwàng**	*visit; call upon*
看中 **kànzhòng**	*take a liking to*
看作 **kànzuò**	*look on ... as; regard ... as*: 把朋友的问题看作是我们的问题 bǎ péngyou de wèntí kànzuò shì wǒmende wèntí (*treat our friends' problems as our problems*)

考 kǎo

examine; take an examination; take a test: 我们明天要考中文 wǒmen míngtiān yào kǎo Zhōngwén (*we are going to have a Chinese exam tomorrow*); 你考得怎么样 nǐ kǎo de zěnmeyàng (*how did you do on your exam?*); 他考了满分 tā kǎo le mǎnfēn (*he got a full score*)

Also appears in the following words: 补考 bǔkǎo (*take a makeup exam*); 参考 cānkǎo (*refer to*); 监考 jiānkǎo (*proctor an exam*)

考察 **kǎochá**	*inspect and investigate* (on site)

考场 kǎochǎng	examination site; examination room. Cl: 处 chù; 个 gè
考古学 kǎogǔxué	archaeology: 考古学家 kǎogǔxuéjiā (archaeologist)
考核 kǎohé	evaluate and assess (a person's performance)
考卷 kǎojuàn	examination paper. Cl: 份 fèn
考虑 kǎolǜ	consider; think over; take into consideration
考生 kǎoshēng	examinee; person who takes the exam. Cl: 个 gè; 位 wèi; 名 míng
考试 kǎoshì	examination; test; take an exam 考试 kǎoshì differs from 考 kǎo in that 考 kǎo is always a verb, whereas 考试 kǎoshì can be used both as a verb and as a noun: When both 考 kǎo and 考试 kǎoshì are used as verbs, 考 kǎo is usually used as a transitive verb that needs to be followed by an object: 考中文 kǎo Zhōngwén (take a test in Chinese); 考大学 kǎo dàxué (take a college entrance exam); and 考试 kǎoshì is used as an intransive verb that cannot be followed by an object: 我们什么时候考试 wǒmen shénme shíhou kǎoshì (when are you going to have an exam?).
考题 kǎotí	examination questions; items on an exam. Cl: 道 dào; 份 fèn

科 kē

1. *academic discipline or department*: 文科 wénkē (*the humanities*); 理科 lǐkē (*the sciences*)

2. *division or section of an organization*: 行政科 xíngzhèngkē (*administrative division*)

科技 kējì	science and technology
科室 kēshì	administrative offices: 科室人员 kēshì rényuán (office personnel)
科学 kēxué	science; scientific: 科学院 kēxuéyuàn (academy of sciences); 科学研究 kēxué yánjiū (scientific research)
科研 kēyán	scientific research

可 kě

1. *may*; *can*, usu. taking the disyllabic form of 可以 kěyǐ: 我可以进来吗 wǒ kěyǐ jìn lái ma (*can I come in?*); 你不可以在这儿吸烟 nǐ bù kěyǐ zài zhèr xī yān (*you can't smoke here*)

2. *be able to*; *be worth doing*; *be good for*; *deserve*, used with a verb: 可爱

117

kě'ài (*loveable*); 可吃 kěchī (*eatable*); 可笑 kěxiào (*laughable*); 可看 kěkàn (*worth seeing*)

3. *presentable; all right; not too bad*: 今天的天气还可以 jīntiān de tiānqì hái kěyǐ (*the weather today is all right*)

4. *but*, usu. taking the disyllabic form of 可是 kěshì

5. *so; such* (for emphasis): 这本书可好了 zhè běn shū kě hǎo le (*this book is so good*); 可别听他的话 kě bié tīng tāde huà (*you should never listen to him*)

Also appears in the following words: 宁可 nìngkě (*rather; prerably*); 认可 rènkě (*authorize*); 许可 xǔkě (v. *permit*)

可耻	**kěchǐ**	*shameful*
可见	**kějiàn**	*it can be concluded*
可靠	**kěkào**	*reliable; dependable*
可怜	**kělián**	*pitiable; pitiful*
可能	**kěnéng**	*possible; probable; possibly; probably; maybe*
可怕	**kěpà**	*scary; fearful*
可是	**kěshì**	*but*
可惜	**kěxī**	*what a pity; what a shame*
可以	**kěyǐ**	**1**. *may; can*: 我可以进来吗 wǒ kěyǐ jìn lái ma (*may I come in?*)
		2. *be able to; be worth doing; be good for; deserve*, used with a verb: 这篇文章可以看 zhè piān wénzhāng kěyǐ kàn (*this article is worth reading*)
		3. *okay; not too bad*, often used with 还 hái: 他的中文还可以 tāde Zhōngwén hái kěyǐ (*his Chinese is not too bad*)

课 kè

lesson; subject; course; class: 中文课 Zhōngwénkè (*Chinese class*); 口语课 kǒuyǔkè (*conversation class*); 上课 shàngkè (*go to class*); 下课 xiàkè (*class is over*); 备课 bèikè (*prepare lessons—for a teacher*); 必修课 bìxiūkè (*required course—for a student*); 补课 bǔkè (*make up a missed lesson*); 讲课 jiǎngkè (*teach a class; lecture*)

课本	**kèběn**	*textbook*. Cl: 册 cè
课表	**kèbiǎo**	*class schedule; school timetable*
课程	**kèchéng**	*course; curriculum*. Cl: 门 mén
课堂	**kètáng**	*classroom*
课外	**kèwài**	*outside of classes; extracurricular*: 课外活动 kèwài huódòng (*extracurricular activities*)
课文	**kèwén**	*text*. Cl: 篇 piān

客 kè

1. *guest; visitor; customer; passenger:* 贵客 guìkè (*distinguished guest*); 乘客 chéngkè (*passenger*); 房客 fángkè (*tenant; boarder*); 顾客 gùkè (*customer*); 游客 yóukè (*tourist*). Cl: 个 gè; 位 wèi; 名 míng

2. *passenger:* 客车 kèchē (*bus; passenger train*). Cl: 节 jié; 列 liè; 辆 liàng; 客机 kèjī (*passenger plane*). Cl: 架 jià

Also appears in the following words: **好客** hàokè (*hospitable*); **请客** qǐngkè (*entertain guests; treat sb. to*); **做客** zuòkè (*be a guest*)

客房 kèfáng	*guest room.* Cl: 间 jiān
客观 kèguān	*objective:* 客观世界 kèguān shìjiè (*objective world; external world*)
客户 kèhù	*client.* Cl: 位 wèi
客满 kèmǎn	(*of theater, etc.*) *full house; sold out*
客气 kèqi	*polite, courteous:* 不客气 bú kèqi (*you are welcome—as a response to* 谢谢 xièxie)
客人 kèrén	*guest.* Cl: 位 wèi; 个 gè
客厅 kètīng	*living room.* Cl: 间 jiān
客栈 kèzhàn	*hostel; inn.* Cl: 家 jiā

空 kōng; kòng

When pronounced as kōng:

1. *empty; hollow:* 空房子 kōng fángzi (*empty house*); 空树 kōng shù (*hollow tree*)

2. *sky; air:* 空中无云 kōng zhōng wú yún (*no cloud in the sky*); 空军 kōngjūn (*air force*)

3. *in vain; for nothing:* 空高兴 kōng gāoxìng (*rejoice too soon*); 空忙 kōng máng (*make fruitless efforts*)

Also appears in the following words: **航空** hángkōng (*aviation*); **太空** tàikōng (*outer space*); **真空** zhēnkōng (*vacuum*)

空洞 kōngdòng	*empty* (*theory, etc.*); *devoid of content*
空话 kōnghuà	*empty or hollow talk.* Cl: 句 jù; 篇 piān
空军 kōngjūn	*air force*
空气 kōngqì	*air*
空前 kōngqián	*unprecedented*
空手 kōngshǒu	*empty-handed*
空谈 kōngtán	*empty talk; armchair talk*
空袭 kōngxí	*air raid*

空想 kōngxiǎng	*fantasy; pipe dream*
空心 kōngxīn	*hollow*
空运 kōngyùn	*airlift; air transport*

When pronounced as kòng:

1. *free time; spare time*: 你今晚有没有空儿 nǐ jīnwǎn yǒu méi you kòngr (*are you free tonight?*)

2. *vacant*: 一块空地 yí kuài kòng dì (*a vacant lot of land*)

口 kǒu

1. *mouth; oral*, used in formal language or set expressions: 口信 kǒuxìn (*oral message*); 口试 kǒushì (*oral examination*)

2. *entrance; opening; exit*: 河口 hékǒu (*estuary*); 入口 rùkǒu (*entrance*)

3. classifier for the total number of people in the family and for certain animals: 我家有四口人 wǒ jiā yǒu sì kǒu rén (*there are four people in my family*); 三口猪 sān kǒu zhū (*three pigs*)

Also appears in the following words: 插口 chākǒu (*socket*); 出口 chūkǒu (*export; exit*); 渡口 dùkǒu (*ferry*); 关口 guānkǒu (*juncture; pass*); 借口 jièkǒu (*excuse; pretext*); 进口 jìnkǒu (*entrance; import*); 门口 ménkǒu (*doorway*); 人口 rénkǒu (*population*)

口岸 kǒu'àn	*port*
口吃 kǒuchī	*stutter*
口袋 kǒudài	*pocket*. Cl: 只 zhī; 个 gè
口号 kǒuhào	*slogan*. Cl: 个 gè; 句 jù
口红 kǒuhóng	*lipstick*. Cl: 支 zhī; 管 guǎn
口气 kǒuqì	*tone; undertone; manner of speaking*
口琴 kǒuqín	*harmonica*. Cl: 把 bǎ
口试 kǒushì	*(academic) oral examination*
口水 kǒushuǐ	*saliva*
口头 kǒutóu	*oral; spoken; verbal*: 口头协议 kǒutóu xiéyì (*verbal agreement*)
口味 kǒuwèi	*taste; preference*: 这种音乐不合我的口味 zhè zhǒng yīnyuè bù hé wǒde kǒuwèi (*this kind of music does not suit my taste*)
口香糖 kǒuxiāngtáng	*chewing gum*. Cl: 片 piàn; 块 kuài
口译 kǒuyì	*oral interpretation; interpreter*
口音 kǒuyīn	*accent*
口语 kǒuyǔ	*spoken language; colloquialism*

快 kuài

1. *fast*; *quick*; *quickly*

2. *hurry up*: 快离开 kuài líkāi (*hurry up and leave*)

3. *soon*; *about to*, used with 了 le: 火车快来了 huǒchē kuài lái le (*the train is about to arrive*); 快下课了 kuài xiàkè le (*the class will be over soon*)

4. *almost*; *about*, followed by a noun: 快三点了 kuài sān diǎn le (*it's almost three o'clock*); 快新年了 kuài xīnnián le (*it is almost the New Year*); 我来美国快十年了 wǒ lái Měiguó kuài shí nián le (*it is almost ten years since I came to America*)

5. *sharp* (knife): 快刀 kuài dāo (*sharp knife*)

6. *quick-witted*

7. *happy*; *gratified*: 快感 kuàigǎn (*gratified feeling*; *pleasant sensation*)

Also appears in the following words: 飞快 fēikuài (*at lightening speed*); 尽快 jǐnkuài (*as soon as possible*); 凉快 liángkuai (*nice and cool*); 外快 wàikuài (*side money*; *extra gains*); 愉快 yúkuài (*delightful*; *cheerful*)

快餐	**kuàicān**	*fast food.* Cl: 份 fèn
快车	**kuàichē**	*express train.* Cl: 辆 liàng; 列 liè
快感	**kuàigǎn**	*pleasant sensation*; *gratified feeling*
快乐	**kuàilè**	*happy*; *cheerful*
快门	**kuàimén**	(camera) *shutter*
快信	**kuàixìn**	*express mail.* Cl: 封 fēng
快要	**kuàiyào**	*soon*; *about to*, used in conjunction with 了 le: 学生们快要毕业了 xuéshengmen kuàiyào bìyè le (*the students are about to graduate*). 要 yào in this expression can be left out. See #3 above.

块 kuài

1. *block*; *chunk*; *cube*; *lump*: 糖块 tángkuài (*candy bar*); 石块 shíkuài (*rock*); 冰块 bīngkuài (*ice cube*)

2. classifier for such cubic-like objects as soap, brick, watch, and bread

3. monetary unit in China, expressed in written language as 元 yuán

---

拉 lā

1. *pull; draw*: 拉门 lā mén (*pull the door*); 马拉车 mǎ lā chē (*the horse is pulling a cart*)

2. *play* (a musical instrument such as the violin or the accordion)

3. *draw out*, often used with 长 cháng or 大 dà: 拉长声音 lā cháng shēngyīn (*drawl*); 拉大距离 lā dà jùlí (*space out; increase the distance*)

4. *solicit; win over; canvass*: 拉广告 lā guǎnggào (*solicit advertisers*); 拉生意 lā shēngyì (*push sales*); 拉选票 lā xuǎnpiào (*canvass votes*)

5. *empty the bowels*

拉倒 **lādǎo**	*forget about it*, used colloquially
拉丁美洲 **Lādīng Měizhōu**	*Latin America*
拉丁文 **Lādīngwén**	*Latin*, also expressed as 拉丁语 Lādīngyǔ
拉肚子 **lā dùzi**	*suffer from diarrhea; have loose bowels*
拉关系 **lā guānxi**	*cultivate connections* (in order to use influence)
拉后腿 **lā hòutuǐ**	*hold sb. back*
拉开 **lā kāi**	**1.** *pull open*: 拉开窗帘 lā kāi chuānglián (*pull open the curtains*)
	2. *increase the distance or gap*: 贫富的距离拉开了 pínfù de jùlí lā kāi le (*the gap between the poor and the rich has been increased*)
拉链 **lāliàn**	*zipper.* Cl: 条 tiáo; 根 gēn
拉手 **lāshǒu**	*doorknob.* Cl: 把 bǎ
拉稀 **lāxī**	*have diarrhea; have loose bowels*

来 lái

1. *come (to); arrive*: 我妈妈明年来美国 wǒ māma míngnián lái Měiguó (*my mother is coming to America next year*); 火车来了 (*the train has arrived*). The subject often follows 来 lái if it is an indefinite noun: 公司来了一个新经理 gōngsī lái le yí ge xīn jīnglǐ (*a new manager has come to the company*)

2. when followed by another verb in a sentence that addresses the same subject, 来 lái indicates an expectation or purpose: 你可以用别的办法来解决这个问题 nǐ kěyǐ yòng biéde bànfǎ lái jiějué zhè ge wèntí (*you may use another method to solve this problem*)

3. *give/bring sth.*, used only in a restaurant or eating setting: 请给我来一杯啤酒 qǐng gěi wǒ lái yì bēi píjiǔ (*please give me a glass of beer*)

4. *write; send*, used with words such as *letter, fax* and *cable*: 我在中国的朋友给我来了一封信 wǒ zài Zhōngguó de péngyou gěi wǒ lái le yì fēng xìn (*my friend in China sent me a letter*)

5. directional complement used after certain verbs such as 到 dào (*go to*), 带 dài (*bring, carry*), 寄 jì (*mail*), 上 shàng (*go up*), 下 xià (*go down*), 进 jìn (*enter*), 出 chū (*exit*), 回 huí (*return*) to show the direction of the action in relation to the speaker. This use of 来 lái is opposed to 去 qù. Cf. 进来 jìn lái (*come in*—in the direction of the speaker) and 进去 jìn qù (*go in*—away from the speaker); 上来 shàng lái (*come up*—the speaker is up) and 上去 shàng qù (*go up*—away from the speaker). If the verb takes an object that indicates a location, the object must be placed between the verb and the directional complement: 我妈妈回家来了 wǒ māma huí jiā lái le (*my mother has come home*). In this case, the aspect marker 了 le cannot be used after the verb, but it is possible to use the modal particle 了 le at the end of the sentence: 他回美国去了 tā huí Méiguó qù le (*he went back to America*). If the object does not indicate a location, it can be placed either between the verb and 来 lái or after 来 lái: 学生们带了书包来 xuéshēngmen méiyou dài shūbāo lái and 学生们带来了书包 xuéshēngmen méiyou dài lái shūbāo (*the students brought their bookbags*). In this case, the aspect particle 了 le can be used, as shown by the examples. If the object appears between the verb and 来 lái, 了 le is used immediately after the verb: 你朋友打了电话来 nǐ péngyou dǎ le diànhuà lái (*your friend called you*). If the object follows 来 lái, 了 le would follow 来 lái as well: 你朋友打电话来了 nǐ péngyou dǎ diànhuà lái le.

6. 来 lái can form a complex directional complement with certain verbs. These verbs include 上 shàng (*go up*), 下 xià (*go down*), 进 jìn (*enter*), 出 chū (*exit*), 回 huí (*return*), 过 guò (*pass*), and 起 qǐ (*rise*). The complex directional complement indicates both a motion and the direction of the motion in relation to the location of the speaker. Cf. 走出来 zǒu chū lái (*walk out*—in the direction of the speaker) and 走出去 zǒu chū qù (*walk out*—away from the speaker). If the verb takes an object that indicates a location, the object must be placed before 来 lái: 运动员们走进体育馆来了 yùndòngyuánmen zǒu jìn tǐyùguǎn lái le (*the athletes walked into the gymnasium*). If the object does not indicate a location, it can be placed either before or after 来 lái. Cf. 我爸爸带回很多书来 wǒ bàba dài huí hěn duō shū lái le (*my father brought back many books*) and 我爸爸带回来很多书 wǒ bàba dài huí lái hěn duō shū.

Also appears in the following words: **本来** běnlái (*originally*); **从来** cónglái (*all along*); **到来** dàolái (*advent; arrival*); **后来** hòulái (*after that; later*); **将来** jiānglái (*in the future*); **历来** lìlái (*always*); **起来** qǐlai (*arise; stand up*); **往来** wǎnglái (*dealings*); **未来** wèilái (*future*); **以来** yǐlái (*since*); **原来** yuánlái (*originally*)

来宾 láibīn   *guest; visitor*. Cl: 位 wèi
来不及 láibùjí   *have not enough time to do; too late for*: 我在上海的时间很短，来不及去看他了 wǒ zài Shànghǎi de shíjiān hěn duǎn, láibùjí qù kàn tā le (*my stay in Shanghai is very short, I won't have time to see him*)

来得及 láidejí	there is still time to do; not too late for: 我们还来得及换衣服吗 wǒmen hái láidejí huàn yīfu ma (do we still have time to change clothes?)
来回 láihuí	make a round trip: 来回票 láihuípiào (round-trip ticket)
来临 láilín	1. arrive; approach
	2. arrival; advent
来往 láiwǎng	dealings; contact: 他们没有来往 tāmen méi you láiwǎng (they are not in contact with each other)
来源 láiyuán	source; origin

老 lǎo

1. (of age and history) old; become old: 这是一座老房子 zhè shì yí zuò lǎo fángzi (this is an old house); 我爸爸不太老 wǒ bàba bú tài lǎo (my father is not very old); 我们是老朋友 (we are old friends). 老 lǎo is used to describe age, but not condition, for which 旧 jiù should be used: 旧书 jiù shū (used book); 旧汽车 jiù qìchē (used car)

2. (of food) overcooked: 菜烧老了 cài shāo lǎo le (the food was overcooked)

3. always: 他老喜欢问这种问题 tā lǎo xǐhuan wèn zhè zhǒng wèntí (he always likes to ask such questions)

4. used to prefix a surname to show intimacy: 老王 Lǎo Wáng

5. used to prefix a number to indicate the birth order of children in the family: 老二 Lǎo Èr (the second oldest child); 老三 Lǎo Sān (the third oldest child). The oldest child is expressed as 老大 Lǎo Dà.

老百姓 lǎobǎixìng	common people. Cl: 个 gè; 群 qún
老板 lǎobǎn	boss. Cl: 位 wèi
老虎 lǎohǔ	tiger. Cl: 只 zhī; 头 tóu; 群 qún
老话 lǎohuà	old saying. Cl: 句 jù
老家 lǎojiā	hometown; birthplace
老练 lǎoliàn	seasoned; experienced
老年 lǎonián	old age: 老年人 (old people)
老婆 lǎopó	wife, used colloquially. Cl: 个 gè
老师 lǎoshī	teacher. Cl: 位 wèi
老实 lǎoshí	honest
老鼠 lǎoshǔ	mouse. Cl: 只 zhī; 群 qún; 窝 wō

了 le

1. aspect particle used to indicate the completion of an action, cf. 我吃早饭 wǒ chī zǎofàn (*I eat breakfast*) and 我吃了早饭 wǒ chī le zǎofàn (*I have eaten breakfast*). In this sense, 了 le cannot be used for cognitive verbs and non-action verbs such as 认识 rènshi (*know*), 喜欢 xǐhuan (*like*), 是 shì (*be*), and 像 xiàng (*resemble*). If there is a series of two verbs in the sentence sharing the same subject, typically with 去 qù (*go*) as the first verb, 了 le must appear after the second verb, not the first one: 他去医院看了他的朋友 tā qù yīyuàn kàn le tāde péngyou (*he went to the hospital to see his friend*). The negative form for a verb with 了 le is 没有 méiyou instead of 不 bù. Once 没有 méiyou is used, 了 le has to be dropped because there is no completed action to speak of. Note also a completed action can take place in the future as well as the past. The following is an example of 了 le used to indicate a completed action as projected from the present time: 我吃了饭去看电影 wǒ chī le fàn qù kàn diànyǐng (*after I've finished eating, I'll go to see a movie*). Since 了 le only indicates the perfect aspect, habitual actions, universal truths or descriptions of a sequence of events, whether in the past or present, can never take 了 le: 我在北京的时候常去故宫 wǒ zài Běijīng de shíhou cháng qù Gùgōng (*I often went to the Palace Museum when I was in Beijing*).

2. modal particle used at the end of a sentence **a)** to indicate that an event has taken place. This use of 了 le differs from the aspect 了 le in that an action may be completed, but the whole event may not have taken place, cf. 我吃了饭就去看电影 wǒ chī le fàn jiù qù kàn diànyǐng (*after eating the meal, I'll go to see the movie*) and 我吃了饭就去看电影了 wǒ chī le fàn jiù qù kàn diànyǐng le (*after eating the meal, I went to see the movie*). When both the completion of the action indicated by the verb and the completion of the event indicated by the sentence have taken place, the use of the second 了 le at the end of the sentence is often determined by the nature of the object in the sentence. If the object is a simple one, i.e. one that is not modified by an attribute such as a number, an adjective or a pronoun, a second 了 le must be used at the end of the sentence, cf. 我吃了中国饭 wǒ chī le Zhōngguó fàn (*I ate Chinese food*—饭 fàn is modified by 中国 Zhōngguó and the second 了 le is not necessary) and 我吃了饭了 wǒ chī le fàn le (*I ate the food*—饭 fàn is not modified and the second 了 le is necessary). Absence of the modal marker 了 le at the end of the sentence when the object is a simple one gives the impression that the sentence is not complete. However, the first 了 le can often be omitted without affecting the meaning. For *I saw a movie yesterday*, both 我昨天看电影了 wǒ zuótiān kàn diànyǐng le and 我昨天看了电影了 wǒ zuótiān kàn le diànyǐng le are correct. If the word 已经 yǐjīng appears in the sentence, the modal particle is used at the end of the sentence: 我姐姐已经毕业了 wǒ jiějie yǐjīng bìyè le (*my older sister has already graduated*). **b)** to indicate a change of condition. This use often suggests a contrast to the present situation: 天冷了 tiān lěng le (*it is* *getting cold*—implying that it is no longer warm), cf. 我没有钱 wǒ méi you qián (*I don't have money*—a statement of fact) and 我没有钱了 wǒ méi you qián le (*I've spent the money*—a temporary situation implying that I had money before). In this usage, 了 le can be used with cognitive and non-action verbs such as 喜欢 xǐhuan (*like*) and 是 shì (*to be*): 我太太现在喜欢吃豆腐了 wǒ tàitai xiànzài xǐhuan chī dòufu le (*my wife now likes to eat tofu*—implying that she didn't like it before); 我们是公民了 wǒmen shì gōngmín le (*we are now citizens*—implying that we were not before). The negative form in this use is 不 bù instead of 没有 méiyou unless the verb is 有 yǒu, then 没 méi should be used: 我不吸烟了 wǒ bù xīyān le (*I no longer smoke*); 他没有汽车了 tā méi you qìchē le (*he no longer has a car*). This use of 了 le can also suggest the emergence of a new situation: 现在四点了，我们上课吧 xiànzài sì diǎn le, wǒmen shàngkè ba (*it's 4 o'clock, let's begin our class*); 我三十岁了 wǒ sānshí suì le (*I'm 30 years old*).

3. Used in a number of set expressions: 太 … 了 tài … le (*very*); 要 … 了 yào … le (*about to*); 别 … 了 bié … le (*don't …*); 极了 jí le (*extremely*); 糟了 zāo le (*terrible*) and so on. If the verb in the sentence is used with a complex directional complement such as 上来 shàng lái and 进去 jìn qù, and takes an object, 了 le should be placed at the end of the sentence. If the verb does not take an object, 了 le can be placed between the verb and the complement: 他走进电影院去了 tā zǒu jìn diànyǐngyuàn qù le (*he walked into the movie theater*); 雨下了起来 yǔ xià le qǐlái (*it started to rain*)

类 lèi

kind; *category*; *class*; *species*: 不同类的事物 bùtóng lèi de shìwù (*things of different categories*); 人类 rénlèi (*human species*)

Also appears in the following words: 败类 bàilèi (*black sheep; scum of a community*); 词类 cílèi (*parts of speech*); 分类 fēnlèi (classify); 同类 tónglèi (*the same type*); 种类 zhǒnglèi (*sort; kind*)

类比 lèibǐ		*analogy*
类别 lèibié		*classification*; *category*: 高校有很多类别 gāoxiào yǒu hěn duō lèibié (*there are many categories of schools of higher education*)
类似 lèisì		*similar*: 类似的例子很少 lèisìde lìzi hěn shǎo (*there are few cases like this*)
类推 lèituī		*reason by analogy*
类型 lèixíng		*type*: 相同类型的机器 xiāngtóng lèixíng de jīqì (*machines of the same type*)

冷 lěng

cold

冷餐	lěngcān	*buffet*
冷藏	lěngcáng	*refrigerate*; *deep freeze*
冷场	lěngchǎng	*awkward silence at a meeting or an event*
冷淡	lěngdàn	*cold, indifferent*: 冷淡的态度 lěngdàn de tàidù (*a frigid attitude*); 反映冷淡 fǎnyìng lěngdàn (*cold response*)
冷静	lěngjìng	*calm*; *sober*
冷门	lěngmén	**1.** *a profession, trade or major that receives little attention* **2.** *an unexpected winner*; *dark house*
冷盘	lěngpán	*cold dish*; *hors d'oeuvres*. Cl: 个 gè; 种 zhǒng; 样 yàng
冷气	lěngqì	*air conditioning*: 冷气机 lěngqìjī (*air conditioner*). Cl: 团 tuán; 股 gǔ
冷清	lěngqīng	*cold and cheerless*
冷饮	lěngyǐn	*cold drinks*. Cl: 种 zhǒng; 样 yàng
冷遇	lěngyù	*cold reception*; *cold shoulder*
冷战	lěngzhàn	*cold war*

离 lí

1. *leave*; *depart from*, usu. used with 开 kāi: 离开医院 líkāi yīyuàn (*leave the hospital*)

2. *away from*; *in reference to* (a point of space); *off*: 学校离我家很远 xuéxiào lí wǒjiā hěn yuǎn (*my school is far from my home*); 银行离公司很近 yínháng lí gōngsī hěn jìn (*the bank is very close to the company*); 离圣诞节还有三天 lí Shèngdànjié hái yǒu sān tiān (*there are three days until Christmas*)

离别	líbié	*leave*; *say good-bye*
离婚	líhūn	*divorce*: 他们决定离婚 tāmen juédìng líhūn (*they have decided to divorce*)
离开	líkāi	*leave*; *depart from*: 代表团明天离开北京 dàibiǎotuán míngtiān líkāi Běijīng (*the delegation is leaving Beijing tomorrow*); 他已经离开了那个公司 tā yǐjing líkāi le nà ge gōngsi (*he has already left that company*)
离奇	líqí	*strange*; *odd*: 离奇的故事 líqíde gùshì (*bizarre story*)
离散	lísàn	*be separated from each other*
离题	lítí	*deviate from the subject*; *off the topic*

里 lǐ

1. *inner; interior*: 里院 lǐyuàn (*inner yard*); 里间 lǐjiān (*inner room*)

2. *in; inside*, used after a noun, as the word is considered as a noun in Chinese, and in conjunction with 在 zài: 在房子里 zài fángzi lǐ (*in the house*); 在海里 zài hǎi lǐ (*in the sea*). 里 lǐ is not used after place nouns: 在美国 zài Měiguó (*in America*); 在北京 zài Běijīng (*in Beijing*); 在学校 zài xuéxiào (*in school*).

3. *at; during*: 夜里 yèlǐ (*at night*); 年里 niánlǐ (*during the year*). 在 zài is normally left out when it appears at the beginning of an existential sentence. 边 biān, 面 miàn or 头 tóu are optionally used with 里 lǐ. In this combination, 边 biān and 头 tóu are pronounced in the neutral tone: 里边 lǐbian; 里头 lǐtou. 里 lǐ used by itself and 里边 lǐbian / 里面 lǐmiàn / 里头 lǐtou are not always interchangeable. When used as an attribute modifying a noun or when used by itself as an adverbial of place, only the disyllabic form is possible: 里边的房间 lǐbian de fángjiān (*the room inside*); 里面有很多人 lǐ miàn yǒu hěn duō rén (*there are many people inside*).

4. *place*, used in collocations with 这 zhè, 那 nà and 哪 nǎ: 这里 zhèlǐ (*here; this place*); 那里 nàlǐ (*there; that place*); 哪里 nǎlǐ (*where; what place*)

里边 **lǐbian**	*in; inside*. See its usage above.
里程 **lǐchéng**	*mileage; course*: 里程碑 líchéngbēi (*milestone*); 里程表 líchéngbiǎo (*odometer*)
里面 **lǐmiàn**	*in; inside*. See its usage above.
里弄 **lǐlòng**	*alleys; neighborhood*
里手 **lǐshǒu**	*expert; skilled hand*
里头 **lǐtou**	*in; inside*. See its usage above.
里子 **lǐzi**	*lining*

理 lǐ

1. *reason; truth*: 那个人不讲理 nà ge rén bù jiǎng lǐ (*that person is not reasonable*); 这件事不合理 zhè jiàn shì bù hé lǐ (*this matter doesn't stand to reason*)

2. *natural sciences*: usu. used to refer to an academic subject: 理科 lǐkē (*science subjects*)

3. *manage; put in order*: 理家 lǐ jiā (*manage the household*); 理财 lǐ cái (*manage finance*)

4. *pay attention to*: 别理他 bié lǐ tā (*ignore him*)

Also appears in the following words: 处理 chǔlǐ (*deal with*); 代理 dàilǐ (*agent*); 道理 dàoli (*reason*; *truth*); 地理 dìlǐ (*geography*); 管理 guǎnlǐ (*manage*); 合理 hélǐ (*reasonable*); 经理 jīnglǐ (*manager*); 物理 wùlǐ (*physics*); 心理 xīnlǐ (*psychology*); 修理 xiūlǐ (*repair*); 整理 zhěnglǐ (*clean up*); 助理 zhùlǐ (*assistant*); 总理 zǒnglǐ (*premier*; *prime minister*)

理发	lǐfǎ	*haircut*; *have a haircut*
理解	lǐjiě	*understand*
理科	lǐkē	*science subjects*
理疗	lǐliáo	*physical therapy*
理论	lǐlùn	*theory*. Cl: 个 gè; 种 zhǒng; 套 tào
理想	lǐxiǎng	*ideal* (n. and adj.). Cl: 个 gè; 种 zhǒng
理由	lǐyóu	*reason*. Cl: 个 gè; 条 tiáo; 点 diǎn

礼 lǐ

1. *ceremony*; *rite*: 婚礼 hūnlǐ (*wedding*); 典礼 diǎnlǐ (*ceremony*); 浸洗礼 jìnxǐlǐ (*baptism*)

2. *courtesy*; *etiquette*; *manners*: 失礼 shī lǐ (*breach etiquette*)

3. *gift*; *present*: 送礼 sòng lǐ (*give a gift*)

礼拜	lǐbài	1. *religious service*: 做礼拜 zuò lǐbài (*go to church*; *attend a religious service*)
		2. *week*: 这个礼拜 zhè ge lǐbài (*this week*); 下个礼拜 xià ge lǐbài (*next week*); 上个礼拜 shàng ge lǐbài (*last week*); 礼拜一 lǐbàiyī (*Monday*); 礼拜二 lǐbài' èr (*Tuesday*); 礼拜三 lǐbàisān (*Wednesday*); 礼拜四 lǐbàisì (*Thursday*); 礼拜五 lǐbàiwǔ (*Friday*); 礼拜六 lǐbàiliù (*Saturday*); 礼拜天 lǐbàitiān (*Sunday*). In this sense, 礼拜 lǐbài means the same as 星期 xīngqī.
礼服	lǐfú	*formal attire*; *ceremonial attire*. Cl: 件 jiàn; 套 tào
礼节	lǐjié	*etiquette*; *protocol*
礼貌	lǐmào	*courtesy*; *manners*; *polite*; *courteous*
礼品	lǐpǐn	*gift*; *present*: 礼品店 (*gift shop*)
礼堂	lǐtáng	*auditorium*. Cl: 座 zuò
礼物	lǐwù	*gift*; *present*. Cl: 件 jiàn; 份 fèn

力 lì

1. *power*; *strength*; *ability*; *energy*: 听力 tīnglì (*listening comprehension*); 人力 rénlì (*manpower*; *human resources*); 体力 tǐlì (*physical strength*)

2. *force*: 动力 dònglì (*motivating force*)

Also appears in the following words: 暴力 bàolì (*violence*); 大力 dàlì (*vigorously*); 电力 diànlì (*electric power*); 能力 nénglì (*ability*); 尽力 jìnlì (*try one's best*); 精力 jīnglì (*energy*); 努力 nǔlì (*try hard*); 潜力 qiánlì (*potential*); 武力 wǔlì (*force*; *military force*); 压力 yālì (*pressure*); 阻力 zǔlì (*resistance*)

力量 lìliang	*power*; *strength*. Cl: 股 gǔ
力气 lìqì	*strength*
力争 lìzhēng	*strive for*

立 lì

1. *stand*, used in literary language or set expressions

2. *upright*; *vertical*: 立式钢琴 lì shì gāngqín (*upright piano*)

3. *live*; *exist*: 自立 zìlì (*self-reliant*)

4. *establish*; *found*; *set up*, usu. used with 成 chéng or 建 jiàn as part of the word: 成立公司 chénglì gōngsī (*set up a company*); 建立国家 jiànlì guójiā (*establish a country*)

Also appears in the following words: 创立 chuànglì (*found*); 独立 dúlì (*independence*); 对立 duìlì (*opposition*); 孤立 gūlì (*isolated*); 私立 sīlì (*private*); 中立 zhōnglì (*neutral*)

立场 lìchǎng	*position*; *stand*
立法 lìfǎ	*legislation*; *legislate*
立即 lìjí	*immediately*; *at once*
立刻 lìkè	*immediately*; *at once*, interchangeable with, but less formal than 立即 lìjí
立足 lìzú	*gain a foothold*

利 lì

1. *sharp*: 利剑 lìjiàn (*sharp sword*)

2. *advantageous*; *favorable*: 这个决定对我们不利 zhè ge juédìng duì wǒmen bú lì (*this decision is not in our favor*)

3. *benefit* (v.): 利己 lìjǐ (*benefit oneself*); 利人 lìrén (*benefit others*)

4. *interest*: 私利 sīlì (*self interest*)

Also appears in the following words: 便利 biànlì (*convenient*); 福利 fúlì (*welfare; benefits*); 吉利 jílì (*auspicious*); 流利 liúlì (*fluent*); 名利 mínglì (*fame and gain*); 权利 quánlì (*rights*); 胜利 shènglì (*victory*); 顺利 shùnlì (*smooth; succcessful*)

利弊	lìbì	*advantages and disadvantages*
利润	lìrùn	*profit*
利息	lìxi	(of money) *interest*
利益	lìyì	*interest*: 为了国家的利益 wèile guójiā de lìyì (*in the interest of the country*)
利用	lìyòng	**1.** *make use of; utilize*: 利用太阳能 lìyòng tàiyángnéng (*make use of the solar energy*)
		2. *take advantage of*: 利用关系牟利 lìyòng guānxi móulì (*seek personal gain by taking advantage of connections*)

连 lián

1. *link; connect; join*: 这两个房子连在一起 zhè liǎng ge fángzi lián zài yìqǐ (*these two houses are joined*)

2. *in succession; back to back; repeatedly*: 连看了三场电影 lián kàn le sān chǎng diànyǐng (*saw three movies in a row*)

3. *even*, usu. used in conjunction with 也 yě or 都 dōu: 这个美国人连上海话也能说 zhè ge Měiguórén lián Shànghǎihuà yě néng shuō (*this American can even speak Shanghai dialect*)

4. *including*: 连今天已经下了四天的雨了 lián jīntiān yǐjīng xià le sì tiān de yǔ le (*including today, it has already been raining for four days*)

连词	liáncí	(gram) *conjunction*
连贯	liánguàn	*coherent*
连接	liánjiē	*join; connect*: 这座桥把两个国家连接起来了 zhè zuò qiáo bǎ liǎng ge guójiā liánjiē qǐlái le (*this bridge connects the two countries*)
连累	liánlěi	*get someone in trouble*
连连	liánlián	*repeatedly*: 连连打喷嚏 liánlián dǎ pēngtì (*repeatedly sneeze*)
连忙	liánmáng	*make haste*
连年	liánnián	*in successive years*
连日	liánrì	*day after day*
连同	liántóng	*together with*
连续	liánxù	*continuous; continuously*: 电视连续剧 diànshì liánxùjù (*TV series; soap opera*); 连续工作了十个小时 liánxù gōngzuò le shí ge xiǎoshí (*worked for ten hours in a row*)

131

连衣裙 liányīqún	dress (n.). Cl: 条 tiáo; 件 jiàn
连用 liányòng	(of words, expressions, etc.) used together: 这两个词不能连用 zhè liǎng ge cí bù néng liányòng (these two words are not to be used together)
连载 liánzǎi	publish in installments

联 lián

join; ally; unite, used as part of another word

联邦 liánbāng	federation: 联邦政府 liánbāng zhèngfǔ (federal government)
联合 liánhé	1. form an alliance: 联合兄弟组织 liánhé xiōngdì zǔzhī (form an alliance with fraternal organizations)
	2. alliance; union
	3. joint; jointly: 联合举办 liánhé jǔbàn (jointly hold an event, etc.); 联合声明 liánhé shēngmíng (joint statement)
联合国 liánhéguó	the United Nations
联结 liánjiē	join; tie; bind: 联结两国人民的语言 liánjiē liǎngguó rénmín de yǔyán (the language that connects the people of the two countries)
联络 liánluò	1. get in touch with: 和我们的同行联络 hé wǒmende tóngháng liánluò (get in touch with our counterpart)
	2. contact (n.); liaison: 失去了联络 shīqù le liánluò (lost contact)
联盟 liánméng	alliance; coalition
联系 liánxì	1. get in touch with; contact; relate: 到后请和我联系 dào hòu qǐng hé wǒ liánxì (please get in touch with me after you arrive). 联系 liánxì is an intransitive verb in Chinese. As such it cannot take an object. The English sentence "please contact me" is expressed in Chinese as 请跟我联系 qǐng gēn wǒ liánxì (literally, with me please get in touch).
	2. connection; relation: 这两个学校的联系很密切 zhè liǎng ge xuéxiào de liánxì hěn mìqiè (the relationship between these two schools is very close)

练 liàn

practice (v.): 练书法 liàn shūfǎ (*practice calligraphy*); 练身体 liàn shēntǐ
(*exercise one's body*); 练口语 liàn kǒuyǔ (*practice spoken language*)

Also appears in the following words: 操练 cāoliàn (*drill*); 教练 jiàoliàn (*coach*);
老练 lǎoliàn (*experienced; sophisticated*); 熟练 shúliàn (*proficient*); 排练 páiliàn
(*dry run; rehearse*); 训练 xùnliàn (*training*)

练习 liànxí   *exercise; practice* (n. & v.). Cl: 个 gè; 项 xiàng

The main differences between 练 liàn and 练习 liànxí are: while 练 liàn is always a
verb, 练习 liànxí can be a verb as well as a noun. When both are used as a verb,
练 liàn is a transitive verb that requires an object, whereas 练习 liànxí can be a
transitive verb as well as an intransitive verb.

量 liáng; liàng

When pronounced liáng:

measure (v.): 量身长 liáng shēncháng (*measure the body length*); 量体重
liáng tǐzhòng (*check the body weight*)

Also appears in the following words: 测量 cèliáng (*survey; measure*); 估量 gūliáng
(*assess*); 商量 shāngliáng (*talk over*)

When pronounced liàng:

1. *quantity*: 菜很好，只是量不够 cài hěn hǎo, zhǐshì liàng bú gòu (*the dish
is excellent, but the portion is not large enough*); 产量 chǎnliàng (*production
output*)

2. *capacity*: 酒量 jiǔliàng (*capacity for drinking alcohol*); 饭量 fànliàng
(*capacity for eating food*)

Also appears in the following words: 大量 dàliàng (*a great deal*); 尽量 jìnliàng (*to
the best of one's abilities*); 力量 lìliàng (*strength*); 数量 shùliàng (*quantity*); 质量
zhìliàng (*quality*); 重量 zhòngliàng (*weight*)

两 liǎng

two, used before nouns to indicate quantity: 两个孩子 liǎng ge háizi (*two
children*); 两把椅子 liǎng bǎ yǐzi (*two chairs*). However, "*two*" is pronounced
èr and written in Chinese as 二 if it appears in the ones' position in a multi-
digit number such as 32 (sānshíèr) and 982 (jiǔbǎi bāshíèr). When number

"*two*" is used for identifying purposes such as in a telephone number or ID number, it is pronounced as èr and written as 二.

both: 两边 liǎngbiān (*both sides*)

两口子	liǎngkǒuzi	*husband and wife*; *a couple*, used colloquially
两面派	liǎngmiànpài	*double faced*; *double dealing*
两难	liǎngnán	*in a dilemma*
两全	liǎngquán	*satisfactory to both sides*
两手	liǎngshǒu	*dual tactics*
两头	liǎngtóu	*both ends*
两栖	liǎngqī	*amphibian*
两性关系	liǎngxìng guānxi	*sexual relationship*
两用	liǎngyòng	*dual purpose*

亮 liàng

bright; *shining*: 天亮了 tiān liàng le (*the day broke*); 房间很亮 fángjiān hěn liàng (*the room is very bright*); 把桌子擦得很亮 bǎ zhuōzi cā de hěn liàng (*wipe the table and make it shiny*)

Also appears in the following words: **明亮** míngliàng (*bright*); **漂亮** piàoliang (*pretty*; *good-looking*); **月亮** yuèliang (*moon*)

另 lìng

1. *another*; *other*, usu. used with 一 yī, whose tone varies according to that of the following word: 另一个人 lìngyí ge rén (*the other person*); 另一本书 lìngyì běn shū (*the other book*)

2. *separately*; *some other*: 另找人吧 lìng zhǎo rén ba (*let's find someone else*); 我另有打算 wǒ lìng yǒu dǎsuan (*I have other plans*)

另外	lìngwài	*in addition*; *moreover*; *besides*
另行	lìngxíng	*separately*: 关于这件事，学校会另行通知 guānyú zhè jiàn shì, xuéxiào huì lìngxíng tōngzhī (*the school will send a separate announcement regarding the matter*)

流 liú

1. *flow*: 黄河流入大海 huánghé liú rù dàhǎi (*the Yellow River flows into the sea*); 流眼泪 liú yǎnlèi (*shed tears*)

2. *current*: 逆流 nì liú (*against the current*); 气流 qìliú (*air current*). Cl: 股 gǔ

3. *rate*; *class*: 一流的旅馆 yì liú de lǚguǎn (*first-rate hotel*)

Also appears in the following words: **潮流** cháoliú (*tide*); **河流** héliú (*river; watercourse*); **交流** jiāoliú (*exchange*); **主流** zhǔliú (*mainstream*)

流产 liúchǎn	*miscarriage*: 人工流产 réngōng liúchǎn (*abortion*)
流畅 liúchàng	(*of writing*) *smooth*
流传 liúchuán	(*of stories, legends, etc.*) *spread; circulate*
流动 liúdòng	*mobile; floating*: 流动人口 liúdòng rénkǒu (*floating population*); 流动医院 liúdòng yīyuàn (*mobile hospital*)
流放 liúfàng	*exile; banish*
流感 liúgǎn	*influenza*
流浪 liúlàng	*wander; roam*: 流浪汉 liúlànghàn (*vagrant*)
流利 liúlì	*fluent*: 说流利的英语 shuō liúlìde Yīngyǔ (*speak fluent English*)
流露 liúlù	*reveal or betray* (*feelings*)
流氓 liúmáng	*hooligan*. Cl: 个 gè; 群 qún
流派 liúpài	*school of thought*
流水线 liúshuǐxiàn	*assembly line*. Cl: 条 tiáo
流行 liúxíng	*trendy; in vogue; in fashion; popular*: 流行音乐 liúxíng yīnyuè (*popular music*)
流血 liúxuě	*bleed*

留 liú

1. *stay on; remain in a place*: 你们去吧，我留在家里 nǐmen qù ba, wǒ liú zài jiā lǐ (*why don't you go and I'll stay home*); 你们应该在中国多留几天 nǐ men yīnggāi zài Zhōngguó duō liú jǐ tiān (*you should stay in China for a few more days*); 下班后，请留一下儿 xiàbān hòu, qǐng liú yíxiàr (*please stay behind for a minute after work*)

2. *leave*: 不要把书留在教室里 bú yào bǎ shū liú zài jiàoshì lǐ (*don't leave your books in the classroom*); 我如果不在，请给我留话 wǒ rúguǒ bú zài, qǐng gěi wǒ liú huà (*if I'm not in, please leave me a message*)

3. *reserve; save*: 请给我留三个座位 qǐng gěi wǒ liú sān ge zuòwèi (*please reserve three seats for me*); 我还留着小时候的很多照片 wǒ hái liú zhe xiǎoshíhou de hěn duō zhàopiàn (*I still keep many childhood photos*); 请留好车票 qǐng liú hǎo chēpiào (*please save your train ticket*)

4. *hold; keep*, used in various words: 保留 bǎoliú (*reserve; retain; keep*); 逗留 dòuliú (*stay*); 拘留 jūliú (*detain; hold in custody*); 停留 tíngliú (*stop over; remain*); 遗留 yíliú (*leave behind; hand down*)

留级 liújí	(of school) *fail to go to the next grade*; *repeat a grade*
留恋 liúliàn	1. *be reluctant to leave a place or part with a person*
	2. *recall with nostalgia*
留心 liúxīn	*be careful*; *take care*; *be observant*
留学 liúxué	*study abroad*: 留学生 liúxuéshēng (*student studying abroad*; *international students*)
留言 liúyán	*leave a message*; *message*
留意 liúyì	*look out*; *keep one's eyes open*

六 liù

six

| 六边形 liùbiānxíng | *hexagon* |
| 六月 liùyuè | *June* |

楼 lóu

1. *storied building*: 大楼 dàlóu (*big building*); 办公楼 bàngōnglóu (*office building*); 行政楼 xíngzhènglóu (*administrative building*). Cl: 个 gè; 座 zuò

2. *floor*: 三楼 sānlóu (*third floor*); 上楼 shàng lóu (*go upstairs*); 下楼 xiàlóu (*go downstairs*)

楼上 lóushàng	*upstairs*
楼梯 lóutī	*stairs*; *staircase*. Cl: 层 céng; 级 jí
楼下 lóuxià	*downstairs*

路 lù

1. *road*; *way*: 公路 (*highway*). Cl: 条 tiáo; 水路 (*waterway*)

2. *distance*: 路很远 lù hěn yuǎn (*the distance is long*)

3. *route*, as a classifier: 这路汽车去不去博物馆 zhè lù qìchē qù bu qù bówùguǎn (*does this bus go to the museum?*)

Also appears in the following words: 半路 bànlù (*halfway*); 道路 dàolù (*road*; *way*); 电路 diànlù (*electric circuit*); 后路 hòulù (*route of retreat*); 马路 mǎlù (*street*); 迷路 mílù (*lose one's way*); 让路 rànglù (*give way*); 思路 sīlù (*train of thought*); 铁路 tiělù (*railroad*); 退路 tuìlù (*leeway*; *route of retreat*); 线路 xiànlù (*line*; *circuit*); 走路 zǒulù (*walk*; *on foot*)

路程 lùchéng	*distance traveled.* Cl: 段 duàn
路灯 lùdēng	*street lamp.* Cl: 盏 zhǎn
路过 lùguò	*pass by*: 从我家到学校要路过公园 cóng wǒ jiā dào xuéxiào yào lùguò gōngyuán (*I'll pass the park on my way to school from my home*)
路口 lùkǒu	*intersection*
路上 lùshang	*on the way*
路线 lùxiàn	*route; itinerary; direction.* Cl: 条 tiáo; 个 gè
路子 lùzi	*way; approach*

落 luò

1. *fall; drop*: 苹果从树上落下 píngguǒ cóng shù shang luò xià (*the apple fell from the tree*); 任务落在他身上 rènwù luò zài tā shēn shang (*the task fell on him*)

2. *fall behind*: 落在队伍后面 luò zài duìwù hòumian (*fall behind the team*)

3. *leave behind*, used with 下 xià: 落下坏名声 luò xià huài míngshēng (*leave behind a bad reputation*)

Also appears in the following words: 部落 bùluò (*tribe*); 降落 jiàngluò (*descend*); 角落 jiǎoluò (*corner*); 衰落 shuāiluò (*decline*)

落成 luòchéng	*complete; completion* (of a building, etc.): 一家新饭店近日落成了 yí jiā xīn fàndiàn jìnrì luòchéng le (*a new hotel has been completed in recent days*)
落后 luòhòu	*fall behind; lag behind; backward; underdeveloped*: 中国队现在落后 Zhōngguó duì xiànzài luòhòu (*the Chinese team is now falling behind*); 那个地区很落后 nà ge dìqū hěn luòhòu (*that region is very underdeveloped*)
落脚 luòjiǎo	*stay for a short time* (at a hotel, etc.): 在朋友家落脚 zài péngyou jiā luòjiǎo (*stay at a friend's house*)
落空 luòkōng	*fall through; fail*: 计划落空 jìhuà luòkōng (*the plan fell through*)
落泪 luòlèi	*shed tears; weep*
落实 luòshí	1. *finalize; make sure*: 出发的日期还没有落实 chūfā de rìqī hái méiyou luòshí (*the date of departure has not been finalized*) 2. *carry out; implement*: 落实政府的政策 luòshí zhèngfǔ de zhèngcè (*implement the government's policy*)
落网 luòwǎng	(of a criminal) *be captured*
落选 luòxuǎn	*lose an election*

吗 ma

Sentence-final particle to indicate a yes/no question: 你好吗 nǐ hǎo ma (*how are you?*); 你有中国朋友吗 nǐ yǒu Zhōngguó péngyou ma (*do you have Chinese friends?*)

妈 mā

mother, usu. taking the disyllabic form of 妈妈 māma

Also appears in the following words: **奶妈** nǎimā (*wet nurse*); **姑妈** gūmā (*paternal aunt*)

马 mǎ

horse. Cl: 匹 pí

马车 **mǎchē**	*horse-drawn carriage.* Cl: 辆 liàng
马虎 **mǎhu**	*careless; casual*
马拉松 **mǎlāsōng**	*marathon*
马马虎虎 **mǎmahūhu**	*so-so; not bad*
马上 **mǎshàng**	*immediately; at once*
马戏 **mǎxì**	*circus.* Cl: 场 chǎng

买 mǎi

buy; purchase: 买东西 mǎi dōngxi (*buy things; go shopping*); 买单 mǎidān (*pay bill in a restaurant*)

Also appears in the following words: **购买** gòumǎi (*purchase*); **收买** shōumǎi (*buy off*)

买方 **mǎifāng**	*buyer*
买卖 **mǎimài**	*buying and selling; business; deal:* 做买卖 zuò mǎimài (*do business*); 买卖人 mǎimàirén (*businessman; trader; merchant*)
买通 **mǎitōng**	*buy off; bribe*
买一送一 **mǎi yī sòng yī**	*buy one get one free*
买主 **mǎizhǔ**	*buyer.* Cl: 个 gè; 位 wèi

卖 mài

sell: 卖完了 mài wán le (*sold out*); 拍卖 pāimài (*auction*)

Also appears in the following words: 出卖 chūmài (*betray*); 贩卖 fànmài (*sell*; *peddle*; *traffic*); 拍卖 pāimài (*auction*; *public sale*); 义卖 yìmài (*charity sale*)

卖方	**màifāng**	*seller*
卖国	**màiguó**	*betray one's country*
卖力	**màilì**	*spare no efforts*; *exert all one's strength*
卖弄	**mài'nòng**	*show off*
卖淫	**màiyín**	*practice prostitution*
卖主	**màizhǔ**	*seller*
卖座	**màizuò**	(*of shows, plays, etc.*) *draw large audiences*: 这个歌剧很卖座 zhè ge gējù hěn màizuò (*this opera draws well*; *tickets for this opera sell very well*)

满 mǎn

1. *full*; *filled*; *packed*, often used as a verb complement: 水池满了 shuǐchí mǎn le (*the pool is filled*); 船上装满了货 chuán shang zhuàng mǎn le huò (*the boat is fully loaded with goods*)

2. *reach*; *to be up to* (a certain age, time, etc.): 我来中国还不满一年 wǒ lái Zhōngguó hái bù mǎn yì nián (*I haven't been in China for one year*); 满十二岁的孩子要买全票 mǎn shí'èr suì de háizi yào mǎi quánpiào (*children who have reached the age of 12 need to pay full price for the tickets*)

3. *all over*: 满街都是人 mǎn jiē dōu shì rén (*people filled the streets*; *there were people all over the streets*); 满脸是汗 mǎn liǎn shì hàn (*sweat all over the face*)

4. *satisfied*; *contented*, used in set expressions: 对工作不满 duì gōngzuò bù mǎn (*dissatisfied with the job*); 自满 zìmǎn (*complacent*; *conceited*; *complacence*; *conceit*)

Also appears in the following words: 充满 chōngmǎn (*full of*); 美满 měimǎn (*happy*); 圆满 yuánmǎn (*satisfactory*); 自满 zìmǎn (*self-complacence*)

满分	**mǎnfēn**	*full marks*; *best grades*
满怀	**mǎnhuái**	*be imbued with*; *full of*: 满怀热情 mǎnhuái rèqíng (*full of enthusiasm*)
满身	**mǎnshēn**	*all over one's body*
满意	**mǎnyì**	*pleased*; *satisfied*: 外国朋友对我们的接待很满意 wàiguó péngyou duì wǒmende jiēdài hěn mǎnyì (*the foreign guests were very satisfied with their treatment*)

满月 mǎnyuè	1. *full moon*
	2. (of newborn babies) *first full month of age*
满足 mǎnzú	1. *content; satisfied,* often used with 于 yú (*with; about*);
	满足现状 mǎnzú xiànzhuàng (*content with the status*
	quo); 满足于已取得的成绩 mánzú yú yǐ qǔdé de chéngji
	(*satisfied with the achievement already made*)
	2. *satisfy; meet the needs of:* 满足学生的要求 mǎnzú
	xuésheng de yāoqiú (*meet the needs of the students*)
满座 mǎnzuò	*full house; house packed*

慢 màn

slow: 汽车开得很慢 qìchē kāi de hěn màn (*the car is driving very slowly*);
你的表慢了 nǐde biǎo màn le (*your watch is slow*)

慢车 mànchē	*local train* (one that makes frequent stops). Cl: 次 cì;
	趟 tàng
慢镜头 mànjìngtóu	(of movies) *slow motion*
慢慢 mànmàn	*slowly; gradually;* 慢慢吃, 不要急 mànmàn chī, búyào jí
	(*eat slowly; there is no hurry*); 我慢慢地学会了开车 wǒ
	mànmànde xuéhuì le kāichē (*I gradually learned to drive*)
慢性 mànxìng	*chronic:* 慢性病 mànxìngbìng (*chronic disease*)
慢性子 mànxìngzi	*phlegmatic temperament; slowpoke*
慢走 mànzǒu	*take care* (used in seeing a visitor off)

忙 máng

busy: 学生们很忙 xuéshengmen hěn máng (*the students are very busy*)

Also appears in the following words: 帮忙 bāngmáng (*help*); 匆忙 cōngmáng (*in a hurry*); 赶忙 gǎnmáng (*make haste*)

忙碌 mánglù	*busy; bustle about*
忙乱 mángluàn	*be in a rush and a muddle*
忙人 mángrén	*busy person.* Cl: 位 wèi; 个 gè

没 méi

Negative word for the verb 有 yǒu (*have*). In this collocation, 有 yǒu is pronounced in the neutral tone: 我没有汽车 wǒ méi you qìchē (*I don't have a car*); 中国城没有日本餐馆 Zhōngguóchéng méi you Rìběn cānguǎn (*there *are no Japanese restaurants in Chinatown)*. When 没 méi is used, 有 yǒu can be left out in spoken language: 他没哥哥 tā méi gēge (*he does not have an older brother*); 家里没人 jiā li méi rén (*there is no one home*).

没法子 **méi fǎzi**	*can't do anything about; have no recourse*
没关系 **méi guānxi**	*it doesn't matter*, often used as a response to 对不起 duìbuqǐ (*sorry*)
没什么 **méi shénme**	*it doesn't matter; you are welcome*, often used as a response to 对不起 duìbuqǐ (*sorry*) or 谢谢 xièxie (*thank you*)
没事儿 **méi shìr**	1. *have nothing to do; be free*
	2. *it's all right; doesn't matter*
没有 **méiyou**	1. negative form of the perfect-aspect verb: 昨天没有下雨 zuótiān méiyou xiàyǔ (*it didn't rain yesterday*); 我们还没有吃晚饭 wǒmen hái méiyou chī wǎnfàn (*we have not had our dinner yet*)
	2. negative form of the progressive-aspect verb: 门没有开着 mén méiyou kāi zhe (*the door is not open*); 学生们没有在看电视 xuéshēngmen méiyou zài kàn diànshì (*the students are not watching TV*)
	3. *not as ... as*: 南京没有北京大 Nánjīng méiyou Běijīng dà (*Nanjing is not as big as Beijing*). 有 yǒu can be left out in spoken language.

每 měi

1. *each; every*, requiring the use of a classifier when used to quantify a noun: 每个人 měi ge rén (*each person*); 每家餐馆 měi jiā cānguǎn (*every restaurant*). 都 dōu is usu. used with 每 měi to emphasize inclusiveness: 我们每天上午都有中文课 wǒmen měitiān shàngwǔ dōu yǒu Zhōngwén kè (*we have a Chinese class every morning*).

2. *on each occasion; whenever*, usu. used with 到 dào: 每到周末，我们都会去爬山 měidào zhōumo, wǒmen dōu huì qù pá shān (*we would go mountain climbing on every weekend*)

每当 **měidāng**	*whenever; every time*: 每当我有困难，他都会帮助我 měidāng wǒ yǒu kùnnan, tā dōu huì bāngzhù wǒ (*whenever I have difficulty, he would help me*)
每隔 **měigé**	*every other*: 每隔一天 měigé yì tiān (*every other day*)

美 měi

1. *pretty*; *beautiful*: 美景 měijǐng (*beautiful scenery*); 美女 měinǚ (*beautiful woman*; *beauty*)

2. *good*; *praiseworthy*: 美文 měiwén (*beautifully written essay*); 美食 měishí (*gourmet food*)

美感	měigǎn	*aesthetic perception*
美观	měiguān	*artistic*; (of objects) *attractive*
美国	Měiguó	*the United States*
美好	měihǎo	*happy*; *glorious*: 美好的生活 měihǎode shēnghuo (*happy life*)
美化	měihuà	*beautify*
美丽	měilì	*beautiful*
美梦	měimèng	*rosy dream*
美妙	měimiào	*wonderful*; *splendid*
美名	měimíng	*good name*; *good reputation*
美容	měiróng	*cosmetology*: 美容院 měiróngyuàn (*beauty parlor*)
美术	měishù	*fine arts*: 美术馆 měishùguǎn (*art gallery*)
美元	měiyuán	*U.S. dollars*
美洲	Měizhōu	*Americas*

们 men

Pronounced in the neutral tone. Suffix used after personal pronouns and human nouns to indicate the plural: 我们 wǒmen (*we*), 你们 nǐmen (*you*), 他们 tāmen (*they*), 老师们 lǎoshīmen (*teachers*). 们 men cannot be used after non-human nouns or inanimate nouns. Additionally, 们 men cannot be used when there is a specifying numeral preceding the noun or when the subject is already plural: 三个老师 sān ge lǎoshī (*three teachers*) and 他们是老师 tāmen shì lǎoshī (*they are teachers*). It is ungrammatical to say, 三个老师们 sān ge lǎoshīmen (*three teachers*) and 他们是老师们 tāmen shì lǎoshīmen (*they are teachers*).

门 mén

1. *door*; *gate*: 前门 qiánmén (*front gate*); 店门 diànmén (*store door*)

2. *way to do something*; *knack*: 我是新手，还没有入门 wǒ shì xīnshǒu, hái méiyou rùmén (*I'm a novice, I have not learned the ropes*)

Also appears in the following words: 部门 bùmén (*department*); 后门 hòumén (*back door*); 热门 rèmén (*popular; in vogue*); 油门 yóumén (*gas pedal*)

门口	ménkǒu	*doorway; entrance*
门类	ménlèi	*category; class*
门面	ménmiàn	*storefront*
门票	ménpiào	*admission ticket.* Cl: 张 zhāng
门市	ménshì	*retail sales*: 门市部 ménshìbù (*retail department; factory outlet*)
门卫	ménwèi	*guard at the gate.* Cl: 个 gè; 名 míng
门诊	ménzhěn	*outpatient service* (in a hospital)

米 mǐ

1. (raw) *rice*

2. *shelled seed*; *husked seed*: 花生米 huāshēngmǐ (*peanut seed*). Cl: 颗 kē; 粒 lì

3. (measure) *meter*

米饭	mǐfàn	(cooked) *rice*
米糕	mǐgāo	*rice cake*
米酒	mǐjiǔ	*rice wine, saké*
米色	mǐsè	*cream-colored*

面 miàn

1. *face*, used in formal language or set expressions

2. *surface*: 水面 shuǐmiàn (*surface of the water*); 路面 lùmiàn (*road surface*)

3. *side; aspect*: 四面 sì miàn (*all sides*)

4. *extent; range*: 他的知识面很广 tāde zhīshimiàn hěn guǎng (*he has a wide range of knowledge*)

5. used as a suffix for direction words and often pronounced in the neutral tone: 前面 qiánmian (*front*); 后面 hòumian (*back*); 左面 zuǒmiàn (*left*); 右面 yòumiàn (*right*)

6. classifier, used for certain objects that either are flat or can unfold: 六面旗子 liù miàn qízi (*six flags*); 三面镜子 sān miàn jìngzi (*three mirrors*)

7. *flour*

8. *powder*: 胡椒面 hújiāo miàn (*ground pepper*)

9. *noodles*

Also appears in the following words: 背面 bèimiàn (*backside*); 表面 biǎomiàn (*surface; appearance*); 当面 dāngmiàn (*face to face; personally*); 见面 jiànmiàn (*meet*); 局面 júmiàn (*situation*); 全面 quánmiàn (*all-round*); 书面 shūmiàn (*in writing*)

面包	miànbāo	*bread.* Cl: 个 gè; 片 piàn; 块 kuài
面对	miànduì	*confront; face* (v.): 面对危险 miànduì wēixiǎn (*face danger*)
面对面	miàn duì miàn	*face to face*
面粉	miànfěn	*flour.* Cl: 袋 dài
面积	miànji	(*of measurement*) *area*
面具	miànjù	*mask.* Cl: 副 fù
面孔	miànkǒng	*face* (n.)
面临	miànlín	*faced with*
面貌	miànmào	*appearance; look*
面洽	miànqià	*discuss business with someone face to face*
面前	miànqián	*in the face of; in front of; ahead*: 我们面前有很多困难 wǒmen miànqián yǒu hěn duō kùnnan (*there are many difficulties ahead of us*)
面色	miànsè	*facial expression*
面生	miànshēng	*look unfamiliar*
面熟	miànshú	*look familiar*
面谈	miàntán	*talk to sb. face to face*
面条	miàntiáo	*noodles*
面向	miànxiàng	*face* (v.)
面子	miànzi	*reputation; face*: 丢面子 diū miànzi (*lose face*)

民 mín

1. *people; folk*

2. *civilian*: 军民关系 jūnmín guānxi (*relationship between the military and civilians*); 民用品 mínyòngpǐn (*products for civilian use*)

Also appears in the following words: 公民 gōngmín (*citizen*); 居民 jūmín (*resident*); 难民 nànmín (*refugee*); 移民 yímín (*immigrant*)

民兵	mínbīng	*militia.* Cl: 位 wèi; 名 míng; 个 gè
民法	mínfǎ	*civil law*
民歌	míngē	*folk song.* Cl: 首 shǒu
民间	mínjiān	*popular; folk*: 民间故事 mínjiān gùshì (*folktale*); 民间艺术 mínjiān yìshù (*folk art*)
民权	mínquán	*civil rights*
民事	mínshì	*civil-law related*: 民事诉讼 mínshì sùsòng (*civil lawsuit*)

民俗	mínsú	folkways; custom
民意	mínyì	public opinion: 民意测验 mínyì cèyàn (public opinion poll)
民用	mínyòng	for civilian use
民主	mínzhǔ	democracy; democratic
民族	mínzú	nation; nationality

明 míng

1. *bright*; *light*: 明月光 míng yuèguāng (*bright moonlight*)

2. *clear*; *clearly*: 情况不明 qíngkuàng bù míng (*the situation is not clear*); 请明说 qǐng míng shuō (*please state it clearly*)

3. *understand*: 不明真相 bù míng zhēnxiàng (*be ignorant of facts*)

Also appears in the following words: 表明 biǎomíng (*indicate*); 聪明 cōngming (*smart*; *intelligent*); 发明 fāmíng (*invent*); 简明 jiǎnmíng (*concise*); 声明 shēngmíng (*make a statement*; *statement*); 说明 shuōmíng (*explain*); 透明 tòumíng (*transparent*); 证明 zhèngmíng (*prove*)

明白	míngbai	**1.** *clear*; *plain*
		2. *explicit*; *frank*
		3. *understand*
明处	míngchù	in the open
明亮	míngliàng	bright; well-lit
明明	míngmíng	obviously, used in a contrastive sentence: 他明明知道这是不对的，可还是做了 tā míngmíng zhīdao zhè shì bú duì de, kě háishì zuò le (*he obviously knew that this was a wrong thing to do, but he still did it*)
明年	míngnián	next year
明确	míngquè	clear; definite; unequivocal
明天	míngtiān	tomorrow
明显	míngxiǎn	clear; obvious
明星	míngxīng	(movie, sports, etc.) star. Cl: 个 gè; 位 wèi
明信片	míngxìnpiàn	postcard. Cl: 张 zhāng

名 míng

1. *name*, often taking the form of 名字 míngzi: 你叫什么名字 nǐ jiào shénme míngzi (*what is your name?*)

2. *famous*; *well-known*: 名演员 míng yǎnyuán (*famous actor*); 名店 míng diàn (*famous store*)

Also appears in the following words: 报名 bàomíng (*sign up*; *register*); 笔名 bǐ míng (*pen name*; *pseudonym*); 出名 chūmíng (*become famous*); 签名 qiānmíng (*sign*; *autograph*); 姓名 xìngmíng (*full name*); 有名 yǒumíng (*famous*); 著名 zhùmíng (*renowned*)

名称	míngchēng	*name* (of an object or a place)
名词	míngcí	*noun*
名次	míngcì	*place* (in a competition or name list)
名单	míngdān	*name list*. Cl: 张 zhāng; 份 fèn
名额	míng'é	*allocation or quota of people*
名利	mínglì	*fame and gain*
名牌	míngpái	*brand name*
名片	míngpiàn	*business card*. Cl: 张 zhāng
名气	míngqì	*reputation*; *fame*
名人	míngrén	*celebrity*. Cl: 位 wèi
名声	míngshēng	*reputation*
名胜	míngshèng	*place of interest*. Cl: 处 chù
名望	míngwàng	*reputation*; *fame*
名义	míngyì	*name*: 以他的名义 yǐ tāde míngyì (*in his name*); 这台电脑名义上是公司的, 但其实是我的 zhè tái diànnǎo míngyì shang shì gōngsī de, dàn qíshí shì wǒde (*this computer belongs to the company only in name, it is actually mine*)
名誉	míngyù	*honorary*: 名誉教授 míngyù jiàoshòu (*honorary professor*)
名字	míngzi	*name*; *given name*

母 mǔ

1. *mother*, usu. taking the disyllabic form of 母亲 mǔqin, which is primarily used as a term of reference as opposed to 妈妈 māma, which is used as a term of address as well as a term of reference

2. *one's female elders*: 伯母 bómǔ (*father's older brother's wife*); 姑母 gūmǔ (*father's brother's wife*); 姨母 yímǔ (*mother's married sister*); 祖母 zǔmǔ (*father's mother*; *grandmother*); 继母 jìmǔ (*stepmother*)

3. *female*, used for animals: 母牛 mǔniú (*cow*); 母鸡 mǔjī (*hen*)

母爱	mǔ'ài	*maternal love*
母老虎	mǔláohǔ	1. *tigress*. Cl: 只 zhī; 头 tóu
		2. *vixen*; *shrew*.
母亲	mǔqin	*mother*. Cl: 个 gè; 位 wèi
母校	mǔxiào	*alma mater*
母语	mǔyǔ	*one's native language*

拿 ná

1. *fetch*; *get*; *go and get*: 谁去拿报纸 shuí qù ná bàozhǐ (*who is going to get the newspaper?*)

2. *hold, carry*: 拿在手里 ná zài shǒu lǐ (*hold in the hand*); 拿来 ná lái (*bring*); 拿去 ná qù (*take*)

3. *use sth. to*, used in conjunction with 做 zuò or 当 dāng: 拿中文做例子 ná Zhōngwén zuò lìzi (*use Chinese as an example*); 他拿我当孩子 tā ná wǒ dāng háizi (*he treats me like a child*)

拿不出手 **ná bù chū shǒu**	*not presentable*: 我的作品拿不出手 wǒde zuòpǐn ná bù chū shǒu (*my works are not presentable*)
拿不准 **ná bù zhǔn**	*not sure*: 我拿不准这个词的意思 wǒ ná bù zhǔn zhè ge cí de yìsi (*I'm not sure about the meaning of the word*)
拿手 **náshǒu**	*good at*: 跳水他很拿手 tiàoshuǐ tā hěn náshǒu (*he is very good at diving*); 拿手好戏 náshǒu hǎoxì (*a game or trick one is good at*)
拿主意 **ná zhǔyì**	*make up one's mind*; *make a decision*

哪 nǎ

which, requiring the use of a classifier when modifying a noun: 哪本书 nǎ běn shū (*which book?*); 哪个人 nǎ ge rén (*which person?*)

哪里 **nǎlǐ**	1. *what place*; *where*, used interchangeably with 哪儿 nǎr: 你在哪里吃中饭 nǐ zài nǎlǐ chī zhōngfàn (*where are you going to eat lunch?*) 2. used to respond to a compliment: **A:** 你帮了我很多忙 nǐ bāng le wǒ hěn duō máng (*you have helped me a lot*) **B:** 哪里 nǎlǐ (*don't mention it*)
哪怕 **nǎpà**	*even*; *even if*; *no matter how*, used in conjunction with 也 yě, 都 dōu or 还 hái: 哪怕再晚，我也要回家 nǎpà zài wǎn, wǒ yě yào huí jiā (*no matter how late, I must go home*)
哪儿 **nǎr**	*what place*; *where*: 厕所在哪儿 cèsuǒ zài nǎr (*where is the bathroom?*)
哪些 **nǎxiē**	*which*, used with a plural reference: 哪些菜是你太太做的 nǎxiē cài shì nǐ tàitai zuò de (*which are the dishes your wife cooked?*); 你看过哪些美国电影 nǐ kàn guo nǎxiē Měiguó diànyǐng (*which American movies have you seen?*)

那 nà

1. *that.* When defining a noun, it usu. requires a classifier: 那个人 nà ge rén (*that person*); 那本书 nà běn shū (*that book*)

2. used at the beginning of a sentence to refer to the previous sentence:

A: 夏天去欧洲的飞机票很贵 xiàtiān qù Ōuzhōu de fēijīpiào hěn guì (*plane tickets are very expensive in the summer for traveling to Europe*)

B: 那我就不去了 nà wǒ jiù bú qù le (*in that case, I won't go there*).

那 nà in this sense can also be expressed as 那么 nàme.

那边 **nàbiān**	*that side*; *over there*
那里 **nàlǐ**	*that place*; *there*, interchangeable with 那儿 nàr
那么 **nàme**	1. *in that event,* often used in conversations to begin a response, alternative with #2 above 2. *so*; *such*; *like that*: 去年的冬天那么冷 qùnián de dōngtiān nàme lěng (*it was so cold last winter*). Both 这么 zhème and 那么 nàme express the same meaning, but 这么 zhème refers to what is close by the speaker and 那么 nàme refers to what is away from the speaker, both temporally and spatially.
那儿 **nàr**	*that place*; *there*, interchangeable with 那里 nàlǐ
那时 **nàshí**	*at that time*; *then*
那些 **nàxiē**	*those*
那样 **nàyàng**	*so*; *such*; *in that event*

难 nán

1. *difficult*; *hard*: 家庭作业很难 jiātíng zuòyè hěn nán (*the homework is very difficult*); 他的口音很难懂 tāde kǒuyīn hěn nán dǒng (*his accent is very hard to understand*)

2. *bad*; *unpleasant*: 难喝 nánhē (*unpleasant to drink*); 难看 nánkàn (*ugly*; *unpleasant to look at*)

难倒 **nándǎo**	*beat*; *baffle*: 这个字难不倒我 zhè ge zì nán bù dǎo wǒ (*this character can't beat me*)
难道 **nándào**	used in rhetorical question: 你难道不知道吗 nǐ nándào bù zhīdao ma (*don't you know it?*)
难得 **nándé**	*rare*; *rarely*: 难得的好天 nándéde hǎotiān (*a rare sunny day*); 难得有空 nándé yǒu kòng (*rarely have free time*)
难点 **nándiǎn**	*difficult point*
难怪 **nánguài**	*no wonder*
难关 **nánguān**	*difficult time*; *barrier*; *crisis.* Cl: 道 dào

难过 nánguò	upset; sad
难看 nánkàn	ugly
难免 nánmiǎn	unavoidable: 难免不犯错误 nánmiǎn bú fàn cuòwù (it is unavoidable not to make mistakes)
难受 nánshòu	feel sick; feel bad
难说 nánshuō	hard to say
难题 nántí	difficult problem. Cl: 道 dào
难听 nántīng	unpleasant to listen to
难忘 nánwàng	memorable; unforgettable
难为情 nánwéiqíng	ashamed; embarrassed; shy
难以 nányǐ	difficult to: 难以想象 nányǐ xiǎngxiàng (difficult to imagine)

南 nán

south; southern: 南部 nánbù (southern part); 南边 nánbian (south side). In expressing southeast and southwest, Chinese places east and west first: 东南 dōngnán (southeast) and 西南 xīnán (southwest).

南方 nánfāng	southern part of a country: 南方人 nánfāngrén (southerner)
南瓜 nánguā	pumpkin
南极 nánjí	the South Pole

男 nán

male; man: 男厕所 náncèsuǒ (men's bathroom); 男衬衫 nánchènshān (men's shirt); 男演员 nányǎnyuán (male actor)

男孩 nánhái	boy
男朋友 nánpéngyou	boyfriend
男人 nánrén	man
男生 nánshēng	schoolboy; male student. Cl: 位 wèi; 名 míng
男士 nánshì	man; gentleman. Cl: 位 wèi; 名 míng
男性 nánxìng	male: 男性朋友 nánxìng péngyou (male friend)
男子 nánzǐ	man. Cl: 个 gè; 位 wèi; 名 míng

呢 ne

sentence-final particle.

1. *what about …*; *how about …*, used to avoid repeating a question previously asked:

> **A:** 你好吗 nǐ hǎo ma (*how are you?*)
> **B:** 我很好, 你呢 wǒ hěn hǎo, nǐ ne (*I'm fine, and you?*)

2. indicating a continued state or action, often used in conjunction with 正 zhèng, 正在 zhèng zài, 在 zài or 着 zhe: 他看书呢 tā kàn shū ne; 他正在看书呢 tā zhèng zài kàn shū ne; 他正看书呢 tā zhèng kàn shū ne; 他看着书呢 tā kàn zhe shū ne (*he is reading*)

3. *speaking of*, used in contrastive or enumerating sentences to mark the topic: 唱歌呢, 我不会; 跳舞呢, 我还可以 chànggē ne, wǒ bú huì; tiàowǔ ne, wǒ hái kěyǐ (*speaking of singing, I'm not good, but in terms of dancing, I can do it*)

4. *where*: 我的钢笔呢 wǒde gāngbǐ ne (*where is my pen?*)

内 nèi

inside; *inner*; *within*; *internal*: used after a noun, as the word is considered as a noun in Chinese: 室内 shìnèi (*indoors*); 国内 guónèi (*within the country*; *domestic*); 一星期内 yì xīngqī nèi (*within a week*)

内部 **nèibù**	*inside*; *internal*: 内部事务 nèibù shìwù (*internal affairs*); 内部使用 nèibù shǐyòng (*for internal use*)
内地 **nèidì**	(of a country) *the interior*
内阁 **nèigé**	(of government) *cabinet*
内行 **nèiháng**	*expert*
内科 **nèikē**	*department of internal medicine*
内伤 **nèishāng**	*internal injury*
内务 **nèiwù**	*internal affairs*
内在 **nèizài**	*inherent*; *intrinsic*; *internal*: 内在原因 nèizài yuányīn (*internal cause*)
内战 **nèizhàn**	*civil war*. Cl: 场 chǎng; 次 cì
内政 **nèizhèng**	(of a country) *domestic affairs*; *internal affairs*

能 néng

1. *can*; *be able to*; *be capable of*: 我们都能游泳 wǒmen dōu néng yóuyǒng (*all of us can swim*)

2. *good at*: 能唱 néng chàng (*good at singing*); 能写 néng xiě (*good at writing*)

3. *possible*: 癌症能治好吗 áizhèng néng zhì hǎo ma (*can cancer be cured?*)

4. *energy*: 太阳能 tàiyangnéng (*solar energy*)

Also appears in the following words: **才能** cáinéng (*talent*); **功能** gōngnéng (*function*); **万能** wànnéng (*omnipotent*); **无能** wúnéng (*inability*); **性能** xìngnéng (*performance*; *property*)

能干 nénggàn	*capable*; *competent*: 他太太很能干 tā tàitai hěn nénggàn (*his wife is very talented*)
能够 nénggòu	*be able to*; *be capable of*, often used interchangeably with 能 néng
能力 nénglì	*ability*; *capability*
能人 néngrén	*able person*. Cl: 个 gè; 位 wèi

你 nǐ

you. It can be used in the possessive sense when defining a place: 你店 nǐ diàn (*your store*); 你校 nǐ xiào (*your school*); 你行 nǐ háng (*your bank*). In this usage, the possessive 的 de is usu. left out and the noun takes the abbreviated form: 商店 shāngdiàn—店 diàn (*store*); 学校 xuéxiào—校 xiào (*school*); 银行 yínháng—行 háng (*bank*).

你的 nǐde	*your*, 的 de is often left out when followed by words for family members, intimate people or places
你们 nǐmen	*you* (plural)
你们的 nǐmende	*your* (plural)

年 nián

year: 今年 jīnnián (*this year*); 明年 míngnián (*next year*); 去年 qùnián (*last year*). 年 nián by itself is not used to indicate a person's age. 岁 suì should be used instead: 我今年三十岁 wǒ jīnnián sānshí suì (*I'm thirty years old this year*)

年代 niándài	(of history) *times*, *age*; *decade*: 50年代 (*the fifties*)
年会 niánhuì	*annual meeting*. Cl: 次 cì; 届 jiè
年级 niánjí	*grade* (in a school). Cl: 个 gè
年纪 niánjì	(a person's) *age*
年龄 niánlíng	(a person's) *age*
年轻 niánqīng	*young*: 年轻人 niánqīngrén (*young people*)

您 nín

you, polite form of the second-person pronoun singular

牛 niú

ox; cattle; cow: 公牛 gōngniú (*bull*); 母牛 mǔniú (*cow*)

牛犊 niúdú	*calf.* Cl: 头 tóu
牛粪 niúfèn	*cow dung*
牛马 niúmǎ	*beasts of burden*, often used figuratively to refer to performing heavy work or working as a slave: 干牛马活 gàn niúmǎ huó (*perform backbreaking work*). 牛 niú and 马 mǎ can be separated in the expression 做牛做马 zuò niú zuò mǎ (*work as a slave*).
牛奶 niúnǎi	*milk*
牛排 niúpái	*beefsteak*
牛棚 niúpéng	*cowshed*
牛皮 niúpí	1. *cowhide.* Cl: 张 zhāng 2. *bragging:* 吹牛皮 chuī niúpí (*brag*)
牛脾气 niúpíqì	*stubborn; obstinate*
牛肉 niúròu	*beef*
牛仔裤 niúzǎikù	*jeans.* Cl: 条 tiáo

农 nóng

1. *agriculture; farming;* often taking of the form of 农业 nóngyè

2. *peasant; farmer,* usu. taking the form of 农民 nóngmín

农场 nóngchǎng	*farm.* Cl: 个 gè; 家 jiā
农村 nóngcūn	*countryside*
农活 nónghuó	*farm work*
农历 nónglì	*the lunar calendar*
农民 nóngmín	*peasant; farmer.* Cl: 个 gè; 位 wèi; 户 hù
农田 nóngtián	*farmland; fields.* Cl: 块 kuài
农业 nóngyè	*agriculture; farming*
农作物 nóngzuòwù	*crops.* Cl: 类 lèi; 种 zhǒng

女 nǚ

1. *female*: 女演员 nǚ yǎnyuán (*actress*); 女学生 nǚ xuésheng (*girl student*)

2. *daughter*, used in set expressions: 儿女 érnǚ (*sons and daughters*); 母女 mǔnǚ (*mother and daughter*)

Also appears in the following words: 处女 chǔnǚ (*virgin*); 妇女 fùnǚ (*woman*); 妓女 jìnǚ (*prostitute*); 美女 měinǚ (*belle; beauty*); 子女 zǐnǚ (*children; sons and daughters*)

女厕所 **nǚcèsuǒ**	*ladies' room*
女儿 **nǚ'ér**	*daughter*
女方 **nǚfāng**	*the bride's side*
女孩 **nǚhái**	*girl*
女皇 **nǚhuáng**	*queen; empress.* Cl: 位 wèi
女朋友 **nǚpéngyou**	*girlfriend*
女人 **nǚrén**	*woman.* Cl: 个 gè
女士 **nǚshì**	*lady; madam.* Cl: 位 wèi
女王 **nǚwáng**	*queen.* Cl: 位 wèi
女婿 **nǚxu**	*son-in-law.* Cl: 个 gè; 位 wèi
女子 **nǚzǐ**	*woman.* Cl: 个 gè; 位 wèi

爬 pá

1. *climb; scale*: 爬山 pá shān (*climb a mountain*); 爬墙 pá qiáng (*scale the wall*)

2. *crawl; creep*: 在地上爬 zài dì shang pá (*crawl on the floor*)

怕 pà

1. *be afraid of; be scared of; fear; dread*: 怕冷 pà lěng (*be afraid of cold weather*); 怕鬼怪 pà guǐguài (*be scared of monsters*); 怕上班 pà shàngbān (*dread of going to work*)

2. *be afraid that; for fear that*: 我怕你忙，所以没有请你帮忙 wǒ pà nǐ máng, suǒyǐ méiyou qǐng nǐ bāngmáng (*I was afraid that you were busy, so I didn't ask you for help*); 她怕信会丢，所以让我带给你 tā pà xìn huì diū, suǒyǐ ràng wǒ dài gěi nǐ (*for fear that the letter might get lost, she asked me to hand it to you*)

Also appears in the following words: 害怕 hàipà (*be afraid*); 可怕 kěpà (*scary*); 恐怕 kǒngpà (*I'm afraid*)

怕人 **pàrén**	1. *shy; timid*: 这儿的鸽子不怕人 zhèr de gēzi bú pàrén (*the pigeons here are not afraid of people*)
	2. *scary*: 那部电影很怕人 nà bù diànyǐng hěn pàrén (*that movie is very scary*)
怕事 **pàshì**	*be afraid of being involved*
怕羞 **pàxiū**	*shy; bashful*

盘 pán

1. *plate; tray; dish*: 茶盘 chápán (*tea tray*); 果盘 guǒpán (*fruit tray*). Cl: 只 zhī; 个 gè

2. *object shaped like or used as a plate or tray*: 硬盘 yìngpán (*hard disk*); 光盘 guāngpán (*CD*). Cl: 张 zhāng; 托盘 tuōpán (*tray*); 棋盘 qípán (*chessboard*). Cl: 副 fù; 张 zhāng

3. *check; examine; interrogate*, often used in various disyllabic forms

Also appears in the following words: 地盘 dìpán (*turf*); 全盘 quánpán (*overall; wholesale*); 算盘 suànpán (*abacus*); 方向盘 fāngxiàngpán (*steering wheel*)

盘查 **pánchá**	*examine thoroughly; question; interrogate and examine*
盘点 **pándiǎn**	*make an inventory of*
盘问 **pánwèn**	*cross-examine; interrogate*
盘子 **pánzi**	*dish; plate.* Cl: 个 gè

旁 páng

1. *side; next to*: 房子旁 fángzi páng (*next to the house*); 路旁 lùpáng (*roadside*); 旁门 pángmén (*side door*)

2. *other*: 旁人 pángrén (*other people*); 旁的学校 pángde xuéxiào (*other schools*)

| 旁边 **pángbiān** | *side; next to*: used after a noun as it is considered as a noun in Chinese: 银行在餐馆的旁边 yínháng zài cānguǎn de pángbiān (*the bank is next to the restaurant*) |
| 旁观 **pángguān** | *look on*: 旁观者 pángguānzhě (*onlooker; bystander*) |

跑 pǎo

1. *run*

2. *flee; escape*: 犯人跑了 fànrén pǎo le (*the prisoner escaped*)

3. *go all over the place*; *visit*: 上个月我跑了好几个城市 shàng ge yuè wǒ pǎo le hǎo jǐ ge chéngshì (*I visited quite a few cities last month*); 他跑了很多商店，但没有买到合适的礼物 tā pǎo le hěn duō shāngdiàn, dàn méiyou mǎi dào héshìde lǐwù (*he went to many stores but didn't find any suitable presents*)

4. *away*, used as a verb complement: 风把纸吹跑了 fēng bǎ zhǐ chuī pǎo le (*the wind blew the paper away*); 小偷被警察吓跑了 xiǎotōu bèi jǐngchá xià pǎo le (*the thieves were frightened away by the police*)

Also appears in the following words: 长跑 chángpǎo (*long-distance running*); 短跑 duǎnpǎo (*sprint*); 赛跑 sàipǎo (*running race*)

跑步	pǎobù	*run* (as an exercise)
跑车	pǎochē	*racing bicycle*. Cl: 辆 liàng
跑道	pǎodào	*race track*. Cl: 条 tiáo
跑马	pǎomǎ	*horse race*: 跑马场 pǎomǎchǎng (*race course*)
跑鞋	pǎoxié	*running shoes*; *athletic shoes*. Cl: 双 shuāng; 只 zhī

皮 pí

1. *skin*; *hide*; *leather*: 皮包 píbāo (*leather bag*; *briefcase*); 皮衣 píyī (*fur coat*); 牛皮 niúpí (*oxhide*; *cowhide*); 香蕉皮 xiāngjiāopí (*banana skin*)

2. *cover*; *wrapper*: 书皮儿 shūpír (*book cover*); 饺子皮儿 jiǎozipír (*dumpling wrapper*)

皮带	pídài	*strap*; *leather belt*. Cl: 条 tiáo; 根 gēn
皮肤	pífū	*skin*: 皮肤病 pífūbìng (*skin disease*)
皮革	pígé	*leather*; *hide*
皮匠	píjiang	*cobbler*; *shoemaker*. Cl: 个 gè; 位 wèi
皮鞋	píxié	*leather shoes*. Cl: 只 zhī; 双 shuāng

片 piàn

1. *small and thin objects*; *piece*; *slice*; *flake*: 麦片 màipiàn (*cereal*); 肉片 ròupiàn (*slices of meat*); 药片 yàopiàn (*pill*); 名片 míngpiàn (*business card*)

2. *classifier*: 一片草地 yí piàn cǎodì (*a stretch of grassland*); 一片雨水 yí piàn yǔshuǐ (*an expanse of rain water*)

Also appears in the following words: 唱片 chàngpiàn (*phonograph record*); 刀片 dāopiàn (*blade*); 图片 túpiàn (*picture*); 影片 yǐngpiàn (*film*); 照片 zhàopiàn (*photograph*)

片段 piànduàn	(of novels, movies, plays, etc.) *episode; passage; scene*
片刻 piànkè	*a short time*: 请等片刻 qǐng děng piànkè (*please wait a little bit*)
片面 piànmiàn	*unilateral; one-sided; prejudiced*: 片面理解 piànmiàn lǐjiě (*prejudiced understanding*)

票 piào

1. *ticket*: 火车票 huǒchēpiào (*train ticket*); 飞机票 fēijīpiào (*plane ticket*); 电影票 diànyǐngpiào (*movie ticket*)

2. *ballot*: 投票 tóupiào (*cast a ballot; vote*)

Also appears in the following words: **彩票** cǎipiào (*lottery*); **传票** chuánpiào (*summons*); **发票** fāpiào (*invoice*); **股票** gǔpiào (*stock*); **门票** ménpiào (*admission ticket*); **邮票** yóupiào (*stamp*); **支票** zhīpiào (*check; cheque*)

票房 piàofáng	*box office; ticket office*
票价 piàojià	*ticket price; admission fee*
票箱 piàoxiāng	*ballot box*
票子 piàozi	*bank note; paper money; bill*. Cl: 张 zhāng

品 pǐn

1. *article; product*: 产品 chǎnpǐn (*product*); 仿制品 fǎngzhìpǐn (*imitation; replica*); 纺织品 fǎngzhīpǐn (*textile products*); 化妆品 huàzhuāngpǐn (*cosmetics*); 纪念品 jìniànpǐn (*souvenir*); 奖品 jiǎngpǐn (*prize; trophy*); 食品 shípǐn (*food; foodstuff*); 药品 yàopǐn (*medicine; drugstuff*)

2. *character; quality*

3. *taste; sample; savor*: 品茶 pǐnchá (*taste the tea*)

Also appears in the following words: **毒品** dúpǐn (*narcotics*); **礼品** lǐpǐn (*gift*); **商品** shāngpǐn (*goods*); **样品** yàngpǐn (*sample*); **作品** zuòpǐn (*works*)

品德 pǐndé	*moral character; morality*
品格 pǐngé	*character and morals*
品牌 pǐnpái	*brand name*. Cl: 个 gè; 种 zhǒng
品味 pǐnwèi	*taste*: 她的品味很好 tāde pǐnwèi hěn hǎo (*she has good taste*)
品质 pǐnzhì	*character; quality*
品种 pǐnzhǒng	*breed; strain; variety*. Cl: 个 gè

平 píng

1. *level*; *plane*; *flat*: 路不平 lù bù píng (*the road is bumpy*)

2. *peaceful*; *calm*, often taking the form of 平静 píngjìng

3. (of a competition or contest) *even*; *draw*: 这两个队打平了 zhè liǎng ge duì dǎ píng le (*these two teams were in a draw*); 比分是十五平 bǐfēn shì shíwǔ píng (*the score is fifteen all*)

Also appears in the following words: 公平 gōngpíng (*fair*); 和平 hépíng (*peace*); 水平 shuǐpíng (*level*)

平安 píng'ān	*safe*; *well*: 祝你一路平安 zhù nǐ yí lù píng'ān (*wish you a pleasant journey*)
平常 píngcháng	**1.** *ordinary*; *common*: 这种事在中国很平常 zhè zhǒng shì zài Zhōngguó hěn píngcháng (*such things are commonplace in China*) **2.** *generally*; *usually*: 我平常不在家吃中饭 wǒ píngcháng bú zài jiā chī zhōngfàn (*I usually don't eat lunch at home*)
平等 píngděng	(of rights) *equal*; *equality*: 男女平等 nán nǚ píngděng (*equality between men and women*); 不平等的待遇 bù píngděngde dàiyù (*unequal treatment*)
平衡 pínghéng	*balance* (v. and n.)
平静 píngjìng	*calm*; *peaceful*
平均 píngjūn	**1.** *average*; *on the average*: 平均分数 píngjūn fēnshù (*average score*); 每班平均有三十个学生 měi bān píngjūn yǒu sānshí ge xuéshēng (*each class has an average of 30 students*) **2.** *equally*: 平均分配 píngjūn fēnpèi (*divide equally*)
平时 píngshí	(of time) *ordinarily*; *regularly*: 他平时不喝酒 tā píngshí bù hē jiǔ (*he ordinarily does not drink*)

破 pò

1. *broken*; *damaged*; *torn*; *worn out*: 头破了 tóu pò le (*got a cut on the head*); 瓶子破了 píngzi pò le (*the bottle was broken*)

2. *break* (a record): 破了纪录 pò le jìlù (*broke a record*)

3. *poor*; *lousy*; *shabby*: 破电影 pò diànyǐng (*bad movie*)

破产 pòchǎn	*go bankrupt*
破费 pòfèi	*spend a lot of money*, used for sb. who spends money on you: 不好意思, 让你破费了 bùhǎoyìsī, ràng nǐ pòfèi le

(*sorry to have caused you to spend money*)

破格 pògé	break a rule; make an exception: 破格提拔 (*break a precedence to promote sb.*)
破坏 pòhuài	*destroy; wreck; undermine; sabotage*
破裂 pòliè	*burst; crack; rupture; split*
破灭 pòmiè	(of hope; dream, etc.) *be shattered; fall through; evaporate*

七 qī

seven

七月 qīyuè	*July*

期 qī

1. *a period of time; duration; phase; stage*: 时期 shíqī (*period; duration*); 学期 xuéqī (*academic term; semester*); 长期 chángqī (*long-term*); 短期 duǎnqī (*short term*); 假期 jiàqī (*vacation; period of leave*)

2. *designated time; appointed time*: 按期 ànqī (*on schedule; on time*); 到期 dàoqī (*expire; be due*); 过期 guòqī (*overdue; expired*); 延期 yánqī (*postpone; defer; put off*); 定期 dìngqī (*regularly; at regular intervals*)

3. (magazine) *issue*: 杂志的第一期 zázhì de dìyī qī (*the first issue of the magazine*)

Also appears in the following words: 日期 rìqī (*date*); 星期 xīngqī (*week*)

期待 qīdài	*look forward to; expect*
期间 qījiān	*duration*: 在比赛期间 (in the course of the competition)
期刊 qīkān	*periodical; journal; magazine.* Cl: 本 běn; 份 fèn
期望 qīwàng	*expectation; expect; anticipate*
期限 qīxiàn	*time limit; deadline*

起 qǐ

1. *rise; get up*: 早睡早起 zǎo shuì zǎo qǐ (*go to bed early and get up early*); 起床 qǐchuáng (*get up*)

2. *develop* (a physical reaction): 起鸡皮疙瘩 qǐ jīpí gēda (*break out in goose bumps*); 起水疱 qǐ shuǐpào (*develop blisters*)

3. *develop; produce*: 起坏心 qǐ huàixīn (*develop evil ideas*); 起作用 qǐ zuòyòng (*produce an effect*)

4. *start from*, used with 从 cóng: 从今天起 cóng jīntiān qǐ (*start from today*)

5. used after a verb to indicate an action that moves from a lower position to a higher position: 举起 jǔ qǐ (*lift up*); 拾起 shí qǐ (*pick up*). If it is preceded by the negative word 不 bù, it suggests inability to afford: 吃不起 chī bù qǐ (*can't afford to eat*); 买不起 mǎi bù qǐ (*can't afford to buy*); 住不起 zhù bù qǐ (*can't afford the rent*)

起初	qǐchū	*at first; originally*
起点	qǐdiǎn	*starting point.* Cl: 个 gè
起飞	qǐfēi	*(of airplanes) take off*
起家	qǐjiā	*build up (a business)*
起来	qǐlái	1. *rise to one's feet; stand up*
		2. used after a verb as a complex directional complement indicating the beginning and the subsequent continuation of an action: 美国客人听了他们的话，就笑了起来 Měiguó kèrén tīng le tāmende huà, jiù xiào le qǐlái (*after hearing what they said, the American guests started laughing*); 天热了起来 tiān rè le qǐlái (*it is getting hot*)
起码	qǐmǎ	*basic; minimum:* 起码的条件 qǐmǎde tiáojiàn (*basic conditions*)
起先	qǐxiān	*at first; in the beginning*
起因	qǐyīn	*cause; reason*
起源	qǐyuán	*origin*

气 qì

1. *air*: 吸气 xīqì (*inhale*); 吐气 tǔqì (*exhale*)

2. *gas*: 毒气 dúqì (*poisonous gas*)

3. *smell; odor*: 香气 xiāngqì (*fragrant smell*). Cl: 股 gǔ

4. *make angry; get angry*: 气死我了 qì sǐ wǒ le (*it greatly angered me*); 她气了 tā qì le (*she is angry*)

5. *get angry because*: 她气我不给她写信 tā qì wǒ bù gěi tā xiě xìn (*she is mad with me because I didn't write to her*)

气氛	qìfēn	*atmosphere:* 节日的气氛 jiérì de qìfēn (*festive atmosphere*)
气愤	qìfèng	*indignant; angry*
气功	qìgōng	*a Chinese system of breathing exercises to keep fit*
气候	qìhòu	*climate*
气魄	qìpò	*boldness of vision*
气球	qìqiú	*balloon.* Cl: 只 zhī; 个 gè

气势 qìshì   *momentum*

气体 qìtǐ   (of physics) *gas*. Cl: 种 zhǒng

气筒 qìtǒng   *bicycle pump*. Cl: 只 zhī; 个 gè

气味 qìwèi   *smell; odor*. Cl: 股 gǔ

气温 qìwēn   *air temperature*

气象 qìxiàng   *meteorology*

汽 qì

steam; vapor

汽车 qìchē   *motor vehicle; automobile*. Cl: 辆 liàng

汽船 qìchuán   *steamboat; steamer*. Cl: 艘 sōu

汽缸 qìgāng   *cylinder*. Cl: 只 zhī; 个 gè

汽水 qìshuǐ   *soda water; soft drink*. Cl: 瓶 píng

汽艇 qìtǐng   *motorboat*. Cl: 艘 sōu; 条 tiáo; 只 zhī

汽油 qìyóu   *gas; gasoline; petrol*. Cl: 桶 tǒng

千 qiān

thousand

千变万化 qiānbiàn wànhuà   *ever changing; capricious*

千方百计 qiānfāng bǎijì   *by every means*

千千万万 qiānqiān wànwàn   *thousands of*: 千千万万的读者 qiānqiān wànwànde dúzhě (*thousands of readers*)

千载难逢 qiānzǎi nánféng   *once in a blue moon; very rare*: 千载难逢的机会 qiānzǎi nánféngde jīhuì (*rare opportunity*)

前 qián

1. *front*: 前门 qiánmén (*front door*); 前线 qiánxiàn (*frontline*)

2. *in front of*, used after a noun, as the word is considered as a noun in Chinese, and in conjunction with 在 zài: 汽车在门前 qìchē zài mén qián (*the car is in front of the gate*); 站在黑板前 zhàn zài hēibǎn qián (*stand in front of the blackboard*). 在 zài is often left out when appearing at the beginning of an existential sentence. See under 在 zài. In this sense, 前 qián is often but not always interchangeable with 前边 qiánbian, 前面 qiánmian, and 前头 qiántou. When used as an attribute modifying a noun or when used by itself as an adverbial of place, only the disyllabic form is possible: 前边的

车 qiánbian de chē (*the car in front*); 前面有座桥 qiánmian yǒu zuò qiáo (*there is a bridge ahead*).

3. *ago*; *before*, used at the end of a phrase or clause, as the word is considered as a noun in Chinese: 三天前 sān tiān qián (*three days ago*); 来美国前，我是医生 lái Měiguó qián, wǒ shì yīshēng (*I was a doctor before coming to America*)

4. *last*: 前几天 qián jǐ tiān (*last few days*)

5. *previous*; *former*: 前妻 qiánqī (*ex-wife*); 前任 qiánrèn (*predecessor*)

6. *forward*; *ahead*: 往前走 wàng qián zǒu (*walk straight ahead*)

Also appears in the following words: 从前 cóngqián (*formerly; once upon a time*); 空前 kōngqián (*unprecedented*); 面前 miànqián (*before; in front of*); 目前 mùqián (*at present*); 事前 shìqián (*in advance*); 提前 tíqián (*bring forward; ahead of time*); 眼前 yǎnqián (*now*); 以前 yǐqián (*in the past; before*)

前边 qiánbian	*in front of; at the head of*	
前程 qiánchéng	*future; future career*	
前方 qiánfāng	*frontline; ahead*	
前后 qiánhòu	**1.** (of time) *around; approximately*: 五点前后 wǔ diǎn qiánhòu (*around 5 o'clock*)	
	2. *from beginning to end*: 这次旅行前后用了四个星期 zhè cì lǚxíng qiánhòu yòng le sì ge xīngqī (*this trip took four weeks from beginning to end*)	
前进 qiánjìn	*move forward; progress; advance*	
前景 qiánjǐng	*prospect*	
前例 qiánlì	*precedent*	
前面 qiánmian	*in front of; at the head of; above; foregoing*	
前任 qiánrèn	*predecessor*	
前提 qiántí	*premise; precondition*. Cl: 个 gè	
前天 qiántiān	*the day before yesterday*	
前头 qiántou	*in front of; at the head of*	
前夕 qiánxi	*eve*	

钱 qián

money

Also appears in the following words: 价钱 jiàqián (*price*); 零钱 língqián (*small change*)

钱包 qiánbāo	*wallet; purse*
钱币 qiánbì	*coin*

强 qiáng

1. *strong*: 强国 qiángguó (*strong state*); 能力很强 nénglì hěn qiáng (*very capable*)

2. *by force*: 强夺 qiáng duó (*seize by force*); 强占 qiáng zhàn (*occupy by force*)

3. *better*, used in comparative sentences: 今年的收成比去年强 jīnnián de shōuchéng bǐ qùnián qiáng (*the harvest this year is better than that of last year*)

Also appears in the following words: 加强 jiāqiáng (*intensify*); 坚强 jiānqiáng (*staunch*); 列强 lièqiáng (*the big powers*); 顽强 wánqiáng (*pertinacity*); 增强 zēngqiáng (*strengthen*)

强大 **qiángdà**	*powerful*: 强大的军队 qiángdàde jūnduì (*powerful army*)
强盗 **qiángdào**	*robber*
强调 **qiángdiào**	*emphasize*
强化 **qiánghuà**	*strengthen*; *intensify*
强加 **qiángjiā**	*impose*: 强加不平等的条约 qiángjiā bù píngděngde tiáoyuē (*impose an unequal treaty*)
强奸 **qiángjiān**	*rape*
强烈 **qiángliè**	*strong*; *strongly*: 强烈抗议 qiángliè kàngyì (*strong protest*; *strongly protest*); 强烈反对 qiángliè fǎnduì (*strongly oppose*)
强迫 **qiǎngpò**	*force*; *compel*, pronounced in the third tone: 强迫交税 qiǎngpò jiāo shuì (*force to pay tax*)
强制 **qiángzhì**	*compel*; *coerce*: 强制执行 qiángzhì zhíxíng (*enforce*)
强壮 **qiángzhuàng**	(*of body and health*) *strong*

亲 qīn

1. *parent*: 双亲 shuānqīn (*father and mother*)

2. *related by blood*: 亲姐妹 qīn jiěmèi (*blood sisters*; *biological sisters*)

3. *relative*: 远亲 yuǎn qīn (*distant relative*)

4. *kiss* (v.)

5. *in person*: 亲笔 qīn bǐ (*in one's own handwriting*)

Also appears in the following words: 父亲 fùqīn (*father*); 母亲 mǔqīn (*mother*); 探亲 tànqīn (*go home to visit one's family*)

亲爱 **qīn'ài**	*dear*; *beloved*: 亲爱的妈妈 qīn'àide māma (*dear mother*)

亲笔 qīnbǐ	in one's own handwriting: 亲笔信 qīnbǐxìn (a personal handwritten letter)
亲近 qīnjìn	be close to; be intimate with
亲密 qīnmì	close; intimate: 亲密的朋友 qīnmìde péngyou (close friend)
亲戚 qīnqi	relatives: 我在英国有很多亲戚 wǒ zài Yīngguó yǒu hěn duō qīnqi (I have many relatives in England). Cl: 个 gè; 位 wèi
亲切 qīnqiè	cordial; kind
亲热 qīnrè	warmhearted; affectionate
亲人 qīnrén	one's family members and relatives. Cl: 个 gè; 位 wèi
亲生 qīnshēng	related by blood; biologically related: 他们不是那个孩子的亲生父母 tāmen bú shì nà ge háizi de qīnshēng fùmǔ (they are not that child's biological parents)
亲友 qīnyǒu	relatives and friends. Cl: 个 gè; 位 wèi
亲自 qīnzì	personally; in person: 经理要亲自和顾客谈 jīnglǐ yào qīnzì hé gùkè tán (the manager wants to talk to the customer in person)

青 qīng

green: 青草 qīngcǎo (green grass)

青菜 qīngcài	green vegetables; greens
青年 qīngnián	youth; young people
青少年 qīngshàonián	teenagers; youngsters
青蛙 qīngwā	frog. Cl: 只 zhī; 个 gè

轻 qīng

1. *light*: 羽毛很轻 yǔmáo hěn qīng (*the feather is very light*); 轻音乐 qīng yīnyuè (*light music*)

2. *slight*; *light* (in age, condition, etc.): 年轻 niánqīng (*young*); 轻伤 qīngshāng (*minor injury*); 责任很轻 zérèn hěn qīng (*the responsibility is very light*)

3. *gently*; *softly*: 轻一点儿说话 qīng yìdiǎnr shuōhuà (*speak softly*); 瓷器要轻放 cíqì yào qīng fàng (*porcelain requires gentle handling*)

4. *easily*; *readily*: 轻信谣言 qīngxìn yáoyán (*easily believe rumors*)

5. *belittle*, used as part of another word

轻便 qīngbiàn	(objects) light; portable
轻活 qīnghuó	light work; easy job
轻快 qīngkuài	brisk (steps); lively (music)

轻慢	qīngmàn	*slight someone*; *treat someone with disrespect*
轻蔑	qīngmiè	*scornful*
轻巧	qīngqiǎo	*dexterous*
轻视	qīngshì	*look down upon*; *underestimate*
轻率	qīngshuài	*rash*; *hasty*: 轻率的决定 qīngshuàide juédìng (*rash decision*)
轻松	qīngsōng	*relaxed*: 轻松的工作 qīngsōngde gōngzuò (*easy job*)
轻微	qīngwēi	*slight*: 轻微的感冒 qīngwēide gǎnmào (*slight cold*)
轻信	qīngxìn	*easily believe* (sb. or sth.)
轻型	qīngxíng	*light-duty*: 轻型卡车 qīngxíng kǎchē (*pickup truck*)
轻易	qīngyì	*easily*; *rashly*

清 qīng

1. *clear*: 清水 qīng shuǐ (*clear water*)

2. *clearly*, used as a verb complement: 说清 shuō qīng (*explain clearly*); 算清 suàn qīng (*calculate clearly*)

3. *completely*: 还清债 huán qīng zhài (*pay off debt*)

清晨	qīngchén	*early morning*
清除	qīngchú	*eliminate* (people or things deemed undesirable)
清楚	qīngchǔ	*clear*; *distinct*
清单	qīngdān	*detailed list*. Cl: 张 zhāng; 份 fèn
清点	qīngdiǎn	*check*; *take inventory*
清洁	qīngjié	*clean*
清理	qīnglǐ	*put in order*; *straighten*
清醒	qīngxǐng	*clear-headed*; *sober*
清真	qīngzhēn	*Islamic*; *Muslim*: 清真教 qīngzhēnjiào (*Islam*)

情 qíng

1. *feeling*; *emotion*; *sentiment*

2. *love*; *affection*: 爱情 àiqíng (*love*); 情欲 qíngyù (*sexual desire*)

3. *situation*; *state*; *condition*: 病情 bìngqíng (*patient's condition*); 灾情 zhāiqíng (*state of disaster*)

Also appears in the following words: **表情** biǎoqíng (*facial expression*); **感情** gǎnqíng (*feeling*; *affection*); **热情** rèqíng (*enthusiastic*; *passionate*); **事情** shìqíng (*matter*; *affair*; *business*); **同情** tóngqíng (*sympathize*); **心情** xīnqíng (*frame of mind*); **友情** yǒuqíng (*friendship*)

情报	qíngbào	*intelligence.* Cl: 份 fèn; 件 jiàn
情敌	qíngdí	*rival in love*
情夫	qíngfū	*lover* (man)
情妇	qíngfù	*mistress*
情感	qínggǎn	*emotion; feeling*
情节	qíngjié	*plot* (of a story)
情景	qíngjǐng	*scene; circumstances*
情况	qíngkuàng	*situation; circumstances; condition.* Cl: 个 gè; 种 zhǒng
情理	qínglǐ	*sense; reason; logic*
情人	qíngrén	*sweetheart; lover.* Cl: 个 gè; 对 duì
情书	qíngshū	*love letter.* Cl: 封 fēng
情形	qíngxing	*situation; circumstances; condition.* Cl: 种 zhǒng
情绪	qíngxù	*mood; feeling; sentiments*
情愿	qíngyuàn	*be willing to; would rather*

请 qǐng

1. *please:* 请进 qǐng jìn (*please come in*); 请喝茶 qǐng hē chá (*please drink tea*)

2. *ask; request:* 我请老师给我解释 wǒ qǐng lǎoshī gěi wǒ jiěshi (*I asked the teacher to explain to me*)

3. *invite; engage:* 中国每年请很多美国老师去教英语 Zhōngguó měi nián qǐng hěn duō Měiguó lǎoshī qù jiāo Yīngyǔ (*China invites many American teachers to go there to teach English every year*)

请假	qǐngjià	*ask for leave*
请教	qǐngjiào	*consult; ask for help* (with a question): 我有个问题向你请教 wǒ yǒu ge wèntí xiàng nǐ qǐngjiào (*I have a question that I'd like to ask you to help with*)
请客	qǐngkè	*play host; treat sb. to sth.:* 今天是老板请客 jīntiān shì lǎobǎn qǐngkè (*it is our boss's treat today*)
请示	qǐngshì	*ask the superior for instruction*
请问	qǐngwèn	*may I please ask,* used as a polite attention-getter
请愿	qǐngyuàn	*petition* (n. and v.)

区 qū

district; region; zone: 学区 xuéqū (*school district*); 商业区 shāngyèqū (*business district*); 免税区 miǎnshuìqū (*duty-free zone*)

Also appears in the following words: 地区 dìqū (*region; area*); 郊区 jiāoqū
(*suburbs*); 山区 shānqū (*mountainous area*); 社区 shèqū (*community*); 市区 shìqū
(*urban district*)

区别 qūbié	1. *distinguish; differentiate*: 区别朋友和敌人 qūbié péngyou hé dírén (*distinguish friends from enemies*) 2. *difference*: 广东菜和湖南菜有很大的区别 Guǎngdōngcài hé Húnáncài yǒu hěn dàde qūbié (*there are major differences between Cantonese food and Hunan food*). Cl: 种 zhǒng; 个 gè
区分 qūfēn	*distinguish; differentiate*: 区分两者的界限 qūfēn liǎngzhě de jièxiàn (*mark the boundary between the two things*)

取 qǔ

1. *go and get; fetch*: 去银行取钱 qù yínháng qǔ qián (*go to the bank to with-draw money*); 我在哪儿取行李 wǒ zài nǎr qǔ xíngli (*where shall I go to claim my luggage?*)

2. *adopt; choose*: 这种方法不可取 zhè zhǒng fāngfǎ bù kě qǔ (*this is not a method to adopt*); 给孩子取名 gěi háizi qǔ míng (*choose a name for the child*)

Also appears in the following words: 采取 cǎiqǔ (*adopt*); 夺取 duóqǔ (*snatch*);
争取 zhēngqǔ (*strive for*)

取材 qǔcái	*gather materials*
取代 qǔdài	*replace; substitute*: 用塑料取代金属 yòng sùliào qǔdài jīnshǔ (*replace metal with plastics*)
取得 qǔde	*obtain; acquire*: 取得谅解 qǔdé liàngjiě (*obtain under-standing*); 取得成功 qǔdé chénggōng (*achieve success*)
取缔 qǔdì	*outlaw; ban*
取决 qǔjué	*be determined by; depend on*: 我能不能去旅行取决于我有没有时间 wǒ néng bu néng qù lǚxíng qǔjué yú wǒ yǒu méi you shíjiān (*whether I can travel depends on whether I have time*)
取暖 qǔnuǎn	*warm oneself; keep warm*
取舍 qǔshě	*accept or reject*: 很难决定取舍 hěn nán juédìng qǔshě (*it is hard to make one's choice whether to accept it*)
取胜 qǔshèng	*win victory; achieve success*
取消 qǔxiāo	*cancel; call off*: 明天的课取消了 míngtiān de kè qǔxiāo le (*tomorrow's class has been canceled*)
取笑 qǔxiào	*make fun of* (someone)

去 qù

1. *go (to)*: 你想去中国吗 nǐ xiǎng qù Zhōngguó ma (*would you like to go to China?*); 他们要去中国城 tāmen yào qù Zhōngguóchéng (*they are going to Chinatown*)

2. (of the year) *last*: 去年 qùnián (*last year*)

3. *write (a letter to)*; *send*: 给客户去信 gěi kèhù qù xìn (*write a letter to the client*); 我们公司去了三个人 wǒmen gōngsī qù le sān ge rén (*our company sent three people*)

4. directional complement used after certain verbs such as 带 dài (*bring*; *carry*), 寄 jì (*mail*), 上 shàng (*go up*), 下 xià (*go down*), 进 jìn (*enter*), 出 chū (*exit*), 回 huí (*return*) to show the direction of the action in relation to the speaker: 孩子们上学去了 háizimen shàng xué qù le (*children went to school—away from the speaker*). This use of 去 qù is opposed to 来 lái. Cf. 进来 jìn lái (*come in—in the direction of the speaker*) and 进去 jìn qù (*go in—away from the speaker*); 上来 shàng lái (*come up—the speaker is up*), and 上去 shàng qù (*go up—away from the speaker*). If the verb takes an object that indicates a location, the object must be placed between the verb and the directional complement: 我妈妈回家去了 wǒ māma huí jiā lái le (*my mother went back home*). In this case, the aspect marker 了 le cannot be used after the verb, but it is possible to use the modal particle 了 le at the end of the sentence: 他回美国去了 tā huí Měiguó qù le (*he returned to America*). If the object does not indicate a location, it can be placed either between the verb and 去 qù or after 去 qù: 学生们带了书包去 xuéshēngmen dài le shūbāo qù and 学生们带去了书包 xuéshēngmen dài qù le shūbāo (*the students took their book bags with them*). In this case, the aspect particle 了 le can be used, as shown by the examples. If the object appears between the verb and 去 qù, 了 le is used immediately after the verb: 我给她写了信去 wǒ gěi tā xiě le xìn qù (*I wrote her a letter*). If the object follows 去 qù, 了 le would follow 去 qù as well: 我给她写信去了 wǒ gěi tā xiě xìn qù le (*I wrote her a letter*).

5. part of a complex directional complement with certain verbs. These verbs include 上 shàng (*go up*), 下 xià (*go down*), 进 jìn (*enter*), 出 chū (*exit*), 回 huí (*return*), 过 guò (*pass*), and 起 qǐ (*rise*). The complex directional complement indicates both a motion and the direction of the motion in relation to the location of the speaker, cf. 走出去 zǒu chū qù (*walk out—away from the speaker*); 走出来 zǒu chū lái (*walk out—towards the speaker*). If the verb takes an object that indicates a location, the object must be placed before 去 qù: 汽车开进车库去了 (*the vehicle drove into the garage*). If the object does not indicate a location, it can be placed either before or after 去 qù, cf. 他买回很多礼物去 tā mǎi huí hěn duō lǐwù qù (*he bought and brought back many gifts*) and 他买回去很多礼物 tā mǎi huí hěn duō lǐwù qù (*he bought and brought back many gifts*).

6. *remove*: 土豆要不要去皮 tǔdòu yào bu yào qù pí (*do you want me to peel the potatoes?*)

去年 qùnián   *last year*

全 quán

1. *whole*; *entire*: 全家 quán jiā (*whole family*); 全国 quán guó (*whole country*)

2. *complete*; *full*: 笔记不全 bǐjì bù quán (*the notes are not complete*)

3. *completely*; *entirely*: 她已经全好了 tā yǐjīng quán hǎo le (*she has completely recovered*)

Also appears in the following words: 安全 ānquán (*safe*; *safety*; *security*); 齐全 qíquán (*complete*); 完全 wánquán (*complete*; *entirely*)

全部 **quánbù**	*whole*; *entire*; *total*; *completely*; *entirely*
全场 **quánchǎng**	*the whole audience*: 全场起立鼓掌 quánchǎng qǐlì gǔzhǎng (*the whole audience stood up to applaud*)
全局 **quánjú**	*overall situation*
全力 **quánlì**	*all out*; *with all one's might*: 全力支持 quánlì zhīchí (*go all out to support*)
全貌 **quánmào**	*the whole picture*
全面 **quánmiàn**	*overall*; *comprehensive*; *comprehensively*: 他们的调查很全面 tāmende diàochá hěn quánmiàn (*their investigation is comprehensive*)
全民 **quánmín**	*people of the whole country*
全球 **quánqiú**	*the whole world*
全然 **quánrán**	*completely*, always used in a negative sentence: 全然不知真相 quánrán bù zhī zhēngxiàng (*completely ignorant of the truth*)
全体 **quántǐ**	*all*; *every*; *entire*: 全体学生 quántǐ xuésheng (*all the students*)
全文 **quánwén**	*full text*
全心全意 **quánxīn quányì**	*wholeheartedly*

群 qún

1. *crowd*; *group*: 人群 rénqún (*crowd*); 羊群 yángqún (*flocks of sheep*)

2. *classifier with the meaning of group*: 一群少年 yì qún shàonián (*a group of teenagers*); 一群鱼 yì qún yú (*a school of fish*)

群情 **qúnqíng**	*public sentiment*
群众 **qúnzhòng**	*masses of people*; *common people*: 群众运动 qúnzhòng yùndòng (*mass campaign*)

然 rán

Used as part of a word: 然而 rán'ér (*yet*; *but*); 然后 ránhòu (*after that*); 当然 dāngrán (*of course*); 自然 zìrán (*nature*)

Also appears in the following words: 不然 bùrán (*otherwise*); 当然 dāngrán (*of course*); 忽然 hūrán (*suddenly*); 既然 jìrán (*since*; *now that*); 自然 zìrán (*nature*; *natural*)

让 ràng

1. *let*; *allow*: 老师不让我们用计算器算 lǎoshī bú ràng wǒmen yòng jìsuànqì suàn (*the teacher does not allow us to calculate with a calculator*)

2. *yield*; *give way*: 汽车应该让行人 qìchē yīnggāi ràng xíngrén (*vehicles should yield to pedestrians*)

3. *make sb. do sth.*: 他让我告诉你 tā ràng wǒ gàosù nǐ (*he asked me to tell you*)

4. *by*, used in the passive construction: 电脑让他修好了 diànnǎo ràng tā xiū hǎo le (*the computer was fixed by him*)

让步	**ràngbù**	*make concessions*; *give in*
让路	**rànglù**	*make way for*
让座	**ràngzuò**	*give up one's seat to sb.*

热 rè

1. *hot*: 天气很热 tiānqì hěn rè (*the weather is very hot*)

2. *to heat*: 饭凉了，要热一热 fàn liáng le, yào rè yi rè (*the food is cold, it needs to be heated*)

3. *fever*: 发热 fārè (*have a fever*)

4. *warm*: 热心 rèxīn (*warmhearted*)

5. *craze*; *fad*: 棒球热 bàngqiúrè (*baseball craze*)

热爱	**rè'ài**	*love* (one's country, people)
热诚	**rèchéng**	*sincerely*; *cordially*: 热诚接待 rèchéng jiēdài (*receive sb. cordially*)
热带	**rèdài**	*the tropics*
热度	**rèdù**	1. *heat* (n.)
		2. *fever*; *temperature*
热恋	**rèliàn**	*be passionately in love*

热烈 **rèliè**	warm; enthusiastic; warmly; enthusiastically: 热烈的掌声 rèliède zhǎngshēng (warm applause); 热烈地欢送 rèliède huānsòng (warmly bid farewell)
热门 **rèmén**	popular; hot; in great demand: 热门商品 rèmén shāngpǐn (merchandise in great demand); 热门话题 rèmén huàtí (hot topics)
热闹 **rènào**	(of a place) bustling with activity: 中国城很热闹 Zhōngguóchéng hěn rènào (Chinatown is bustling with activity)
热能 **rènéng**	heat energy
热情 **rèqíng**	1. enthusiasm; zeal: 学习的热情 xuéxi de rèqíng (enthusiasm with which to study). Cl: 股 gǔ 2. warm; warmly; warmheartedly: 这儿的服务员都很热情 zhèr de fúwùyuán dōu hěn rèqíng (the waiters here are all very warm and kind); 热情对待顾客 rèqíng duìdài gùkè (treat the customers warmheartedly)
热线 **rèxiàn**	hotline

人 rén

1. person; people

2. used after the names of countries to form nationality words: 中国人 Zhōngguórén (Chinese); 美国人 Měiguórén (Americans); 法国人 Fǎguórén (French)

Also appears in the following words: 别人 biérén (others; someone else); 敌人 dírén (enemy); 动人 dòngrén (moving; touching); 犯人 fànrén (criminal); 夫人 fūrén (madam; lady); 工人 gōngrén (worker); 客人 kèrén (guest); 老人 lǎorén (old person); 名人 míngrén (famous person; celebrity); 男人 nánrén (man); 女人 nǚrén (woman); 情人 qíngrén (lover); 穷人 qióngrén (poor people)

人才 **réncái**	talent
人家 **rénjiā**	1. household 2. other people: 这是人家的事，请不要多管 zhè shì rénjiā de shì, qǐng búyào duō guǎn (this is other people's business, please don't meddle)
人口 **rénkǒu**	population
人类 **rénlèi**	humanity; human species
人们 **rénmen**	people
人民 **rénmín**	people. This is a political term, used in such expressions as 中国人民 Zhōngguó rénmín (Chinese people) and 美国人民 Měiguó rénmín (American people).

人情 **rénqíng**	compassion; *favor*: 我欠了他一个人情 wǒ qiàn le tā yí ge rénqíng (*I owe him a favor*)
人手 **rénshǒu**	*manpower*
人选 **rénxuǎn**	*candidate*. Cl: 个 gè
人员 **rényuán**	*personnel*. Cl: 个 gè; 位 wèi; 名 míng
人造 **rénzào**	*man-made*; *artificial*

认 rèn

1. *recognize; make out*: 对不起, 我刚刚没有认出你来 duìbuqǐ, wǒ gānggāng méiyou rèn chū nǐ lái (*sorry that I didn't recognize you just now*); 这个字很难认 zhè ge zì hěn nán rèn (*this character is difficult to recognize*)

2. *adopt*: 认她做女儿 rèn tā zuò nǚ'ér (*adopt her as a daughter*)

3. *accept as given; resign oneself to*: 今年又要加税; 我们只有认了 jīnnián yòu yào jiā suì; wǒmen zhǐyǒu rèn le (*tax is going up again this year, but we can do nothing but accept it*)

Also appears in the following words: 否认 fǒurèn (*deny; negate*); 确认 quèrèn (*affirm*)

认错 **rèncuò**	*admit a mistake*
认得 **rènde**	*know; recognize*: 你还认得这个地方吗 nǐ hái rènde zhè ge dìfāng ma (*do you still recognize this place?*)
认可 **rènkě**	*approval*: 这所学校没有得到政府的认可 zhè suǒ xuéxiào méiyou dédào zhèngfǔ de rènkě (*this school did not receive the government's approval*)
认识 **rènshi**	**1.** *know; understand; recognize*: 我不认识他太太 wǒ bú rènshi tā tàitai (*I don't know his wife*); 你认识去火车站的路吗 nǐ rènshi qù huǒchēzhàn de lù ma (*do you know the way to the train station?*) **2.** *understanding*: 这位学者对文学的认识很深刻 zhè wèi xuézhě duì wénxué de rènshi hěn shēnkè (*this scholar has a deep understanding of literature*)
认为 **rènwéi**	*think; believe; to be of the opinion*
认真 **rènzhēn**	*serious; earnest; seriously; earnestly* (towards study, work, etc.): 你们要认真学习 nǐmen yào rènzhēn xuéxí (*you should study seriously*); 他工作不认真 tā gōngzuò bú rènzhēn (*he is not serious with his work*)
认字 **rènzì**	*learn to read; can read; be literate*
认罪 **rènzuì**	*admit guilt*

日 rì

1. *sun*

2. *day*: 今日 jīnrì (*today*); 昨日 zuórì (*yesterday*); 明日 míngrì (*tomorrow*); 星期日 xīngqīrì (*Sunday*). More formal than 今天 jīntiān (*today*); 昨天 zuótiān (*yesterday*); 明天 míngtiān (*tomorrow*), and 星期天 xīngqītiān (*Sunday*)

日报 rìbào	*daily.* Cl: 张 zhāng; 份 fèn	
日本 Rìběn	*Japan*; 日本人 Rìběnrén (*Japanese person*)	
日常 rìcháng	*day-to-day; routine*	
日场 rìchǎng	*matinee*	
日光 rìguāng	*sunlight*	
日记 rìjì	*diary.* Cl: 篇 piān; 段 duàn; 本 běn	
日历 rìlì	*calendar.* Cl: 本 běn; 页 yè	
日期 rìqī	*date*	
日夜 rìyè	*day and night*	
日语 rìyǔ	*Japanese language*	
日子 rìzi	*day; date; time; life*	

肉 ròu

flesh; meat: 烤肉 kǎoròu (*barbecue*); 牛肉 niúròu (*beef*); 猪肉 zhūròu (*pork*); 羊肉 yángròu (*mutton; lamb*)

肉店 ròudiàn	*butcher's.* Cl: 家 jiā
肉麻 ròumá	*nauseating; sickening*
肉末 ròumò	*minced meat; ground meat*
肉丝 ròusī	*shredded meat*
肉刑 ròuxíng	*corporal punishment*
肉眼 ròuyǎn	*naked eye*
肉汁 ròuzhī	*gravy*

如 rú

1. *like; as*: 四季如春 sì jì rú chūn (*all four seasons are like spring; perennially spring*); 如鱼得水 rú yú dé shuǐ (*feel like a fish in water*); 如我预言 rú wǒ yùyán (*as I predicted*)

2. *comparable with; as good as,* always in the negative: 我的中文不如你的中文 wǒde Zhōngwén bù rú nǐde Zhōngwén (*my Chinese is not as good as yours*)

3. *for example*: 中国有很多大城市，如北京和上海 Zhōngguó yǒu hěn duō dà chéngshì, rú Běijīng hé Shànghǎi (*there are many large cities in China, for example, Beijing and Shanghai*)

4. *in keeping with; in accordance with*: 万事如意 wànshì rúyì (*may everything go your way*); 一切如愿 yíqiè rúyuàn (*one's wishes have been fulfilled*)

Also appears in the following words: 比如 bǐrú (*for example*); 假如 jiǎrú (*if; in case*); 例如 lìrú (*for example*)

如此 rúcǐ		*like this*
如果 rúguǒ		**1.** *if*, used to introduce a conditional clause and optionally followed by 的话 dehuà at the end of the clause: 你如果现在忙（的话），我改天再来 nǐ rúguǒ xiànzài máng (dèhua), wǒ gǎitiān zài lái (*if you are busy now, I'll come another day*). The conditional clause is usu. placed before the main clause.
		2. *what if*, followed by 呢 ne at the end of the sentence:
		A: 你可以用电脑学中文 nǐ kěyǐ yòng diànnǎo xué Zhōngwén (*you can study Chinese using the computer*)
		B: 我如果没有电脑呢 wǒ rúguǒ méi you diànnǎo ne (*what if I don't have a computer?*)
如何 rúhé		*how*, usu. used in formal language
如今 rújīn		*nowadays*
如来 rúlái		*Buddha*
如同 rútóng		*like; as*
如意 rúyì		*as one wishes*

入 rù

1. *enter*: 入关 rù guān (*go through customs*); 入境 rù jìng (*enter another country*)

2. *join*: 入党 rù dǎng (*join the party*); 入会 rù huì (*join the association*)

3. *income*, often taking the form of 收入 shōurù

Also appears in the following words: 加入 jiārù (*join*); 进入 jìnrù (*enter*); 收入 shōurù (*income*); 输入 shūrù (*import; input*); 投入 tóurù (*plunge into; jump in*)

入伙 rùhuǒ		*join a partnership*
入口 rùkǒu		*entrance.* Cl: 个 gè; 处 chù
入门 rùmén		**1.** *get the hang of it; learn the rudiments of*: 我刚学开车，还没有入门 wǒ gāng xué kāi chē, hái méiyou rùmén (*I have just started learning to drive and I have not got the hang of it*)

2. *elementary course*, often used in a book title: 电脑入门 Diànnǎo Rùmén (*Computer Basics*)

入迷 **rùmí**	*be carried away; be held spellbound*
入侵 **rùqīn**	*invade*
入睡 **rùshuì**	*fall asleep*
入学 **rùxué**	*start school; be enrolled in a school*

三 sān

three

三角 **sānjiǎo**	*triangle*
三轮车 **sānlúnchē**	*tricycle*. Cl: 辆 liàng
三月 **sānyuè**	*March*

色 sè

1. *color*. When used without modification, it usu. takes the disyllabic form of 颜色 yánsè: 红色 hóngsè (*red*); 黄色 huángsè (*yellow*).

2. *look; appearance; countenance*: 脸色 liǎnsè (*look on the face*)

3. *type*: 各色各样的产品 gèsè gèyàngde chǎnpǐn (*various types of products*)

Also appears in the following words: 彩色 cǎisè (*multi-color*); 景色 jǐngsè (*scenery*); 角色 juésè (*role*); 特色 tèsè (*characteristic; feature*)

色彩 **sècǎi**	*color; shade*
色情 **sèqíng**	*sex; pornography*

山 shān

mountain; hill

Also appears in the following words: 火山 huǒshān (*volcano*); 靠山 kàoshān (*backer*)

山地 **shāndì**	*hilly area; mountainous region*
山顶 **shāndǐng**	*top of a mountain; summit*
山洞 **shāndòng**	*cave*
山脚 **shānjiǎo**	*foot of a mountain*
山区 **shānqū**	*mountainous area*
山羊 **shānyáng**	*goat*. Cl: 只 zhī; 头 tóu
山芋 **shānyù**	*sweet potato*

商 shāng

1. *trade; commerce; business*: 经商 jīngshāng (*be engaged in business*); 通商 tōngshāng (*have trade relations*)

2. *businessman; trader; merchant*: 出口商 chūkǒushāng (*exporter*); 代理商 dàilǐshāng (*agent*); 零售商 língshòushāng (*retailer*); 珠宝商 zhūbǎoshāng (*jeweler*). When not modified, it needs to take the disyllabic form of 商人 shāngrén.

3. *discuss; consult*, usu. in such words as 商量 shāngliàng (*discuss; talk over*), 商谈 shāngtán (*discuss; confer; negotiate*), and 商议 shāngyì (*discuss; confer*)

Also appears in the following words: **协商** xiéshāng (*negotiate about*); **智商** zhìshāng (*IQ*)

商标 **shāngbiāo**	*trade mark.* Cl: 种 zhǒng	
商场 **shāngchǎng**	*shopping center; mall; bazaar.* Cl: 家 jiā	
商店 **shāngdiàn**	*store; shop.* Cl: 家 jiā; 个 gè	
商会 **shānghuì**	*chamber of commerce*	
商量 **shāngliàng**	*discuss; talk over*	
商品 **shāngpǐn**	*merchandise; goods; commodity.* Cl: 个 gè; 件 jiàn; 批 pī	
商人 **shāngrén**	*businessman; businessperson; merchant.* Cl: 个 gè; 位 wèi; 名 míng	
商务 **shāngwù**	*business affairs; commercial affairs*	
商谈 **shāngtán**	*discuss; confer; negotiate*	
商业 **shāngyè**	*business; commerce*	
商议 **shāngyì**	*discuss; confer*	

上 shàng

1. *upper; up*: 上身 shàngshēn (*upper part of the body*); 上游 shàngyóu (*upstream*)

2. *on; over; above; on the surface of; on top of*, used after a noun, as the word is considered as a noun in Chinese, and in conjunction with 在 zài; 上 shàng in this sense is pronounced in the neutral tone: 在桌子上 zài zhuōzi shang (*on the table*); 在天上 zài tiān shang (*in the sky*). 在 zài is often left out when appearing at the beginning of an existential sentence. See under 在 zài. In this sense, 上 shàng is often but not always interchangeable with 上边 shàngbian, 上面 shàngmian, and 上头 shàngtou. When used as an attribute modifying a noun or when used by itself as an adverbial of place, only the disyllabic form is possible: 上边的书 shàngbian de shū (*the book on top*); 上面没有词典 shàngmian méi you cídiǎn (*there are no dictionaries up there*).

3. *in*, pronounced in the neutral tone: 世界上 shìjiè shang (*in the world*); 报纸上 bàozhǐ shang (*in the newspaper*); 课堂上 kètáng shang (*in the classroom*)

4. *in the field of; regarding; in terms of*, pronounced in the neutral tone: 在工作上 zài gōngzuò shang (*regarding work*); 在原则问题上不能让步 zài yuánzé wèntí shang bù néng ràngbù (*no concession can be made on matters of principle*); 我们在人力上占优势 wǒmen zài rénlì shang zhàn yōushì (*we have an advantage in manpower*)

5. *go up*: 上山 shàng shān (*go up the mountain*); 上楼 shàng lóu (*go upstairs*)

6. used in conjunction with 来 lái or 去 qù to form a complex directional complement to indicate the movement of the action in relation to where the speaker is. If the preceding verb takes an object that indicates a location, the object is placed between 上 shang and 来 lái / 去 qù. If the object does not indicate a location, it follows 来 lái / 去 qù: 爬上山来 pá shang shān lái (*climb up the mountain*); 从井里提上来水 cóng jǐng lǐ tí shang lái shuǐ (*fetch water from the well*). In this usage, 上 shàng is pronounced in the neutral tone.

7. *go to* (following a routine schedule): 上班 shàngbān (*go to work*); 上学 shàngxué (*go to school*); 上课 shàngkè (*go to class*)

8. *last*: 上次 shàng cì (*last time*); 上个月 shàng ge yuè (*last month*); 上个星期 shàng ge xīngqī (*last week*)

Also appears in the following words: 马上 mǎshàng (*at once*); 世上 shìshàng (*on earth*); 早上 zǎoshàng (*morning*)

上班	**shàngbān**	*go to work*
上边	**shàngbian**	*on; over; above; on the surface of; on top of*
上层	**shàngcéng**	*upper strata*: 上层社会 shàngcéng shèhuì (*upper-class society*)
上床	**shàngchuáng**	*go to bed*
上当	**shàngdàng**	*be taken in; be ripped off*
上等	**shàngděng**	*first-rate; superior*
上帝	**shàngdì**	*God*
上吊	**shàngdiào**	*hang oneself*
上级	**shàngjí**	*higher authorities; superior*
上街	**shàngjiē**	*go to the street*
上课	**shàngkè**	*(for students) go to class; (for teachers) conduct a class*
上面	**shàngmian**	*on; over; above; on the surface of; on top of*
上身	**shàngshēn**	*upper part of the body*
上市	**shàngshì**	**1.** *(of vegetables and fruits) go on the market.*
		2. *(of companies) get listed in the stock exchange*: 上市公司 shàngshì gōngsī (*publicly traded companies*)

上司 **shàngsī**	superior; boss. Cl: 个 gè; 位 wèi
上诉 **shàngsù**	(of law) appeal
上台 **shàngtái**	come to power; assume power
上头 **shàngtou**	on; over; above; on the surface of; on top of
上午 **shàngwǔ**	morning
上下文 **shàngxiàwén**	context
上旬 **shàngxún**	the first ten days of a month
上衣 **shàngyī**	jacket. Cl: 件 jiàn
上游 **shàngyóu**	upper reaches (of a river)
上涨 **shàngzhǎng**	(of water, price, etc.) go up; rise

少 shǎo

1. *few; little*, often used as a predicative adjective: 我的钱少，他的钱多 wǒde qián shǎo, tāde qián duō (*I have little money, he has a lot*); 这个学校的学生很少 zhè ge xuéxiào de xuésheng hěn shǎo (*there are not many students at this school*)

2. *less*: 少说多做 shǎo shuō duō zuò (*say little but do more*); 印度的人比中国的人少 Yìndù de rén bǐ Zhōngguó de rén shǎo (*there are not as many people in India as there are in China*)

3. *lose; have less; be missing*: 这学期我们班少了五个学生 zhè xuéqī wǒmen bān shǎo le wǔ ge xuésheng (*we have five fewer students this semester*)

| 少量 **shǎoliàng** | a small quantity; a little: 放少量的糖 fàng shǎoliàngde táng (put in a little sugar) |
| 少数 **shǎoshù** | minority; a small part: 少数民族 shǎoshù mínzú (ethnic minorities) |

社 shè

organization; association; society; agency: 报社 bàoshè (*newspaper office*); 出版社 chūbǎnshè (*publishing house*); 旅行社 lǚxíngshè (*travel agency*). Cl: 家 jiā

社会 **shèhuì**	society; social: 中国传统社会 Zhōngguó chuántǒng shèhuì (traditional Chinese society); 社会地位 shèhuì dìwèi (social status); 社会学 shèhuìxué (sociology); 社会主义 shèhuìzhǔyì (socialism)
社交 **shèjiāo**	socializing; social contact
社论 **shèlùn**	editorial. Cl: 篇 piān

身 shēn

body: 健身 jiànshēn (*exercise one's body; bodybuilding*)

Also appears in the following words: 单身 dānshēn (*unmarried*); 随身 suíshēn (*carry on one's person; take with one*); 自身 zìshēn (*oneself*)

身边 **shēnbiān**	*at one's side*: 她的子女不在身边 tāde zǐnǚ bú zài shēnbiān (*her children are not at her side*)
身材 **shēncái**	*stature; figure*: 身材苗条 shēncái miáotiáo (*a slender figure*)
身份 **shēnfèn**	*status; identity; capacity*: 有身份的人 yǒu shēnfèn de rén (*a person with high status*); 证明身份 zhèngmíng shēnfèn (*prove one's identity*)
身上 **shēnshàng**	*on or with one*: 你身上有没有钱 nǐ shēnshàng yǒu méi you qián (*do you have any money on you?*)
身体 **shēntǐ**	*body; health*

什 shén

Only used in conjunction with 么 me.

1. *what*: 你叫什么名字 nǐ jiào shénme míngzi (*what is your name?*); 这是什么 zhè shì shénme (*what is this?*)

2. *something; anything*: 老师好象在看什么 lǎoshī hǎoxiàng zài kàn shénme (*the teacher seems to be reading something*)

3. *any*: 你会说什么外语吗 nǐ huì shuō shénme wàiyǔ ma (*do you speak any foreign languages?*); 食堂里没有什么好吃的菜 shítáng lǐ méi you shénme hǎochīde cài (*there are not any good dishes at the cafeteria*)

4. used with 也 yě or 都 dōu before a verb to indicate emphasis: 你什么时候来都可以 nǐ shénme shíhou lái dōu kěyǐ (*you can come anytime*); 我什么也不想吃 wǒ shénme yě bù xiǎng chī (*I don't want to eat anything*)

生 shēng

1. *give birth to*: 生孩子 shēng háizi (*give birth to a child*)

2. *birth*: 从生到死 cóng shēng dào sǐ (*from birth to death*)

3. *be struck with; be inflicted with*: 生病 shēng bìng (*get sick*)

4. *raw; unripe; uncooked*: 生鱼 shēngyú (*raw fish*); 生菜 shēngcài (*uncooked dish*)

5. *unfamiliar; strange:* 生词 shēngcí (*new words*); 生人 shēngrén (*stranger*).

Cl: 个 gè

Also appears in the following words: 产生 chǎnshēng (*produce*); 出生 chūshēng (*be born*); 发生 fāshēng (*happen*); 天生 tiānshēng (*innate; natural*); 新生 xīnshēng (*a new lease of life*); 学生 xuésheng (*student*); 医生 yīshēng (*doctor*)

生产	shēngchǎn	*production; produce*
生动	shēngdòng	*lively; vivid*
生活	shēnghuó	*life; live; livelihood*
生理	shēnglǐ	*physiology*
生命	shēngmìng	*life*
生气	shēngqì	*become angry; get mad*
生日	shēngrì	*birthday*
生意	shēngyi	*business*
生长	shēngzhǎng	*grow*

声 shēng

1. *voice; sound:* 女声 nǚshēng (*female voice*); 大声 dàshēng (*loud voice*); 回声 huíshēng (*echo*)

2. *tone* (in Chinese): 第一声 dìyī shēng (*first tone*); 第三声 dìsān shēng (*third tone*)

3. *reputation,* used as part of another word: 名声 míngshēng (*reputation*); 声誉 shēngyù (*reputation; fame*)

声带	shēngdài	*vocal cord*
声调	shēngdiào	*tone* (of a Chinese word)
声明	shēngmíng	*state; declare; statement; declaration.* Cl: 项 xiàng; 篇 piān
声势	shēngshì	*fanfare; show of strength*
声望	shēngwàng	*prestige; popularity*
声音	shēngyīn	*voice; sound*
声誉	shēngyù	*reputation; fame*

师 shī

1. *teacher,* usu. taking the disyllabic form of 老师 lǎoshī

2. *person with skill in a certain profession:* 建筑师 jiànzhùshī (*architect*); 技师 jìshī (*technician*); 厨师 chúshī (*chef; cook*); 导师 dǎoshī (*academic advisor*); 工程师 gōngchéngshī (*engineer*); 理发师 lǐfàshī (*barber*), 律师 lùshī (*attorney; lawyer; counselor*); 面包师 miànbāoshī (*baker*); 魔术师 móshùshī (*magician*); 设计师 shèjìshī (*designer*); 摄影师 shèyǐngshī (*photographer*); and 园艺师 yuányìshī (*gardener*). Cl: 名 míng; 位 wèi; 个 gè

师范 **shīfàn**		*teacher training*: 师范学院 shīfàn xuéyuàn (*teachers' college*)
师傅 **shīfu**		*master worker* (as opposed to apprentice). Also used as a term of address for certain skilled workers such as taxi drivers and factory workers.

十 shí

ten

十分 **shífēn**		*very; extremely*: 十分生气 shífēn shēngqì (*very angry*)
十全十美 **shíquánshíměi**		*perfect*
十月 **shíyuè**		*October*

时 shí

1. *time when; times*: 古时 gǔshí (*ancient times*); 那时 nàshí (*that time*); 我在中国时 wǒ zài Zhōngguó shí (*when I was in China*); 过时 guòshí (*obsolete; out of date; outdated*). In spoken language, 时 in the sense of *time when* is usu. expressed as 时候 shíhou. Since it is a noun in Chinese, it appears at the end of a clause or verbal phrase: 吃饭的时候，不要说话 chīfàn de shíhou, búyào shuōhuà (*don't talk while eating*); 我在中国的时候，去过青岛 wǒ zài Zhōngguó de shíhou, qù guo Qīngdǎo (*I had been to Qingdao when I was in China*).

2. *hour*: 报时 bào shí (*announce the hour*); 三时 sān shí (*three o'clock*)

3. (gram) *tense*: 现在时 xiànzàishí (*present tense*); 过去时 guòqùshí (*past tense*)

Also appears in the following words: 当时 dàngshí (*at that time*); 费时 fèishí (*time-consuming; take time*); 及时 jíshí (*in time*); 平时 píngshí (*regularly*); 随时 suíshí (*at any time*); 小时 xiǎoshí (*hour*); 有时 yǒushí (*sometimes*); 准时 zhǔnshí (*on time*)

时差 **shíchā**	*time difference*
时常 **shícháng**	*often; frequently*
时代 **shídài**	*times; age; era; epoch*
时候 **shíhou**	*time; time when*
时机 **shíjī**	*opportunity; opportune moment*

时间 shíjiān	*time.* 时间 shíjiān differs from 时候 shíhou in that 时间 shíjiān indicates a point of time, whereas 时候 shíhou indicates a duration of time. In comparison to English, 什么时候 shénme shíhou is equivalent to *when,* whereas 什么时间 shénme shíjiān is equivalent to *what time.* Since 什么时候 shénme shíhou commands a larger scope, it can be used for 什么时间 shénme shíjiān, but not vice versa.
时刻 shíkè	*moment; juncture:* 时刻表 shíkèbiǎo (*timetable; schedule*)
时髦 shímáo	*stylish; fashionable*
时期 shíqī	*period; stage:* 和平时期 (*peacetime*)
时时 shíshí	*often; constantly*
时态 shítài	(gram) *tense*
时事 shíshì	*current affairs*
时钟 shízhōng	*clock.* Cl: 座 zuò

实 shí

solid; true; real; actual

Also appears in the following words: 诚实 chéngshí (*honest*); 果实 guǒshí (*fruit*); 结实 jiēshi (*sturdy*); 老实 lǎoshi (*honest*); 确实 quèshí (*indeed*); 如实 rúshí (*truthfully*); 事实 shìshí (*fact*); 现实 xiànshí (*reality*); 真实 zhēnshí (*true*)

实地 shídì	*on site; on the spot:* 实地考察 shídì kǎochá (*onsite inspection*)
实干 shígàn	*no-nonsense:* 实干精神 shígàn jīngshen (*no-nonsense approach*)
实话 shíhuà	*truth.* Cl: 句 jù
实际 shíjì	*reality:* 实际上 shíjì shang (*in reality; in actuality*); *realistic*
实践 shíjiàn	*practice*
实况 shíkuàng	*live broadcast*
实力 shílì	*actual strength*
实施 shíshī	*implement; carry out*
实物 shíwù	*actual object*
实习 shíxí	*practice* (a profession); *internship; practicum:* 实习生 (*intern* n.)
实现 shíxiàn	*realize; make happen; come true*
实效 shíxiào	*actual effect*
实行 shíxíng	*implement; carry out*
实验 shíyàn	*experiment:* 做实验 zuò shíyàn (*do an experiment*)
实用 shíyòng	*practical*
实在 shízài	*honestly; really; indeed*

| 实质 **shízhí** | *essence*; *substance* |

识 shí

know; *recognize*, used in set collocations or as part of the word 认识 rènshi (*know*): 识趣 shí qù (*know how to behave in a delicate situation*); 老马识途 lǎo mǎ shí tú (*old horse knows its way*)

Also appears in the following words: 常识 chángshí (*common sense*; *general knowledge*); 意识 yìshi (*realize*; *consciousnesss*); 知识 zhīshi (*knowledge*)

识别 **shíbié**	*distinguish*; *detect*; *discern*: 识别谎言 shíbié huǎngyán (*detect lies*)
识破 **shípò**	*see through*: 识破伪装 shípò wěizhuāng (*see through disguise*)
识字 **shízì**	*know the words*; *learn to read*; *literate*

使 shǐ

1. *cause*; *make*: 使人高兴 shǐ rén gāoxìng (*make one happy*)

2. *envoy*: 大使 dàshǐ (*ambassador*); 特使 tèshǐ (*special envoy*)

3. *use*, often taking the form of 使用 shǐyòng

Also appears in the following words: 促使 cùshǐ (*urge*); 迫使 pòshǐ (*compel*); 天使 tiānshǐ (*angel*); 主使 zhǔshǐ (*incite*)

使出 **shǐchū**	*use*; *exert*: 使出全部力量 shǐchū quánbù lìliàng (*use all strength*)
使得 **shǐde**	*cause*; *make*, followed by a clause: 新年的到来使得我们很激动 xīnnián de dàolái shǐde wǒwen hěn jīdòng (*the arrival of the New Year made us very excited*)
使馆 **shǐguǎn**	*embassy*; *consulate*
使命 **shǐmìng**	*mission*
使用 **shǐyòng**	*use*; *employ*: 使用各种方法 shǐyòng gè zhǒng fāngfǎ (*use various methods*); 使用两种语言 shǐyòng liǎng zhǒng yǔyán (*use two languages*)

是 shì

1. *to be*, used between two nouns to indicate identity. Different from verb *to be* in English, 是 shì in Chinese is only used when the subject and the

predicative have the same referent: 我妈妈是医生 wǒ māma shì yīshēng (*my mother is a doctor*); 这是他们的学校 zhè shì tāmende xuéxiào (*this is their school*). If the predicative indicates a condition or a description in the form of an adjective, or a location in the form of a prepositional phrase, 是 shì is not used: 日本的东西很贵 Rìběn de dōngxi hěn guì (*things in Japan are very expensive*); 中国银行在中国城 Zhōngguó Yínháng zài Zhōngguóchéng (*Bank of China is in Chinatown*). 是 shì can be left out when the predicative indicates date, time, age, etc.: 今天（是）星期三 jīntiān (shì) xīngqīsān (*today is Wednesday*); 现在（是）八点 xiànzài (shì) bā diǎn (*it is eight o'clock now*)

2. *exist*, used in an existential or presentational sentence: 美国的北边是加拿大 Měiguó de běibian shì Jiānádà (*north of the United States is Canada*). Note that the item following 是 shì, which is the real subject, must be definite or specified. If it is not, 有 yǒu should be used instead: 美国的北边只有一个国家 Měiguó de běibian zhǐ yǒu yí ge guójiā (*there is only one country north of the United States*).

3. used before a verb or an adjective for emphasis, concurrence or rebuttal: 高铁是很快 (*the high-speed train is indeed fast*); 我是在银行工作 (*I do work at the bank*)

是不是 **shì bu shì**   used to form a question at the beginning of a sentence or after the subject to seek confirmation of a supposition: 你是不是在银行工作 nǐ shì bu shì zài yínháng gōngzuò (*is it true that you work at a bank?*). 是不是中国人都用筷子吃饭 shì bu shì Zhōngguórén dōu yòng kuàizi chīfàn (*is it true that every Chinese eats with chopsticks?*). In colloquial speech, 是不是 shì bu shì can also appear at the end of the sentence: 你会说法语，是不是 nǐ huì shuō Fǎyǔ, shì bu shì (*you speak French, right?*). 是不是 shì bu shì has the same effect as a disjunctive question in English such as *you work at a bank, don't you?; Chinese people all eat with chopsticks, don't they?* The answer to the question formed by 是不是 shì bu shì is either 是 shì (*yes*) or 不是 bú shì (*no*), or 对 duì (*correct*) or 不对 bú duì (*not correct*).

是吗 **shì ma?**   1. used at the end of a question to mean the same as 是不是 shì bu shì: 韩国在东亚，是吗? Hánguó zài Dōngyà, shì ma (*Korea is in East Asia, isn't it?*). The answer to the question is either 是 shì (*yes*) or 不是 bú shì (*no*), or 对 duì (*correct*) or 不 bú duì (*not correct*).

2. used as a response to suggest surprise and disbelief with the meaning of "*really?*"

是啊 **shì a**   used as a response to suggest agreement

是 ... 的 shì ... de | **1.** used to emphasize or contrast the subject and the adverbial (time, place, manner of the action) in a sentence, similar to the "*it is ... that ...*" structure in English. 是 shì appears before the item to be emphasized and 的 de comes at the end of the sentence: 是我晚上在学校学中文的 shì wǒ wǎnshang zǎi xuéxiào xué Zhōngwén de (*it is I who studies Chinese in the evening at school*); 我是晚上在学校学中文的 wǒ shì wǎnshang zài xuéxiào xué Zhōngwén de (*it is in the evening that I study Chinese in a school*); 我晚上是在学校学中文的 wǒ wǎnshang shì zài xuéxiào xué Zhōngwén de (*it is at school that I study Chinese in the evening*).

2. used to ask questions about the time, place and manner of a past event, where 是 shì can be omitted: 他 (是) 什么时候去中国的 tā (shì) shénme shíhou qù Zhōngguó de (*when did he go to China?*); 你今天 (是) 怎么来的 nǐ jīntiān (shì) zěnme lái de (*how did you come today?*). When the verb is a transitive one, 的 de is usu. placed between the verb and the object: 你今天 (是) 在哪儿吃的中饭 nǐ jīntiān (shì) zài nǎr chī de zhōngfàn (*where did you eat lunch today?*). 你 (是) 在哪儿上的大学 nǐ (shì) zài nǎr shàng de dàxué (*where did you go to college?*). Note that the response to the questions above should take the same form. If the object is a pronoun or if it is a noun followed by a directional complement, 的 de must be placed at the end of the sentence: 你是在哪儿认识他的 nǐ shì zài nǎr rènshi tā de (*where did you meet him?*). 他是昨天寄来这封信的 tā shì zuótiān jì lái zhè fēng xìn de (*he sent this letter yesterday*).

3. used to emphasize purpose. This usage involves two verbs, the first of which is often a verbal phrase introduced by 来 lái (*come*) or 去 qù (*go*): 我是去中国工作的 wǒ shì qù Zhōngguó gōngzuò de (*I'm going to China to work—implying that I'm not going there for pleasure*).

事 shì

1. *matter; things to do*: 好事 hǎo shì (*good thing*); 我今天有很多事要做 wǒ jīntiān yǒu hěn duō shì yào zhuò (*come*)

2. *trouble*: 省事 shěng shì (*save trouble*); 费事 fèi shì (*troublesome*)

3. *job; work*: 你在哪儿做事 nǐ zài nǎr zuò shì (*where do you work?*)

Also appears in the following words: 从事 cóngshì (*undertake*); 董事 dǒngshì (*trustee*; *board member*); 故事 gùshì (*story*); 军事 jūnshì (*military affairs*); 领事 lǐngshì (*consul*); 启事 qǐshì (*notice*); 人事 rénshì (*personnel matters*); 时事 shíshì (*current affairs*); 外事 wàishì (*foreign affairs*); 刑事 xíngshì (*criminal affairs*)

事故 shìgù	*accident*. Cl: 起 qǐ; 次 cì	
事件 shìjiàn	*incident*; *event*. Cl: 起 qǐ	
事情 shìqing	*matter*; *things to do*, often shortened to 事 shì. Cl: 件 jiàn	
事实 shìshí	*fact*	
事务 shìwù	*routine work*; *affair*; *matter*	
事物 shìwù	*things*	
事先 shìxiān	*in advance*: 事先通知 shìxiān tōngzhī (*notify in advance*)	
事业 shìyè	*cause*; *career*	

市 shì

1. *city*; *municipality*: 市政府 shì zhèngfǔ (*municiple government*); 市中心 shì zhōngxīn (*center of the city*; *downtown*)

2. *market*: 菜市 càishì (*food market*); 夜市 yèshì (*evening market*); 超市 (*supermarket*). Cl: 个 gè; 家 jiā

市场 shìchǎng	*market*; *marketplace*: 股票市场 gǔpiào shìchǎng (*stock market*)
市民 shìmín	*townspeople*; *city resident*. Cl: 位 wèi; 群 qún
市区 shìqū	*urban area*; *city proper*
市长 shìzhǎng	*mayor*

室 shì

room: 教室 jiàoshì (*classroom*); 实验室 shíyànshì (*lab*); 温室 wēnshì (*greenhouse*); 卧室 wòshì (*bedroom*); 休息室 xiūxīshì (*lounge*); 浴室 yùshì (*bathroom*; *shower room*); 阅览室 yuèlǎnshì (*reading room*); 暗室 ànshì (*darkroom*); 办公室 bàngōngshì (*office*); 工作室 gōngzuòshì (*studio*). Cl: 间 jiān; 个 gè

室内 shì'nèi	*indoor*; *interior*: 室内设计 shìnèi shèjì (*interior design*)
室温 shìwēn	*room temperature*

试 shì

try; *test*; *attempt*, often in various collocations: 测试 cèshì (*test*; *testing*); 尝试 chángshì (*attempt*; *try*); 考试 kǎoshì (*take an exam*; *examination*); 面试 miànshì (*job interview*); 笔试 bǐshì (*written exam*); 口试 kǒushì (*oral exam*). 试 shì is often used with another verb in the sense of *doing sth. on the trial basis*: 试飞 shìfēi (*test flight*; *trial flight*); 试航 shìháng (*trial voyage*); 试用 shìyòng (*on probation*; *use on trial basis*).

试点 **shìdiǎn**	1. *launch a pilot project*	
	2. *place where an experiment is conducted*	
	Cl: 个 gè	
试管 **shìguǎn**	*test tube*: 试管婴儿 shìguǎn yīng'ér (*test-tube baby*).	
	Cl: 支 zhī; 根 gēn	
试讲 **shìjiǎng**	(of teachers) *give a demo class*	
试卷 **shìjuàn**	*examination paper*; *test paper*. Cl: 张 zhāng; 份 fèn	
试题 **shìtí**	*examination questions*	
试图 **shìtú**	*attempt*; *try*	
试行 **shìxíng**	*try out*	
试验 **shìyàn**	*experiment*; *test*; *trial*	
试用 **shìyòng**	*on probation*; *use on trial basis*; *try out*	

收 shōu

1. *accept*: 中国的餐馆不收小费 Zhōngguó de cānguǎn bù shōu xiǎofèi (*restaurants in China do not accept tips*)

2. *receive*, often used with the verb complement 到 dào: 这个收音机能收多少台 zhè ge shōuyīnjī néng shōu duōshao tái (*how many stations can this radio receive?*); 我收到了你的信 wǒ shōu dào le nǐde xìn (*I've received your letter*)

3. *put away*: 老师让学生们把书收起来 lǎoshī ràng xuéshengmen bǎ shū shōu qǐlái (*the teacher asked the students to put away their books*)

4. *collect*: 收学费 shōu xuéfèi (*collect tuition*); 收作业 shōu zuòyè (*collect homework*)

Also appears in the following words: **回收** huíshōu (*reclaim*; *recycle*); **接收** jiēshōu (*take over*); **没收** mòshōu (*confiscate*); **吸收** xīshōu (*absorb*)

收藏 **shōucáng**	*collect* (art works, etc.): 收藏家 shōucángjiā (*art collector*)
收费 **shōufèi**	*collect fees*
收回 **shōuhuí**	*take back*; *recall*; *regain*; *withdraw*: 收回命令 shōuhuí

	mìnglìng (*take back the order*); 收回建议 shōuhuí jiànyì (*withdraw the suggestion*); 收回领土 shōuhuí lǐngtǔ (*regain territory*)
收获 shōuhuò	*achievement*; *reward*; *gain*: 听了他的讲座，我有很大的收获 tīng le tāde jiǎngzuò, wǒ yǒu hěn dàde shōuhuò (*I gained a lot from his lecture*)
收集 shōují	*collect*; *gather*: 收集邮票 shōují yóupiào (*collect stamps*)
收据 shōujù	*receipt*. Cl: 张 zhāng
收入 shōurù	*income*. Cl: 项 xiàng; 笔 bǐ
收拾 shōushi	1. *put in order*; *clean*; *straighten*: 收拾房间 shōushi fángjiān (*clean the room*) 2. *pack*: 收拾行李 shōushi xíngli (*pack luggage*)
收尾 shōuwěi	*wind up* (work, etc.); *end* (of a story, etc.)
收效 shōuxiào	*produce effects or results*: 这个广告没有收效 zhè ge guǎnggào méi you shōuxiào (*this advertisement did not produce any result*)
收信人 shōuxìnrén	*recipient of a letter*; *addressee*
收养 shōuyǎng	*adopt* (a child)
收音机 shōuyīnjī	*radio*. Cl: 台 tái; 架 jià; 个 gè
收支 shōuzhī	*income and expenses*

手 shǒu

1. *hand*

2. *person with certain skills*: 水手 shuǐshǒu (*sailor*); 副手 fùshǒu (*assistant*); 歌手 géshǒu (*singer*). Cl: 位 wèi; 名 míng; 个 gè

Also appears in the following words: **帮手** bāngshou (*helper*); **对手** duìshǒu (*opponent*); **分手** fēnshǒu (*part company*; *break up*); **新手** xīnshǒu (*novice*)

手表 shǒubiǎo	*wrist watch*. Cl: 块 kuài
手段 shǒuduàn	*means*; *measure*; *method*
手法 shǒufǎ	*skill*; *style*
手风琴 shǒufēngqín	*accordion*. Cl: 架 jià
手工 shǒugōng	*handwork*
手工艺 shǒugōngyì	*handicraft*
手机 shǒujī	*cell phone*
手巾 shǒujīn	*towel*. Cl: 条 tiáo; 块 kuài
手绢 shǒujuàn	*handkerchief*. Cl: 块 kuài
手铐 shǒukào	*handcuff*. Cl: 副 fù
手枪 shǒuqiāng	*pistol*. Cl: 把 bǎ
手势 shǒushì	*gesture*; *hand sign*
手术 shǒushù	*surgery*

手提包 **shǒutíbāo**	*handbag.* Cl: 只 zhī
手头 **shǒutóu**	*at hand*
手续 **shǒuxù**	*procedures; formalities*
手艺 **shǒuyì**	*skill; craftsmanship.* Cl: 门 mén
手掌 **shǒuzhǎng**	*palm*
手指 **shǒuzhǐ**	*finger.* Cl: 根 gēn

受 shòu

1. *suffer; be subject to:* 受批评 shòu pīping (*get criticized*); 受罚 shòufá (*be penalized*)

2. *receive; accept:* 受训练 shòu xùnliàn (*receive training*); 受贿 shòu huì (*accept bribery*)

3. *stand; endure; tolerate:* often used in the negative sense with 不了 bùliǎo: 受不了那儿的夏天 shòu bùliǎo nàr de xiàtiān (*can't stand the summer there*)

Also appears in the following words: 感受 gǎnshòu (*experience*); 接受 jiēshòu (*accept*); 难受 nánshòu (*feel ill; feel unhappy*); 享受 xiǎngshòu (*enjoy; enjoyment*)

受害 **shòuhài**	*be victimized; be adversely affected:* 受害者 shòuhàizhě (*victim*).
受惊 **shòujīng**	*be frightened*
受苦 **shòukǔ**	*suffer hardship*
受凉 **shòuliáng**	*catch cold*
受骗 **shòupiàn**	*be ripped off; be taken in*
受权 **shòuquán**	*be authorized*
受伤 **shòushāng**	*be injured*
受审 **shòushěn**	*stand trial*
受托 **shòutuō**	*be commissioned; be entrusted with*
受益 **shòuyì**	*benefit from*
受孕 **shòuyùn**	*become pregnant*
受灾 **shòuzāi**	*be hit by a natural disaster*

书 shū

1. *book*

2. *document:* 毕业证书 bìyè zhèngshū (*diploma*); 协议书 xiéyìshū (*written agreement*). Cl: 份 fèn; 张 zhāng

3. *write,* used in literary language or set expressions

Also appears in the following words: 读书 dúshū (*read*; *study*; *attend school*); 教书 jiāoshū (*teach*); 秘书 mìshū (*secretary*); 情书 qíngshū (*love letter*); 说明书 shuōmíngshū (*manual*; *instructions*)

书包	shūbāo	*book bag*
书店	shūdiàn	*bookstore*
书法	shūfǎ	*calligraphy*
书画	shūhuà	*painting and calligraphy*. Cl: 幅 fú
书籍	shūjí	(*collective*) *books*
书记	shūjì	*secretary* (in a political party)
书架	shūjià	*bookshelf*. Cl: 个 gè
书刊	shūkān	*books and periodicals*
书面	shūmiàn	*in writing*: 书面答复 shūmiàn dáfù (*reply in writing*)
书评	shūpíng	*book review*. Cl: 篇 piān
书签	shūqiān	*bookmark*. Cl: 张 zhāng
书信	shūxìn	*letter*. Cl: 封 fēng

数 shǔ; shù

When pronounced shǔ:

1. *count* (v.): 数钱 shǔ qián (*count money*)

2. *be regarded as*: 中国数哈尔滨最冷 Zhōngguó shǔ Hārbīn zuì lěng (*Harbin is regarded as the coldest place in China*)

When pronounced shù:

number

Also appears in the following words: 单数 dānshù (*odd number*; *singular*); 多数 duōshù (*majority*); 分数 fēnshù (*fraction*); 复数 fùshù (*plural*)

数据	shùjù	*data*
数量	shùliàng	*quantity*; *amount*
数学	shùxué	*mathematics*
数字	shùzi	*numeral*

术 shù

1. *skill*; *technique*; *art*: 美术 měishù (*fine arts*); 技术 jìshù (*technique*; *technology*; *skill*); 艺术 yìshù (*art*); 算术 suànshù (*arithmetic*)

2. *method*; *tactics*: 战术 zhànshù (*tactic*). Cl: 套 tào; 种 zhǒng

Also appears in the following words: 魔术 móshù (*magic*); 手术 shǒushù (*operation*; *surgery*); 武术 wǔshù (*martial art*); 学术 xuéshù (*learning*; *academic*)

术语 shùyǔ　　　　　　*technical terms*; *terminology*

双 shuāng

1. *two*; *twin*; *both*; *dual*

2. *pair*: 一双袜子 yì shuāng wàzi (*a pair of socks*); 两双手套 liǎng shuāng shǒutào (*two pairs of gloves*); 三双筷子 sān shuāng kuàizi (*three pairs of chopsticks*)

3. *even*: 双号 shuānghào (*even number*)

4. *double*; *twofold*

双胞胎 shuāngbāotāi	*twins*. Cl: 对 duì
双边 shuāngbiān	*bilateral*: 双边条约 shuāngbiān tiáoyuē (*bilateral treaty*)
双层 shuāngcéng	*double-deck*; *two layers*: 双层床 shuāngcéngchuáng (*double-deck bed*)
双重 shuāngchóng	*double*; *duel*: 双重标准 shuāngchóng biāozhǔn (*double standards*); 双重国籍 shuāngchóng guójí (*double citizenship*)
双方 shuāngfāng	*both sides*; *two parties*
双亲 shuāngqīn	*parents*; *father and mother*
双人床 shuāngrénchuáng	*double bed*
双语 shuāngyǔ	*bilingual*; *dual languages*

谁 shuí; shéi

Both pronunciations are in common use.

1. *who*, 谁是你的中文老师 shuí shì nǐde Zhōngwén lǎoshī (*who is your Chinese teacher?*); 你和谁去看电影 nǐ hé shuí qù kàn diànyīng (*who are you going to see the movie with?*)

2. *anyone*, *no one* (in the negative), usu. used with 都 dōu: 苏州的园林，谁都说漂亮 Sūzhōu de yuánlín, shuí dōu shuō piàoliang (*anyone would say that the gardens in Suzhou are beautiful*); 谁都不愿意做这种事 shuí dōu bú yuànyì zuò zhè zhǒng shì (*no one would want to do something like this*)

谁的 shuíde	*whose*: 这是谁的书 zhè shì shuíde shū (*whose book is this?*)

水 shuǐ

water

Also appears in the following words: 风水 fēngshui (*geomancy*); 洪水 hóngshuǐ (*flood*); 开水 kāishuǐ (*boiling water; boiled water*); 汽水 qìshuǐ (*soda*); 薪水 xīnshui (*salary*)

水兵	**shuǐbīng**	*seaman; sailor*
水彩	**shuǐcǎi**	*watercolor*: 水彩画 shuǐcǎihuà (*watercolor painting*)
水池	**shuǐchí**	*pond; pool*
水稻	**shuǐdào**	*rice paddy*
水果	**shuǐguǒ**	*fruit*
水饺	**shuǐjiǎo**	*dumplings*
水库	**shuǐkù**	*reservoir*. Cl: 个 gè; 座 zuò
水路	**shuǐlù**	*water route*
水泥	**shuǐní**	*cement*. Cl: 袋 dài
水牛	**shuǐniú**	*water buffalo*. Cl: 头 tóu
水平	**shuǐpíng**	*level; standard*: 英语水平 Yīngyǔ shuǐpíng (*level of English*); 生活水平 shēnghuó shuǐpíng (*living standard*)

睡 shuì

sleep; go to bed: 睡得早 shuì de zǎo (*go to bed early*); 睡得好 shuì de hǎo (*had a good sleep*)

睡觉 **shuìjiào**	*sleep; go to bed*. 睡觉 shuìjiào is interchangeable with 睡 shuì in expressing *to go to bed*: 你要早点儿睡觉 nǐ yào zǎo diǎnr shuìjiào (*you should go to bed early*); it is equally correct to say 你要早点儿睡 nǐ yào zǎo diǎnr shuì. When used in the sense of *to sleep*, 睡 shuì can directly take a complement, whereas 睡觉 shuìjiào can't, because 睡觉 shuìjiào is actually a VO (verb-object) structure. As such, 觉 jiào in 睡觉 shuìjiào can be modified by a noun phrase or an adjective. Cf. 我睡了五个小时 wǒ shuì le wǔ ge xiǎoshí (*I slept for five hours*); 我睡了五个小时的觉 wǒ shuì le wǔ ge xiǎoshí de jiào (*I slept for five hours*); 我睡得好 wǒ shuì de hǎo (*I had a good sleep*); 我睡了一个好觉 wǒ shuì le yí ge hǎo jiào (*I had a good sleep*).
睡眠 **shuìmián**	*sleep* (n.): 睡眠不足 shuìmián bù zú (*insufficient sleep*)
睡醒 **shuìxǐng**	*wake up*
睡衣 **shuìyī**	*pajamas; nightgown*. Cl: 件 jiàn

说 shuō

1. *say*; *speak*; *tell*; *talk*: 你会说中文吗 nǐ huì shuō Zhōngwén ma (*do you speak Chinese?*); 请大声说 qǐng dàshēng shuō (*please speak loudly*); 这个词用中文怎么说 zhè ge cí yòng Zhōngwén zěnme shuō (*how do you say this word in Chinese?*)

2. *explain*: 孩子不知道怎么向家长说 háizi bù zhīdao zěnme xiàng jiāzhǎng shuō (*the child does not know how to explain to his parents*)

3. *criticize*; *scold*: 他常迟到，老师今天说了他 tā cháng chídào, lǎoshī jīntiān shuō le tā (*he is often late, so the teacher scolded him today*)

Also appears in the following words: 传说 chuánshuō (*legend*); 听说 tīngshuō (*hear of*; *be told*); 小说 xiǎoshuō (*novel*; *fiction*); 再说 zàishuō (*besides*; *what's more*)

说不定 **shuō bu dìng**	*maybe*; *perhaps*
说不过去 **shuō bu guòqù**	*unjustifiable*
说法 **shuōfa**	*way of saying things*
说服 **shuōfú**	*persuade*; *convince*
说好 **shuō hǎo**	*reach an agreement or understanding*
说话 **shuōhuà**	*talk* (v.)
说谎 **shuōhuǎng**	*tell a lie*
说明 **shuōmíng**	*explain*; *elucidate*
说情 **shuōqíng**	*plead for mercy or forgiveness for someone*

死 sǐ

1. *die*: 鱼死了 yú sǐ le (*the fish died*); 死于癌症 sì yú áizhèng (*die of cancer*). 死 sǐ is often used as a verb complement to indicate a result: 打死 dǎ sǐ (*beat to death*); 杀死 shā sǐ (*kill*); 病死 bìng sǐ (*die of a disease*).

2. *dead*: 死鱼 sǐ yú (*dead fish*); 死人 sǐ rén (*dead person*)

3. *extremely*; *to death*: 饿死了 è sǐ le (*starving*; *extremely hungry*); 忙死了 máng sǐ le (*extremely busy*)

4. *fixed*; *inflexible*; *tight*, often used as a verb complement: 死结 sǐ jié (*fast knot*), 门关死了 mén guān sǐ le (*the door is shut tight*); 他把话说死了 tā bǎ huà shuō sǐ le (*he didn't leave any room for negotiation in his talk*)

5. *inactive*: 死水 sǐ shuǐ (*stagnant water*); 死火山 sǐ huǒshān (*inactive volcano*)

死地 **sǐdì**	*a fatal position*
死角 **sǐjiǎo**	*blind angle*

死路	**sǐlù**	road to destruction. Cl: 条 tiáo
死尸	**sǐshī**	corpse
死亡	**sǐwáng**	death
死心	**sǐxīn**	forget about an idea forever; have no more illusion about: 他对当律师没有死心 tā duì dāng lǜshī méiyou sǐxīn (he hasn't given up the idea of becoming a lawyer)
死刑	**sǐxíng**	death penalty; capital punishment
死者	**sǐzhě**	the dead; the diseased

四 sì

four

| 四处 | **sìchù** | everywhere; in all directions |
| 四月 | **sìyuè** | April |

送 sòng

1. *give as a present*: 他送给他的女朋友一个戒指 tā sòng gěi tāde nǚpéngyou yí ge jièzhi (*he gave his girlfriend a ring as a present*)

2. *see sb. off; escort sb. to*: 送客人去机场 sòng kèrén qù jīchǎng (*take the guests to the airport*); 送孩子到学校 sòng háizi dào xuéxiào (*take the child to school*)

3. *deliver*: 送信 sòng xìn (*deliver a letter*); 送饭 sòng fàn (*deliver food*)

Also appears in the following words: **护送** hùsòng (*escort*); **欢送** huānsòng (*send off*); **运送** yùnsòng (*v. ship*)

送还	**sònghuán**	return a borrowed item in person
送货	**sònghuò**	make a delivery
送交	**sòngjiāo**	deliver sth. to sb.; hand over
送礼	**sònglǐ**	give a present: 他们结婚的那天, 有很多人送礼 tāmen jiéhūn de nà tiān, yǒu hěn duō rén sònglǐ (*many people gave them presents on their wedding day*)
送行	**sòngxíng**	see sb. off; give sb. a send-off party
送葬	**sòngzàng**	attend a funeral procession

算 suàn

1. *calculate*; *compute*

2. *count*; *include*: 不算他，我们一共有十个人 bú suàn tā, wǒmen yígòng yǒu shí ge rén (*not counting him, we have ten people altogether*)

3. *consider*; *count as*: 这算是我们的一点儿心意 zhè suànshì wǒmende yìdiǎnr xīnyì (*this counts as our little token of thanks*)

4. *carry weight*; *mean*; *count*, often used with 说 shuō: 他常常说话不算话 tā chángcháng shuōhuà bú suàn huà (*he often doesn't mean what he says*); 我们家我妈妈说了算 wǒmen jiā wǒ māma shuò le suàn (*in our house, my mother is the boss*)

5. *at long last*; *finally*: 他的病算好了 tāde bìng suàn hǎo le (*he finally recovered from his sickness*)

6. *forget about it*; *let it pass*, used with 了 le: 既然没有人能来，这个晚会就算了 jìrán méi you rén néng lái, zhè ge wǎnhuì jiù suàn le (*since no one can make it, let's forget about the evening party*)

Also appears in the following words: 打算 dǎsuan (*plan*); 计算 jìsuàn (*compute*; *calculate*); 预算 yùsuàn (*budget*); 总算 zǒngsuàn (*finally*; *at long last*)

算命	suànmìng	*fortune-telling*
算盘	suànpán	*abacus*. Cl: 把 bǎ; 个 gè
算是	suànshì	*at long last*; *finally*
算术	suànshù	*arithmetic*
算数	suànshù	*carry weight*; *mean*; *count*: 他不是老板，他说的话不算数 tā bú shì lǎobǎn, tā shuō de huà bú suànshù (*he is not the boss, what he says doesn't count*). 算数 suànshù can also be expressed as 算话 suànhuà.
算帐	suànzhàng	*do accounts*; *balance the books*; *settle a score*

岁 suì

1. *year*, used in formal language: 今岁 jīn suì (*this year*); 岁收 suìshōu (*annual revenue*)

2. (of a person's age) *year*: 三十岁 sānshí suì (*thirty years old*)

岁数	suìshù	*age*: 他岁数不大 tā suìshù bú dà (*he is very young*)
岁月	suìyuè	*years*; *times*: 艰难的岁月 jiānnán de suìyuè (*difficult years*)

所 suǒ

1. *place*: 厕所 cèsuǒ (*bathroom*); 研究所 yánjiūsuǒ (*research institute*)

2. classifier used for schools, hospitals, etc.

3. used before a transitive verb in the nominalizing structure; the object can often be left out: 他所说的 (话) 和他所做的 (事) 不一样 tā suǒ shuō de (huà) hé tā suǒ zuò de (shì) bù yíyàng (*what he said is not the same as what he did*). 所 suǒ is often left out in colloquial speech without affecting the meaning of the sentence.

Also appears in the following words: 厕所 cèsuǒ (*restroom*; *toilet*); 场所 chǎngsuǒ (*location*; *place*); 诊所 zhěnsuǒ (*clinic*; *doctor's office*)

所得 **suǒdé**	*income*: 所得税 suǒdéshuì (*income tax*)
所谓 **suǒwèi**	*so-called*: 所谓春节就是中国新年 suǒwèi chūnjié jiù shì Zhōngguó xīnnián (*the so-called Spring Festival is the Chinese New Year*)
所以 **suǒyǐ**	*therefore*, always used at the beginning of the second clause; the first clause indicating the cause is usu. introduced by 因为 yīnwei or 由于 yóuyú.
所有 **suǒyǒu**	*whole*; *all*: 所有的住房 suóyǒude zhùfáng (*all the residential houses*)

他 tā

1. *he*; *him*

2. *other*: 他人 tārén (*other people*); 他国 tāguó (*other countries*)

Also appears in the following words: 吉他 jítā (*guitar*); 其他 qítā (*other*; *else*)

他的 **tāde**	*his*; 的 de is often left out when followed by words for family members or intimate people or places.
他们 **tāmen**	*they*; *them*
他们的 **tāmende**	*their*

她 tā

she; *her*

她们 **tāmen**	*they*; *them* (all females)
她们的 **tāmende**	*their* (all females)

它 tā

it. When used to refer to an object for the first time, 它 tā is not to be used. Words such as 这 or 那 should be used: 这是什么 zhè shì shénme (*what is this?*); 那是什么 nà shì shénme (*what is that?*)

它的 tāde	*its*
它们 tāmen	*they*, standing for non-human nouns only
它们的 tāmende	*their*, followed by non-human nouns only

太 tài

1. *too; excessively*: 太快 tài kuài (*too fast*); 太贵 tài guì (*too expensive*)

2. *very; extremely*, usu. used in conjunction with 了 le at the end of the phrase or sentence: 太好了 tài hǎo le (*great*); 太累了 tài lèi le (*exhausted*)

太极拳 tàijíquán	*traditional Chinese shadow boxing*
太平 tàipíng	*peace and prosperity*
太平洋 Tàipíngyáng	*the Pacific Ocean*
太太 tàitai	**1.** *Mrs.*, used before the surname: 王太太 Wáng Tàitai (*Mrs. Wang*)
	2. *wife*: 我太太 wǒ tàitai (*my wife*)
太阳 tàiyáng	*the sun*

谈 tán

talk; chat; discuss: 和谈 hétán (*peace talk*); 会谈 huìtán (*talk*); 交谈 jiāotán (*conversation; converse*); 空谈 kōngtán (*empty talk*); 面谈 miàntán (*interview; speak to sb. face to face*). 谈 tán differs from 说 shuō in that it implies the participation of two interlocutors.

谈话 tánhuà	*talk; chat; conversation; statement*
谈判 tánpàn	*negotiation; negotiate*
谈天 tántiān	*chat; talk*
谈心 tánxīn	*heart-to-heart talk*

特 tè

1. *Unusually; exceptionally*, often taking the disyllabic form of 特别 tèbié: 特别好看 tèbié hǎokàn (*exceptionally pretty*)

2. *specially*; *in particular*, often used in conjunction with 地 dì: 他特地来看你 tā tèdì lái kàn nǐ (*he came specially to see you*)

Also appears in the following words: **独特** dútè (*unique*); **模特** mótè (*model*); **奇特** qítè (*oddity; peculiar*)

特别 tèbié	1. *unusually; exceptionally*: 今天的风特别大 jīntiān de fēng tèbié dà (*the wind today is unusually strong*) 2. *extraordinary; special*: 特别的礼物 tèbiéde lǐwù (*special gift*); 特别的待遇 tèbiéde dàiyù (*special treatment*)
特产 tèchǎn	*special product*; (local) *specialty*. Cl: 种 zhǒng; 样 yàng
特长 tècháng	*strongpoint; specialty*. Cl: 种 zhǒng
特地 tèdì	*specially*: 这是特地为你买的 zhè shì tèdì wèi nǐ mǎi de (*this is specially bought for you*)
特定 tèdìng	*given; specific; specified*: 特定的环境 tèdìngde huánjìng (*specific circumstances*)
特快 tèkuài	*express* (mail, train, etc.)
特权 tèquán	*privilege*. Cl: 种 zhǒng
特色 tèsè	*characteristic; distinctive feature*. Cl: 个 gè; 种 zhǒng
特殊 tèshū	*special; exceptional*
特效 tèxiào	*special effect*
特征 tèzhēng	*characteristic; feature; trait*. Cl: 个 gè; 种 zhǒng

疼 téng

ache; pain; sore: 头疼 tóuténg (*headache*); 肚子疼 dùziténg (*stomachache*); 嗓子疼 sǎngziténg (*sore throat*)

疼爱 téng'ài	*be very fond of; love dearly*. The object is usually a child.
疼痛 téngtòng	*ache; pain; painful, sore*

提 tí

1. *carry or hold* (in one's hand with the arm down): 提篮子 tí lánzi (*carry the basket*)

2. *raise*: 提工资 tí gōngzī (*raise the salary*); 提速度 tí sùdù (*accelerate the speed*)

3. *move up* (a time or date): 提早到学校 tízǎo dào xuéxiào (*go to school earlier*); 提前下班 tíqián xiàbān (*get off work earlier*)

4. *bring up; raise*: 提问题 tí wèntí (*raise a question*); 提条件 tí tiáojiàn (*lay down conditions*)

5. *withdraw* (money); *extract*: 提钱 tí qián (*withdraw money*)

6. *mention*, used with 到 dào: 这本书提到那位作家 zhè běn shū tí dào nà wèi zuòjiā (*this book mentioned that author*)

提案	**tí'àn**	*motion; proposal.* Cl: 条 tiáo
提拔	**tíbá**	*promote (a person to a higher position)*
提倡	**tíchàng**	*advocate; encourage; promote (an idea, etc.)*
提出	**tíchū**	*put forward; bring up (a suggestion, issue, etc.)*
提法	**tífǎ**	*wording; formulation*
提高	**tígāo**	*heighten; raise; improve*: 提高生活水平 tígāo shēnghuó shuǐpíng (*raise living standards*); 提高英语能力 tígāo Yīngyǔ nénglì (*improve English ability*)
提供	**tígòng**	*provide; supply*
提交	**tíjiāo**	*submit (a proposal, etc.)*
提名	**tímíng**	*nominate*
提前	**tíqián**	*move up a date; in advance*
提升	**tíshēng**	*promote (a person to a higher position)*
提问	**tíwèn**	*put a question to*
提醒	**tíxǐng**	*remind*
提要	**tíyào**	*summary; abstract*
提议	**tíyì**	*propose; proposal; motion*
提早	**tízǎo**	*move up a date; in advance*

题 tí

1. *title; subject; topic*: 话题 huàtí (*topic of conversation*); 标题 biāotí (*title; headline*). Cl: 个 gè

2. (academic) *question; problem*: 数学题 shùxuétí (*mathematics problem*); 难题 nántí (*difficult question*). Cl: 道 dào

Also appears in the following words: 离题 lítí (*off subject*); 问题 wèntí (*problem; question*); 主题 zhǔtí (*subject; theme*)

题材	**tícái**	*subject matter*
题目	**tímù**	*title; subject; topic*

体 tǐ

1. *body*: 人体 réntǐ (*human body*); 体态 tǐtài (*posture; state*)

2. *state of a substance*: 液体 yètǐ (*liquid state*); 气体 qìtǐ (*gas state*); 固体 gùtǐ (*solid state*). Cl: 种 zhǒng

3. *literary or calligraphic style*

4. *system*: 政体 zhèngtǐ (*polity; system of a government*)

Also appears in the following words: 集体 jítǐ (*collective*); 解体 jiětǐ (*disintegrate*); 具体 jùtǐ (*concrete*); 立体 lìtǐ (*solid*); 裸体 luǒtǐ (*nude*); 全体 quántǐ (*whole*); 身体 shēntǐ (*body; health*); 尸体 shītǐ (*corpse*)

体裁	tǐcái	*literary genre.* Cl: 种 zhǒng
体操	tǐcāo	*gymnastics*
体罚	tǐfá	*corporal punishment*
体格	tǐgé	*physique;* (physical) *constitution; build* (n.)
体积	tǐjī	*volume*
体力	tǐlì	*physical; physical strength; stamina*: 体力工作 tǐlì gōngzuò (*physical work*)
体谅	tǐliang	*make allowances for*
体面	tǐmiàn	*grace; graceful*
体贴	tǐtiē	*be considerate; show consideration for*
体温	tǐwēn	*body temperature*
体系	tǐxì	*system.* Cl: 种 zhǒng; 套 tào
体现	tǐxiàn	*embody; show*
体形	tǐxíng	(body) *figure*
体育	tǐyù	*physical education; sports*: 体育课 tǐyùke (*gym class*); 体育馆 tǐyùguan (*gymnasium*)
体质	tǐzhì	*physical constitution*

天 tiān

1. *sky; heaven*: 天上没有云 tiān shang méi you yún (*there are no clouds in the sky*)

2. *day*: 每天 měi tiān (*every day*); 冷天 lěng tiān (*cold day*). 天 tiān both serves as a classifier and a noun, so it can directly follow a number or a demonstrative pronoun: 三天 sān tiān (*three days*); 那天 nà tiān (*that day*).

3. *season*: 春天 chūntiān (*spring*); 夏天 xiàtiān (*summer*); 秋天 qiūtiān (*fall*); 冬天 dōngtiān (*winter*)

4. *weather*: 天下雨了 tiān xiàyǔ le (*it started raining*); 天热了 tiān rè le (*it is getting hot*)

天才	tiāncái	*genius; talent.* Cl: 个 gè; 位 wèi
天花板	tiānhuābǎn	*ceiling*
天空	tiānkōng	*sky*
天气	tiānqì	*weather*
天桥	tiānqiáo	*overpass.* Cl: 个 gè; 座 zuò

天然	tiānrán	natural
天生	tiānshēng	innate; inborn; inherent
天堂	tiāntáng	paradise; heaven
天文	tiānwén	astronomy: 天文学家 tiānwénxuéjiā (astronomer)
天线	tiānxiàn	antenna. Cl: 根 gēn
天性	tiānxìng	natural instincts
天灾	tiānzāi	natural disaster
天真	tiānzhēn	naive; innocent

条 tiáo

1. *a long narrow piece*; *strip*: 纸条 zhǐtiáo (*informal note*); 布条 bùtiáo (*a strip of cloth*)

2. *an item in a document*: 合同的第三条 hétóng de dì sān tiáo (*the third clause in the contract*)

3. classifier used mostly for long and narrow or belt-like objects, such as a tie, pants, street, river, belt, snake, etc.

条件	tiáojiàn	condition; circumstances; terms; requirement: 旅馆的条件 lǚguǎn de tiáojiàn (condition of the hotel); 我们不能接受这样的条件 wǒmen bú néng jiēshòu zhèyàngde tiáojiàn (we can't accept such terms); 需要具备什么样的条件才能当老师 xūyào jùbèi shénmeyàng de tiáojiàn cái néng dāng lǎoshī (what requirements does one need to meet in order to become a teacher?). Cl: 个 gè; 项 xiàng
条款	tiáokuǎn	clause or provision in a contract or treaty. Cl: 项 xiàng
条理	tiáolǐ	well-organized
条例	tiáolì	regulations; rules. Cl: 项 xiàng
条约	tiáoyuē	treaty; pact. Cl: 项 xiàng; 个 gè
条子	tiáozi	a brief informal note

跳 tiào

1. *jump*; *leap*

2. *beat*; *bounce*: 心跳 xīn tiào (*heartbeat*)

3. *skip*; *bypass*, used with the verb complement 过 guò: 跳过下一课 tiào guò xià yī kè (*skip the next lesson*); 跳过中间人 tiào guò zhōngjiānrén (*bypass the middleman*)

| 跳板 | tiàobǎn | springboard; diving board. Cl: 块 kuài; 个 gè |
| 跳动 | tiàodòng | (of heart) beat; pulsate |

跳高 tiàogāo	high jump
跳马 tiàomǎ	vaulting horse; horse-vaulting
跳皮筋 tiàopíjīn	rubber band skipping (popular game for young children in China)
跳棋 tiàoqí	Chinese checkers. Cl: 副 fù
跳伞 tiàosǎn	parachute (v.)
跳绳 tiàoshéng	rope skipping
跳水 tiàoshuǐ	dive
跳台 tiàotái	diving platform. Cl: 座 zuò
跳舞 tiàowǔ	dance (v.)
跳远 tiàoyuǎn	long jump
跳蚤 tiàozǎo	flea. Cl: 只 zhī

听 tīng

listen: 听音乐 tīng yīnyuè (*listen to music*); 听收音机 tīng shōuyīnjī (*listen to the radio*)

听话 tīnghuà	be obedient to an elder, parent or superior
听见 tīngjiàn	hear
听觉 tīngjué	sense of hearing
听课 tīngkè	audit or observe a class
听力 tīnglì	listening comprehension
听说 tīngshuō	be told; hear of: 听说明天要下雪 tīngshuō míngtiān yào xiàxuě (*I heard that it is going to snow tomorrow*)
听写 tīngxiě	dictation; give a dictation
听众 tīngzhòng	audience; listeners

停 tíng

1. *stop; cease; halt*: 车停了 chē tíng le (*the car has stopped*); 飞机在路上停不停 fēijī zài lù shang tíng bu tíng (*will the plane stop on the way?*)

2. *stay; stop by*: 她在这儿只停了一晚上 tā zài zhèr zhǐ tíng le yì wǎnshang (*she only stayed here one night*)

3. *park* (v.); *anchor*: 你的车停在哪儿 nǐde chē tíng zài nǎr (*where did you park your car?*); 岸边停着很多船 ànbiān tíng zhe hěn duō chuán (*many boats are anchored along the shore*)

停产 tíngchǎn	stop production
停车 tíngchē	(of vehicles and trains) stop; pull over; park
停电 tíngdiàn	power failure; blackout

停顿 tíngdùn	pause
停火 tínghuǒ	cease-fire
停靠 tíngkào	(of boats and ships) berth (at)
停留 tíngliú	stay; make a brief stop
停学 tíngxué	drop out of school; be suspended from school
停业 tíngyè	close down business
停战 tíngzhàn	armistice; truce
停止 tíngzhǐ	stop; cease
停滞 tíngzhì	stagnate: 经济陷于停滞状况 jīngjì xiàn yú tíngzhì zhuàngkuàng (the economy is in a state of stagnation)

通 tōng

1. *be put through; open*: 水管不通 shuǐguǎn bù tōng (*the tube is clogged*); 路通了 lù tōng le (*the road was opened*)

2. *through*, used as a verb complement: 电话接通了 diànhuà jiē tōng le (*the phone call was put through*); 这个方法行不通 zhè ge fāngfǎ xíng bù tōng (*this method won't work*)

3. *go to; lead to*: 这条路通不通火车站 zhè tiáo lù tōng bu tōng huǒchēzhàn (*does this road lead to the train station?*)

4. *exchange; connect*: 这两个国家通商 zhè liǎng ge guójiā tōngshāng (*these two countries have trade relations*)

5. *expert; be knowledgeable about*: 中国通 Zhōngguótōng (*expert on China*); 我不通日语 wǒ bù tōng Rìyǔ (*I don't understand Japanese*)

Also appears in the following words: 沟通 gōutōng (*communicate*); 交通 jiāotōng (*traffic; transportation*); 精通 jīngtōng (*mastery; proficient*); 流通 liútōng (*circulation*); 普通 pǔtōng (*common*)

通病 tōngbìng	common problem
通常 tōngcháng	generally; normally
通告 tōnggào	public notice. Cl: 份 fèn; 张 zhāng; 个 gè
通过 tōngguò	1. *go through; pass through*: 火车通过了隧道 huǒchē tōngguò le suìdào (*the train passed through the tunnel*) 2. *through*: 通过翻译交谈 tōngguò fānyì jiāotán (*talk through the interpreter*) 3. *adopt; pass* (a resolution, etc.) 4. *approve*: 你的申请没有通过 nǐde shēnqǐng méiyou tōngguò (*your application was not approved*)
通俗 tōngsú	popular; easy to understand: 通俗的语言 tōngsúde yǔyán (*plain language*)
通信 tōngxìn	correspond; exchange letters

通讯 **tōngxùn**	*communication*; *telecommunication*: 通讯社 tōngxùnshè (*news agency*); 通讯员 tōngxùnyuán (*news correspondent*)
通用 **tōngyòng**	1. *interchangeable*: 这两个词可以通用 zhè liǎng ge cí kěyǐ tōngyòng (*these two words are interchangeable*) 2. *in common use*: 通用术语 tōngyòng shùyǔ (*terminology in common use*)
通知 **tōngzhī**	*notify*; *notification*. Cl: 个 gè; 张 zhāng; 份 fèn

---

同 tóng

1. *same*; *of one*, usu. used with 一 yī: 同一个人 tóngyī ge ren (*the same person*); 同一本书 tóngyī běn shū

2. *with*; *as ... as*: 谁同我一起去 shuí tóng wǒ yìqǐ qù (*who is going with me?*); 同美国比，中国大一点儿 tóng Měiguǒ bǐ, Zhōngguó dà yìdiǎnr (*compared with the United States, China is a little larger*); 这个电脑同那个电脑一样快 zhè ge diànnǎo tóng nà ge diànnǎo yíyàng kuài (*this computer is as fast as that computer*)

3. *to*: 经理在同客户谈话 jīnglǐ zài tóng kèhù tánhuà (*the manager is talking to the customers*)

Also appears in the following words: 共同 gòngtóng (*common*; *jointly*); 合同 hétong (*contract*; *compact*); 陪同 péitóng (*accompany*); 相同 xiāngtóng (*identical*); 一同 yìtóng (*together*)

同伴 **tóngbàn**	*companion*. Cl: 个 gè; 位 wèi
同等 **tóngděng**	*of the same class, rank or importance*
同行 **tóngháng**	*of the same profession*. Cl: 个 gè; 位 wèi
同居 **tóngjū**	*cohabit*
同路 **tónglù**	*go in the same direction*
同盟 **tóngméng**	*alliance*
同情 **tóngqíng**	*sympathize with*; *sympathy*
同时 **tóngshí**	*at the same time*; *simultaneously*
同事 **tóngshì**	*colleague*; *co-worker*. Cl: 个 gè; 位 wèi
同乡 **tóngxiāng**	*fellow townsman*. Cl: 个 gè; 位 wèi
同学 **tóngxué**	*classmate*. Cl: 个 gè; 位 wèi
同样 **tóngyàng**	*same*; *equally*; *in the same way*: 同样的东西 tóngyàngde dōngxi (*the same stuff*); 同样处理 tóngyàng chùlǐ (*handle in the same way*)
同义词 **tóngyìcí**	*synonym*
同意 **tóngyì**	*agree*; *consent*
同志 **tóngzhì**	*comrade*. Cl: 个 gè; 位 wèi

头 tóu

1. *head*

2. *top*; *end*: 山头 shāntóu (*top of a mountain*); 北头 běitóu (*northern end*)

3. *beginning*: 从头来 cóng tóu lái (*start from the beginning*)

4. *end*; *butt*: 粉笔头 fěnbǐtóu (*chalk stub*); 香烟头 xiāngyāntóu (*cigarette butt*)

5. *chief*; *leader*, often taking the form of 头儿 tóur: 谁是你们的头儿 shuí shì nǐmende tóur (*who is your leader?*)

6. *first*: 头两天 tóu liǎng tiān (*first two days*); 头三排 tóu sān pái (*the first three rows*)

7. classifier, used for certain domestic animals such as cow, pig, donkey, sheep: 三头猪 sān tóu zhū (*three pigs*); 五头牛 wǔ tóu niú (*five cow*)

Also appears in the following words: **插头** chātóu (*plug*); **镜头** jìngtóu (*lens*); **码头** mǎtóu (*wharf*); **指头** zhítou (*finger*)

头版 tóubǎn	*front page* (of a newspaper)	
头等 tóuděng	*first class*; *first-rate*: 头等舱 tóuděngcāng (*first-class cabin*)	
头顶 tóudǐng	*top of the head*	
头发 tóufa	*hair* (on the human head). Cl: 根 gēn	
头号 tóuhào	*number one*	
头昏 tóuhūn	*dizzy*	
头脑 tóunǎo	*brain*; *mind*: 头脑清醒 tóunǎo qīngxǐng (*clear-headed*)	
头皮 tóupí	*scalp*	
头疼 tóuténg	*have a headache*, interchangeable with 头痛 tóutòng	
头痛 tóutòng	*have a headache*, interchangeable with 头疼 tóuténg	
头衔 tóuxián	*title of a position*. Cl: 个 gè; 种 zhǒng	
头晕 tóuyūn	*dizzy*	
头子 tóuzi	*chieftain*; *leader*, often in a pejorative sense. Cl: 个 gè	

土 tǔ

1. *soil*; *earth*; *clay*: 肥土 féitǔ (*fertile soil*); 土墙 tǔqiáng (*earthen wall*); 土路 tǔlù (*dirt road*)

2. *land*: 国土 guótǔ (*territory of a country*)

3. *local*; *native*: 土话 tǔhuà (*local dialect*); 土产 tǔchǎn (*local products*)

4. *homemade*; *indigenous*: 土方法 tǔ fāngfǎ (*indigenous method*)

5. *provincial*; *rustic*; *uncouth*

Also appears in the following words: 尘土 chéntǔ (*dust*); 出土 chūtǔ (*excavated*); 领土 lǐngtǔ (*territory*)

土产	tǔchǎn	*local products*
土地	tǔdì	*land.* Cl: 块 kuài; 片 piàn
土豆	tǔdòu	*potato*
土匪	tǔfěi	*bandit*
土话	tǔhuà	*local dialect*; *local saying*
土气	tǔqì	*provincial*; *rustic*; *uncouth*
土壤	tǔrǎng	*soil*
土语	tǔyǔ	*local saying*; *local dialect*

团 tuán

1. *a ball-like object*: 汤团 tāngtuán (*rice dumplings*); 面团 miàntuán (*dough*); 纸团 zhǐtuán (*paper rolled into a ball*). Cl: 个 gè

2. *group*; *organization*: 旅行团 lǚxíngtuán (*travel group*); 代表团 dàibiǎotuán (*delegation*); 剧团 jùtuán (*drama troupe*). Cl: 个 gè

3. classifier for ball-like objects: 一团线 yì tuán xiàn (*a ball of thread*); 一团泥 yì tuán ní (*a lump of clay*)

Also appears in the following words: 财团 cáituán (*financial group*; *consortium*); 集团 jítuán (*bloc*; *group*); 社团 shètuán (*community groups*)

团结	tuánjié	*unite*; *united*
团聚	tuánjù	*get-together*; *reunion*
团体	tuántǐ	*group*; *organization*: 民间团体 mínjiān tuántǐ (*non-governmental organization*). Cl: 个 gè
团圆	tuányuán	*family reunion*

推 tuī

push; *shove*: 推车 tuī chē (*push a cart*); 推门 tuī mén (*push the door*)

推测	tuīcè	*speculation*; *guess*; *speculate*; *infer*
推迟	tuīchí	*defer*; *postpone*; *put off*
推动	tuīdòng	*push*; *urge*: 推动力 tuīdònglì (*impetus*; *urge*; *motive*)
推翻	tuīfān	*overthrow*
推荐	tuījiàn	*recommend*; *recommendation*: 推荐信 tuījiànxìn (*recommendation letter*)
推进	tuījìn	*push on*; *carry forward*; *advance*
推理	tuīlǐ	*deduction*; *inference*; *deduce*; *infer*

推算 tuīsuàn	calculate; reckon
推土机 tuītǔjī	bulldozer. Cl: 台 tái; 辆 liàng
推卸 tuīxiè	shirk: 推卸责任 tuīxiè zérèn (shirk responsibility)
推销 tuīxiāo	promote sales; market: 推销员 tuīxiāoyuán (salesperson)

退 tuì

1. *retreat; move back; recede*: 败退 bàituì (*retreat in defeat*); 撤退 chètuì (*of troops: retreat, withdraw*); 倒退 dàotuì (*go backwards; retreat*); 后退 hòutuì (*retreat; draw back*); 衰退 shuāituì (*of economy, health, etc.: degenerate, decline*)

2. *withdraw from; quit*: 退学 tuìxué (*quit school*)

3. *return; give back; refund*: 退货 tuìhuò (*return purchase; return goods*)

退步 tuìbù	lag behind; retrogress
退出 tuìchū	withdraw from (a process); quit; back out
退还 tuìhu	return (an object); send back
退货 tuìhuò	return purchase; return goods
退款 tuìkuǎn	refund (n. & v.)
退路 tuìlùàn	path of return; leeway; room for maneuver
退伍 tuìwǔ	be demobilized; be discharged from active military service: 退伍军人 tuìwǔ jūnrén (veterans)
退休 tuìxiū	retire; retired: 退休金 tuìxiūjīn (pension)

外 wài

1. *outer; external*: 外间 wàijiān (*outer room*); 外界 wàijiè (*external world*)

2. *outside*, used after a noun, as the word is considered as a noun in Chinese, and in conjunction with 在 zài: 在院子外 zài yuànzi wài (*outside the yard*); 在校外 zài xiào wài (*outside the school*). 在 zài is normally left out when it appears at the beginning of an existential sentence. 边 biān, 面 miàn, or 头 tóu are optionally used with 外 wài. In this combination, 边 biān, 面 miàn, and 头 tóu are pronounced in the neutral tone: 外边 wàibian; 外面 wàimian; 外头 wàitou. 外 wài used by itself and 外边 wàibian / 外面 wàimian / 外头 wàitou are not always interchangeable. When used as an attribute modifying a noun or when used by itself as an adverbial of place, only the disyllabic form is possible: 外边的房间 wàibian de fángjiān (*the room outside*); 外面有很多人 wàimian yǒu hěn duō rén (*there are many people outside*)

3. *foreign*: 外国 wàiguó (*foreign country*); 外贸 wàimào (*foreign trade*)

206

Also appears in the following words: 除外 chúwài (*except*); 此外 cǐwài (*besides*);
海外 hǎiwài (*abroad; overseas*); 课外 kèwài (*after school; extracurricular*); 野外
yěwài (*field*); 以外 yǐwài (*beyond; apart from*); 意外 yìwài (*accident*)

外币 wàibì	*foreign currency*
外边 wàibian	*outside*
外表 wàibiǎo	*outward appearance*
外宾 wàibīn	*foreign guest*. Cl: 个 gè; 位 wèi; 名 míng
外公 wàigōng	*maternal grandfather*
外国 wàiguó	*foreign country*: 外国人 wàiguórén (*foreigner*)
外行 wàiháng	*layman; nonprofessional*. Cl: 个 gè; 位 wèi
外号 wàihào	*nickname*. Cl: 个 gè
外汇 wàihuì	*foreign exchange*. Cl: 笔 bǐ
外交 wàijiāo	*diplomacy; foreign affairs*: 外交部 wàijiāobù (*Ministry of Foreign Affairs*); 外交关系 wàijiāo guānxi (*diplomatic relations*)
外科 wàikē	*surgical department* (in a hospital): 外科医生 wàikē yīshēng (*surgeon*)
外贸 wàimào	*foreign trade*: 外贸公司 wàimào gōngsī (*import and export company*)
外面 wàimian	*outside*
外婆 wàipó	*maternal grandmother*
外孙 wàisūn	*daughter's son; grandson*
外孙女 wàisūnnǚ	*daughter's daughter; granddaughter*
外套 wàitào	*overcoat; outer garment*. Cl: 件 jiàn
外头 wàitou	*outside*
外文 wàiwén	*foreign language*. Cl: 门 mén; 种 zhǒng
外语 wàiyǔ	*foreign language*. Cl: 门 mén; 种 zhǒng

完 wán

1. *finish; be over; run up; use up*, often used as a verb complement: 电影完了
diànyǐng wán le (*the movie was over*); 看完了书 kàn wán le shū (*finished
reading the book*); 钱花完了 qián huā wán le (*the money was all spent*)

2. *whole; intact*: 完美 wánměi (*whole and perfect*)

完成 wánchéng	*accomplish; complete*
完工 wángōng	*complete* (a construction project, etc.)
完结 wánjié	*complete; finish* (an event, deal, etc.)
完美 wánměi	*perfect*
完全 wánquán	*complete; whole; completely; totally*: 这个句子不完全 zhè ge jùzi bù wánquán (*this sentence is not complete*);

这个句子完全错了 zhè ge jùzi wánquán cuò le (*this sentence is totally wrong*)

完善 wánshàn *perfect* (v. and adj.); 设备不完善 shèbèi bù wánshàn (*the facility is not perfect*); 完善制度 wánshàn zhìdù (*perfect the system*)

完整 wánzhěng *complete*; *intact*: 完整的记录 wánzhěngde jìlù (*complete records*)

玩 wán

1. *play; have fun*: 玩牌 wán pái (*play cards*); 玩游戏 wán yóuxì (*play a game*); 去亚洲玩 qù Yàzhōu wán (*travel to Asia for pleasure*); 你们玩得怎么样 nǐmen wán de zěnmeyàng (*did you have a good time?*)

2. *enjoy; find pleasure in*: 玩邮票 wán yóupiào (*collect stamps as a hobby*)

3. *employ; resort to*, with a pejorative meaning: 玩手段 wán shǒuduàn (*employ underhand means*)

Also appears in the following words: **古玩** gǔwán (*curio; antique*); **好玩** hǎowán (*amusing; fun*); **游玩** yóuwán (*amuse oneself; play*)

玩花招 wán huāzhāo *play tricks*

玩具 wánjù *toy.* Cl: 个 gè; 件 jiàn; 套 tào; 种 zhǒng

玩弄 wánnòng **1.** *dally with; flirt with*
2. *employ; resort to*, with a pejorative meaning

玩笑 wánxiào *joke; jest*: 开玩笑 kāi wánxiào (*crack a joke*). Cl: 句 jù; 个 gè

晚 wǎn

1. *late*: 很晚了，店都关门了 hěn wǎn le, diàn dōu guānmén le (*it's getting late and the stores have all closed*)

2. *evening; night*, often taking the disyllabic form of 晚上 wǎnshang: 昨晚 zuówǎn (*last night*); 昨天晚上 zuótiān wǎnshang (*last night*)

晚安 wǎn'ān *good night*

晚班 wǎnbān *evening shift*

晚报 wǎnbào *evening paper.* Cl: 张 zhāng; 份 fèn

晚辈 wǎnbèi *younger generation*

晚餐 wǎncān *dinner.* Cl: 顿 dùn; 份 fèn

晚点 wǎndiǎn *behind schedule*: 飞机晚点了 fēijī wǎndiǎn le (*the flight is late*)

晚饭 wǎnfàn *dinner.* Cl: 顿 dùn; 份 fèn

晚年 **wǎnnián**   *old age; in ones' advanced age*

晚期 **wǎnqī**   *late period; late stage*

万 wàn

1. *ten thousand*: 五万 wǔ wàn (*fifty thousand*)

2. *every; a vast number of*: 万物生长靠太阳 wànwù shēngzhǎng kào tàiyáng (*the growth of everything depends on the sun*)

万分 **wànfēn**   *extremely*: 万分激动 wànfēn jīdòng (*extremely excited*)

万能 **wànnéng**   *omnipotent; all powerful*

万万 **wànwàn**   *absolutely*, used before a negative word to indicate emphasis: 我万万没有想到他是电影明星 wǒ wànwàn méiyou xiǎng dào tā shì diànyīng míngxīng (*it never occurred to me that he was a movie star*)

万一 **wànyī**   *just in case*: 万一没有人接你，你就坐出租车 wànyī méi you rén jiē nǐ, nǐ jiù zuò chūzūchē (*in case no one comes to pick you up, just take a taxi*)

往 wǎng

1. *in the direction of; toward*: 往右转 wǎng yòu zhuǎn (*turn right*); 往山下看 wǎng shān xià kàn (*look down the mountain*)

2. used after certain verbs, such as 开 kāi (*drive*), 通 tōng (*lead to*), 送 sòng (*deliver*), 寄 jì (*mail*), 运 yùn (*ship*), 派 pài (*dispatch*), 飞 fēi (*fly*), to indicate the destination of the action expressed by the verb: 这列火车开往香港 zhè liè huǒchē kāi wǎng Xiānggǎng (*this train goes to Hong Kong*); 寄往东京的信 jì wǎng Dōngjīng de xìn (*the letter to mail to Tokyo*)

3. *go*: 我叫他往东，他偏往西 wǒ jiào tā wǎng dōng, tā piān wǎng xī (*I wanted him to go east, but he insisted on going west*)

4. *past*: 往事 wǎngshì (*past events*)

Also appears in the following words: 交往 jiāowǎng (*associate*); 来往 láiwǎng (*come and go*); 前往 qiánwǎng (*head for*); 往往 wǎngwǎng (*often; frequently*)

往常 **wǎngcháng**   *in the past; used to*: 往常夏天没有这么热 wǎngcháng xiàtiān méiyou zhème rè (*summer didn't used to be so hot*)

往返 **wǎngfǎn**   *go back and forth*: 校车往返学校和火车站之间 xiàochē wǎngfǎn xuéxiào hé huǒchēzhàn zhījiān (*the school bus shuttles between the school and the train station*); 往返票 wǎngfǎn piào (*a round-trip ticket*)

往后 wǎnghòu	*from now on; in the future*
往来 wǎnglái	*contact; dealing*: 我们两家来往很密切 wǒmen liǎng jiā láiwǎng hěn mìqiè (*our two families are in close contact*)
往年 wǎngnián	*in years past*
往日 wǎngrì	*in old days*
往往 wǎngwǎng	*often; frequently*: 上下班的时候往往很难找到出租车 shàngxiàbān de shíhou wǎngwǎng hěn nán zhǎo dào chūzūchē (*it is often very hard to find a taxi during rush hours*)

忘 wàng

forget, always followed by 了 le in affirmative and imperative sentences: 对不起，我忘了你的名字 duìbuqǐ, wǒ wàng le nǐde míngzi (*sorry that I forgot your name*); 别忘了关灯 bié wàng le guān dēng (*don't forget to turn off the lights*); 难忘 nánwàng (*memorable; unforgettable*)

忘掉 wàngdiào	*forget about; let slip from one's mind*: 忘掉这件不愉快的事 wàngdiào zhè jiàn bú yúkuài de shì (*forget about this unpleasant event*)
忘恩负义 wàng'ēn fùyì	*ungrateful*
忘记 wàngjì	*forget*
忘我 wàngwǒ	*selfless; oblivious of oneself*: 忘我地工作 wàngwǒ de gōngzuò (*work selflessly*)

望 wàng

1. *expect; hope; look forward to*: 望你工作顺利 wàng nǐ gōngzuò shùnlì (*hope that you are successful with your work*). It is often expressed as 希望 xīwàng.

2. *look into the distance*: 登山远望 dēng shān yuǎn wàng (*climb the mountain to look far*)

Also appears in the following words: **绝望** juéwàng (*despair*); **期望** qīwàng (*expectation*); **声望** shēngwàng (*prestige; reputation*); **失望** shīwàng (*despond; disappointment*); **希望** xīwàng (*hope*)

| 望见 wàngjiàn | *see; catch sight of* |
| 望远镜 wàngyuǎnjìng | *telescope; binoculars*. Cl: 架 jià; 台 tái |

围 wéi

surround; encircle; gather around: 围着营火跳舞 wéi zhe yínghuǒ tiàowǔ (*dance around the campfire*); 学生们围着老师问问题 xuéshengmen wéi zhe lǎoshī wèn wèntí (*the students gathered around the teacher to ask questions*)

Also appears in the following words: 包围 bāowéi (*encircle*); 范围 fànwéi (*scope; range*); 周围 zhōuwéi (*surrounding*)

围攻	wéigōng	*lay siege to*
围巾	wéijīn	*scarf*. Cl: 条 tiáo
围棋	wéiqí	*go* (a board game with black and white pieces). Cl: 副 fù
围墙	wéiqiáng	*fencing wall*. Cl: 道 dào
围绕	wéirào	*center around*: 围绕这个话题讨论 wéirào zhè ge huàtí tǎolùn (*hold a discussion on this topic*)

为 wèi

1. *preposition indicating the beneficiary or the purpose of an action*: 他为孩子买衣服 tā wèi háizi mǎi yīfu (*he buys clothes for his children*); 为我们的合作干杯 wèi wǒmende hézuò gān bēi (*toast to our collaboration*)

2. *in order to; for the sake of; because of*, usu. used with 了 le: 为了和中国人交流，他开始学中文 wèile hé Zhōngguórén jiāoliú, tā kāishǐ xué Zhōngwén (*in order to communicate with the Chinese people, he started to study Chinese*); 为了工作，他常常忘了吃饭 wèile gōngzuò, tā chángcháng wàng le chīfàn (*he often forgets to eat because of work*)

3. used with 什么 shénme to mean *why*. As an adverb, it is usu. placed immediately before the verb: 你为什么不多穿一点儿衣服 nǐ wèishénme bù duō chuān yìdiǎnr yīfu (*why didn't you put on a little more clothes?*).

位 wèi

1. *place; status*, used in conjunction with various words: 学位 xuéwèi (*academic degree status*); 地位 dìwèi (*status*); 职位 zhíwèi (*title; rank*)

2. *seat*: 王位 wángwèi (*throne*)

3. *classifier for people in a polite sense*: 两位客人 liǎng wèi kèrén (*two guests*); 三位老师 sān wèi lǎoshī (*three teachers*)

位于	wèiyú	*situated*: 中国位于亚洲的东部 Zhōngguó wèiyú Yàzhōu de dōngbù (*China is situated in East Asia*)
位置	wèizhi	*position; location*

位子 **wèizi**   *seat.* Cl: 个 gè; 排 pái

文 **wén**

1. *language*: 中文 Zhōngwén (*Chinese*); 英文 Yīngwén (*English*); 外文 wàiwén (*foreign language*)

2. *writing; script*

3. *culture*: 文物 wénwù (*cultural relics*). Cl: 件 jiàn; 套 tào

4. *civilian*: 文职 wénzhí (*civilian post*)

Also appears in the following words: **公文** gōngwén (*document*); **论文** lùnwén (*paper; thesis; dissertation*); **课文** kèwén (*text*); **散文** sǎnwén (*essay*); **天文** tiānwén (*astronomy*); **作文** zuòwén (*composition*)

文笔 **wénbǐ**	*style of writing*
文法 **wénfǎ**	*grammar*, interchangeable with 语法 yǔfǎ
文化 **wénhuà**	*culture.* Cl: 种 zhǒng
文件 **wénjiàn**	*document; paper.* Cl: 个 gè; 份 fèn
文具 **wénjù**	*stationery.* Cl: 种 zhǒng
文科 **wénkē**	*liberal arts subjects*
文盲 **wénmáng**	*illiterate; illiteracy; illiterate person.* Cl: 个 gè
文明 **wénmíng**	*civilization*
文人 **wénrén**	*scholar.* Cl: 个 gè; 位 wèi
文体 **wéntǐ**	*literary style*
文学 **wénxué**	*literature*
文言 **wényán**	*classical Chinese*
文艺 **wényì**	*literature and art*
文章 **wénzhāng**	*article.* Cl: 篇 piān; 段 duàn
文字 **wénzì**	*characters; written language.* Cl: 种 zhǒng; 段 duàn; 篇 piān

---

问 **wèn**

ask; question; inquire: 问问题 wèn wèntí (*ask questions*); 问路 wènlù (*ask for direction*). 问 wèn is not used in Chinese to express the meaning of asking sb. to do sth. The meaning is expressed by either 请 qǐng or 让 ràng: 我请他告诉你 wǒ qǐng tā gàosù nǐ (*I asked him to tell you*); 他让我告诉你 tā ràng wǒ gàosù nǐ (*he asked me to tell you*)

Also appears in the following words: **访问** fǎngwèn (*visit*); **顾问** gùwèn (*advisor; consultant*); **请问** qǐngwèn (*may I ask?*); **提问** tíwèn (*put a question to*); **学问** xuéwen (*learning; knowledge*)

问答 wèndá	questions and answers
问好 wènhǎo	say hello to; give regards to: 向你妈妈问好 xiàng nǐ māma wènhǎo (say hello to your mother)
问号 wènhào	question mark
问候 wènhòu	extend greetings to; give regards to, interchangeable with 问好 wènhǎo
问路 wènlù	ask for directions
问题 wèntí	question. Cl: 个 gè

我 wǒ

I. The customary order of a series of personal pronouns in Chinese is to place the first person pronoun first: 我和你 wǒ hé nǐ (*I and you*) and 我你他 wǒ nǐ tā (*I, you, and he*). 我 wǒ can often be used in the sense of *our* when referring to a country, a business or an organization, but the noun generally has to be monosyllabic: 我国 wǒ guó (*our country*); 我校 wǒ xiào (*our school*); 我方 wǒ fāng (*our side*). Otherwise, the plural possessive form 我们的 wǒmende should be used: 我们的国家 wǒmende guójiā (*our country*); 我们的学校 wǒmende xuéxiào (*our school*).

我的 wǒde	my; 的 de is often left out when followed by words for family members or intimate people or places
我们 wǒmen	we; us
我们的 wǒmende	our

无 wú

no; nothing; without, used in formal language or set expressions: 无偿 wúchǎng (*gratis; free*); 无力 wúlì (*powerless*); 无籽 wúzǐ (*seedless*)

无比 wúbǐ	unequalled; matchless: 无比高兴 wúbǐ gāoxìng (*happy beyond description*); 无比愤怒 wǔbǐ fènnù (*furiously indignant*)
无不 wúbù	all; without exception: 听到这个消息, 大家无不激动 tīng dào zhè ge xiāoxi, dàjiā wúbù jīdòng (*after hearing the news, everyone became excited*)
无耻 wúchǐ	shameless
无敌 wúdí	matchless; invincible
无端 wúduān	for no reason, used in a pejorative sense: 无端争吵 wúduān zhēngchǎo (*quarrel for no reason*)
无法 wúfǎ	unable; incapable: 我没有电话, 无法和你联系 wǒ méi you diànhuà, wúfǎ hé nǐ liánxì (*I didn't have a phone, so I was not able to get in touch with you*)

无妨 **wúfáng**	*no harm in doing sth.*	
无非 **wúfēi**	*nothing but*: 无非是闲聊 wúfēi shì xiánliáo (*nothing but chatting*)	
无辜 **wúgū**	*innocent*	
无故 **wúgù**	*without reason*: 他被无故解雇了 tā bèi wúgù jiěgù le (*he was fired for no reason*)	
无关 **wúguān**	*have nothing to do*: 事故和天气无关 shìgù hé tiānqì wúguān (*this accident had nothing to do with the weather*)	
无理 **wúlǐ**	*unreasonable; unjustifiable*: 无理要求 wúlǐ yāoqiú (*unreasonable demands*)	
无力 **wúlì**	*powerless; incapable*: 我们无力解决这个问题 wǒmen wúlì jiějué zhè ge wèntí (*we are incapable of solving this problem*)	
无聊 **wúliáo**	*bored; dull; senseless*	
无论 **wúlùn**	*no matter*: 无论谁 wúlùn shuí (*no matter who*); 无论什么 wúlùn shénme (*no matter what*); 无论什么时候 wúlùn shénme shíhou (*no matter when*); 无论哪儿 wúlùn nǎr (*no matter where*); 无论怎么 wúlùn zěnme (*no matter how*)	
无论如何 **wúlùn rúhé**	*in any case; at any rate*	
无能 **wúnéng**	*incompetent*	
无情 **wúqíng**	*heartless; coldhearted*	
无尚 **wúshàng**	*supreme*	
无视 **wúshì**	*disregard*, used in a pejorative sense	
无数 **wúshù**	*numerous; countless*	
无私 **wúsī**	*selfless*	
无所谓 **wúsuǒwèi**	*be indifferent; not care*: 我无所谓吃什么 wǒ wúsuǒwèi chī shénme (*I don't care what to eat*)	
无条件 **wútiáojiàn**	*unconditional; unconditionally*	
无限 **wúxiàn**	*infinite; boundless*	
无效 **wúxiào**	*invalid*	
无形 **wúxíng**	*invisible*	
无疑 **wúyí**	*doubtless*	
无意 **wúyì**	1. *have no intention*: 她无意去 tā wúyì qù (*she has no intention to go*) 2. *not on purpose; unintentionally*: 无意犯了错误 wúyì fàn le cuòwù (*unintentionally made the mistake*)	
无意识 **wúyìshi**	*unconscious*	
无用 **wúyòng**	*useless*	
无知 **wúzhī**	*ignorant*	
无罪 **wúzuì**	*innocent; not guilty*	

五 wǔ

five

五边形	wǔbiānxíng	*pentagon*
五官	wǔguān	*the five sense organs* (ears, eyes, lips, nose, and tongue)
五金	wǔjīn	*metals; hardware*: 五金店 wǔjīndiàn (*hardware store*)
五线谱	wǔxiànpǔ	(music) *staff*
五月	wǔyuè	*May*

午 wǔ

noon; midday; meridiem. When used unmodified, it takes the disyllabic form of 中午 zhōngwǔ. Words for morning and afternoon both use 午 wǔ as a reference point: 上午 shàngwǔ (*morning*); 下午 xiàwǔ (*afternoon*).

午餐	wǔcān	*lunch*. Cl: 顿 dùn
午饭	wǔfàn	*lunch*, synonymous with 午餐 wǔcān except that 午餐 wǔcān is a little bit more formal. Cl: 餐 cān; 顿 dùn
午觉	wǔjiào	*afternoon nap*
午休	wǔxiū	*noon break; noontime rest; lunch hour*
午夜	wǔyè	*midnight*

物 wù

matter; thing: 文物 wénwù (*cultural relics*); 公物 gōngwù (*public property*). Cl: 件 jiàn; 套 tào; 博物馆 bówùguǎn (*museum*). Cl: 座 zuò; 个 gè

Also appears in the following words: 产物 chǎnwù (*outcome; product*); 动物 dòngwù (*animal*); 读物 dúwù (*reader; reading matter*); 废物 fèiwù (*rubbish; crap*); 怪物 guàiwù (*monster*); 礼物 lǐwù (*gift*); 人物 rénwù (*character*); 生物 shēngwù (*organism*); 食物 shíwù (*food stuff*); 植物 zhíwù (*plant*)

物价	wùjià	*price of goods*
物理	wùlǐ	*physics*
物品	wùpǐn	*goods; article*. Cl: 件 jiàn; 种 zhǒng
物色	wùsè	*seek out; select* (talented people)
物资	wùzī	*supply; material*. Cl: 种 zhǒng; 批 pī

西 xī

west; western: 西部 xībù (*western part*); 西边 xībian (*west side*)

西餐 **xīcān**	*Western food.* Cl: 顿 dùn
西方 **xīfāng**	*the West*
西瓜 **xīguā**	*watermelon.* Cl: 个 gè; 块 kuài
西红柿 **xīhóngshì**	*tomato*
西式 **xīshì**	*Western-style*
西医 **xīyī**	*Western medicine; doctor practicing Western medicine.* Cl: 位 wèi; 个 gè
西装 **xīzhuāng**	*Western-style clothing; suit.* Cl: 套 tào

喜 xǐ

1. *like*, usu. taking the disyllabic form of 喜欢 xǐhuan

2. *happy event; occasion for celebration*: 报喜 bàoxǐ (*report good tidings*)

喜爱 **xǐ'ài**	*favor; like; love; be fond of*
喜欢 **xǐhuan**	*like*
喜剧 **xǐjù**	*comedy*: 喜剧演员 xǐjù yǎnyuán (*comedian*)
喜庆 **xǐqìng**	*festive; celebrate*

洗 xǐ

1. *wash; clean*: 洗手 xǐ shǒu (*wash hands*); 干洗 gānxǐ (*dry-clean*)

2. *develop* (film): 洗照片 xǐ zhàopiàn (*develop a film*)

洗发液 **xǐfàyè**	*shampoo*
洗劫 **xǐjié**	*loot; ransack*
洗手间 **xǐshǒujiān**	*restroom*
洗碗机 **xǐwǎnjī**	*dishwasher* (碗 wǎn actually means *bowl*)
洗衣店 **xǐyīdiàn**	*laundry* (*shop*)
洗衣机 **xǐyījī**	*washing machine; washer.* Cl: 台 tái
洗衣房 **xǐyīfáng**	*laundry room*
洗衣粉 **xǐyīfěn**	*washing powder.* Cl: 袋 dài
洗澡 **xǐzǎo**	*take a bath/shower*

下 xià

1. *lower; down:* 下身 xiàshēn (*lower part of the body*); 下游 xiàyóu (*downstream*)

2. *under, underneath; below,* used after a noun, as the word is considered as a noun in Chinese, and in conjunction with 在 zài: 在桌子下 zài zhuōzi xià (*under the table*); 在桥下 zài qiáo xià (*under the bridge*). 在 zài is left out when appearing at the beginning of a sentence. See under 在 zài. In this sense, 下 xià is often but not always interchangeable with 下边 xiàbian, 下面 xiàmian, and 下头 xiàtou. When used as an attribute modifying a noun or when used by itself as an adverbial of place, only the disyllabic form is possible: 下边的书 shàngbian de shū (*the book underneath*).

3. *go down; get off* (a vehicle, boat, plane, etc.): 下山 xià shān (*go down the mountain*); 下楼 xià lóu (*go downstairs*); 下船 xià chuán (*get off a boat*). 下 xià is often used in conjunction with 来 lái or 去 qù to form a complex directional complement to indicate the movement of the action in relation to where the speaker is: 石头滚下山来 shítou gǔn xià shān lái (*the rock rolled down the mountain*). If the preceding verb takes an object that indicates a location, the object is placed between 下 xià and 来 lái / 去 qù. If the object does not indicate a location, it can be placed either before or after 来 lái / 去 qù. Cf. 从书架上拿下来三本书 cóng shūjià shang ná xià lái sān běn shū (*took three books from the bookshelf*) and 从书架上拿下三本书来 cóng shūjià shang ná xià sān běn shū lái (*took three books from the bookshelf*).

4. (of rain, snow, etc.) *fall:* 下雨 xiàyǔ (*it rains*); 下雪 xiàxuě (*it snows*)

5. *get off* (following a routine schedule): 下班 xiàbān (*get off work*); 下学 xiàxué (*school is over*); 下课 xiàkè (*class is dismissed*)

6. *next:* 下次 xià cì (*next time*), 下个月 xià ge yuè (*next month*); 下个星期 xià ge xīngqī (*next week*)

7. *boil; cast:* 下面条 xià miàntiáo (*cook noodles*); 下饺子 xià jiǎozi (*boil dumplings*); 下鱼网 xià yúwǎng (*cast fishing nets*)

8. *off,* used after a verb: 脱下衣服 tuō xià yīfu (*take off clothes*); 卸下货 xiè xià huò (*unload merchandise*)

9. *able to hold,* used with verbs such as 装 zhuāng (*load*), 放 fàng (*put*), 住 zhù (*live*), 站 zhàn (*stand*), 坐 zuò (*sit*), etc.: 这个汽车坐不下六个人 zhè ge qìchē zuò bú xià liù ge rén (*this car is not big enough to seat six people*); 书包装不下这么多书 shūbāo zhuāng bú xià zhème duō shū (*the bookbag can't hold so many books*)

下巴 **xiàba**		*the lower jaw*
下班 **xiàbān**		*get off work*
下边 **xiàbian**		*under, underneath; below*

下层 **xiàcéng**	lower strata: 下层社会 xiàcéng shèhuì (low society; bottom of society).	
下功夫 **xiàgōngfu**	make an effort; devote time and energy	
下级 **xiàjí**	subordinate; lower level	
下降 **xiàjiàng**	descend; drop	
下流 **xiàliú**	indecent; obscene	
下面 **xiàmian**	1. under, underneath; below	
	2. next: 下面请看电影 xiàmian qǐng kàn diànyǐng (please see the movie next)	
下棋 **xiàqí**	play a chess game	
下去 **xià qù**	continue, used as a complex complement: 看下去 kàn xià qù (read on); 走下去 zǒu xià qù (walk on)	
下台 **xiàtái**	step down from office; be removed from office	
下头 **xiàtou**	under, underneath; below	
下午 **xiàwǔ**	afternoon	
下乡 **xiàxiāng**	go to the countryside	
下旬 **xiàxún**	the last ten days of a month	
下游 **xiàyóu**	lower reaches of a river	

先 **xiān**

first; earlier: 先走后跑 xiān zǒu hòu pǎo (first walk, and then run); 先洗手再吃饭 xiān xǐ shǒu zài chīfàn (wash your hands before you eat); 我太太比我先下班 wǒ tàitai bǐ wǒ xiān xiàbān (my wife gets off work earlier than I)

Also appears in the following words: 事先 shìxiān (in advance; ahead of time); 首先 shǒuxiān (first of all); 优先 yōuxiān (precedence; priority)

先辈 **xiānbèi**	old generation; fathers. Cl: 位 wèi	
先进 **xiānjìn**	advanced: 先进技术 xiānjìn jìshù (advanced technology); 先进学生 xiānjìn xuésheng (honor or meritorious student)	
先例 **xiānlì**	precedence	
先前 **xiānqián**	previously; before	
先生 **xiānsheng**	1. Mr. (used before the surname); gentleman: 王先生 Wáng Xiānsheng (Mr. Wang); 女士们，先生们 nǚshìmen, xiānshengmen (Ladies and Gentlemen)	
	2. husband: 我先生 wǒ xiānsheng (my husband)	
先兆 **xiānzhào**	omen; indication	

现 xiàn

1. *now; present,* usu. taking the disyllabic form of 现在 xiànzài

2. *newly; on the spot:* 现学的技术 xiàn xué de jìshù (*newly acquired skills*)

3. *ready; on hand:* 现金 xiànjīn (*cash*); 现房 (*house ready for occupancy or purchase*)

Also appears in the following words: 表现 biǎoxiàn (*manifest; manifestation*); 出现 chūxiàn (*appear*); 发现 fāxiàn (*discover; discovery*); 实现 shíxiàn (*realize*); 体现 tǐxiàn (*materialize; embody*)

现场 xiànchǎng	**1.** *scene of a crime or accident*
	2. *on the spot; live*
现成 xiànchéng	*ready-made*
现代 xiàndài	*modern*
现金 xiànjīn	*cash*
现实 xiànshí	*reality; realistic*
现象 xiànxiàng	*phenomenon*
现在 xiànzài	*now; at present*
现状 xiànzhuàng	*current status*

相 xiāng

each other, usu. used in formal and set expressions: 相见 xiāngjiàn (*see each other*); 相隔 xiānggé (*separate from each other*)

Also appears in the following words: 互相 hùxiāng (*each other; mutually*); 争相 zhēngxiāng (*vie with each other*)

相比 xiāngbǐ	*compare with each other:* 和昨天相比, 今天很暖和 hé zuótiān xiāngbǐ, jīntiān hěn nuǎnhe (*as compared with yesterday, it is very warm today*)
相差 xiāngchà	*differ:* 飞机的票价和火车的票价相差很多 fēijī de piàojià hé huǒchē de piàojià xiāngchà hěn duō (*airfare differs greatly from train fare*)
相称 xiāngchèn	*match* (v.); *commensurate with:* 工资和责任不相称 gōngzī hé zérèn bù xiāngchèn (*the salary is not commensurate with the responsibility*)
相处 xiāngchǔ	*get along with:* 他和同事们相处得很好 tā hé tóngshìmen xiāngchǔ de hěn hǎo (*he gets along with his colleagues very well*)
相当 xiāngdāng	**1.** *match; correspond; be commensurate with,* used with the preposition 于 yú when followed by an object: 这两件

上衣大小相当 zhè liǎng jiàn shàngyī dàxiǎo xiāngdāng (*these two jackets are about the same size*); 中国的省相当于美国的州 Zhōngguó de shěng xiāngdāng yú Měiguó de zhōu (*provinces in China are equivalent to states in the U.S.*)

2. *very; quite; considerably*: 相当困难 xiāngdāng kùnnan (*very difficult*)

相等 **xiāngděng** *be equivalent to; same*: 这两个学校的学生相等 zhè liǎng ge xuéxiào de xuésheng xiāngděng (*these two schools have the same number of students*)

相对 **xiāngduì** **1.** *be opposed to*: 白和黑相对 bái hé hēi xiāngduì (*white is opposed to black*)

2. *comparatively; relatively*: 相对安全 xiāngduì ānquán (*relatively safe*)

相反 **xiāngfǎn** *contrary to*: 你做的和我说的相反 nǐ zuò de hé wǒ shuō de xiāngfǎn (*what you did is contrary to what I said*)

相符 **xiāngfú** *conform to*: 和要求相符 hé yāoqiú xiāngfú (*conform to requirements*)

相关 **xiāngguān** *relate to*: 天气和农业相关很大 tiānqì hé nóngyè xiāngguān hěn dà (*weather has a lot to do with agriculture*)

相互 **xiānghù** *each other; mutually*: 相互了解 xiānghù liáojiě (*understand each other*)

相识 **xiāngshí** *acquainted with each other*

相似 **xiāngsì** *similar to each other*

相同 **xiāngtóng** *the same as; identical*: 他们的答案是相同的 tāmende dá'àn shì xiāngtóngde (*their answers are the same*)

相象 **xiāngxiàng** *similar to each other*

相信 **xiāngxìn** *believe*

相应 **xiāngyìng** *corresponding to; relevant*: 相应的人员 xiāngyìng de rényuán (*relevant personnel*)

想 xiǎng

1. *think; feel; believe*

2. *would like to*: 你想喝什么 nǐ xiǎng hē shénme (*what would you like to drink?*)

3. *miss; long for*: 想家 xiǎng jiā (*miss home*)

Also appears in the following words: 幻想 huànxiǎng (*illusion; fantasy*); 理想 lǐxiǎng (*ideal*); 梦想 mèngxiǎng (*dream*); 思想 sīxiǎng (*thought; thinking*)

想不到 **xiǎng bú dào** *unexpected; never expected*

想出 **xiǎng chū**	*hit an idea; come up with an idea*
想当然 **xiǎngdāngrán**	*take for granted; assume*
想到 **xiǎngdào**	*think of; realize*
想法 **xiǎngfǎ**	*opinion; idea; thought.* Cl: 个 gè
想念 **xiǎngniàn**	*miss (a person or place)*
想起来 **xiǎng qǐlái**	*recall; come to mind:* 我想不起来她的名字 wǒ xiǎng bù qǐlái tāde míngzi (*I can't recall her name*)
想象 **xiǎngxiàng**	*imagine; imagination*

向 xiàng

1. *face* (v.): 中国皇帝的王位总是向南 Zhōngguó huángdì de wángwèi zǒngshì xiàng nán (*Chinese emperors' thrones always faced the south*)

2. *in the direction of; towards; from:* 流向大海 liú xiàng dàhǎi (*flow towards the sea*); 向右转 xiàng yòu zhuǎn (*turn right*); 向她学习 xiàng tā xuéxí (*learn from her*)

3. *direction:* 风向 fēngxiàng (*wind direction*)

Also appears in the following words: **方向** fāngxiàng (*direction*); **倾向** qīngxiàng (*tendency; trend*); **趋向** qūxiàng (*trend*)

向导 **xiàngdǎo**	*guide.* Cl: 个 gè; 位 wèi; 名 míng
向来 **xiànglái**	*always; all along*
向日葵 **xiàngrìkuí**	*sunflower.* Cl: 棵 kē
向往 **xiàngwǎng**	*yearn for*
向着 **xiàngzhe**	*side with*

象 xiàng

elephant

Also appears in the following words: 抽象 chōuxiàng (*abstract*); 对象 duìxiàng (*object; target*); 气象 qìxiàng (*meteorology*); 现象 xiànxiàng (*phenomenon*)

| 象棋 **xiàngqí** | *Chinese chess* |
| 象征 **xiàngzhēng** | *symbolize; symbol* |

像 xiàng

1. *portrait; likeness; image:* 画像 huàxiàng (*draw a portrait*); 图像 túxiàng (*image; picture*); 雕像 diāoxiàng (*statue*); 肖像 xiāoxiàng (*portrait*); 照像 zhàoxiàng (*take a picture*)

2. *resemble; take after; look like*: 儿子长得像爸爸 érzi zhǎng de xiàng bàba (*the son takes after his father*); 上海很像香港 Shànghǎi hěn xiàng Xiānggǎng (*Shanghai resembles Hong Kong a lot*); 这里像我自己的家一样 zhèlǐ xiàng wǒ zìjǐ de jiā yíyàng (*this place is just like my own home*)

3. *such as, like*: 像这样的商店 xiàng zhèyàng de shāngdiàn (*stores such as this*); 像这样的问题不能问老师 xiàng zhèyàng de wèntí bù néng wèn lǎoshī (*you can't ask the teacher questions like this*)

4. *look as if; seem*: 天像要下雨了 tiān xiàng yào xiàyǔ le (*it looks like rain*)

小 xiǎo

1. *small; little; petty*

2. *become small* or *less intense*: 雨小了 yǔ xiǎo le (*the rain has become lighter*)

3. *younger*, used in comparative sentences: 我妹妹比我小三岁 wǒ mèimei bǐ wǒ xiǎo sān suì (*my sister is three years younger than I am*)

4. used before a surname of a young person as an address form to show intimacy

小报 **xiǎobào**	*tabloid.* Cl: 张 zhāng; 份 fèn
小便 **xiǎobiàn**	*urinate; urine*
小菜 **xiǎocài**	*pickles*
小产 **xiǎochǎn**	*miscarriage*
小吃 **xiǎochī**	*snack food*: 小吃店 xiǎochīdiàn (*snack bar*)
小丑 **xiǎochǒu**	*clown*
小道消息 **xiǎodàoxiāoxi**	*hearsay; grapevine*
小儿科 **xiǎo'érkē**	*pediatrics; pediatric department*
小贩 **xiǎofàn**	*peddler*
小费 **xiǎofèi**	*tip* (for a waiter, etc.)
小孩 **xiǎohái**	*child; children*
小看 **xiǎokàn**	*look down upon*
小朋友 **xiǎopéngyou**	*child; children*, often used as an address form for children. Cl: 个 gè; 群 qún
小气 **xiǎoqì**	*stingy*
小时侯 **xiǎoshíhou**	*during one's childhood*
小说 **xiǎoshuō**	*novel; fiction.* Cl: 篇 piān; 本 běn; 部 bù
小提琴 **xiǎotíqín**	*violin.* Cl: 把 bǎ
小偷 **xiǎotōu**	*thief; pickpocket*
小心 **xiǎoxīn**	*be careful; be cautious*
小学 **xiǎoxué**	*elementary school*: 小学生 xiǎoxuéshēng (*elementary school student*). Cl: 所 suǒ
小组 **xiǎozǔ**	*group*

笑 xiào

smile; laugh

Also appears in the following words: 嘲笑 cháoxiào (*jeer; sneer*); 好笑 hǎoxiào (*laughable; ridiculous*); 取笑 qǔxiào (*make fun of; tease*); 玩笑 wánxiào (*joke; jest*)

笑柄 **xiàobǐng**	*laughing stock*
笑话 **xiàohuà**	*joke*: 说笑话 shuō xiàohuà (*crack a joke*)

些 xiē

1. suffix used after 一 yī and demonstrative pronouns 这 zhè, 那 nà, and 哪 nǎ to indicate an indeterminate or unspecified amount: 一些 yìxiē (*some*); 这些 zhèxiē (*these*), 那些 nàxiē (*those*), and 哪些 nǎxiē (*which ones*). Note that 些 xiē is not a plural suffix. If what follows 这 zhè or 那 nà is a specific number, 些 xiē cannot be used: 这三本书 zhè sān běn shū (*these three books*); 那五个人 nà wǔ ge rén (*those five people*).

2. *a little bit; somewhat*: 她的心情好一些了 tāde xīnqíng hǎo yìxiē le (*her mood has improved a little bit*). 一 yī in 一些 yìxiē can be left out as long as it does not appear at the beginning of a sentence: 病人喝了些水 bìngrén hē le xiē shuǐ (*the patient drank some water*).

写 xiě

write

写生 **xiěshēng**	*paint outdoors from nature.*
写意 **xiěyì**	*free sketch* (in traditional Chinese painting)
写照 **xiězhào**	*portrayal*
写字台 **xiězìtái**	*writing desk*
写作 **xiězuò**	*writing*: 写作课 xiězuòkè (*composition class*); 写作技巧 xiězuò jìqiǎo (*writing techniques*)

谢 xiè

thank: 我忘了谢他 wǒ wàng le xiè tā (*I forgot to thank him*). When used as a vocative, it always takes the reduplicated form of 谢谢 xièxie: 谢谢你 xièxie nǐ (*thank you*); 谢谢你的帮助 xièxie nǐde bāngzhù (*thank you for your help*).

Also appears in the following words: **多谢** duōxiè (*many thanks!*); **感谢** gǎnxiè (*thank; express thanks*); **感谢信** gǎnxièxìn (*letter of thanks*)

谢绝 xièjué	*decline with thanks*
谢天谢地 xiè tiān xiè dì	*thank God; thank goodness*
谢谢 xièxie	*thank you; thanks*
谢意 xièyì	*gratitude; thankfulness*

心 xīn

1. *heart*

2. *sense; feeling; intention; thoughts:* 责任心 zérènxīn (*sense of responsibility*); 羞耻心 xiūchǐxīn (*sense of shame*); 伤心 shāng xīn (*hurt one's feelings*)

3. *center:* 菜心 càixīn (*the heart of the vegetable*); 手心 shǒuxīn (*the hollow of the palm*)

Also appears in the following words: **安心** ānxīn (*set one's heart at rest*); **变心** biànxīn (*change heart*); **担心** dānxīn (*worry*); **点心** diǎnxin (*refreshment; snack*); **放心** fàngxīn (*be at ease*); **关心** guānxīn (*concern; care about*); **小心** xiǎoxīn (*be careful; beware*)

心理 xīnlǐ	*state of mine; mentality:* 心理学 xīnlǐxué (*psychology*)
心情 xīnqíng	*mood; state of mind*
心事 xīnshì	*load on one's mind; something to worry about.* Cl: 件 jiàn
心跳 xīntiào	*heartbeat*
心意 xīnyì	*intention; token of thanks.* Cl: 片 piàn
心脏 xīnzàng	*heart;* 心脏病 (*heart disease*)

新 xīn

new; newly: 新书 xīn shū (*new book*); 新买的书 xīn mǎi de shū (*newly bought book*)

Also appears in the following words: **重新** chóngxīn (*again; anew*); **创新** chuàngxīn (*innovate*); **崭新** zhǎnxīn (*brand new*)

新房 xīnfáng	*bridal chamber.* Cl: 间 jiān
新婚 xīnhūn	*newly married*
新居 xīnjū	*new home*
新郎 xīnláng	*bridegroom*
新年 xīnnián	*New Year*
新娘 xīnniáng	*bride*
新奇 xīnqí	*novel* (adj.)

新式	xīnshì	new style; latest fashion
新手	xīnshǒu	novice; inexperienced. Cl: 个 gè; 名 míng
新闻	xīnwén	news: 新闻记者 xīnwén jìzhě (reporter; journalist). Cl: 条 tiáo; 则 zé
新鲜	xīnxian	fresh
新兴	xīnxìng	new; rising; emerging; vigorous: 新兴的城市 xīnxìngde chéngshì (rising new city)

信 xìn

1. *believe; have faith in*: 信教 xìnjiào (*believe in religion*); 不信谣言 bú xìn yáoyán (*not believe rumors*)

2. *letter*: 写信 xiě xìn (*write a letter*)

信封	xìnfēng	envelope
信号	xìnhào	signal (n.)
信任	xìnrèn	trust; have confidence in
信守	xìnshǒu	abide by (an agreement)
信徒	xìntú	disciple. Cl: 个 gè; 名 míng
信息	xìnxī	information. Cl: 条 tiáo
信箱	xìnxiāng	mailbox. Cl: 只 zhī; 个 gè
信心	xìnxīn	confidence
信用	xìnyòng	1. credit: 信用卡 xìnyòngkǎ (credit card) 2. trustworthiness
信誉	xìnyù	prestige; reputation

星 xīng

star, often taking the disyllabic form of 星星 xīngxīng: 天上有很多星星 tiān shàng yǒu hěn duō xīngxīng (*there are many stars in the sky*); 五星饭店 wǔxīng fàndiàn (*five-star hotel*). Also used metaphorically in 歌星 gēxīng (*singing star; famous singer*); 电影明星 diànyǐng míngxīng (*movie star*). Cl: 个 gè; 位 wèi; 名 míng

Also appears in the following words: 流星 liúxīng (*meteor*); 明星 míngxīng (*star; celebrity*); 卫星 wèixīng (*satellite*); 影星 yǐngxīng (*movie star*)

星河	xīnghé	the Milky Way
星火	xīnghuǒ	spark
星期	xīngqī	week: 这个星期 zhè ge xīngqī (this week); 上个星期 shàng ge xīngqī (last week); 下个星期 xià ge xīngqī (next week); 三个星期 sān gè xīngqī (three weeks); 星期一

xīngqīyī (*Monday*); 星期二 xīngqī'èr (*Tuesday*); 星期三 xīngqīsān (*Wednesday*); 星期四 xīngqīsì (*Thursday*); 星期五 xīngqīwǔ (*Friday*); 星期六 xīngqīliù (*Saturday*); 星期天 xīngqītiān (*Sunday*). Cl: 个 gè

星星 xīngxīng *star*. Cl: 个 gè; 颗 kē

行 xíng

1. *all right; permitted*: 没有铅笔，用钢笔也行 méi you qiānbǐ, yòng gāngbǐ yě xíng (*if you don't have a pencil, it is okay for you to use a pen*); 来晚不行 lái wǎn bù xíng (*it is not okay to be late*)

2. *go; move*: 行走 xíngzǒu (*walk*); 人行道 rénxíngdào (*pedestrian crossing*). Cl: 条 tiáo; 段 duàn

3. *do; perform*: 行医 xíngyī (*practice medicine*); 行贿 xínghuì (*bribe*)

4. *capable; resourceful*: 我朋友修汽车很行 wǒ péngyou xiū qìchē hěn xíng (*my friend is very good at fixing cars*)

Also appears in the following words: **暴行** bàoxíng (*atrocity*); **步行** bùxíng (*walk*); **飞行** fēixíng (*flying; flight*); **进行** jìnxíng (*carry out; proceed*); **举行** jǔxíng (*hold; convene*); **流行** liúxíng (*be the rage; in vogue*); **旅行** lǚxíng (*travel*); **言行** yánxíng (*words and deeds*); **游行** yóuxíng (*parade; march*)

行不通 xíng bù tōng *won't work*: 这个办法行不通 zhè ge bànfǎ xíng bù tōng (*this method won't work*)

行程 xíngchéng *distance of travel; itinerary*

行动 xíngdòng *movement; action*

行李 xíngli *luggage*. Cl: 件 jiàn

行为 xíngwéi *behavior*

行凶 xíngxiōng *commit a violent crime*

行医 xíngyī *practice medicine*

行政 xíngzhèng *administrative*

姓 xìng

surname; family name: 您贵姓 nín guì xìng (*what is your family name?*); 我姓王 wǒ xìng Wáng (*my family name is Wang*). 姓 xìng in the last example is used as a verb.

姓名 xìngmíng *full name; family name and given name*

性 xìng

1. *gender; sex:* 男性 nánxìng (*male; man*); 女性 nǚxìng (*female; woman*)

2. *character; disposition*

3. *suffix used to indicate property or manner:* 可能性 kěnéngxìng (*possibility*); 适应性 shìyìngxìng (*adaptability*)

Also appears in the following words: 本性 běnxìng (*nature*); 词性 cíxìng (*part of speech*); 恶性 èxìng (*malignant*); 个性 gèxìng (*personality; individuality*); 惯性 guàn xìng (*inertia*); 记性 jìxìng (*memory*); 理性 lǐxìng (*reason; rationality*); 慢性 mànxìng (*chronic*); 人性 rénxìng (*human nature*); 特性 tèxìng (*characteristic*); 天性 tiānxìng (*nature*)

性别 **xìngbié**	*gender*
性格 **xìnggé**	*personality; temperament*
性急 **xìngjí**	*impatient*
性命 **xìngmìng**	*life*
性能 **xìngnéng**	(of a machine, device, etc.) *function; property; performance*
性器官 **xìngqìguān**	*sexual organ*
性欲 **xìngyù**	*sexual desire*
性质 **xìngzhì**	*nature; character:* 工作的性质 gōngzuò de xìngzhì (*the nature of the work*)
性子 **xìngzi**	*temper*

学 xué

1. *study; learn:* 学英语 xué Yīngyǔ (*study English*); 学开车 xué kāi chē (*learn to drive*)

2. *imitate:* 学狗叫 xué gǒu jiào (*mimic dogs' barking*)

3. *subject of study; branch of learning:* 文学 wénxué (*literature*); 经济学 jīngjìxué (*economics*); 数学 shùxué (*mathematics*)

4. *school:* 小学 xiǎoxué (*elementary school*); 中学 zhōngxué (*secondary school*); 大学 dàxué (*university*). Cl: 个 gè

Also appears in the following words: 放学 fàngxué (*classes are over; let out*); 教学 jiàoxué (*teaching*); 开学 kāixué (*school opens*); 科学 kēxué (*science*); 留学 liúxué (*study abroad*); 上学 shàngxué (*go to school*); 同学 tóngxué (*classmate*); 文学 wénxué (*literature*)

学费 **xuéfèi**	*tuition*
学分 **xuéfēn**	*academic credit.* Cl: 个 gè
学科 **xuékē**	*academic discipline*
学历 **xuélì**	*curriculum vitae*

学龄 **xuélíng**	*school-age:* 学龄儿童 xuélíng értóng (*school-age children*)	
学派 **xuépài**	*school of thought*	
学期 **xuéqī**	*semester; term.* Cl: 个 gè	
学生 **xuésheng**	*student.* Cl: 名 míng; 个 gè	
学士 **xuéshì**	*bachelor degree*	
学说 **xuéshuō**	*theory; doctrine.* Cl: 种 zhǒng	
学位 **xuéwèi**	*academic degree*	
学问 **xuéwèn**	*learning; knowledge; scholarship.* Cl: 门 mén	
学习 **xuéxí**	*study.* Although 学习 xuéxí and 学 xué can be used interchangeably from time to time, there are two differences between them. While 学 xué is always a verb, 学习 xuéxí can be used both as a verb and as a noun: 他学习中文 tā xuéxí Zhōngwén (*he studies Chinese*); 他的学习很好 tāde xuéxi hěn hǎo (*he is good with his studies*). When both 学习 xuéxí and 学 xué are used as verbs, 学 xué is a transitive verb only but 学习 xuéxi can be used both transitively or intransitively: 我哥哥学（习）中文 wǒ gēge xué(xí) Zhōngwén (*my older brother studies Chinese*); 他在纽约大学学习 tā zài Niǔ Yuē Dàxué xuéxí (*he studies at New York University*), where it is incorrect to use 学 xué.	
学校 **xuéxiào**	*school.* Cl: 所 suǒ; 个 gè	
学院 **xuéyuàn**	*college; institute.* Cl: 所 suǒ	
学者 **xuézhě**	*scholar.* Cl: 位 wèi; 个 gè	

雪 xuě

snow: 大雪 dà xuě (*heavy snow*); 小雪 xiǎo xuě (*light snow*). Cl: 场 chǎng. Note that 雪 xuě in Chinese is always a noun. The expression for *to snow* is 下雪 xià xuě.

雪白 **xuěbái**	*snow-white:* 雪白的床单 xuěbáide chuángdān (*clean white bed sheet*)
雪堆 **xuěduī**	*snow drift*
雪花 **xuěhuā**	*snowflake.* Cl: 片 piàn
雪茄 **xuějiā**	*cigar.* Cl: 根 gēn; 支 zhī; 盒 hé
雪亮 **xuěliàng**	*shiny* (car, etc.); *sharp* (eyes, etc.)
雪撬 **xuěqiào**	*sleigh.* Cl: 只 zhī
雪人 **xuěrén**	*snowman*
雪山 **xuěshān**	*snow-capped mountain.* Cl: 座 zuò

眼 yǎn

1. *eye*, usu. taking the disyllabic form of 眼睛 yǎnjīng. Cl: 只 zhī; 个 gè; 双 shuāng; 对 duì

2. *look*; *glance*: 只看了一眼 zhǐ kàn le yì yǎn (*only gave one look*)

眼光 **yǎnguāng**	*eyesight*; *perspective*: 眼光敏锐 yǎnguāng mǐnruì (*sharp eyes*); 历史眼光 lìshǐ yǎnguāng (*historical perspective*)
眼红 **yǎnhóng**	*jealous*
眼界 **yǎnjiè**	*field of vision*: 开眼界 kāi yǎnjiè (*broaden one's horizon*; *be an eye-opener*)
眼镜 **yǎnjìng**	*glasses*; *spectacles*. Cl: 副 fù
眼睛 **yǎnjīng**	*eye*. Cl: 只 zhī; 个 gè; 双 shuāng; 对 duì
眼科 **yǎnkē**	*ophthalmology*: 眼科医生 yǎnkē yīshēng (*ophthalmologist*)
眼泪 **yǎnlèi**	*tears*. Cl: 滴 dī
眼看 **yǎnkàn**	**1.** *see sth. about to happen*: 眼看就要到新年 yǎnkàn jiù yào dào xīn nián (*the New Year is about to arrive*) **2.** *look on*; *watch helplessly*: 我们不能眼看他有困难而不帮 wǒmen bú néng yǎnkàn tā yǒu kùnnán ér bù bāng (*we can't just watch him in difficulty without lending a helping hand*)

阳 yáng

the sun, usu. taking the form of 太阳 tàiyáng

阳光 **yángguāng**	*sunlight*; *sunshine*
阳历 **yánglì**	*solar or Western calendar*
阳伞 **yángsǎn**	*parasol*; *sunshade*. Cl: 把 bǎ
阳台 **yángtái**	*balcony*

样 yàng

1. *shape*; *appearance*: 同样 tóngyàng (*same*); 不一样 bù yíyàng (*different*)

2. *kind*; *type*, used as a classifier: 两样东西 liǎng yàng dōngxi (*two kinds of things*)

Also appears in the following words: 式样 shìyàng (*style*); 一样 yíyàng (*the same*; *alike*)

样品 **yàngpǐn**	*sample*. Cl: 个 gè; 件 jiàn; 种 zhǒng

样式 yàngshì	(of clothing) *style; cut.* Cl: 个 gè; 种 zhǒng
样子 yàngzi	*appearance; look; manner:* 这个玩具的样子很好 zhè ge wánjù de yàngzi hěn hǎo (*the toy has a good appearance*)

要 yào

1. *want; intend; desire*

2. modal verb used in conjunction with another verb to mean *wish* or *would like*: 我要喝茶 wǒ yào hē chá (*I'd like to drink tea*). The negative form is 不想 bù xiǎng: 我不想喝茶 wǒ bù xiǎng hē chá (*I don't want to drink tea*).

3. *need; should; must,* often used in imperative sentences: 吃饭前要洗手 chīfàn qián yào xǐ shǒu (*you should wash your hands before eating the meal*). The negative form is usu. 不用 búyòng (*don't have to; don't need to*) or 不要 búyào (*don't*): 上公立学校不用付学费 shàng gōnglì xuéxiào búyòng fù xuéfèi (*you don't need to pay tuition for attending a public school*); 请不要吸烟 qǐng búyào xī yān (*please don't smoke*).

4. *require; cost,* the subject is usu. an action or an event: 从北京坐火车到上海要五个小时 cóng Běijīng zuò huǒchē dào Shànghǎi yào wǔ ge xiǎoshí (*it takes 5 hours to go from Beijing to Shanghai by train*); 这件大衣要三百块 zhè jiàn dàyī yào sān bǎi kuài (*this overcoat costs $300*)

5. *about to happen,* used with a verb followed by 了 le: 我妈妈要来美国了 wǒ māma yào lái Měiguó le (*my mother is coming to America soon*). 要 yào in this sense is often preceded by 就 jiù or 快 kuài for additional emphasis.

6. *important:* 要人 yàorén (*important person*); 要事 yàoshì (*important matter*); 要点 yàodiǎn (*gist; major points*)

Also appears in the following words: 必要 bìyào (*need; necessity*); 需要 xūyào (*demand; need; require*); 重要 zhòngyào (*important*); 主要 zhǔyào (*main; primary*)

要不 yàobù	*otherwise:* 快走吧，要不就晚了 kuài zǒu ba, yàobù jiù wǎn le (*let's hurry up, otherwise, we'll be late*)
要不是 yàobúshì	*if it were not for:* 要不是有电脑，这个工作要一个星期 yàobúshì yǒu diànnǎo, zhè ge gōngzuò yào yí ge xīngqī (*if it were not for the computer, the job would take a week*)
要是 yàoshì	*if ... then:* 要是有计算器，我们很快就能解决这个问题 yàoshì yǒu jìsuànqì, wǒmen hěn kuài jiù néng jiějué zhè ge wèntí (*if we had a calculator, we would be able to solve this problem right away*)

也 yě

1. *also*; *too*; *either*, used in both affirmative and negative sentences: 我是中国人，我太太也是中国人 wǒ shì Zhōngguórén, wǒ tàitai yě shì Zhōngguórén (*I'm Chinese and my wife is also Chinese*); 我不是中国人，我太太也不是中国人 wǒ bú shì Zhōngguórén, wǒ tàitai yě bú shì Zhōngguórén (*I'm not Chinese and my wife is not Chinese, either*)

2. used with interrogative words or words such as 一点儿 yìdiǎnr and 连 lián, etc. to indicate emphasis: 我什么地方也没去 wǒ shénme dìfāng yě méiyou qù (*I didn't go anywhere*); 他一点儿东西也没有吃 tā yìdiǎnr yě méiyou chī (*he didn't eat anything*); 这个中文学生连 "大" 字也不会写 zhè ge Zhōngwén xuésheng lián "dà" zì yě bú huì xiě (*this student of Chinese cannot even write the character for "big"*)

3. used to indicate concession: 你不告诉我，我也知道 nǐ bú gàosù wǒ, wǒ yě zhīdao (*even though you refused to tell me, I knew it anyway*)

也好 **yěhǎo**	*it may not be a bad idea*: 你没带钱也好 nǐ méi dài qián yě hǎo (*it may not have been a bad idea if you had not brought any money*)
也许 **yěxǔ**	*maybe*; *perhaps*

夜 yè

night

夜班 **yèbān**	*night shift*
夜景 **yèjǐng**	*night scene*
夜里 **yèlǐ**	*at night*
夜校 **yèxiào**	*evening school*. Cl: 所 suǒ
夜总会 **yèzǒnghuì**	*nightclub*. Cl: 家 jiā

业 yè

1. *profession*; *trade*; *business*: 行业 hángyè (*profession*; *line of business*); 创业 chuàngyè (*start a business*); 农业 nóngyè (*agriculture*)

2. *job*; *work*: 就业 jiùyè (*get employed*); 失业 shīyè (*lose a job*)

3. *property*; *estate*: 业主 yèzhǔ (*home owner*); 家业 jiāyè (*family property*)

4. *program of study*: 学业 xuéyè (*course of academic study*)

Also appears in the following words: 毕业 bìyè (*graduate*); 行业 hángyè (*trade*; *profession*); 结业 jiéyè (*complete a course*); 事业 shìyè (*cause*; *undertaking*);

营业 yíngyè (*to do business*); 专业 zhuānyè (*specialty; major*); 作业 zuòyè (*school assignment*)

业绩 **yèjí**	*work performance.* Cl: 项 xiàng
业务 **yèwù**	*business one handles; line of business.* Cl: 项 xiàng; 种 zhǒng
业余 **yèyú**	1. *spare time; leisure time* 2. *amateur:* 业余摄影师 yèyú shèyǐngshī (*amateur photographer*)

一 yi

一 yi is pronounced in the first tone when **a)** it is read in isolation; **b)** it serves a designating or identifying function rather than indicating a quantity such as in a telephone number and account number: (telephone number) 212-744-8181 (èr yī èr qī sì sì bā yī bā yī); or **c)** it appears in the ones and tens position of a number: 511 (wǔ bǎi yī shí yī). Otherwise it is pronounced in the fourth tone before a first tone, a second tone, or a third tone word: 一本书 yì běn shū (*one book*), and in the second tone before a fourth tone word: 一次 yí cì (*once*). In an ordinal number, 一 yi is always pronounced in the first tone: 第一家餐馆 dìyī jiā cānguǎn (*the first restaurant*); 一月 yīyuè (*January*). If pronounced in isolation as in a designating number that consists of three or more digits, 一 yi can be read as yāo.

1. *one*

2. used between duplicated monosyllabic verbs to suggest that the action is brief, informal or tentative. As such, it is pronounced in the neutral tone: 看一看 kàn yi kàn (*have a look*); 听一听 tīng yi tīng (*listen for a minute*); 等一等 děng yi děng (*wait a minute*). 一 yī in these expressions can be omitted without affecting the meaning.

3. *whole; entire; full:* 我们一家人昨天去了博物馆 wǒmen yì jiā rén zuótiān qù le bówùguǎn (*our whole family went to the museum yesterday*); 昨天他工作了一天 zuótiān tā gōngzuò le yìtiān (*he worked the whole day yesterday*). Unless it appears at the beginning of a sentence, 一 yī can be omitted when used with a classifier to qualify a noun: 我想买（一）件毛衣 wǒ xiǎng mǎi (yí) jiàn máoyī (*I'd like to buy a sweater*); 她是（一）个好老师 tā shì (yí) ge hǎo lǎoshī (*she is a good teacher*).

Also appears in the following words: 单一 dānyī (*single; only*); 同一 tóngyī (*the same; identical*); 万一 wànyī (*in case*)

一 ... 就 ... **yī ... jiù ...** *as soon as:* 他一来我就走 tā yì lái wǒ jiù zǒu (*as soon as he comes, I'll leave*). Note that **a)** the main clause (in this case, 我就走 wǒ jiù zǒu) always follows the subordinate clause, and **b**) the subject of the main clause (in this case 我 wǒ) always precedes 就 jiù instead of following it.

一般 yìbān
1. *usually*; *generally*
2. *ordinary*; *average*; *regular*

一边 ... 一边 ...
yìbiān ... yìbiān ...
Used in pairs to indicate that two actions are taking place simultaneously: 他喜欢一边看书一边听音乐 tā xǐhuan yìbiān kànshū yìbiān tīng yīnyuè (*he likes to listen to music while reading*). If the two verbs share the same subject, 一 yì in the expression can often be left out; otherwise, it must be present: 他喜欢边看书边听音乐 tā xǐhuan biān kànshū biān tīng yīnyue (*he likes to listen to music while reading*); 你一边说，我一边记 nǐ yìbiān shuō, wǒ yìbiān jì (*while you were talking, I took notes*). 边 biān in 一边 yìbiān can often be substituted by 面 miàn.

一点儿 yìdiǎnr
a little: 会说一点儿中文 huì shuō yìdiǎnr Zhōngwén (*know how to speak a little Chinese*); 吃了一点儿 chī le yìdiǎnr (*ate a little*)

一定 yídìng
1. *definitely*; *certainly*; *must be*: 纽约一定有中国城 Niǔyuē yídìng yǒu Zhōngguóchéng (*there must be a Chinatown in New York*)
2. *certain*; *given*; *necessary*: 做这样的事, 必须有一定的条件 zuò zhèyàng de shì, bìxū yǒu yídìngde tiáojiàn (*to do such a thing, there must be necessary conditions*)
3. *must*, used in imperative sentences, often with verbs such as 要 yào (*need*) or 得 děi (*have to*): 你一定要早来 nǐ yídìng yào zǎo lái (*you must come early*)

一方面 ... 一方面
yìfāngmiàn ... yìfāngmiàn
on one hand; *on the other hand*

一会儿 yíhuìr
a little while: 看了一会儿书 kàn le yíhuìr shū (*read for a little while*)

一起 yìqǐ
together: 一起去看电影 yìqǐ qù kàn diànyǐng (*go to the movies together*)

一下儿 yíxiàr
Used after a verb to suggest that an action takes place briefly, informally, casually or tentatively: 请来一下儿 qǐng lái yíxiàr (*please come here for a minute*); 我介绍一下儿上海 wǒ jièshào yíxiàr Shànghǎi (*let me say a few words about Shanghai*). 一下儿 yíxiàr can be used interchangeably with the "verb 一 yi verb structure": 坐一坐/坐一下儿 zuò yi zuò/zuò yíxiàr (*have a seat*); 用一用/用一下儿 yòng yi yòng/yòng yíxiàr (*use for a minute*).

一些 yīxiē
1. *some*; *a few*: 一 yī can be omitted if it does not appear

at the beginning of the sentence: 我昨天去书店买了一些书 wǒ zuótiān qù shūdiàn mǎi le yīxiē shū (*I went to the bookstore yesterday and bought a few books*).

2. used before 什么 shénme (*what*) in a question to soften the speech. 一 yī is usu. left out in this usage: 你们想吃些什么 nǐmen xiǎng chī xiē shénme (*what would you like to eat?*).

3. *somewhat*, used after an adjective with a comparative implication. 一 yī is usu. left out: 我妈妈的身体现在好些了 wǒ māma de shēntǐ xiànzài hǎo xiē le (*my mother's health is a little better now*).

一样 **yíyàng**
1. *same*: 一样的书 yíyàngde shū (*the same book*): 你的汽车和我的汽车颜色一样 nǐde qìchē hé wǒde qìchē yánsè yíyàng (*your car is of the same color as my car*).

2. *similarly; as ... as*: 苏州和杭州一样好玩 Sūzhōu hé Hángzhōu yíyàng hǎowán (*Suzhou is just as fun as Hangzhou*). If the negative word 不 bù is used in **1** and **2**, it precedes 一样 yíyàng instead of 跟 gēn / 和 hé: 中餐跟西餐不一样 Zhōngcān gēn Xīcān bù yíyàng (*Chinese food is not the same as Western food*).

3. *like*, used with 像 xiàng: 今天像冬天一样 jīntiān xiàng dōngtiān yíyàng (*it is just like winter today*)

衣 yī

clothes; clothing: 便衣 biànyī (*plain clothes*); 大衣 dàyī (*overcoat*); 风衣 fēngyī (*trench coat*); 毛衣 máoyī (*sweater*); 皮衣 píyī (*leather coat*); 睡衣 shuìyī (*pajamas*)

衣橱 **yīchú**	*wardrobe*. Cl: 个 gè
衣服 **yīfu**	*clothes; clothing*. Cl: 件 jiàn; 套 tào
衣柜 **yīguì**	*wardrobe*. Cl: 个 gè
衣架 **yījià**	*coat hanger*. Cl: 个 gè
衣料 **yīliào**	*material for clothing; fabric*. Cl: 块 kuài

医 yī

1. *doctor*, when used with a descriptive word. Otherwise, it takes the disyllabic form of 医生 yīshēng: 牙医 yáyī (*dentist*); 兽医 shòuyī (*veterinary*); 中医 zhōngyī (*doctor practicing Chinese medicine*). Cl: 个 gè; 位 wèi; 名 míng.

2. *medicine; medical science:* 学医 xuéyī (*study medicine*); 中医 zhōngyī
(*Chinese medicine*); 西医 xīyī (*Western medicine*)

3. *cure; treat:* 给病人医病 gěi bìngrén yī bìng (*treat patients*)

医疗 **yīliáo**	*medical treatment; medical:* 公费医疗 gōngfèi yīliáo (*public health services*)
医生 **yīshēng**	*doctor.* Cl: 个 gè; 位 wèi; 名 míng
医务室 **yīwùshì**	*dispensary; clinic*
医学 **yīxué**	*medical science:* 医学院 yīxuéyuàn (*medical school*)
医药 **yīyào**	*treatment and medicine;* 医药费 yīyàofèi (*medical expenses*)
医院 **yīyuàn**	*hospital.* Cl: 所 suǒ; 家 jiā; 个 gè; 座 zuò
医治 **yīzhì**	*cure; treat; heal*

以 yǐ

1. *with; using:* 以公司的名义 yǐ gōngsī de míngyì (*in the name of the company*)

2. *in order to,* used between two verbal phrases: 他送给你这束花以表示谢意 tā sòng gěi nǐ zhè shù huā yǐ biǎoshì xièyì (*he gave you this bouquet of flowers to show his appreciation*)

3. *treat as,* used with the preposition 为 wéi: 以诚实为荣 yǐ chéngshi wéi róng (*regard honesty as pride*)

4. *according to:* 以天计算 yǐ tiān jìsuàn (*calculate according to the number of the days*)

5. *because of; for:* 纽约以高楼闻名 Niǔyuē yǐ gāo lóu wénmíng (*New York is famous for its tall buildings*)

Also appears in the following words: 可以 kěyǐ (*can; may*); 难以 nányǐ (*difficult to*); 所以 suǒyǐ (*therefore*)

以便 **yǐbiàn**	*in order to; so that,* used at the beginning of the second phrase to indicate purpose: 老师说得很慢以便学生记下 lǎoshī shuō de hěn màn yǐbiàn xuésheng jì xià (*the teacher spoke slowly so that the students could take notes*)
以后 **yǐhòu**	**1.** *later, in the future:* 我以后要当老师 wǒ yǐhòu yào dāng lǎoshī (*I would like to become a teacher in the future*) **2.** *after,* used at the end of a clause or verbal phrase: 1900年以后 1900 nián yǐhòu (*after 1900*); 下课以后，他们要去看电影 xià kè yǐhòu, tāmen yào qù kàn diànyǐng (*they are going to see a movie after class*). 以后 yǐhòu is considered as a noun in Chinese.

以及 yǐjí

as well as: 这儿有咖啡，茶以及橘子汁 zhèr yǒu kāfēi, chá yǐjí júzizhī (*there is coffee, tea as well as orange juice here*)

以来 yǐlái

since: 退休以来，他已经写了两本书了 tuìxiū yǐlái, tā yǐjing xiě le liáng běn shū le (*since retirement, he has already written two books*). 以来 yǐlái is considered as a noun in Chinese.

以内 yǐnèi

inside; within: 十天以内 shítiān yǐnèi (*within ten days*); 公司以内 gōngsī yǐnèi (*within the company*). 以内 yǐnèi is considered as a noun in Chinese.

以免 yǐmiǎn

lest: 我早到了一个小时以免没有位子 wǒ zǎo dào le yí ge xiǎoshí yǐmiǎn méi you wèizi (*I arrived an hour earlier lest there would be no seat*)

以前 yǐqián

1. *before; previously*: 她以前是老师 tā yǐqián shì lǎoshī (*she used to be a teacher*); 我以前没有吃过广东菜 wǒ yǐqián méiyou chī guo Guǎngdōng cài (*I have never had Cantonese food before*)

2. *before; ago*, used at the end of a phrase or a clause: 三天以前 sān tiān yǐqián (*three days ago*); 你来美国以前会不会说英语 nǐ lái Měiguó yǐqián huì bu huì shuō Yīngyǔ (*did you know how to speak English before you came to America?*). 以前 yǐqián is considered as a noun in Chinese.

以上 yǐshàng

above; beyond; over: 以上是我的看法 yǐshàng shì wǒde kànfǎ (*the above is my opinion*); 一个星期以上 yí ge xīngqī yǐshàng (*over one week*). 以上 yǐshàng is considered as a noun in Chinese.

以外 yǐwài

besides, often used in conjunction with 除了 chúle: 除了音乐以外，你还喜欢什么 chúle yīnyuè yǐwài, nǐ hái xǐhuan shénme (*what else do you like besides music?*). 以外 yǐwài is considered as a noun in Chinese.

以往 yǐwǎng

in the past; previously: 以往电视都是黑白的 yǐwǎng diànshì dōu shì hēibái de (*in the past, television was all black and white*). 以往 yǐwǎng is considered a noun in Chinese.

以为 yǐwéi

1. *think*
2. (mistakenly) *thought*

以下 yǐxià

below; under; as follows: 12岁以下的儿童不要票 12 suì yǐxià de értóng bú yào piào (*children under 12 do not need to pay for the tickets*); 以下是我们的计划 yǐxià shì wǒmende jìhuà (*the following is our plan*). 以下 yǐxià is considered as a noun in Chinese.

已 yǐ

already, often taking the disyllabic form of 已经 yǐjīng: 雨已停了 yǔ yǐ tíng le (*the rain has already stopped*); 电影已经开始了 diànyǐng yǐjīng kāishǐ le (*the movie has already started*)

已经 **yǐjīng**	*already*
已知 **yǐzhī**	*known*; *given*: 已知信息 yǐzhī xìnxī (*known information*)

意 yì

1. *meaning*; *idea*: often taking the form of 意思 yìsi. Cl: 个 gè; 种 zhǒng

2. *intention*: 好意 hǎoyì (*good intention*); 恶意 èyì (*malicious intention*)

Also appears in the following words: 大意 dàyì (*general idea*); 故意 gùyì (*deliberately*; *on purpose*); 介意 jièyì (*v. mind*); 满意 mǎnyì (*satisfied*); 生意 shēngyi (*business*); 特意 tèyì (*especially*; *for express purposes of*); 愿意 yuànyì (*be willing*); 主意 zhǔyi (*idea*); 注意 zhùyì (*pay attention to*)

意见 **yìjian**	**1.** *opinion*; *viewpoint* **2.** *objection*; *different opinion* Cl: 个 gè; 条 tiáo; 点 diǎn
意念 **yìniàn**	*idea*; *thought*
意识 **yìshí**	**1.** *consciousness*: 失去意识 shī qù yìshí (*lose consciousness*) **2.** *be aware of*; *realize*; *consciousness*, usu. followed by 到 dào: 我刚刚意识到我们今天没有课 wǒ gānggāng yìshi dào wǒmen jīntiān méi you kè (*I just realized that we don't have classes today*)
意思 **yìsi**	**1.** *meaning*; *idea*. Cl: 个 gè; 种 zhǒng **2.** *Intention*. Cl: 个 gè; 种 zhǒng **3.** *token of thanks*: 这是我的一点儿意思 zhè shì wǒde yìdiǎnr yìsi (*this is my little token of thanks*) **4.** *interest*; *fun*, used with the verb 有 yǒu: 北京很有意思 Běijīng hěn yǒu yìsi (*Beijing is a fun place*); 那本书没有意思 nà běn shū méi you yìsi (*that book is not interesting*)
意图 **yìtú**	*intention*. Cl: 个 gè; 种 zhǒng
意外 **yìwài**	**1.** *unexpected*; *surprised* **2.** *accident*: 遇到意外 yùdào yìwài (*involved in an accident*)
意味着 **yìwèizhe**	*imply*; *mean*: 他不说话意味着他不同意 tā bù shuōhuà yìwèizhe tā bù tóngyì (*his silence means that he does not agree*)
意向 **yìxiàng**	*intention*. Cl: 个 gè; 种 zhǒng
意义 **yìyì**	*meaning*; *significance*

| 意愿 yìyuàn | *desire*; *wish*. Cl: 个 gè; 种 zhǒng |
| 意志 yìzhì | *will* (n.) |

因 yīn

because of; *due to*: 因公出差 yīn gōng chūchāi (*travel on business*); 因故没
有来 yīngù méiyou lái (*didn't come for some reason*)

因此 yīncǐ	*for this reason*; *therefore*
因果 yīnguǒ	*cause and effect*
因素 yīnsù	*factor*. Cl: 个 gè; 种 zhǒng
因为 yīnwèi	*because*, placed either at the beginning of the clause or after the subject: 因为下大雪，学校决定停课/学校因为下大雪决定停课 yīnwéi xià dà xuě, xuèxiào juédìng tíng kè/ xuéxiào yīnwèi xià dà xuě juédìng tíng kè (*because of the heavy snow, the school decided to suspend its classes*). When 因为 yīnwèi appears in the first clause, the second clause is usu. introduced by 所以 suǒyǐ: 我因为很忙，所以没有及时给你写信 wǒ yīnwèi hěn máng, suǒyǐ méiyou jíshí gěi nǐ xiě xìn (*I have been very busy, so I didn't write to you promptly*).

音 yīn

sound; *voice*: 你的音发得很准 nǐde yīn fā de hěn zhǔn (*your sounds are
pronounced very accurately*)

Also appears in the following words: 发音 fāyīn (*pronounce*; *pronounciation*); 回音
huíyīn (*echo*; *reply*); 口音 kǒuyīn (*accent*); 拼音 pīnyīn (*pinyin*); 声音 shēngyīn
(*sound*; *voice*)

音调 yīndiào	*tone*
音节 yīnjié	*syllable*
音量 yīnliàng	*volume of sound*
音响 yīnxiǎng	*acoustics*: 音响效果 yīnxiǎng xiàoguǒ (*acoustic effects*)
音信 yīnxìn	*news*; *mail*: 失踪的人没有音信 shīzōng de rén méi you yīnxìn (*there is no news of the missing people*)
音译 yīnyì	*transliteration*
音乐 yīnyuè	*music*: 音乐家 yīnyuèjiā (*musician*); 音乐会 yīnyuèhuì (*concert*)

应 yīng

should; *ought to*, often taking the disyllabic form of 应该 yīnggāi or 应当 yīngdāng

应当 **yīngdāng**	*should*; *ought to*
应该 **yīnggāi**	*should*; *ought to*
应有 **yīngyǒu**	*due*; *deserved*: 应有的权利 yīngyǒude quánlì (*deserved rights*)

用 yòng

1. *use*; *employ*; *apply*: 我还不会用中文字典 wǒ hái bú huì yòng diànnǎo (*I still don't know how to use the Chinese dictionary*)

2. *use* (n.): 学英语很有用 xué Yīngyǔ hěn yǒu yòng (*it's very useful to learn English*)

3. *need*; usu. used in negative sentences: 你不用给我钱 nǐ bú yòng gěi wǒ qián (*you don't have to give me money*)

4. *in*; *with*: 用中文说 yòng Zhōngwén shuō (*speak in Chinese*); 用铅笔写 yòng qiānbǐ xiě (*write in pencil*)

5. *eat*; *drink*, used on polite or formal occasions: 请用茶 qǐng yòng chá (*please drink tea*); 在宾馆用餐 zài bīnguǎn yòng cān (*eat the meal at the guesthouse*)

Also appears in the following words: 采用 cǎiyòng (*adopt*); 费用 fèiyòng (*cost; expenditure*); 利用 lìyòng (*make use of*); 日用 rìyòng (*of everyday use*); 实用 shíyòng (*practical*); 使用 shǐyòng (*use; employ*); 信用 xìnyòng (*credit; honor*); 作用 zuòyòng (*effect*)

用处 **yòngchù**	*use* (n.); *the good*: 电脑的用处很大 diànnǎo de yòngchù hěn dà (*the computer can do a lot of things*). Cl: 个 gè; 种 zhǒng
用法 **yòngfǎ**	*method of use*; *usage*. Cl: 种 zhǒng
用功 **yònggōng**	(of students) *diligent*; *hardworking*
用户 **yònghù**	*consumer*, usu. of commercial products
用具 **yòngjù**	*utensil*; *appliance*. Cl: 种 zhǒng
用品 **yòngpǐn**	*necessities*. Cl: 种 zhǒng
用途 **yòngtú**	*use* (n.). Cl: 种 zhǒng
用心 **yòngxīn**	1. *diligently*; *attentively* 2. *motive*; *intention*
用意 **yòngyì**	*purpose*; *intention*
用语 **yòngyǔ**	*diction*; *wording*

游 yóu

1. *swim*, often taking the disyllabic form of 游泳 yóuyǒng with the difference that 游泳 yóuyǒng is always a sport, whereas 游 yóu refers simply to the action of moving in water

2. *tour*: 春游 chūnyóu (*spring outing*); 游长城 yóu Chángchéng (*tour the Great Wall*)

3. *part of a river*; *reach*: 上游 shàngyóu (*the upper reaches*); 下游 xiàyóu (*the lower reaches*)

Also appears in the following words: 导游 dǎoyóu (*tour guide*); 旅游 lǚyóu (*tour*)

游客 **yóukè**	*visitor*; *sightseer*; *tourist*. Cl: 个 gè; 位 wèi; 名 míng	
游览 **yóulǎn**	*go sightseeing*; *tour*	
游人 **yóurén**	*visitor*; *sightseer*; *tourist*. Cl: 个 gè; 名 míng	
游艇 **yóutǐng**	*yacht*. Cl: 条 tiáo; 只 zhī	
游玩 **yóuwán**	*amuse oneself*; *play*	
游戏 **yóuxì**	*game*; *pastime*	
游行 **yóuxíng**	*parade*; *demonstration*; *rally*	
游泳 **yóuyǒng**	*swim*: 游泳池 yóuyǒngchí (*swimming pool*); 游泳衣 yóuyǒngyī (*bathing suit*)	

邮 yóu

mail; *post*; *postal*, in various combinations

邮编 **yóubiān**	*zip code*
邮差 **yóuchāi**	*mailman*; *postman*. Cl: 个 gè; 名 míng
邮戳 **yóuchuō**	*postmark*. Cl: 个 gè
邮递员 **yóudìyuán**	*mailman*; *postman*. Cl: 个 gè; 位 wèi; 名 míng
邮购 **yóugòu**	*mail order*
邮寄 **yóujì**	*mail* (v.)
邮件 **yóujiàn**	*mail* (n.): 电子邮件 diànzi yóujiàn (*email*)
邮局 **yóujú**	*post office*. Cl: 所 suǒ; 个 gè
邮票 **yóupiào**	*stamp*. Cl: 张 zhāng; 套 tào
邮箱 **yóuxiāng**	*mailbox*; *postbox*. Cl: 个 gè
邮资 **yóuzī**	*postage*

由 yóu

1. *by way of; from*: 由纽约去华盛顿 yóu Niǔyuē qù Huáshèngdùn (*go to Washington by way of New York*); 由远而近 yóu yuǎn ér jìn (*from far to near*)

2. *by*: 会议由主席主持 huìyì yóu zhǔxí zhǔchí (*the meeting was presided over by the chairman*). 由 yóu differs from 被 yong in that 由 yóu carries the meaning of *it is the responsibility/obligation of sb. to*. As such, it is usu. followed by a human noun: 这件事由我们通知他 zhè jiàn shì yóu wǒmen tōngzhī tā (*we'll be responsible for notifying him*).

3. *be up to*: 去不去由你 qù bu qù yóu nǐ (*it's up to you whether to go*)

Also appears in the following words: 理由 lǐyóu (*reason*); 自由 zìyóu (*free; freedom*)

由不得 yóu bùde	*not up to sb. to decide*: 这事由不得我 zhè shì yóu bùde wǒ (*this matter is not up to me to decide*)
由此 yóucǐ	*because of this; in view of this*
由来 yóulái	*original cause*
由于 yóuyú	*due to; because of*: 由于食物不干净，他生了病 yóuyú shíwù bù gānjìng, tā shéng le bìng (*due to unclean food, he got sick*)
由衷 yóuzhōng	*from the bottom of one's heart; sincere*: 由衷的感谢 yóuzhōngde gǎnxiè (*heartfelt thanks*)

有 yǒu

1. *have; possess*: 我有一本中文书 wǒ yǒu yì běn Zhōngwén shū (*I have a Chinese book*). The negative of 有 yǒu is 没 méi instead of 不 bù. When 有 yǒu is preceded by 没 méi, it is pronounced in the neutral tone: 我没有汽车 wǒ méi you qìchē (*I don't have a car*); 我们学校没有美国老师 wǒmen xuéxiào méi you Měiguó lǎoshī (*our school does not have American teachers*).

2. *exist; be present*: (在) 银行的东边有三个店 (zài) yínháng de dōngbian yǒu sān ge diàn (*there are three stores to the east of the bank*); (在) 桥的下边有两条船 (zài) qiáo de xiàbian yǒu liǎng tiáo chuán (*there are two boats under the bridge*). Note that the prepositional phrase of location must precede the verb 有 yǒu and 在 zài in the phrase is always left out. Additionally, what follows 有 yǒu must be an indefinite or unspecified item. If it is definite or specified, 是 shì must be used in place of 有 yǒu, cf. 中国的北边有两个国家 Zhōngguó de běibian yǒu liǎng ge guójiā (*there are two countries north of China—unspecified*) and 中国的北边是蒙古和俄国 Zhōngguó de běibian shì Ménggǔ hé Éguó (*to the north of China are Mongolia and Russia*).

3. indicator of degree, often used for measurements: 他有六英尺高 tā yǒu liù yīngchǐ gāo (*he is six feet tall*); 长江有多长 Chángjiāng yǒu duō cháng (*how long is the Yangtze River?*); 非洲有多热 Fēizhōu yǒu duō rè (*how hot is it in Africa?*)

4. used to postpone an indefinite or unspecified item. Similar to English, there is a tendency in Chinese to place an indefinite or unspecified item towards the end of the sentence and a definite or specified item at the beginning of the sentence, but if an unspecified item has to be placed at the beginning of a sentence, 有 yǒu is used before it to soften the bluntness or abruptness: 有一个人上午来找你 yǒu yí ge rén shàngwǔ lái zhǎo nǐ (*someone came to see you this morning*); 有个书店卖这本书 yǒu ge shūdiàn mài zhè běn shū (*there is a bookstore that sells this book*).

5. used in the form of 有的…有的 … yǒude … yǒude … to mean *some ... others* ...: 有的是美国人，有的是英国人 yǒude shì Měiguórén, yǒude shì Yīngguórén (*some are Americans, and others are British*). Note that 有的 yǒude plus the noun it modifies can only be placed at the subject position, but not at the object position: 有的菜我喜欢，有的菜我不喜欢 yǒude cài wǒ xǐhuan, yǒude cài wǒ bù xǐhuan (*I like some dishes, but not others*). It is ungrammatical to say, 我喜欢有的菜，不喜欢有的菜 wǒ xǐhuan yǒude cài, bù xǐhuan yǒude cài. A variation of this form is 有的时候…有的时候… yǒude shíhou … yǒude shíhou … (*sometimes ... sometimes ...*). 有的时候 yǒude shíhou is often shortened to 有时 yǒushí: 我有时在家吃中饭，有时在公司吃中饭 wǒ yǒushí zài jiā chī zhōngfàn, yǒushí zài gōngsī chī zhōngfàn (*I sometimes eat lunch at home, sometimes at work*).

6. used in comparative sentences to mean, *A is up to B; A is comparable to B* or *A is as much as B*. This use occurs more often in questions and negative forms: 四川菜有广东菜好吃吗 Sìchuāncài yǒu Guǎngdōngcài hǎochī ma (*does Sichuan food taste as good as Guangdong food?*); 香港的东西没有东京的东西贵 Xiāng Gǎng de dōngxi méiyou Dōngjīng de dōngxi guì (*things in Hong Kong are not as expensive as things in Tokyo*).

7. used in the expression 没有 méiyou to express the negative of a completed action or a progressive action: 他今天没有去上班 tā jīntiān méiyou qù shàngbān (*he didn't go to work today*); 学生们没有在学习 xuéshēngmen méiyou zài xuéxí (*the students are not studying*). When used with 没 méi, 有 yǒu can often be omitted: 我没（有）弟弟 wǒ méi (you) dìdi (*I don't have a younger brother*); 汽车没来 qìchē méi lái (*the bus didn't come*).

有的 **yǒude**　　some: 有的人是中国人，有的人是韩国人 yǒude rén shì Zhōngguórén, yǒude rén shì Hánguórén (*some are Chinese and others are Korean*)

有点儿 **yǒudiǎnr**　　a little; somewhat, usu. used for conditions that are undesirable: 有点儿累 yǒudiǎnr lèi (*a little tired*); 有点儿不高兴 yǒudiǎnr bù gāoxìng (*somewhat upset*)

有关 **yǒuguān**	*having to do*; *relevant*: 有关战争的电影 yǒuguān zhànzhēng de diànyǐng (*movie about the war*; *war movies*); 有关人员 yǒuguān rényuán (*personnel concerned*)
有害 **yǒuhài**	*harmful*
有理 **yǒulǐ**	*justified*; *reasonable*
有力 **yǒulì**	*forceful*; *powerful*
有利 **yǒulì**	*favorable*; *beneficial*: 有利的条件 yǒulìde tiáojiàn (*favorable conditions*)
有名 **yǒumíng**	*famous*; *well-known*
有钱 **yǒuqián**	*rich*; *wealthy*
有趣 **yǒuqù**	*interesting*; *funny*
有时 **yǒushí**	*sometimes*
有事 **yǒushì**	*be busy*; *be engaged* (in something)
有限 **yǒuxiàn**	*limited*
有效 **yǒuxiào**	*effective*
有些 **yǒuxiē**	*some*
有益 **yǒuyì**	*beneficial*; *useful*
有意 **yǒuyì**	*deliberately*; *on purpose*
有意思 **yǒuyìsī**	*interesting*
有用 **yǒuyòng**	*useful*; *helpful*

友 yǒu

friend, used in formal language or expressions with modification: 探亲访友 tàn qīn fǎng yǒu (*visit relatives and friends*); 笔友 bǐyǒu (*pen pal*); 男友 nányǒu (*boyfriend*); 女友 nǔyǒu (*girlfriend*); otherwise taking the disyllabic form of 朋友 péngyou

友邦 **yǒubāng**	*friendly nation*
友好 **yǒuhǎo**	*friendly*: 那个国家的人民很友好 nà ge guójiā de rénmín hěn yǒuhǎo (*people in that country are very friendly*); 友好访问 yǒuhǎo fǎngwèn (*friendly visit*)
友情 **yǒuqíng**	*friendly sentiments*; *friendship*
友人 **yǒurén**	*friend*. Cl: 位 wèi
友谊 **yǒuyí**	*friendship*

又 yòu

1. *again*: 我昨天去了银行，今天又去了银行 wǒ zuótiān qù le yínháng, jīntiān yòu qù le yínháng (*I went to the bank yesterday. I went there again today*). 又 yòu differs from 再 zài in that 又 yòu indicates a repeated action that has already taken place, whereas 再 zài indicates an action that is yet to

243

take place. Cf. 他今年又去了中国 tā jīnnián yòu qù le Zhōngguó (*he went to China again this year*); 欢迎再来中国 huānyíng zài lái Zhōngguó (*welcome to come to China again*).

2. *both … and*: 又吃又喝 yòu chī yòu hē (*both eat and drink*); 又唱又跳 yòu chàng yòu tiào (*both sing and dance*); 又年轻又漂亮 yòu niánqīng yòu piàoliang (*both young and pretty*)

3. *on top of; moreover; besides*: 我不会说英语，又没有人教我，所以我在美国很困难 wǒ bú huì shuō Yīngyǔ, yòu méi you rén jiāo wǒ, suǒyǐ wǒ zài Měiguó hěn kùnnan (*I don't speak English, besides, there is no one to teach me. It is therefore very difficult for me in America*)

4. used after a whole number to indicate a fraction: 一年又四个月 yì nián yòu sì ge yuè (*a year and four months*); 五小时又二十分 wǔ xiǎoshí yòu èrshí fēn (*five hours and twenty minutes*)

右 yòu

the right side; right: 右手 yòushǒu (*right hand*); 向右转 xiàng yòu zhuǎn (*turn right*)

右边	yòubian	*right*
右面	yòumiàn	*right*
右翼	yòuyì	*right wing*

于 yú

Preposition left over from classic Chinese. The time or place expression it introduces follows the verb instead of preceding it.

1. *in; at*: 这部电影拍于1930年 zhè bù diànyǐng pāi yú 1930 nián (*this movie was produced in 1930*); 邓小平生于四川 Dèng Xiǎopíng shēng yú Sìchuān (*Deng Xiaoping was born in Sichuan*)

2. *to*: 我们的公寓属于公司 wǒmende gōngyù shǔ yú gōngsī (*our apartments belong to the company*); 功劳归于大家 gōngláo guī yú dàjiā (*success should be credited to everyone*); 致力于文学研究 zhìlì yú wénxué yánjiù (*engaged in literary study*)

3. *than*: 这学期的成绩好于上学期的成绩 zhè xuéqī de chéngji hǎo yú shàng xuéqī de chéngji (*the grades this semester are better than those last semester*); 北京的大学多于上海的大学 Běijīng de dàxué duō yú Shànghǎi de dàxué (*there are more universities in Beijing than Shanghai*)

Also appears in the following words: 等于 děngyú (*equal to*; *tantamount to*); 对于 duìyú (*to*; *as far as ... is concerned*); 关于 guānyú (*concerning*; *regarding*); 属于 shǔyú (*belong to*); 由于 yóuyú (*due to*; *as a result of*) and 至于 zhìyú (*as for*)

于是 **yúshì**		*as a result*; *consequently*: 大家都说电影不好看，于是我就没去看 dàjiā dōu shuō diànyǐng bù hǎokàn, yúshì wǒ jiù méi qù kàn (*everyone said that the movie was not interesting, so I didn't go to see it*)

雨 yǔ

rain: 大雨 dà yǔ (*heavy rain*); 小雨 xiǎo yǔ (*light rain*). Cl: 场 chǎng. Note that the word 雨 yǔ is always a noun in Chinese. The expression for *to rain* is 下雨 xiàyǔ.

Also appears in the following words: 雷雨 léiyǔ (*thunderstorm*); 毛毛雨 máomáoyǔ (*drizzle*)

雨点 **yǔdiǎn**	*raindrop*. Cl: 个 gè
雨季 **yǔjì**	*rainy season*
雨量 **yǔliàng**	*rainfall*
雨伞 **yǔsǎn**	*umbrella*. Cl: 把 bǎ
雨衣 **yǔyī**	*raincoat*. Cl: 件 jiàn

语 yǔ

language; *words*: 俄语 éyǔ (*Russian language*); 汉语 hànyǔ (*Chinese language*); 外语 wàiyǔ (*foreign language*); 口语 kǒuyǔ (*spoken language*); 母语 mǔyǔ (*mother tongue*); 手语 shǒuyǔ (*sign language*); 双语 shuāngyǔ (*bilingual*; *dual languages*). When used without modification, it takes the disyllabic form of 语言 yǔyán: 你会说什么语言 nǐ huì shuō shénme yǔyán (*what languages do you speak?*)

Also appears in the following words: 标语 biāoyǔ (*slogan*); 成语 chéngyǔ (*idiom*); 词语 cíyǔ (*words and expressions*); 短语 duǎnyǔ (*phrase*); 耳语 ěryǔ (*whisper*); 国语 guóyǔ (*Mandarin*); 术语 shùyǔ (*term*; *nomenclature*)

语调 **yǔdiào**	*intonation*
语法 **yǔfǎ**	*grammar*
语气 **yǔqì**	*tone*; *manner of speaking*; *mood*
语态 **yǔtài**	(gram) *voice*
语序 **yǔxù**	*word order*
语言 **yǔyán**	*language*: 语言学 yǔyánxué (*linguistics*); 语言学家 yǔyánxuéjiā (*linguist*)

语义 yǔyì	semantic: 语义学 yǔyìxué (semantics)
语音 yǔyīn	pronunciation: 语音学 yǔyīnxué (phonetics)

园 yuán

1. *garden; plot; plantation:* 果园 guǒyuán (*orchard*); 花园 huāyuán (*flower garden*); 葡萄园 pútáoyuán (*vineyard*); 种植园 zhòngzhíyuán (*plantation*); 植物园 zhíwùyuán (*botanical garden*). Cl: 处 chù; 座 zuò; 个 gè

2. *park; place of recreation:* 公园 gōngyuán (*park*); 动物园 dòngwùyuán (*zoo*). Cl: 个 gè; 所 suǒ

Also appears in the following words: 花园 huāyuán (*garden*); 校园 xiàoyuán (*campus*); 幼儿园 yòu'éryuán (*kindergarten*)

园丁 yuándīng	gardener. Cl: 个 gè; 位 wèi; 名 míng
园林 yuánlín	gardens; park. Cl: 处 chù; 片 piàn
园艺 yuányì	gardening: 园艺师 yuányìshī (gardener)

员 yuán

1. *person; personnel,* used as a suffix: 服务员 fúwùyuán (*waiter; waitress; attendant*); 售货员 shòuhuòyuán (*salesclerk*); 打字员 dǎzìyuán (*typist*); 队员 duìyuán (*team member*); 飞行员 fēixíngyuán (*pilot*); 分析员 fēnxīyuán (*analyst*); 公安员 gōng'ānyuán (*public security officer; police*); 公务员 gōngwùyuán (*civil servant*); 官员 guānyuán (*officer; official*); 售货员 shòuhuóyuán (*salesman; salesperson*); 图书馆员 túshūguǎnyuán (*librarian*); 演员 yǎnyuán (*actor; performer*). Cl: 个 gè; 位 wèi; 名 míng

2. *member:* 会员 huìyuán (*association member*); 党员 dǎngyuán (*party member*). Cl: 个 gè; 位 wèi; 名 míng

Also appears in the following words: 成员 chéngyuán (*member*); 船员 chuányuán (*seaman*); 店员 diànyuán (*shop assistant; salesclerk*); 动员 dòngyuán (*mobilize*); 雇员 gùyuán (*employee*); 官员 guānyuán (*official*); 海员 hǎiyuán (*seaman*); 人员 rényuán (*personnel*); 学员 xuéyuán (*student*); 演员 yǎnyuán (*actor*); 议员 yìyuán (*assemblyman; councilman*)

员工 yuángōng	staff; personnel. Cl: 个 gè; 名 míng

原 yuán

1. *former; original; formerly; originally*: 原意 yuányì (*original intention*);
原以为 yuán yǐwéi (*originally believed*)

2. *unprocessed; raw; crude*: 原油 yuányóu (*crude oil*); 原料 yuánliào (*raw material*)

3. *plain* (n): 草原 cǎoyuán (*grassland*); 高原 gāoyuán (*highland*); 平原 píngyuán (*plains*). Cl: 片 piàn

原告 **yuángào**	*plaintiff*. Cl: 个 gè; 名 míng	
原来 **yuánlái**	*former; original; formerly; originally*: 原来的公司 yuánláide gōngsī (*the former company*); 我原来不想来 wǒ yuánlái bù xiǎng lái (*initially, I didn't want to come*)	
原谅 **yuánliàng**	*forgive*	
原料 **yuánliào**	*raw material*. Cl: 种 zhǒng	
原始 **yuánshǐ**	1. *primitive*: 原始社会 yuánshǐ shèhuì (*primitive society*) 2. *primary; firsthand*: 原始资料 yuánshǐ zīliào (*firsthand data*)	
原文 **yuánwén**	*original text*. Cl: 段 duàn; 句 jù; 篇 piān	
原因 **yuányīn**	*reason; cause*. Cl: 个 gè; 种 zhǒng; 条 tiáo	
原则 **yuánzé**	*principle*. Cl: 个 gè; 项 xiàng; 条 tiáo	

远 yuǎn

far; remote: 火车站离飞机场不远 huǒchēzhàn lí fēijīchǎng bù yuǎn (*the train station is not far from the airport*)

Also appears in the following words: **长远** chángyuǎn (*long-range*); **久远** jiǔyuǎn (*ancient; far away*); **永远** yǒngyuǎn (*forever*)

远大 **yuǎndà**	*long-range; ambitious*: 远大的目标 yuǎndàde mùbiāo (*long-range goal*)
远东 **yuǎndōng**	*the Far East*
远方 **yuǎnfāng**	*distant place*
远景 **yuǎnjǐng**	*long-range prospect*
远亲 **yuǎnqīn**	*distant relatives*

院 yuàn

1. *courtyard*; *yard*; *compound*: 前院 qiányuàn (*front yard*); 后院 hòuyuàn (*back yard*). When used without modification, it takes the disyllabic form of 院子 yuànzi.

2. *government offices and public places*: 参议院 cānyìyuàn (*the Senate*); 众议院 zhòngyìyuàn (*House of Representatives*); 法院 fǎyuàn (*court*); 电影院 diànyǐngyuàn (*movie theater*); 剧院 jùyuàn (*theater*). Cl: 家 jiā; 座 zuò

3. *college*; *academy*: 学院 xuéyuàn (*college*; *institute*); 研究生院 yánjiūī shēngyuàn (*graduate school*); 医学院 yīxuéyuàn (*medical school*). Cl: 所 suǒ

4. *hospital*: 住院 zhùyuàn (*be hospitalized*); 出院 chūyuàn (*be discharged from the hospital*)

院子 yuànzi　　　　*courtyard*; *yard*. Cl: 个 gè; 座 zuò

月 yuè

1. *the moon*, often taking the disyllabic form of 月亮 yuèliang
2. *month*

月饼 yuèbǐng	*moon cake* (for Mid-Autumn Festival). Cl: 个 gè; 块 kuài
月经 yuèjīng	*menstruation*; *period*
月刊 yuèkān	*monthly* (magazine, newspaper, etc.). Cl: 期 qī; 份 fèn; 本 běn
月亮 yuèliang	*the moon*
月票 yuèpiào	*monthly pass* (for bus, train, etc.). Cl: 张 zhāng

---

越 yuè

1. *climb over*; *go over*; *jump over*, usu. followed by 过 guò: 越过高山 yuè guò gāoshān (*climb over tall mountains*)

2. *exceed*; *overstep*; *go beyond*, usu. followed by 过 guò: 越过权限 yuè guò quánxiàn (*exceed one's authority*)

Also appears in the following words: **超越** chāoyuè (*surmount*; *exceed*); **跨越** kuàyuè (*cross over*; *span*); **优越** yōuyuè (*superiority*)

越发 yuèfā	*all the more*; *even more*: 夏天的到来对庄稼越发有利 xiàtiān de dàolái duì zhuāngjia yuèfā yǒulì (*the arrival of the summer is even more favorable to the crops*)
越轨 yuèguǐ	*transgress*: 越轨行为 yuèguǐ xíngwéi (*transgression*)

越过 yuèguò	pass; cross; surmount: 越过障碍 yuèguò zhàng'ài (surmount obstacles)
越来越 yuèláiyuè	more and more: 天气越来越冷 tiānqì yuèláiyuè lěng (the weather is getting colder and colder); 你的中文越来越好 nǐde Zhōngwén yuèláiyuè hǎo (your Chinese is getting better and better)
越南 Yuènán	Vietnam: 越南人 Yuènánrén (Vietnamese people); 越南语 Yuènányǔ (Vietnamese language)
越权 yuèquán	overstep one's authority
越狱 yuèyù	break prison; escape from prison
越 … 越 … yuè … yuè …	the more … the more …: 越多越好 yuè duō yuè hǎo (the more, the better); 我越学越有兴趣 wǒ yuè xué yuè yǒu xìngqù (the more I study, the more interested I become)

运 yùn

1. *transport; ship*: 运货 yùn huò (*transport goods*); 海运 hǎi yùn (*ocean shipping*)

2. *move; use in a deliberate way*: 运球 yùn qiú (*dribble*); 运笔 yùn bǐ (*wield the pen*).

3. *fortune; luck*: 好运 hǎo yùn (*good luck*); 坏运 huài yùn (*bad luck*)

Also appears in the following words: 搬运 bānyùn (*carry; ship*); 货运 huòyùn (*freight transport*); 空运 kōngyùn (*ship by air*); 托运 tuōyùn (*consign for shipment*); 幸运 xìngyùn (*luck*); 走运 zǒuyùn (*have one's day; luck up*)

运动 yùndòng	1. *move; movement; campaign*: 政治运动 zhèngzhì yùndòng (*political movement*); 敌军向我方运动 díjūn xiàng wǒfāng yùndòng (*the enemy troops are moving in our direction*) 2. *sports; exercise*: 你喜欢什么运动 nǐ xǐhuan shénme yùndòng (*what sports do you like?*); 我每天早上都要运动 wǒ měitiān zǎoshang dōu yào yùndòng (*I always exercise in the morning*); 运动会 yùndònghuì (*sports meet*); 运动员 yùndòngyuán (*athletes*)
运费 yùnfèi	shipping charge
运河 yùnhé	canal. Cl: 条 tiáo
运气 yùnqì	fortune; luck
运输 yùnshū	transport: 运输公司 yùnshū gōngsī (*shipping company*)
运用 yùnyòng	apply; utilize: 运用先进的技术 yùnyòng xiānjìnde jìshù (*apply advanced technology*)
运转 yùnzhuǎn	(of machinery) work; operate: 机器运转正常 jīqì yùnzhuǎn zhèngcháng (*the machines are running well*)

在 zài

1. *at, in, on,* used to indicate time, locations or direction: 故事发生在古代 gùshi fāshēng zài gǔdài (*the story took place in ancient times*); 天安门在北京 Tiānānmén zài Běijīng (*Tiananmen is in Beijing*); 厕所在三楼 cèsuǒ zǎi sān lóu (*the bathroom is on the third floor*). In most cases, the adverbial phrase introduced by 在 zài precedes the verb to indicate a setting: 我妈妈在医院工作 wǒ māma zài yīyuàn gōngzuò (*my mother works at a hospital*); 他在家吃中饭 tā zài jiā chī zhōngfàn (*he eats lunch at home*), but with some verbs, such as 住 zhù (*live*), 出生 chūshēng (*be born*), and 发生 fāshēng (*happen*), the 在 zài phrase can be placed either before or after the verb: 在纽约住 zài Niǔyuē zhù / 住在纽约 zhù zài Niǔyuē (*live in New York*); 在英国出生 zài Yīngguó chūshēng / 出生在英国 chūshēngzài Yīngguó (*born in England*). Other verbs that also have such flexibility with 在 zài include 放 fàng (*put*), 写 xiě (*write*), 躺 tǎng (*lie*), 站 zhàn (*stand*), 存 cún (*deposit*), and 挂 guà (*hang*). When placed after the verb, the 在 zài phrase suggests a destination involving a temporal sequence: 放在桌子上 fàng zài zhuōzi shang (*put on the table*—the action started somewhere else and rested on the table); 挂在墙上 guà zài qiáng shang (*hang on the wall*—the action started somewhere else and rested on the wall).

2. *exist; be present*: 20年过去了，那家商店还在 èrshí nián guò qù le, nà jiā shāngdiàn hái zài (*20 years have passed, but that store is still there*); 对不起，我们的经理现在不在 duìbuqǐ wǒmende jīnglǐ xiànzài bú zài (*sorry that our manager is not in right now*)

3. aspect marker used before a verb to indicate that an action is in progress. The particle 呢 ne can optionally be used at the end of the sentence: 经理在打电话（呢）jīnglǐ zài dǎ diànhuà (ne) (*the manager is making a phone call*); 我先生在睡觉（呢）wǒ xiānsheng zài shuìjiào (ne) (*my husband is sleeping*). For emphasis, 在 zài can be preceded by the adverb 正 zhèng (*right, just*): 他来的时候，我正在开会 tā lái de shíhou, wǒ zhèng zài kāi huì (*when he came, I was in the middle of a meeting*). When either 正 zhèng or 呢 ne appears in the sentence, 在 zài can be omitted: 他正看书（呢）tā zhèng kàn shū (ne) (*he is reading*); 他们谈话呢 tāmen tánhuà ne (*they are talking*). The negative form of the progressive aspect marker is 没有 méiyou instead of 不 bù: 外边没有在下雨 wàibian méiyou zài xiàyǔ (*it is not raining outside*). 在 zài is always left out in the existential or presentational sentences where the adverbial phrase it introduces appears at the beginning of a sentence: （在）公园里有一个动物园 (zài) gōngyuán lǐ yǒu yí ge dòngwùyuán (*there is a zoo in the park*). However 在 zài cannot be left out if the sentence is not existential or presentational even if the adverbial phrase appears at the beginning of the sentence: 在中国，很多人骑自行车上班 zài Zhōngguó, hěn duō rén qí zìxíngchē shàngbān (*in China, many people go to work by bike*).

Also appears in the following words: 存在 cúnzài (*exist*); 潜在 qiánzài (*potential*);
实在 shízài (*indeed; actuality*); 现在 xiànzài (*now*)

在场 **zàichǎng**	*be present*	
在行 **zàiháng**	*be good at; be expert in*	
在乎 **zàihu**	*care; mind*: 我是北方人，不在乎冷天 wǒ shì běifāngrén, bù zàihu lěngtiān (*I'm from the north and I don't mind the cold weather*)	
在意 **zàiyì**	*care; mind*, used interchangeably with 在乎 zàihu	
在于 **zàiyú**	*lie in; depend on*: 问题在于你没有兴趣 wèntí zàiyú nǐ méi you xìngqù (*the problem lies in your lack of interest*); 我能不能去旅行在于我有没有时间 wǒ néng bu néng qù lǚxíng zàiyú wǒ yǒu méi you shíjiān (*whether I can travel depends on whether I have the time*)	
在职 **zàizhí**	*in service; on the job*: 在职训练 zàizhí xùnliàn (*in-service training*)	

再 zài

1. *again; once more*: 再见 zàijiàn (*good-bye*, literally "*see again*"); 再来 zài lái (*come again*). The action indicated by the verb is yet to happen; otherwise, 又 yòu should be used: 我昨天去了图书馆, 今天又去了那儿 wǒ zuótiān qù le túshūguǎn, jīntiān yòu qù le nàr (*I went to the library yesterday and I went there again today*).

2. *then*: 先洗手再吃饭 xiān xǐ shǒu zài chīfàn (*first wash your hands and then eat*)

3. (of time) *in*: 再过一个星期, 我们就要放假了 zài guò yí ge xīngqī, wǒmen jiù yào fàngjià le (*we'll be on vacation in a week*)

4. used to indicate that an action will take place at a specific time in the future: 动物园今天关门, 我们明天再去吧 dòngwùyuán jīntiān guānmén, wǒmen míngtiān zài qù ba (*the zoo is closed today, let's go there tomorrow*)

5. *even if; no matter how*, usu. used in conjunction with 也 yě or 还是 háishì: 我再抄这个字, 还是记不住 wǒ zài chāo zhè ge zì, háishí jì bú zhù (*no matter how many times I copied the character, I still couldn't remember it*); 山再高, 我们也要爬 shān zài gāo, wǒmen yě yào pá (*no matter how high the mountain is, we'll scale it*)

6. used in the negative in conjunction with 也 yě to indicate an action that will not happen or has never happened: 他再也不来了 tā zài yě bù lái le (*he will never come again*); 离开中国后, 我再也没吃过中国菜 líkāi Zhōngguó hòu, wǒ zài yě méi chī guo Zhōngguócài (*since I left China, I have never had Chinese food*)

再婚 **zàihūn**	*remarry*

再见 zàijiàn   *good-bye*

再三 zàisān   *over and over again; repeatedly*

再说 zàishuō   **1.** *some other time*: 这件事, 我们再说吧 zhè jiàn shì, wǒmen zàishuō ba (*let's talk about the matter some other time*)

     2. *what is more; besides*: 我没有时间去旅行, 再说我也没有钱 wǒ méi you shíjiān qù lǚxíng, zàishuō wǒ yě méi you qián (*I don't have time to travel. Besides, I don't have money*)

咱 zán

1. *I*, used in certain dialects

2. *we*, used colloquially and in certain dialects

咱们 zánmen   *we*; 咱们 zánmen differs from 我们 wǒmen in that 咱们 zánmen includes both the speaker and the listener, whereas 我们 wǒmen does not necessarily include the listener.

早 zǎo

1. *early*: 早班 zǎobān (*early shift*); 请早点儿来 qǐng zǎo diǎnr lái (*please come a little early*)

2. *long ago; for a long time*: 早知道今天没有课, 我就不来了 zǎo zhīdao jīntiān méi you kè, wǒ jiù bù lái le (*had I known that there would be no class today, I would not have come*)

3. (greeting) *good morning*

Also appears in the following words: 趁早 chènzǎo (*as early as possible*); 迟早 chízǎo (*sooner and later*); 清早 qīngzǎo (*early morning*)

早安 zǎo'ān   (greeting) *good morning*

早班 zǎobān   *morning shift*

早餐 zǎocān   *breakfast* (formal). Cl: 顿 dùn

早晨 zǎochén   *early morning*

早饭 zǎofàn   *breakfast* (informal). Cl: 顿 dùn

早期 zǎoqī   *early time; early stage*

早上 zǎoshang   *morning*

早先 zǎoxiān   *previously*

早已 zǎoyǐ   *long ago*: 他早已毕业了 tā zǎoyǐ bìyè le (*he graduated a long time ago*)

造 zào

1. *make*; *build*, *manufacture*: 造桥 zào qiáo (*build a bridge*); 造汽车 zào qìchē (*manufacture cars*); 造纸 zào zhǐ (*make paper*)

2. *invent*; *fabricate*: 造假证据 zào jiǎ zhèngjù (*fabricate evidence*)

Also appears in the following words: 创造 chuàngzào (*create*); 改造 gǎizào (*rebuild*; *recast*); 构造 gòuzào (*structure*); 建造 jiànzào (*build*); 人造 rénzào (*man-made*; *artificial*); 制造 zhìzào (*make*; *manufacture*)

造成 **zàochéng**	*create*; *bring about*; *cause*: 造成损失 zàochéng sǔnshī (*cause damage*); 造成影响 zàochéng yǐngxiǎng (*create an impact*)
造反 **zàofǎn**	*rise in rebellion*
造价 **zàojià**	*cost* (of making or building): 这种机器的造价很高 zhè zhǒng jīqì de zàojià hěn gāo (*the cost of making this kind of machine is very high*)
造句 **zàojù**	*sentence-making*
造谣 **zàoyáo**	*create or spread a rumor*

怎 zěn

Not used by itself apart from being part of another word or expression.

怎么 **zěnme**	**1.** *how*: 你怎么去上班 nǐ zěnme qù shàngbān (*how do you go to work?*)
	2. *why*; *how come*, implying surprise or blame: 你怎么迟到了 nǐ zěnme chídào le (*how come you are late?*)
	3. used in the negative to mean *not quite*; *not particularly*: 这儿的冬天不怎么冷 zhèr de dōngtiān bù zěnme lěng (*winter here is not so cold*); 我不怎么相信他的话 wǒ bù zěnme xiāngxìn tāde huà (*I don't quite believe what he says*)
	4. *no matter how*; *however*, used in conjunction with 也 yě or 都 dōu: 我怎么写也写不好 wǒ zěnme xiě yě xiě bù hǎo (*no matter how I write, I can't get it right*)
怎么了 **zěnme le**	*what's the matter with*; *what's wrong*, used for situations where there is a problem: 你怎么了 nǐ zěnme le (*what's the matter with you?*)
怎么样 **zěnmeyàng**	**1.** *how are things*: 你最近怎么样 nǐ zuìjìn zěnmeyàng (*how have you been recently?*)
	2. *how do you like*; *what do you think of*, used to solicit

253

opinions: 这本书怎么样 zhè běn shū zěnmeyàng (*what do you think of the book?*); 我们去中国城怎么样 wǒmen qù Zhōngguóchéng zěnmeyàng (*let's go to Chinatown, shall we?*)
3. used in the negative to mean *not that great*: 这部电影不怎么样 zhè bù diànyǐng bù zěnmeyàng (*this movie is not that great*)

怎样 **zěnyàng**
1. *how*, used more in written language
2. *what kind of*, used to modify a noun: 怎样的人 zěnyàng de rén (*what kind of person*); 怎样的公司 zěnyàng de gōngsī (*what kind of company*)

站 zhàn

1. *stand*: 站在舞台上 zhàn zài wǔtái shang (*stand on the stage*)

2. *station; stop*: 火车站 huǒchēzhàn (*train station*); 汽车站 qìchēzhàn (*bus stop*)

3. *service station; service center*: 加油站 jiāyóuzhàn (*gas station*); 网站 wǎngzhàn (*website*)

站队 **zhànduì**		*line up; stand in line*
站岗 **zhàngǎng**		*stand sentry*
站台 **zhàntái**		*(railroad) platform*
站住 **zhàn zhù**		*(command) halt; freeze; stop*
站住脚 **zhàn zhù jiǎo**		*hold water; be tenable*: 这个解释站不住脚 zhè ge jiěshì zhàn bu zhù jiǎo (*this explanation is not tenable*)

张 zhāng

1. *spread; open*: 张嘴 zhāng zuǐ (*open mouth*); 张网打鱼 zhāng wǎng dǎ yú (*cast the net to catch fish*)

2. classifier used for things such as beds, tables, paper, and tickets: 一张床 yì zhāng chuáng (*one bed*); 两张桌子 liǎng zhāng zhuōzi (*two tables*); 三张纸 sān zhāng zhǐ (*three sheets of paper*)

Also appears in the following words: 紧张 jǐnzhāng (*strain; tense*); 扩张 kuòzhāng (*expand*); 纸张 zhǐzhāng (*paper*)

长 zhǎng

1. *older*: 他长我三岁 tā zhǎng wǒ sān suì (*he is three years older than I am*)

2. *oldest*: 长子 zhǎngzǐ (*oldest son*); 长孙 zhǎngsūn (*oldest grandson*)

3. *grow; form*: 花长得很好 huā zhǎng de hěn hǎo (*the flower is growing well*)

4. *acquire* (knowledge): 去了一次中国, 他长了不少见识 qù le yí cì Zhōngguó, tā zhǎng le bù shǎo jiànshi (*after his trip to China, he became knowledgeable about many things*)

5. *chief*: 市长 shìzhǎng (*mayor*); 校长 xiàozhǎng (*head of a school*)

长辈 **zhǎngbèi**	*elders*	
长大 **zhǎng dà**	*grow up*: 你长大后想做什么 nǐ zhǎng dà hòu xiǎng zuò shénme (*what would you like to do when you grow up?*)	
长进 **zhǎngjìn**	*progress*	

找 zhǎo

1. *look for*: 找工作 zhǎo gōngzuò (*look for a job*)

2. *find*, followed by the verb complement 到 dào: 你有没有找到钱包 nǐ yǒu méiyou zhǎo dào qiánbāo (*have you found your wallet?*)

3. *come to see; call on*: 有人找你 yǒu rén zhǎo nǐ (*someone is here to see you*)

4. *give change to*, used with 钱 qián: 少找了我钱 shǎo zhǎo le wǒ qián (*didn't give me enough change*)

找麻烦 **zhǎo máfan**	*look for trouble*
找钱 **zhǎoqián**	*give change*
找死 **zhǎosǐ**	*court death*
找寻 **zhǎoxún**	*search; seek*

照 zhào

1. *illuminate; light up; shine*: 月光照在水面上 yuèguāng zhào zài shuǐmiàn shang (*the moonlight shines on the surface of the water*)

2. *reflect; mirror* (v.): 照镜子 zhào jìngzi (*look in the mirror*)

3. *take* (a picture): 照照片 zhào zhàopiàn (*take a picture*)

4. *photograph*: 人物照 rénwùzhào (*portrait*); 风景照 fēngjǐngzhào (*landscape photo*)

5. *license; permit*: 车照 chēzhào (*driver's license*); 护照 hùzhào (*passport*).
Cl: 本 běn; 种 zhǒng

6. *according to*: 照规定办事 zhào guīdìng bànshì (*handle business according to regulations*)

Also appears in the following words: **按照** ànzhào (*according to*); **对照** duìzhào (*contrast*); **关照** guānzhào (*look after*); **拍照** pāizhào (*take a picture*); **牌照** páizhào (*license plate*); **执照** zhízhào (*license*); **遵照** zūnzhào (*act in accordance with*)

照办 **zhàobàn**	*act accordingly*	
照常 **zhàocháng**	*as usual*: 照常办公 zhàocháng bàngōng (*business as usual*)	
照抄 **zhàochāo**	*copy word for word*	
照顾 **zhàogù**	1. *look after; care for*: 照顾孩子 zhàogù háizi (*look after children*)	
	2. *consideration; give consideration to*: 病人需要特别的照顾 bìngrén xūyào tèbiéde zhàogù (*patients need special consideration*)	
照旧 **zhàojiù**	*as usual*: 工作分配照旧 gōngzuò fēnpèi zhàojiù (*the work assignment is as usual*)	
照看 **zhàokàn**	*look after; keep an eye on*: 你能不能照看一下儿我的行李 nǐ néng bu néng zhàokàn yíxiàr wǒde xíngli (*can you keep an eye on my luggage?*)	
照片 **zhàopiàn**	*photo*. Cl: 张 zhāng	
照相 **zhàoxiàng**	*take a picture*: 照相机 zhàoxiàngjī (*camera*)	
照样 **zhàoyàng**	*in the same way; all the same*: 没有帮助，我们照样能成功 méi you bāngzhù, wǒmen zhàoyàng néng chénggōng (*without help, we can still succeed*)	

着 zhe

Pronounced in the neutral tone. Grammatical particle used after a verb:

1. to indicate a continuous aspect of an action, often used with 在 zài, 正 zhèng, or 正在 zhèng zài: 他们在喝着茶，说着话 tāmen zài hē zhe chá, shuō zhe huà (*they are drinking tea and chatting*)

2. to indicate the continuous state of an action: 门开着 mén kāi zhe (*the door is open*); 杯子在桌子上放着 bēizi zài zhuōzi shang fàng zhe (*the cups are lying on the table*). Contrast these with 门开了 mén kāi le (*the door was opened*); 他把杯子放在桌子上 tā bǎ bēizi fàng zài zhuōzi shang (*he put the cups on the table*). In these cases, the verbs are instantaneous rather than durative. The negative form of a verb followed by 着 zhe is 没有 méiyou + verb: 门没有开着 mén méiyou kāi zhe (*the door is not open*).

256

3. to indicate an accompanying or secondary action: 笑着说 xiào zhe shuō (*say while smiling*); 走着看 zǒu zhe kàn (*read while walking*)

者 zhě

person; *personnel*: suffix used after nouns, verbs and adjectives: 作者 zuòzhě (*author*); 医疗工作者 yīliáo gōngzuòzhě (*medical worker*); 读者 dúzhě (*reader*). Cl: 个 gè; 位 wèi; 名 míng

Also appears in the following words: 或者 huòzhě (*or*); 记者 jìzhě (*reporter*); 学者 xuézhě (*scholar*)

这 zhè

this. When used to define a noun, it usu. requires a classifier to go with it because it is considered as a veiled form of *this one*: 这家餐馆 zhè jiā cānguǎn (*this restaurant*); 这个城市 zhè ge chéngshì (*this city*). When a noun is defined by both a possessive pronoun and 这 zhè, 这 zhè follows the possessive pronoun: 我的这位朋友 wǒde zhè wèi péngyou (*this friend of mine*).

这儿 / 这里 zhèr / zhèlǐ These two terms are often used interchangeably.
1. *here*; *this place*: 这儿没有银行 zhèr méi you yínháng (*there is no bank here*); 这里是我的家 zhèlǐ shì wǒde jiā (*this place is my home*)
2. placed after a personal pronoun to indicate a place: 我们这儿冬天常常下雪 wǒmen zhèr dōngtiān chángcháng xiàxuě (*it often snows in our place in winter*); 我这儿没有日语书 wǒ zhèr méi you Rìyǔ shū (*there are no Japanese books at my place*)

这么 zhème
1. *so*; *such*: 今天这么热 jīntiān zhème rè (*it's so hot today!*); 雨下得这么大 yǔ xià de zhème dà (*what a downpour!*); 这么好看的电影 zhème hǎokàn de diànyǐng (*such an interesting movie!*). Both 这么 zhème and 那么 nàme express the same meaning, but 这么 zhème refers to what is close by the speaker and 那么 nàme refers to what is away from the speaker, both temporally and spatially.
2. *in this way*: 这个字该这么写 zhè ge zì gāi zhème xiě (*this character should be written like this*)

真 zhēn

real; *true*; *really*; *truly*: 真话 zhēn huà (*true words*); 真事 zhēn shì (*real event*); 真冷 zhēn lěng (*really cold*). When used as the predicative, 真 zhēn usu. takes the form of 真的 zhēnde: 这个故事不是真的 zhè ge gùshì bú shì zhēnde (*this story is not true*).

Also appears in the following words: **果真** guǒzhēn (*indeed*; *really*); **清真** qīngzhēn (*Islamic*; *Muslim*); **认真** rènzhēn (*earnest*; *serious*); **天真** tiānzhēn (*naive*; *simple*)

真诚 zhēnchéng	*sincere*; *genuine*	
真的吗 zhēn de ma?	*really?*	
真情 zhēnqíng	*real or true situation*; *truth*; *facts*	
真实 zhēnshí	*real*, *true*: 真实的故事 zhēnshíde gùshì (*true story*)	
真心 zhēnxīn	*sincere*; *heartfelt*	
真正 zhēnzhèng	*true*; *genuine*: 真正的朋友 zhēnzhèngde péngyou (*true friends*)	

整 zhěng

1. *whole*; *complete*; *sharp*: 整天 zhěngtiān (*the whole day*); 十点整 shí diǎn zhěng (*ten o'clock sharp*)

2. *neat*; *tidy*, often used as part of another word (see below)

Also appears in the following words: **平整** píngzhěng (*level*); **调整** tiáozhěng (*adjust*); **完整** wánzhěng (*complete*); **修整** xiūzhěng (*repair and maintain*)

整顿 zhěngdùn	*rectify*; *reorganize*; *strengthen*: 整顿组织 zhěngdùn zǔzhí (*restructure the organization*); 整顿市场 zhěngdùn shìchǎng (*clean up the market*)
整个 zhěnggè	*whole*; *entire*: 整个社会 zhěnggè shèhuì (*the entire society*); 整个公司 zhěnggè gōngsī (*the whole company*).
整洁 zhěngjié	*clean*; *tidy*; *neat*: 学生们的卧室很整洁 xuéshengmen de wòshì hěn zhěngjié (*the students' bedrooms are very clean*)
整理 zhěnglǐ	*put in order*; *straighten out*; *sort out*: 整理房间 zhěnglǐ fángjiān (*straighten the room*)
整齐 zhěngqí	*in good order*; *neat*: 街道很整齐 jiēdào hěn zhěngqí (*the streets are neatly laid out*)
整体 zhěngtǐ	*overall*: 整体规划 zhěngtǐ guīhuà (*overall planning*)
整天 zhěngtiān	*the whole day*; *all day long*: 玩了一整天 wán le yì zhěngtiān (*played the whole day*)
整修 zhěngxiū	*rebuild*; *renovate*

整整　zhěngzhěng　　　*whole*; *full*, *exactly*, followed by a measurement: 在台湾住了整整三年 zài Táiwān zhù le zhěngzhěng sān nián (*lived in Taiwan for three whole years*); 存了整整三万块钱 cún le zhěngzhěng sān wàn yuán qián (*saved exactly 30,000 dollars*)

整治　zhěngzhì　　　*repair*; *dredge*: 整治河流 zhěngzhì héliú (*dredge a river*)

正　zhèng

1. *straight*; *upright*: 墙上的画不正 qiáng shang de huà bú zhèng (*the picture on the wall is not straight*)

2. (of houses and rooms) *main*: 正室 zhèng shì (*the main room*); 正门 zhèng mén (*the main gate*)

3. *correct*; *honest*: 他做事很正 tā zuò shì hěn zhèng (*he is very honest in doing things*)

4. *exactly*; *just*: 衣服的长短正合适 yīfu de chángduǎn zhèng héshi (*the length of the clothes is exactly right*); 正如我说 zhèng rú wǒ shuō (*just as I said*)

5. used before a verb to indicate a progressive action; if the verb has no modifier, 正 zhèng must be accompanied by 在 zài (before the verb), or 着 zhe (after the verb), or 呢 ne (at the end of the sentence) or both 着 zhe and 呢 ne: 妈妈正在厨房做饭 māma zhèng zài chúfáng zuòfàn (*mother is cooking in the kitchen*); 工人们正修着路 gōngrénmen zhèng xiū zhe lù (*the workers are repairing the road*); 老师正和家长谈话呢 lǎoshī zhèng hé jiāzhǎng tánhuà ne (*the teacher is talking to the parents*).

6. *just about*; *just when*: 我正要找你 wó zhèng yào zhǎo nǐ (*I was just about to look for you*)

Also appears in the following words: 纯正 chúnzhèng (*pure*; *genuine*); 反正 fǎnzhèng (*anyway*); 改正 gǎizhèng (*correct*; *rectify*); 更正 gēngzhèng (*make corrections*); 公正 gōngzhèng (*equity*; *honesty*); 真正 zhēnzhèng (*true*)

正常　zhèngcháng　　　*normal*; *regular*

正当　zhèngdāng　　　**1.** *proper*; *legitimate*; *appropriate*; *justifiable*: 正当的自卫 zhèngdāngde zìwèi (*justifiable self-defense*)
　　　　　　　　　　2. *just when*: 正当我要离开的时候 zhèngdāng wǒ yào líkāi de shíhou (*just when I was going to leave*)

正点　zhèngdiǎn　　　(of trains, planes, etc.) *on time*

正方形　zhèngfāngxíng　　　*square*

正规　zhèngguī　　　*regular*: 正规学校 zhèngguī xuéxiào (*regular school*)

正好　zhènghǎo　　　**1.** *by chance*; *it happens that*: 他在图书馆的时候，我正

好也在那儿 tā zài túshūguǎn de shíhou, wǒ zhènghǎo yě zài nàr (*when he was in the library, I happened to be there too*).

2. *just right*: 你做这个工作正好 nǐ zuò zhè ge gōngzuò zhènghǎo (*you are the right person to do the job*)

正面 **zhèngmiàn** **1.** *front*: 戏院的正面 xìyuàn de zhèngmiàn (*the front of the theater*)

2. *positive*: 正面人物 zhèngmiàn rénwù (*positive character; good guy*)

3. *the obverse side* (of an object): 纸的正面 zhǐ de zhèngmiàn (*the right side of the paper*)

正巧 **zhèngqiǎo** *by chance; it happens that*, interchangeable with the first sense of 正好 zhènghǎo above

正确 **zhèngquè** *correct; right*

正式 **zhèngshì** *formal; official*

正统 **zhèngtǒng** *orthodox*

正直 **zhèngzhí** (of a person) *upright; honest*

证 zhèng

1. *certificate; certifying document; card*: 出生证 chūshēngzhèng (*birth certificate*); 借书证 jièshūzhèng (*library card*); 身份证 shēnfènzhèng (*ID card*); 毕业证 bìyèzhèng (*diploma*)

2. *evidence; proof; testimony*: 旁证 pángzhèng (*circumstantial evidence; collateral evidence*); 物证 wùzhèng (*material evidence; exhibit*); 罪证 zuìzhèng (*evidence of a crime*); 作证 zuòzhèng (*testify; give evidence*); 公证 gōngzhèng (*notarization*)

Also appears in the following words: 保证 bǎozhèng (*guarantee*); 见证 jiànzhèng (*testimony; witness*); 人证 rénzhèng (*testimony of a witness*); 工作证 gōngzuòzhèng (*employee's ID*)

证件 **zhèngjiàn** *credentials; papers; ID*. Cl: 份 fèn; 个 gè

证据 **zhèngjù** *evidence; proof*

证明 **zhèngmíng** **1.** *certificate; proof*

2. *prove; bear out; certify*

Cl: 份 fèn; 个 gè

证券 **zhèngquàn** *bond; security*: 证券交易所 zhèngquàn jiāoyìsuǒ (*stock exchange*)

证人 **zhèngrén** *witness* (n.). Cl: 个 gè; 位 wèi; 名 míng

证实 **zhèngshí** *confirm; verify*

证书 **zhèngshū** *certificate; credentials*. Cl: 份 fèn; 张 zhāng

---

知 zhī

know; be aware of, usu. taking the disyllabic form of 知道 zhīdao

Also appears in the following words: **通知** tōngzhī (*inform; give notice*); **无知** wúzhī (*ignorant*)

知道 **zhīdao**	*know; be aware of*
知己 **zhījǐ**	*intimate:* 知己朋友 zhījǐ péngyou (*intimate friend*)
知觉 **zhījué**	*consciousness*
知名 **zhīmíng**	*famous; renowned:* 知名学者 zhīmíng xuézhě (*renowned scholar*)
知识 **zhīshi**	*knowledge; learning*

之 zhī

Particle left over from classic Chinese.

1. used between a modifier and a noun to indicate a noun-modifying relationship: 老人之家 lǎorén zhī jiā (*senior citizens' home*); 无价之宝 wújià zhī bǎo (*priceless treasure*)

2. used in set expressions, such as 之一 zhī yī and 百分之 bǎifēn zhī to indicate a whole-part relationship: 广州是中国最大的城市之一 Guǎngzhōu shì Zhōngguó zuìdàde chéngshì zhī yī (*Guangzhou is one of the largest cities in China*); 四分之三 sìfēn zhī sān (*three-fourths*); 百分之一 bǎifēn zhī yī (*one percent*). Note that whole precedes part in Chinese.

之后 **zhīhòu**	*later; after:* 五年之后 wǔ nián zhīhòu (*five years later*). 之后 zhīhòu can be used interchangeably with 以后 yǐ hòu, but is not as common in colloquial speech.
之间 **zhījiān**	*between:* 你我之间 nǐ wǒ zhījiān (*between you and me*); 纽约在华盛顿和波士顿之间 Niǔyuē zài Huáshèngdùn hé Bōshìdùn zhījiān (*New York lies between Washington and Boston*)
之前 **zhīqián**	*before, ago:* 来美国之前 lái Měiguó zhīqián (*before coming to America*). 之前 zhīqián can be used interchangeably with 以前 yǐqián, but is not as common in colloquial speech.

Note: All of the above expressions are considered as nouns (time words) in Chinese.

直 zhí

1. *straight* (adj.): 直线 zhíxiàn (*straight line*). Cl: 条 tiáo

2. *straightforward*; *frank*: 直言 zhíyán (*straight talk*)

3. *just*; *upright*: 为人正直 wéi rén zhèngzhí (*upright in conducting oneself*)

4. *straight* (adv.): 直走 zhí zǒu (*walk straight ahead*); 直飞上海 zhí fēi Shànghǎi (*nonstop flight to Shanghai*)

Also appears in the following words: **笔直** bǐzhí (*perfectly straight*); **简直** jiǎnzhí (*simply*); **一直** yìzhí (*all along*; *all the while*); **正直** zhèngzhí (*honesty*; *integrity*)

直达 **zhídá**	*nonstop* (train or bus)	
直飞 **zhífēi**	*direct* (flight)	
直接 **zhíjiē**	*direct*; *directly*	
直径 **zhíjìng**	*diameter*	
直觉 **zhíjué**	*intuition*	
直升飞机 **zhíshēngfēijī**	*helicopter*. Cl: 架 jià	
直率 **zhíshuài**	*frank*; *candid*	

只 zhǐ; zhī

When pronounced in the third tone:

only; always used as an adverb preceding a verb

只不过 **zhǐbuguò**	*nothing but*: 这只不过是一个谣言 zhè zhǐbuguò shì yí ge yáoyán (*this is nothing but a rumor*)
只得 **zhǐde**	*have no alternative but*, used interchangeably with 只好 zhǐhǎo: 现在已经没有汽车了，我只得走回家 xiànzài yǐjing méi you qìchē le, wǒ zhǐde zǒu huí jiā (*there is no bus now, so I have to walk home*)
只顾 **zhǐgù**	*be only concerned with*: 不要只顾自己，不顾别人 búyào zhǐgù zìjǐ, bú gù biérén (*don't just care about yourself, and show no concern for others*)
只管 **zhǐguǎn**	*by all means*; *feel free*: 你只管用我的字典 nǐ zhǐguǎn yòng wǒde zìdiǎn (*feel free to use my dictionary*)
只好 **zhǐhǎo**	*have no alternative but*, used interchangeably with 只得 zhǐde
只是 **zhǐshì**	**1.** *merely*; *simply*: 只是打雷，没有下雨 zhǐshì dǎléi, méiyou xiàyǔ (*there was only thunder, but no rain*) **2.** *except that*: 我不累，只是有点儿渴 wǒ bú lèi, zhǐshì yǒudiǎnr kě (*I'm not tired except that I'm a little thirsty*)

| 只要 zhǐyào | *as long as*, usu. used in conjunction with 就 jiù: 你只要多说，就能 流利 nǐ zhǐyào duō shuō, jiù néng liúlì (*as long as you speak more, you will become fluent*) |
| 只有 zhǐyǒu | *only when*; *only if*, usu. used in conjunction with 才 cái: 你只有上大学才能找到好工作 nǐ zhǐyǒu shàng dàxué cái néng zhǎo dào hǎo gōngzuò (*you can only find a good job when you go to college*) |

When pronounced in the first tone:

used as a classifier, used for such animals as chicken, duck, cat, and puppy, and such object as a shoe, a sock, and a glove

---

指 zhǐ

1. *point at*: 指人不礼貌 zhǐ rén bù lǐmào (*it is not polite to point at people*); 看我指的地方 kàn wǒ zhǐ de dìfāng (*look at where I point*)

2. *refer to*: 你指的是谁 nǐ zhǐ de shì shuí (*who are you referring to?*)

3. *finger*, often taking the disyllabic form of 手指 shǒuzhǐ. Cl: 根 gēn

Also appears in the following word: 戒指 jièzhǐ (*ring*)

指标 zhǐbiāo	*quota*; *goal*; *target*. Cl: 项 xiàng
指出 zhǐchū	*point out*
指导 zhǐdǎo	*direct*; *guide*
指点 zhǐdiǎn	*give direction*; *give advice*
指定 zhǐdìng	*designate*; *appoint*
指挥 zhǐhuī	**1.** *command*; *direct*; *conduct*
	2. *commander*; *conductor*. Cl: 名 míng; 位 wèi
指教 zhǐjiào	*give direction*; *give advice*
指望 zhǐwàng	*count on*; *depend on*

纸 zhǐ

paper: 墙纸 qiángzhǐ (*wallpaper*); 卫生纸 wèishēngzhǐ (*toilet paper*; *bathroom tissue*); 报纸 bàozhǐ (*newspaper*). Cl: 张 zhāng; 种 zhǒng

Also appears in the following words: 剪纸 jiǎnzhǐ (*paper-cut*); 图纸 túzhǐ (*blueprint*; *drawing*); 折纸 zhézhǐ (*paper folding*; *origami*)

纸币 zhǐbì	*paper money*; *note*. Cl: 张 zhāng
纸盒 zhǐhé	*carton*
纸片 zhǐpiàn	*scraps of paper*

纸条	zhǐtiáo	*slip of paper*
纸箱	zhǐxiāng	*carton*
纸张	zhǐzhāng	(collective n.) *paper*: 不要浪费纸张 bú yào làngfèi zhǐ zhāng (*don't waste paper*)

治 zhì

1. *manage; rule; govern*: 治国 zhì guó (*govern a country*); 治校 zhì xiào (*manage a school*); 自治 zìzhì (*self-rule; autonomy*)

2. *control; transform*: 治水 zhì shuǐ (*harness a river*); 治山 zhì shān (*transform the mountain*)

3. *treat* (a disease); *cure*: 治病 zhì bìng (*treat a disease*)

治安	zhì'ān	*public security; public order*: 那个地方的治安不好 nà ge dìfāng de zhì'ān bù hǎo (*that place is not safe*)
治理	zhìlǐ	1. *rule; govern; manage*
		2. *control; transform*
治疗	zhìliáo	*treat; cure*: 他正在治疗中 tā zhèng zài zhìliáo zhōng (*he is being treated*)

中 zhōng

1. *in*, used after a noun: 家中 jiā zhōng (*in the house*); 水中 shuǐ zhōng (*in the water*); 讲话中 jiǎnghuà zhōng (*in the speech*)

2. *middle*: 中学 zhōngxué (*middle school*); 中秋 zhōngqiū (*mid-autumn*)

3. *in the middle of; among; in the course of; in the process of*: used after a noun, as the word is considered as a noun in Chinese, and often in conjunction with 在 zài: (在 zài) 假期中 jiàqī zhōng (*during the vacation*); (在 zài) 学生中 xuésheng zhōng (*among the students*); (在 zài) 修理中 xiūlǐ zhōng (*being repaired*)

Also appears in the following words: 集中 jízhōng (*centralize; concentrate*); 其中 qízhōng (*thereinto; among*); 折中 zhézhōng (*compromise*)

中部	zhōngbù	*middle section*; (of a country) *central region*
中餐	zhōngcān	*Chinese food* (中 zhōng short for 中国 Zhōngguó, "*China*"); *lunch* (中 zhōng short for 中午 zhōngwǔ, "*midday*"). Cl: 顿 dùn
中产阶级	zhōngchǎn jiējí	*middle class*
中等	zhōngděng	*medium-sized*
中断	zhōngduàn	*discontinue; suspend*: 中断合作 zhōngduàn hézuò (*suspend cooperation*)

中饭 zhōngfàn		*lunch*
中国 Zhōngguó		*China*
中级 zhōngjí		*middle rank; intermediate*
中间 zhōngjiān		**1.** *middle; between; among*: 井在院子的中间 jǐng zài yuànzi de zhōngjiān (*the well is in the middle of the yard*); 餐馆在商店和银行的中间 cānguǎn zài shāngdiàn hé yínháng de zhōngjiān (*the restaurant is between the store and the bank*); 学生中间有很多人会说法语 xuéshēng zhōngjiān yǒu hěn duō rén huì shuō Fǎyǔ (*among the students, many speak French*) **2.** *during*: 学期中间没有假 xuéqī zhōngjiān méi you jià (*there is no vacation during the semester*). 中间 zhōngjiān is considered as a noun in Chinese.
中立 zhōnglì		*neutrality; neutral*: 保持中立 bǎochí zhōnglì (*remain neutral*)
中年 zhōngnián		*middle age*: 中年人 zhōngniánrén (*middle-aged person*)
中式 zhōngshì		*Chinese style*: 中式服装 zhōngshì fúzhuāng (*Chinese-style clothes*)
中途 zhōngtú		*midway; halfway; on the way*
中文 Zhōngwén		*Chinese language*
中午 zhōngwǔ		*midday; noon*
中心 zhōngxīn		*center*
中学 zhōngxué		*middle school*: 中学生 zhōngxuésheng (*middle school student*)
中旬 zhōngxún		*the middle ten days of a month*: 九月中旬 jiǔ yuè zhōngxún (*the middle ten days of September*)
中央 zhōngyāng		**1.** *center; middle* **2.** *central authority*: 中央政府 zhōngyāng zhèngfǔ (*central government*); 中央银行 zhōngyāng yínháng (*central bank*)
中药 zhōngyào		*herbal medicine; traditional Chinese medicine*. Cl: 副 fù
中医 zhōngyī		**1.** *traditional Chinese medicine* **2.** *doctor of traditional Chinese medicine*. Cl: 个 gè; 位 wèi; 名 míng
中游 zhōngyóu		*middle reaches* (of a river)
中止 zhōngzhǐ		*discontinue; suspend*: 中止合同 zhōngzhǐ hétóng (*terminate a contract*)

钟 zhōng

1. *clock; bell*: 警钟 jǐngzhōng (*alarm bell*); 闹钟 nàozhōng (*alarm clock*); 钟楼 zhōnglóu (*bell tower*)

2. *time* (as measured by hours and minutes); *o'clock*: 5点钟 wǔ diǎnzhōng (*5 o'clock*); 10点钟 shí diǎnzhōng (*10 o'clock*); 15 分钟 shíwǔ fēnzhōng (*15 minutes*)

钟表 **zhōngbiǎo**	*timepiece; clocks and watches*: 钟表店 zhōngbiǎodiàn (*watchmaker's store*)	
钟楼 **zhōnglóu**	*bell tower; belfry; clock tower*	
钟头 **zhōngtóu**	*hour*: 我等了你一个钟头 wǒ děng le nǐ yí ge zhōngtóu (*I have been waiting for you for an hour*). Synonymous with 小时 xiǎoshí, 钟头 zhōngtóu is used more in spoken language. Cl: 个 gè	

种 zhǒng; zhòng

When pronounced zhǒng:

1. *seed*, usu. used in the disyllabic form of 种子 zhǒngzi. Cl: 颗 kē; 粒 lì

2. *kind; type*: 这种方法 zhè zhǒng fāngfǎ (*this kind of method*); 各种各样 gè zhǒng gè yàng (*various kinds of*)

3. *race*: 白种人 bái zhǒng rén (*white people*)

种类 **zhǒnglèi**	*variety; kind; type*
种子 **zhǒngzi**	*seed*. Cl: 颗 kē; 粒 lì
种族 **zhǒngzú**	(ethnic) *race*

When pronounced zhòng:

grow; plant; cultivate: 种花 zhòng huā (*grow flowers*); 种地 zhòng dì (*till the land*)

重 zhòng

1. *heavy*: 责任很重 zérèn hěn zhòng (*the responsibility is heavy*); 很重的口音 hěn zhòng de kǒuyīn (*thick accent*)

2. *serious*: 重病 zhòng bìng (*serious illness*)

3. *emphasize*: 重工轻农 zhòng gōng qīng nóng (*emphasize industry to the neglect of agriculture*)

Also appears in the following words: 贵重 guìzhòng (*precious; valuable*); 看重 kànzhòng (v. *value*); 隆重 lóngzhòng (*grand; solemn*); 慎重 shènzhòng (*cautious*); 体重 tǐzhòng (*body weight*); 严重 yánzhòng (*grave; severe*); 珍重 zhēnzhòng (v. *treasure*); 尊重 zūnzhòng (*respect; defer to*)

重大	**zhòngdà**	*major; weighty*: 重大事件 zhòngdà shìjiàn (*major event*)
重担	**zhòngdàn**	*difficult task; heavy responsibility*
重点	**zhòngdiǎn**	*emphasis; major point; key*: 语音是我们的重点 yǔyīn shì wǒmende zhòngdiǎn (*pronunciation is our emphasis*); 重点学校 zhòngdiǎn xuéxiào (*key school*)
重活	**zhònghuó**	*heavy work*
重量	**zhòngliàng**	*weight*
重视	**zhòngshì**	*attach importance to; emphasize*
重要	**zhòngyào**	*important*

周 zhōu

1. *week*: 下周 xiàzhōu (*next week*); 上周 shàngzhōu (*last week*); 周五 zhōuwǔ (*Friday*); 周日 zhōurì (*weekday*). 周 zhōu is synonymous with 星期 xīngqī in this sense except that it is not used with a classifier when preceded by a number or words such as 这 zhè, 上 shàng, and 下 xià, whereas the classifier 个 ge is usually required for 星期 xīngqī, as in 三个星期 sān ge xīngqī (*three weeks*); 这个星期 zhè ge xīngqī (*this week*), 上个星期四 shàng ge xīngqīsì (*last Thursday*), 下个星期一 xià ge xīngqīyī (*next Monday*).

2. *circumference; periphery; circuit*, in various combinations

3. *all; whole; all over*: 周游世界 zhōuyóu shìjiè (*travel all over the world*); 众所周知 zhòngsuǒ zhōuzhī (*as is known to all*)

周长	**zhōucháng**	*circumference; perimeter*
周到	**zhōudào**	*thoughtful; considerate*
周刊	**zhōukān**	(magazine) *weekly*. Cl: 期 qī; 份 fèn; 本 běn
周密	**zhōumì**	*careful; thorough; meticulous*
周末	**zhōumò**	*weekend*
周年	**zhōunián**	*anniversary*
周期	**zhōuqī**	*cycle; period*
周围	**zhōuwéi**	*surroundings*
周折	**zhōuzhé**	*twists and turns; setbacks*
周转	**zhōuzhuǎn**	(financial) *turnover; turn over*

主 zhǔ

1. *owner*; *proprietor*; *master*: 厂主 chǎngzhǔ (*factory owner*); 店主 diànzhǔ (*store owner*)

2. *host*; often taking the form of 主人 zhǔrén

3. *main*; *principal*; *chief*: 主编 zhǔbiān (*editor-in-chief*); 主演 zhǔyǎn (*lead actor or actress*). Cl: 个 gè; 位 wèi; 名 míng

Also appears in the following words: 公主 gōngzhǔ (*princess*); 买主 mǎizhǔ (*buyer*); 卖主 màizhǔ (*seller*); 民主 mínzhǔ (*democracy*); 自主 zìzhǔ (*autonomous*; *independence*)

主办	zhǔbàn	*sponsor*; *organize* (an event)
主持	zhǔchí	*preside over*
主动	zhǔdòng	*initiate*; *take an active role*
主妇	zhǔfu	*housewife*. Cl: 位 wèi
主观	zhǔguān	*subjective*
主见	zhǔjiàn	*independent idea*; *thoughts of one's own*
主角	zhǔjué	*leading actor*; *leading character*. Cl: 个 gè; 位 wèi; 名 míng
主流	zhǔliú	*mainstream*
主权	zhǔquán	*sovereignty*
主人	zhǔrén	*master*; *host*
主任	zhǔrèn	*director*. Cl: 个 gè; 位 wèi; 名 míng
主食	zhǔshí	*staple food*. Cl: 种 zhǒng
主题	zhǔtí	*subject*; *theme*
主席	zhǔxí	*chairman*. Cl: 个 gè; 位 wèi; 名 míng
主修	zhǔxiū	*major in*; *specialize in*
主演	zhǔyǎn	*act the leading character*; *leading actor or actress*
主要	zhǔyào	*main*; *principal*
主义	zhǔyì	*doctrine*; *-ism*
主意	zhǔyì	*idea*; *thought*
主张	zhǔzhāng	*advocate*; *propose*; *proposal*. Cl: 个 gè; 项 xiàng

---

住 zhù

1. *live*; *reside*; the location phrase can be placed either before it or after it: 在学校住 zài xuéxiào zhù (*live on campus*) or 住在学校 zhù zài xuéxiào. When the location appears after 住 zhù, 在 zài can be left out: 住学校 zhù xuéxiào.

2. *stop*: 雨住了 yǔ zhù le (*the rain has stopped*); 住口 zhùkǒu (*shut up*; *stop talking*); 住手 zhùshǒu (*halt your hand*)

3. used as a verb complement to mean *firmly* or *tightly*: 拿住 ná zhù (*hold tightly*); 站住 zhàn zhù (*stand still*); 记住 jì zhù (*remember*)

住处 zhùchù	residence; dwelling
住房 zhùfáng	house; housing
住口 zhùkǒu	shut up; stop talking
住手 zhùshǒu	stay one's hand, used to order someone to stop using physical force
住院 zhùyuàn	be hospitalized
住宅 zhùzhái	residence; dwelling
住址 zhùzhǐ	(residence) address

祝 zhù

wish (v.): 祝你好运 zhù nǐ hǎoyùn (*good luck!*); 祝你一路平安 zhù nǐ yílù píng'ān (*wish you a pleasant journey!*); 祝你成功 zhù nǐ chénggōng (*wish you success!*); 祝你新年快乐 zhù nǐ xīnnián kuàilè (*wish you Happy New Year!*)

祝福 zhùfú	wish happiness; bless
祝贺 zhùhè	congratulate; congratulation
祝酒 zhùjiǔ	propose a toast
祝愿 zhùyuàn	wish; offer best wishes; best wishes; blessings

转 zhuǎn; zhuàn

When pronounced zhuǎn:

1. *transfer; forward*: 转学 zhuǎn xué (*transfer to another school*); 转车 zhuǎn chē (*transfer to another bus or train*); 请把我的信转给我 qǐng bǎ wǒde xìn zhuǎn gěi wǒ (*please forward my mail to me*)

2. *turn; change*: 向右转 xiàng yòu zhuǎn (*turn right*); 天气好转 tiānqì hǎo zhuǎn (*the weather is improving*)

Also appears in the following words: **好转** hǎozhuǎn (*improve; mend*); **婉转** wǎnzhuǎn (*tactful*); **中转** zhōngzhuǎn (*transfer; change trains*)

转变 zhuǎnbiàn	change (n. and v.); *transform*: 转变观点 zhuǎnbiàn guāndiǎn (*change viewpoints*); 他的行为有很大的转变 tāde xíngwéi yǒu hěn dàde zhuǎnbiàn (*there is a great change in his behavior*)
转达 zhuǎndá	convey (a message, etc.)
转告 zhuǎn'gào	pass on (information, word): 请转告同学们明天的课取消了 qǐng zhuǎn'gào tóngxuémen míngtiān de kè qǔxiāo le (*please let your classmates know that the class for tomorrow has been cancelled*)

转化 zhuǎnhuà	transform
转机 zhuǎnjī	a turn for the better: 股票市场大有转机 gǔpiào shìchǎng dà yǒu zhuǎnjī (there is a great prospect for a turn for the better with the stock market)
转交 zhuǎnjiāo	pass on (an object): 请把这封信转交给你太太 qǐng bǎ zhè fēng xìn zhuǎnjiāo gěi nǐ tàitai (please pass this letter to your wife)
转身 zhuǎnshēn	face about; turn around
转弯 zhuǎnwān	make a turn: 转弯时不要开得太快 zhuǎnwān shí búyào kāi de tài kuài (don't drive too fast when you make a turn)
转眼 zhuǎnyǎn	in the twinkle of an eye
转移 zhuǎnyí	transfer; shift: 转移资产 zhuǎnyí zīchǎn (transfer asset); 转移注意力 zhuǎnyí zhùyìlì (shift attention)

When pronounced zhuàn:

turn; revolve; rotate: 月亮围地球转 yuèliang wéi dìqiú zhuàn (the moon revolves around the earth)

| 转动 zhuàndòng | turn; revolve; rotate: 机器在转动 jīqì zài zhuàndòng (the machine is moving) |
| 转椅 zhuànyǐ | swivel chair. Cl: 把 bǎ |

装 zhuāng

1. *load*; *pack*; *put*: 装车 zhuāng chē (*load the car*); 把书装在书包里 bǎ shū zhuāng zài shūbāo lǐ (*put the book in the schoolbag*)

2. *install*; *equip*: 装电话 zhuāng diànhuà (*install a phone*); 装煤气 zhuāng méiqì (*install a gas stove*)

3. *act*; *play the part of* (in a movie or play): 他在电影里装军人 tā zài diànyǐng lǐ zhuāng jūnrén (*he played a soldier in the movie*)

4. *pretend*; *feign*: 装死 zhuāng sǐ (*feign death*); 装不知道 zhuāng bù zhīdao (*pretend not to know*)

5. *clothing*; *garment*: 服装 fúzhuāng (*clothes*); 女装 nǚzhuāng (*women's garment*). Cl: 件 jiàn; 套 tào

Also appears in the following words: 便装 biànzhuāng (*slack suit*); 军装 jūnzhuāng (*military uniform*); Cl: 件 jiàn; 套 tào; 伪装 wěizhuāng (*camouflage*); 武装 wǔzhuāng (v. *arm*)

| 装扮 zhuāngbàn | disguise; masquerade, often used with 成 chéng: 装扮成小丑 zhuāngbàn chéng xiǎochǒu (masqueraded as a clown) |

装备	zhuāngbèi	*equip; equipment.* Cl: 套 tào
装订	zhuāngdìng	*bind* (a book)
装门面	zhuāng ménmiàn	*put up a (false) front*
装配	zhuāngpèi	*assemble*
装饰	zhuāngshì	*decorate; decoration*
装蒜	zhuāngsuàn	*pretend ignorance,* used in a pejorative sense
装卸	zhuāngxiè	*load and unload*
装修	zhuāngxiū	*fix up; renovate*
装运	zhuāngyùn	*load and transport; ship*

准 zhǔn

1. *accurate; exact:* 今天的天气预报不准 jīntiān de tiānqì yùbào bù zhǔn (*today's weather forecast is not accurate*); 我的表很准 wǒde biǎo hěn zhǔn (*my watch is very accurate*).

2. *certainly; definitely:* 老师准会让我们重写作文 lǎoshī zhǔn huì ràng wǒmen chóng xiě zuòwén (*the teacher will definitely ask us to rewrite the composition*)

3. *allow; permit:* 博物馆里不准照相 bówùguǎn lǐ bù zhǔn zhàoxiàng (*no photography is allowed in the museum*)

4. *standard; norm,* used as part of another word: 标准 (*standard*); 准则 (*norm*). Cl: 条 tiáo; 项 xiàng

Also appears in the following words: 批准 pīzhǔn (*approve*); 水准 shuǐzhǔn (*level; standard*)

准备	zhǔnbèi	**1.** *prepare; get ready:* 妈妈在准备晚餐 māma zài zhǔnbèi wǎncān (*mother is preparing dinner*); 明天考试，我们已经准备好了 míngtiān kǎoshì, wǒmen yǐjīng zhǔnbèi hǎo le (*there is an exam tomorrow and we are ready for it*) **2.** *plan:* 你今年准备在哪儿过年 nǐ jīnnián zhǔnbèi zài nǎr guò nián (*where are you planning to spend your New Year this year?*)
准确	zhǔnquè	*accurate; precise*
准时	zhǔnshí	*punctual; on time*
准许	zhǔnxǔ	*permit; allow*
准则	zhǔnzé	*norm; standard:* 外交准则 wàijiāo zhǔnzé (*diplomatic norms*). Cl: 条 tiáo; 项 xiàng

子 zi; zǐ

When pronounced zi:

Used with certain monosyllabic nouns to distinguish them from other homophonic monosyllabic words: 筷子 kuàizi (*chopsticks*) (Cl: 枝 zhī; 支 zhī; 根 gēn; 双 shuāng; 把 bǎ); 桌子 zhuōzi (*table*) (Cl: 个 gè; 张 zhāng); 鞋子 xiézi (*shoes*) (Cl: 双 shuāng; 只 zhī); 儿子 érzi (*son*) (Cl: 个 gè)

Also appears in the following words: **包子** bāozi (*steamed stuffed bun*); **本子** běnzi (*notebook*); **点子** diǎnzi (*idea*); **电子** diànzǐ (*electronic*); **肚子** dǔzi (*stomach*); **个子** gèzi (*body height*); **瓜子** guāzǐ (*melon seeds*); **架子** jiàzi (*shelf*); **句子** jùzǐ (*sentence*); **骗子** piànzi (*swindler*); **样子** yàngzi (*manner; appearance*)

When pronounced zǐ:

1. *person*, used after certain nouns: 男子 nánzǐ (*man*); 女子 nǔzǐ (*woman*). Cl: 个 gè; 位 wèi; 名 míng

2. *son*; *child*, often used in conjunction with its opposites: 母子 mǔzǐ (*mother and son*); 子女 zǐnǔ (*son and daughter*)

自 zì

1. *self*, used as a prefix to a verb: 自杀 zìshā (*commit suicide; suicide*); 自卫 zìwèi (*defend oneself; self defense*); 自夸 zìkuā (*brag about oneself*)

2. *from ... on*; *since*, often used with 起 qǐ or 以来 yǐlái: 自今天起 zì jīntiān qǐ (*from today on*); 自古以来 zì gǔ yǐlái (*since ancient times*)

Also appears in the following words: **独自** dúzì (*alone; by oneself*); **各自** gèzì (*each; respective*); **亲自** qīnzì (*in person*); **私自** sīzì (*privately; without permission*)

自卑 **zìbēi**	*feel inferior about oneself*
自称 **zìchēng**	*profess; claim oneself to be*
自从 **zìcóng**	*since*, often used in conjunction with 以来 yǐlái: 自从我学中文以来 zìcóng wǒ xué zhōngwén yǐlái (*since I started studying Chinese*)
自动 **zìdòng**	*automatic*: 自动洗衣机 zìdòng xǐyījī (*automatic wash machine*)
自己 **zìjǐ**	1. *self; one's own*: 我自己 wǒ zìjǐ (*myself*); 你自己 nǐ zìjǐ (*yourself*); 他自己 tā zìjǐ (*himself*); 我自己的房子 wǒ zìjǐ de fángzi (*my own house*)
	2. *by oneself; alone*: 你自己去还是和别人去 nǐ zìjǐ qù háishi hé biérén qù (*are you going alone or with somebody else?*)

自然 zìrán   *nature; naturally*

字 zì

character: 汉字 hànzì (*Chinese character*)

Also appears in the following words: 打字 dǎzì (*type; typewrite*); 汉字 hànzì (*Chinese characters*); 名字 míngzi (*name*); 数字 shùzì (*number*); 文字 wénzì (*writing script*)

字典 zìdiǎn	*dictionary*. Cl: 本 běn; 部 bù
字画 zìhuà	*calligraphy and painting*. Cl: 幅 fú; 张 zhāng
字迹 zìjì	*handwriting*
字母 zìmǔ	*letters of an alphabet*
字幕 zìmù	(of movies) *subtitles*
字体 zìtǐ	*style of calligraphy; font*

总 zǒng

1. *general; total*: 总形势 zǒng xíngshì (*general situation*); 总人口 zǒng rénkǒu (*total population*)

2. *chief*: 总经理 zǒng jīnglǐ (*general manager*); 总司令 zǒng sīlìng (*commander in chief*)

3. *always*: 我儿子总喜欢在学习的时候听音乐 wǒ érzi zǒng xǐhuan zài xuéxí de shíhou tīng yīnyuè (*my son always likes to listen to music while studying*)

4. *sooner or later; eventually*: 我总有一天会有自己的房子 wǒ zǒng yǒu yìtiān huì yǒu zìjǐde fángzi (*sooner or later, I'll have my own house*)

总的来说 zǒngdéláishuō	*generally speaking*
总共 zǒnggòng	*in total; altogether*: 总共100个人 zǒnggòng 100 ge rén (*100 people altogether*)
总机 zǒngjī	*switchboard*
总结 zǒngjié	*sum up; summarize; summary*
总理 zǒnglǐ	*prime minister; premier*
总数 zǒngshù	*total; sum total*
总算 zǒngsuàn	*at long last*: 我总算写完了这本书 wǒ zǒngsuàn xiě wán le zhè běn shū (*I have at long last finished writing the book*)
总统 zǒngtǒng	*president* (of a country)
总之 zǒngzhī	*in short; in a word*

走 zǒu

1. *walk; move:* 汽车不走了 qìchē bù zǒu le (*the bus stopped moving*); 孩子会走了 háizi huì zǒu le (*the child has learned to walk*)

2. *leave; go:* 我们应该走了 wǒmen yīnggāi zǒu le (*we should be leaving*); 火车站怎么走 huǒchēzhàn zěnme zǒu (*how do I go to the train station?*)

3. *away;* used after a verb: 请不要把书拿走 qǐng bú yào bǎ shū ná zǒu (*please don't take away the books*)

走读	zǒudú	*attend a school as a commuter student:* 走读生 zǒudúshēng (*commuter student*)
走狗	zǒugǒu	*lackey.* Cl: 条 tiáo
走后门	zǒu hòumén	*gain advantage by using influence or connection*
走廊	zǒuláng	*corridor; hallway.* Cl: 条 tiáo
走路	zǒulù	*walk:* 你走路去还是坐车去 nǐ zǒulù qù háishi zuò chē qù (*are you going on foot or by bus?*). Note: 路 lù in 走路 zǒulù can be left out.
走私	zǒusī	*smuggle*
走运	zǒuyùn	*be in luck:* 他走了运, 赢了彩票 tā zǒu le yùn, yíng le cǎipiào (*he is lucky, he has won a lottery prize*)

最 zuì

most: 最大 zuì cháng (*the longest*); 最高兴 zuì gāoxìng (*happiest*); 最喜欢 zuì xǐhuan (*like the most*)

最初	zuìchū	*at the beginning*
最多	zuìduō	*at most; maximum*
最高	zuìgāo	*supreme*
最好	zuìhǎo	*it is better that:* 你最好上公立学校 nǐ zuìhǎo shàng gōnglì xuéxiào (*it would be better for you to attend a public school*)
最后	zuìhòu	*final; last; ultimate; finally; ultimately.* When used as an attributive adjective, the word 一 (*one*) needs to be used after it, as it actually means *last one:* 最后一天 zuìhòu yì tiān (*the last day*); 最后一个人 zuìhòu yí ge rén (*the last person*)
最近	zuìjìn	*recently; soon*
最少	zuìshǎo	*at least; minimum*
最终	zuìzhōng	*ultimate; final*

左 zuǒ

the left side; *left*: 左手 zuǒshǒu (*left hand*); 向左转 xiàng zuǒ zhuǎn (*turn left*)

左边 **zuǒbian**	*left*
左轮手枪 **zuǒlún shǒuqiāng**	*revolver*. Cl: 把 bǎ
左面 **zuǒmiàn**	*the left side*
左撇子 **zuǒpiězi**	*left-handed person*
左翼 **zuǒyì**	*left wing*
左右 **zuǒyòu**	**1.** *control*; *influence*; *manipulate*: 我们不能受他的左右 wǒmen bù néng shòu tāde zuǒyòu (*we can't subject ourselves to his manipulation*) **2.** *more or less*; *approximately*: 三点左右 sān diǎn zuǒyòu (*about 3 o'clock*); 一百人左右 yì bǎi rén zuǒyòu (*about 100 people*)
左右手 **zuǒyòushǒu**	*right-hand man*

做 zuò

1. *make*; *do*; *produce*: 做饭 zuò fàn (*cook*, literally *make food*); 做生意 zuò shēngyì (*do business*); 做家具 zuò jiājù (*make furniture*)

2. *act as*; *work as*: 做老师 zuò lǎoshī (*work as a teacher*); 做我们的翻译 zuò wǒmende fānyì (*act as our interpreter*)

3. *write*; *create*: 做诗 zuò shī (*write a poem*); 做文章 zuò wénzhāng (*write an article*)

做到 **zuòdào**	*accomplish*; *achieve*; *succeed in doing*: 我很难做到你所说的 wǒ hěn nán zuòdào nǐ suǒ shuǒ de (*it is very difficult for me to do what you said*)
做东 **zuòdōng**	*play the host*: 今天是老板做东，我们不必付钱 jīntiān shì lǎobǎn zuòdōng, wǒmen búbì fùqián (*it's on the boss today, we don't need to pay*)
做法 **zuòfǎ**	*way of doing things*; *method*; *practice*
做工 **zuògōng**	*work as a manual laborer*
做客 **zuòkè**	*be a guest*
做礼拜 **zuò lǐbài**	*go to church*
做梦 **zuòmèng**	*have a dream*
做事 **zuòshì**	*work*: 在邮局做事 zài yóujú zuòshì (*work at a post office*)

作 zuò

1. *do*; *make*: 作家庭作业 zuò jiātíng zuòyè (*do homework*)

2. *as*; *used after a verb*: 把他看作朋友 bǎ tā kàn zuò péngyou (*treat him as a friend*)

3. *act as*: 谁作你的翻译 shuí zuò nǐde fānyì (*who is going to be your interpreter?*)

Also appears in the following words: 创作 chuàngzuò (*create*; *write*); 工作 gōngzuò (*work*); 合作 hézuò (*collaborate*; *cooperate*); 杰作 jiézuò (*masterpiece*); 写作 xiězuò (*compose*; *write*); 著作 zhùzuò (*published work*; *book*)

作案 zuò'àn	*commit a crime*	
作弊 zuòbì	*cheat*; *engage in fraud*	
作法 zuòfa	*way of doing things*	
作废 zuòfèi	*become invalid*	
作家 zuòjiā	*writer*; *author*. Cl: 个 gè; 位 wèi; 名 míng	
作品 zuòpǐn	(*literary or artistic*) *work*. Cl: 篇 piān; 部 bù; 本 běn; 件 jiàn	
作曲 zuòqǔ	*compose*	
作为 zuòwéi	*as*; *treat as*: 作为老师, 我们应该给学生树立一个榜样 zuòwéi lǎoshī, wǒmen yīnggāi gěi xuéshēng shùlì yí ge bǎngyàng (*as teachers, we should set an example for the students*); 把音乐课作为选修课 bǎ yínyuè kè zuòwéi xuǎnxiū kè (*treat the music class as an elective class*)	
作文 zuòwén	(*academic*) *composition*. Cl: 篇 piān	
作业 zuòyè	*school assignment*; *homework*. Cl: 篇 piān; 本 běn	
作用 zuòyòng	*effect*; *function*; *use*	
作者 zuòzhě	*author*. Cl: 个 gè; 位 wèi; 名 míng	
作主 zuòzhǔ	*make a decision*	

坐 zuò

1. *sit*: 坐在地上 zuò zài dì shang (*sit on the floor*)

2. *travel by* (*bus, train, boat, plane, etc.*): 坐地铁去学校 zuò dìtiě qù xuéxiào (*go to school by subway*)

坐垫 zuòdiàn	*cushion*
坐牢 zuòláo	*do time in jail*; *be imprisoned*
坐立不安 zuòlì bù'ān	*be on pins and needles*
坐落 zuòluò	*be situated*: 博物馆坐落在湖边 bówùguǎn zuòluò zài húbiān (*the museum is situated by the lake*)

座 zuò

1. *seat*, often taking the disyllabic form of 座位 zuòwèi: 请入座 qǐng rù zuò (*please take your seat*); 这是你的座位 zhè shì nǐde zuòwèi (*this is your seat*)
2. classifier for buildings; sculptures; mountains, etc.: 一座楼 yí zuò lóu (*a building*); 两座山 liǎng zuò shān (*two mountains*); 三座塑像 sān zuò sùxiàng (*three sculptures*)

Also appears in the following words: 插座 chāzuò (*socket*); 讲座 jiǎngzuò (*lecture*); 卖座 màizuò (*draw large audience*)

座谈 **zuòtán**	*have an informal discussion*; *informal discussion*: 座谈会 zuòtánhuì (*forum*; *symposium*)
座右铭 **zuòyòumíng**	*motto*; *maxim*

FREQUENCY INDEX

Freq.	Char.	Pinyin	Pg.
61	同	tóng	203
62	老	lǎo	124
63	中	zhōng	264
64	十	shí	180
65	从	cóng	31
66	自	zì	272
67	面	miàn	143
69	前	qián	160
70	头	tóu	204
71	道	dào	40
72	它	tā	196
73	后	hòu	88
74	然	rán	169
75	走	zǒu	274
76	很	hěn	88
77	象	xiàng	221
78	见	jiàn	100
79	两	liǎng	133
80	用	yòng	239
81	她	tā	195
82	国	guó	81
83	动	dòng	52
84	进	jìn	110
85	成	chéng	25
86	回	huí	92
87	什	shén	178
88	边	biān	12
89	作	zuò	276
90	对	duì	55
91	开	kāi	115
92	假	jiǎ; jià	99
93	些	xiē	223
94	现	xiàn	219
95	山	shān	174

Freq.	Char.	Pinyin	Pg.
96	民	mín	144
97	经	jīng	111
98	发	fā	58
99	工	gōng	74
100	向	xiàng	221
101	事	shì	184
102	给	gěi	73
103	长	cháng	35
104	水	shuǐ	191
105	几	jǐ	97
106	三	sān	174
107	声	shēng	179
108	于	yú	244
109	高	gāo	71
110	正	zhèng	259
111	妈	mā	138
112	手	shǒu	187
113	知	zhī	261
114	理	lǐ	128
115	眼	yǎn	229
116	点	diǎn	47
117	心	xīn	224
118	站	zhàn	254
119	二	èr	58
120	问	wèn	212
121	但	dàn	38
122	身	shēn	178
123	方	fāng	60
124	像	xiàng	221
125	实	shí	181
126	吃	chī	26
127	做	zuò	275
128	叫	jiào	105
129	当	dāng	38

Freq.	Char.	Pinyin	Pg.	Freq.	Char.	Pinyin	Pg.
130	住	zhù	268	164	五	wǔ	215
131	听	tīng	201	165	第	dì	46
132	打	dǎ	32	166	使	shǐ	182
133	呢	ne	150	167	写	xiě	223
134	真	zhēn	258	168	军	jūn	114
135	全	quán	168	169	吧	ba; bā	2
136	才	cái	19	170	文	wén	212
137	四	sì	193	171	运	yùn	249
138	已	yǐ	237	172	再	zài	251
139	所	suǒ	195	173	果	guǒ	81
140	之	zhī	260	174	怎	zěn	253
141	最	zuì	274	175	定	dìng	50
142	光	guāng	80	176	快	kuài	121
143	产	chǎn	22	177	明	míng	145
144	长	zhǎng	255	178	行	xíng	226
145	情	qíng	164	179	因	yīn	238
146	路	lù	136	180	别	bié	15
147	分	fēn	64	181	飞	fēi	62
148	总	zǒng	273	182	外	wài	206
149	条	tiáo	200	183	物	wù	215
150	白	bái	3	184	活	huó	93
151	话	huà	89	185	部	bù	18
152	东	dōng	51	186	门	mén	142
153	次	cì	31	187	无	wú	213
154	亲	qīn	162	188	往	wǎng	209
155	如	rú	172	189	船	chuán	29
156	被	bèi	9	190	望	wàng	210
157	花	huā	89	191	新	xīn	224
158	口	kǒu	120	192	带	dài	35
159	放	fàng	61	193	队	duì	56
160	儿	ér	57	194	先	xiān	218
161	常	cháng	23	195	力	lì	130
162	西	xī	216	196	完	wán	207
163	气	qì	159	197	间	jiān	100

Freq.	Char.	Pinyin	Pg.	Freq.	Char.	Pinyin	Pg.
198	代	dài	36	232	原	yuán	247
199	员	yuán	246	233	拿	ná	147
200	机	jī	94	234	群	qún	168
201	更	gèng	74	235	各	gè	73
202	九	jiǔ	112	236	六	liù	136
203	您	nín	152	237	本	běn	9
204	每	měi	141	238	解	jiě	108
205	风	fēng	65	239	立	lì	130
206	跟	gēn	73	240	河	hé	86
207	笑	xiào	223	241	爸	bà	3
208	啊	à; a	1	242	八	bā	2
209	孩	hái	84	243	难	nán	148
210	万	wàn	209	244	早	zǎo	252
211	少	shǎo	177	245	吗	ma	138
212	直	zhí	262	246	共	gòng	76
213	意	yì	237	247	让	ràng	169
214	夜	yè	231	248	相	xiāng	219
215	比	bǐ	10	249	今	jīn	109
216	连	lián	131	250	书	shū	188
217	车	chē	24	251	坐	zuò	276
218	重	zhòng	266	252	接	jiē	105
219	马	mǎ	138	253	应	yīng	239
220	哪	nǎ	147	254	关	guān	78
221	化	huà	90	255	信	xìn	225
222	太	tài	196	256	性	xìng	227
223	指	zhǐ	263	257	死	sǐ	192
224	变	biàn	13	258	步	bù	18
225	社	shè	177	259	男	nán	149
226	者	zhě	257	260	反	fǎn	59
227	干	gàn; gān	68	261	处	chǔ; chù	28
228	满	mǎn	139	262	记	jì	97
229	日	rì	172	263	将	jiāng	102
230	决	jué	114	264	千	qiān	160
231	百	bǎi	4	265	找	zhǎo	255

Freq.	Char.	Pinyin	Pg.
266	或	huò	94
267	师	shī	179
268	管	guǎn	79
269	结	jié	106
270	块	kuài	121
271	跑	pǎo	154
272	谁	shéi; shuí	190
273	草	cǎo	20
274	谈	tán	196
275	越	yuè	248
276	字	zì	273
277	加	jiā	98
278	紧	jǐn	109
279	爱	ài	1
280	等	děng	44
281	怕	pà	153
282	月	yuè	248
283	青	qīng	163
284	半	bàn	5
285	火	huǒ	93
286	法	fǎ	59
287	题	tí	198
288	建	jiàn	101
289	赶	gǎn	68
290	位	wèi	211
291	唱	chàng	24
292	海	hǎi	84
293	七	qī	158
294	女	nǚ	153
295	件	jiàn	101
296	感	gǎn	69
297	准	zhǔn	272
298	张	zhāng	254
299	团	tuán	205

Freq.	Char.	Pinyin	Pg.
300	离	lí	127
301	色	sè	174
302	片	piàn	155
303	科	kē	117
304	倒	dǎo; dào	39
305	利	lì	130
306	病	bìng	15
307	刚	gāng	70
308	喜	xǐ	216
309	由	yóu	241
310	送	sòng	193
311	星	xīng	225
312	晚	wǎn	208
313	表	biǎo	14
314	够	gòu	76
315	整	zhěng	258
316	认	rèn	171
317	雪	xuě	228
318	流	liú	134
319	场	chǎng	24
320	该	gāi	66
321	期	qī	158
322	并	bìng	16
323	底	dǐ	45
324	平	píng	157
325	电	diàn	48
326	忙	máng	140
327	提	tí	197
328	近	jìn	111
329	亮	liàng	134
330	轻	qīng	163
331	讲	jiǎng	102
332	农	nóng	152
333	古	gǔ	77

Freq.	Char.	Pinyin	Pg.
334	黑	hēi	87
335	告	gào	71
336	拉	lā	122
337	名	míng	145
338	远	yuǎn	247
339	土	tǔ	204
340	清	qīng	164
341	阳	yáng	229
342	照	zhào	255
343	办	bàn	5
344	另	lìng	134
345	改	gǎi	67
346	酒	jiǔ	112
347	转	zhuǎn;	269
		zhuàn	
348	画	huà	90
349	造	zào	253
350	单	dān	37
351	治	zhì	264
352	北	běi	9
353	语	yǔ	245
354	必	bì	12
355	服	fú	65
356	留	liú	135
357	雨	yǔ	245
358	穿	chuān	29
359	父	fù	66
360	内	nèi	150
361	识	shí	182
362	传	chuán	29
363	业	yè	231
364	菜	cài	19
365	爬	pá	153
366	睡	shuì	191

Freq.	Char.	Pinyin	Pg.
367	量	liáng; liàng	133
368	咱	zán	252
369	体	tǐ	198
370	皮	pí	155
371	通	tōng	202
372	合	hé	86
373	交	jiāo	103
374	双	shuāng	190
375	友	yǒu	243
376	度	dù	54
377	米	mǐ	143
378	术	shù	189
379	饭	fàn	60
380	公	gōng	75
381	旁	páng	154
382	房	fáng	61
383	极	jí	96
384	南	nán	149
385	客	kè	119
386	读	dú	53
387	岁	suì	194
388	空	kōng; kòng	119
389	收	shōu	186
390	算	suàn	194
391	安	ān	1
392	证	zhèng	260
393	市	shì	185
394	落	luò	137
395	钱	qián	161
396	室	shì	185
397	特	tè	196
398	围	wéi	211
399	教	jiāo; jiào	104
400	院	yuàn	248

Freq.	Char.	Pinyin	Pg.
401	热	rè	169
402	包	bāo	6
403	歌	gē	72
404	类	lèi	126
405	强	qiáng	162
406	数	shǔ; shù	189
407	音	yīn	238
408	答	dá	32
409	旧	jiù	113
410	座	zuò	277
411	帮	bāng	6
412	错	cuò	32
413	美	měi	142
414	受	shòu	188
415	跳	tiào	200
416	非	fēi	63
417	牛	niú	152
418	取	qǔ	166
419	入	rù	173
420	掉	diào	49
421	种	zhǒng; zhòng	266
422	装	zhuāng	270
423	顶	dǐng	49
424	谢	xiè	223
425	急	jí	95
426	联	lián	132
427	停	tíng	201
428	搬	bān	4
429	请	qǐng	165
430	区	qū	165
431	衣	yī	234
432	报	bào	7
433	母	mǔ	141

Freq.	Char.	Pinyin	Pg.
434	慢	màn	140
435	钟	zhōng	266
436	背	bēi; bèi	8
437	城	chéng	26
438	礼	lǐ	129
439	冷	lěng	127
440	低	dī	45
441	医	yī	234
442	费	fèi	63
443	楼	lóu	136
444	品	pǐn	156
445	街	jiē	106
446	周	zhōu	267
447	破	pò	157
448	贵	guì	80
449	玩	wán	208
450	忘	wàng	210
451	节	jié	107
452	店	diàn	48
453	坏	huài	91
454	餐	cān	20
455	园	yuán	245
456	游	yóu	240
457	推	tuī	205
458	买	mǎi	138
459	试	shì	186
460	差	chā; chà; chāi	21
461	午	wǔ	215
462	号	hào	87
463	戴	dài	36
464	纸	zhǐ	263
465	笔	bǐ	11
466	馆	guǎn	79

Freq.	Char.	Pinyin	Pg.
467	肉	ròu	172
468	商	shāng	175
469	班	bān	4
470	短	duǎn	54
471	杯	bēi	7
472	参	cān	19
473	汉	hàn	86
474	换	huàn	91
475	退	tuì	206
476	层	céng	21
477	左	zuǒ	275
478	词	cí	30
479	挂	guà	77
480	懂	dǒng	51
481	卖	mài	139
482	盘	pán	154
483	洗	xǐ	216

Freq.	Char.	Pinyin	Pg.
484	右	yòu	244
485	刀	dāo	39
486	遍	biàn	13
487	借	jiè	108
488	蛋	dàn	37
489	汽	qì	160
490	茶	chá	22
491	鸡	jī	95
492	票	piào	156
493	练	liàn	133
494	姓	xìng	226
495	祝	zhù	269
496	疼	téng	197
497	寄	jì	97
498	课	kè	118
499	订	dìng	50
500	邮	yóu	240

CHARACTER INDEX

(By Number of Strokes)